Modern Constitutions

DEMOCRACY, CITIZENSHIP, AND CONSTITUTIONALISM

Rogers M. Smith and Mary L. Dudziak, Series Editors

Modern Constitutions

Edited by
Rogers M. Smith and Richard R. Beeman

PENN

UNIVERSITY OF PENNSYLVANIA PRESS

PHILADELPHIA

Published by
University of Pennsylvania Press
Philadelphia, Pennsylvania 19104-4112
www.upenn.edu/pennpress

Printed in the United States of America on acid-free paper

10 9 8 7 6 5 4 3 2 1

A Cataloguing-in-Publication record is available from the Library of Congress

ISBN 978-0-8122-5234-7

CONTENTS

Introduction

Rogers M. Smith with Richard R. Beeman

The Tasks of Constitution-Making

Aristotle is said to have compiled a collection of ancient constitutions that informed his studies of politics, writings that retain lasting influence after more than two millennia (e.g., Armstrong 1981, 71). But for Aristotle, constitutions largely distilled and described the distinctive patterns of political life established over time in many differing ways in many places. What constitutionalism has come to mean in the modern era originates chiefly in the late eighteenth century and primarily with the United States Constitution, written in 1787 and made effective in 1789, and the various French constitutions that began in 1791.

In some of their elements, especially in their adoption of representative assemblies, both of these first modern written constitutions were influenced by the prior example of Great Britain's "unwritten constitution" and its parliamentary institutions. With the global expansion of the British Empire through the end of the nineteenth century, the British model of constitutionalism continued to have far-ranging impact, along with the French and the American. Even the constitutions of Russia and the Union of Soviet Socialist Republics after the Bolshevik Revolution drew on these traditions, especially French constitutionalism (Pipes 1990, 161, 516). Then, after World War II brought an end to the age of European empires and a new emphasis in international law on human rights and human dignity, postcolonial nations began crafting new constitutions, a trend that only accelerated through the beginning of the twenty-first century. Beginning with the influential Indian Constitution of 1950, many of these new constitutions started to incorporate a broader range of social rights and recognitions for claims of cultural communities and disadvantaged groups than their historical predecessors, causing many scholars to classify them as instances of "transformative" constitutionalism (Dinghra 2014). As part of the "left turn" in Latin American politics during the early twenty-first century, Latin American nations especially were in the forefront of adopting new constitutions that expanded commitments to "social, economic, and cultural" rights of long-marginalized groups, though efforts to implement the new constitutional guarantees often met with strong resistance (Gargarella 2018, 203).

Today, the practice of formally adopting, if not necessarily governing by, constitutions is nearly universal. The Comparative Constitutions Project, directed by Professors Zachary Elkins and James Melton along with Thomas Ginsburg, a law professor, political scientist, and contributor to this volume, has collaborated with Google to provide online access to all of today's constitutions—a far more massive and fast-changing documentary endeavor than Aristotle confronted, abetted by technology of which he could only dream. Their project currently includes 195 national constitutions. Of those, 132 were adopted in 1975 or later; 65 were adopted in 1995 or later; and many others have been significantly modified during those years.[1] Though it is reasonable to doubt the efficacy of written constitutions in many contexts, it cannot be denied that in the modern era an enormous amount of political effort has been devoted to constitution-making. The twenty-first century shows no signs of it slowing, much less ceasing.

In regard to the central goals of the world's early modern constitution-makers, however, there are now signs that the efficacy of modern constitutionalism may be waning, or at least that constitutionalism is being substantially redirected in many regimes. At the end of the second decade of the twenty-first century, politics and law within many lands and also across national lines have been reshaped by the rise of insurgencies labeled "populist." These movements, most often on the right though sometimes on the left, frequently treat constitutions solely as vehicles for, not as checks upon, the direct expression of the will of the majority, or the will of leaders that claim to speak for majorities. The editors of one recent volume warn that "the global momentum toward constitutional democracy" has now "stalled and perhaps has begun to reverse" (Graber, Levinson, and Tushnet 2018, 2).

A leading student of contemporary populism, Jan-Werner Müller, argues somewhat differently. He holds that not only do modern populist movements claim to speak for democratic "peoples," they also profess to support constitutionalism. But rather than seeing constitutionalism as an effort to guide and limit governmental power through the rule of law, they treat a constitution as "a purely partisan instrument to capture the polity" (Müller 2016, 68). If so, then constitutionalism in the twenty-first century is coming to mean something very different from what "modern" constitutionalism meant in the eighteenth, nineteenth, and twentieth centuries, and something that does entail the decline of many older liberal conceptions of constitutional democracy.

These developments may only mean, however, that modern constitution-makers are in many countries giving different responses to the fundamental issues that constitutionalism always addresses. Reflection suggests that all constitution-making requires answers to at least six broad and basic questions.

First, who has the authority to write a constitution or to propose amendments to that constitution? Can and should it be committees in the legislatures in existing regimes, or executive branch officials, or special teams of experts appointed by one or the other, or members of an elected or appointed constitutional convention, or some other procedure?

Second, who has the authority to enact a constitution in a way that makes it legitimately authoritative? An existing legislature, chief executive, a popular referendum, or elected or appointed ratifying conventions? Or perhaps, as in the case of South Africa's 1996 constitution, might an existing constitutional court have some special role in ratification?

Third and closely related, should a constitution be difficult to amend, so that it can provide enduring structures, limits, and guides for governing? Or should it be more easily alterable, so as always to be responsive to the evolving will of the sovereign people—perhaps as embodied in a populist leader or party?

Fourth, should the constitution be fully written as a single document (even though written amendments can be added)? Or can it instead be in significant measure "unwritten," composed of venerated statutes, long-established customs and norms, and a developing body of judicial precedents, as in the classic British model?

Fifth and broadest, what sorts of governing institutions should a constitution establish—a Westminster-style parliamentary system in which the dominant coalition in the legislature appoints a prime minister or president, as well as all the other major ministers who head the executive branch that directly governs? Or a system like that in the United States, with a separately elected president, and no prime minister, even if there are powerful leaders of the legislative chambers? Or a hybrid, as in modern France, with both a prime minister and a separately elected president? What sorts of judicial institutions are appropriate, and what should their relationship to the other branches be—should there be a special constitutional court disconnected from the regular judicial system, or should constitutional review be a function of some or all regular courts, or should courts defer to the elected legislature or the executive branch on constitutional issues? What should be the division of powers between the national government and any state or provincial governments or autonomous groups and regions, or local levels of government? And there are many other institutional choices to be made—far too many to list here.

Sixth, finally, and perhaps most important: what should the purposes of a constitution be? Should it simply authorize the sovereign people of a society to pursue whatever aims they find desirable, or should it specify shared aims in ways that are meant to serve as bounds as well as guides for what governments can legitimately do? If the latter, should those aims include establishing a national church, or a military authorized to engage in offensive wars, or powers to promote specific kinds of economic activity and social and moral conduct, or to combat group economic inequalities or entrenched patterns of racial, ethnic, gender, class, or regional discrimination?

Out of their fierce opposition to absolutist monarchies, many early modern constitution-makers, especially the Americans, were more concerned to limit the governments they authorized than to prescribe whole ways of life to their communities, in the manner Aristotle found to be characteristic of ancient constitutions. Even so, their constitutions suggested some content for the kinds of lives that could—and could not—be pursued by the populations governed by those constitutions. As noted, modern constitutions often strive to do much more, either by enshrining a broad variety of rights, in the cases of many transformative constitutions, or by enhancing the power of those who claim to speak for the people, in the cases of many populist ones.

America's Example

In this volume, scholars from different disciplines specializing in different parts of the world provide discussions that exhibit many of the answers that modern constitution-makers have given and are giving to most if not all of these questions in their varied settings. They offer reflections on why particular answers have been adopted and how far they may be judged successful. The three chapters in Part I consider the example of the U.S. Constitution. Because it was the first modern written constitution, many analysts, especially American ones, have long approached constitutionalism around the world through the lens of the U.S. example. After the Bolshevik Revolution in Russia, political scientist Henry Jones Ford did contend that "the constitution of the French republic" had come to exceed the American one in influence, as it was more congenial to socialist systems (Ford 1920, 3). Then, as the United States became the world's leading military and economic power at the end of World War II, the power of its constitutional example resurged.

In recent years, however, more and more writers have questioned this focus on American constitutionalism, in light of the long-standing, broad-ranging influence of the British and French constitutions and, especially, in light of the dramatic departures in modern transformative constitutions from the U.S. Constitution's emphasis on a small range of so-called negative rights. The Ecuador's 2008 constitution, for example, includes "positive" rights to education, food, water, health, income supports, and jobs, as well as a broad range of antidiscrimination and affirmative action requirements that go well beyond anything contemplated by the American framers in 1787.[2] Yet, still more recently, as populists have challenged understandings of constitutionalism as imposing limits, the scholarly pendulum has begun to swing the other way, with renewed calls for the relevance of early American constitutional conceptions of negative rights and bounded authorizations of governmental powers (Graber, Levinson, and Tushnet 2018, 5–9).

One prominent contribution to this continuing debate over the global importance of America's constitutional example appears here in updated form. In 2012, David S. Law and Mila Versteeg caused a stir when they argued for "the declining influence of the U.S. Constitution" (Law and Versteeg 2012). Then and still, Law and Versteeg contend that in most of its leading structural particulars, including a presidential rather than a parliamentary system, the systems of representation in the Congress, a presidential selection system involving the electoral college, its forms of federalism and separated powers, as well as its articulation of basic constitutional rights, the U.S. Constitution has few imitators today. Indeed, they argue, *no* other national system has been modeled closely on the American constitutional system as a whole. They also do not see any other model as hegemonic, however; and they are skeptical about the impact of modern populist movements on eroding constitutionalism as a whole. They perceive great diversity in constitutions around a world that has in many respects left the hard-to-amend U.S. Constitution far behind.

Not long after Law and Versteeg first wrote, various writers responded, many arguing that these contentions missed the forest for the trees. Perhaps most prominent was law professor Akhil Amar. He maintained that the U.S. Constitution can be seen as nothing less than the "hinge of world history," because before it, there simply were no large-scale national democratic systems, much less ones with written constitutions—and today, despite all the variations in particulars Law and Versteeg identify, these basic features of government are very much global norms (Amar 2012b). Amar has also long insisted that the model of the U.S. Constitution has over time reshaped the contents of what are now fifty American *state* constitutions, which collectively govern almost 330 million people—making this model of great contemporary significance, even if many other countries have chosen to depart from many of its elements (Amar 2006, 2012a).

There is clearly power in both arguments. Furthermore, discussions of the impact of American constitutionalism should probably not be confined to the 1787 Constitution and the subsequent Bill of Rights. As historian David Armitage has shown, the 1776 Declaration of Independence has had an even more pervasive global influence, fostering the core concepts that governments exist by the consent of the governed and are created in order to secure basic rights (Armitage 2007).

The other two chapters in Part I offer arguments that are pertinent to the question of whether the American state constitutions demonstrate the power of the example of the U.S. national constitution, while the essays in Part II present analyses that can help us consider its influence abroad, among other major issues. In Chapter 2, the often iconoclastic constitutional scholar Sanford Levinson weighs in on what might at first be seen as the Law and Versteeg side of this debate. Levinson calls into question, as he has done in range of works, whether the U.S. Constitution really deserves to be seen as a large-scale democracy that exemplifies governance by the consent of the governed (Levinson 2006, 2012). In the manner of Amar, however, Levinson stresses that the more amendable American state constitutions take commitments to democratic self-governance further than the original U.S. Constitution did. He urges greater attention to, and reliance on, *these* American constitutions.

In Chapter 3, political scientist Emily Zackin shows that state constitutions in America also have more in common with recent transformative constitutions than the U.S. national constitution has ever had. Over time, many state constitutions have included some "positive" rights for education, labor, environmental protection, and more. She contends that scholars should regard these state provisions as features of American constitutionalism, along with those found in the harder-to-change U.S. Constitution. Doing so diminishes to some degree the contrasts between American constitutionalism and patterns of constitutional contents elsewhere in the world. Zackin's work suggests that American constitutionalism, taken as a whole and analyzed in its historical evolution, shows more continuities with recent constitutions in other countries than many analysts have recognized. These continuities include both the establishment over time of a broader range of constitutional rights, and the emphasis on courts upholding the rule of law to limit governments that many of those concerned about populist excesses wish to reassert.

Global Patterns and Problems

The chapters in Part II display these continuities in modern constitutionalism in different parts of the world, as well as significant variations. They make it clear that the commitments to government by consent and explicitly republican self-governance found in the American Declaration of Independence and the original Constitution, as well as the concerns to insure that governments honor basic rights that are central to both, have indeed become pervasive features of the rhetoric and often the practice of constitutionalism everywhere in the ensuing centuries. Nonetheless, different countries have adopted very different answers to the questions of who can write a constitution, who can authorize it, whether it should be easily alterable, whether it can and should be strictly "written," as well as what sorts of basic institutions and purposes it should have.

In Part II's opening chapter, law professor Christopher McCrudden discerns a growing trend around the world to understand constitutions as designed to secure human rights that express fundamental values of human dignity. In keeping with David Armitage's argument about the influence of the American Declaration of Independence, this feature of modern global constitutionalism can reasonably be seen as in part a descendant of the insistence in the Declaration's preamble that governments must secure natural rights of all persons. The widespread emphasis on human dignity has, however, multiple sources. They include Catholic traditions that were probably far from the deist Thomas Jefferson's mind, along with more secular calls for recognizing intrinsic human dignity that proliferated as the world grasped the horrors of the Nazi Holocaust. In the modern era, proponents of many religious traditions and moral philosophies have reinforced those calls. In this still-burgeoning global landscape of avowed and institutionalized commitments to human dignity and human rights, we may perhaps see sources of constructive convergence in world politics.

McCrudden is careful to point out, however, that the rhetoric of human dignity is far more widely shared than understandings of just what tasks and limits are set for governments by dignity norms. They can be used to argue for rights of democratic self-governance and for a great variety of negative and positive rights, but for that very reason, sometimes they can serve as instruments of radical social transformations, sometimes as conservative bulwarks against reconstructive schemes. What seems beyond question is that the heightened focus on human dignity represents a developing pattern in global constitutionalism that merits close and continuing attention.

In Chapter 5, Tom Ginsburg contributes a counterpart argument. He, too, documents how some features of constitutionalism are being very widely adopted in the twenty-first century. In contrast to most versions of human dignity values, however, these features are ones that do only a little to diminish the fundamental differences between authoritarian and democratic regimes. Using an array of examples, Ginsburg shows that not only many regimes typically deemed democratic but also many regimes frequently classified as authoritarian display commitments to significant forms of the rule of law, stable institutional structures, and accountability for unconstitutional conduct by lower officials. To be sure, all such classifications of regimes are subject to reasonable disputes. But as Ginsburg explains, even undeniably authoritarian regimes can have strong incentives to attract foreign investors, limit domestic discontent, and make the consequences of their own governing decisions more predictable by establishing courts and other governing mechanisms that can, on a wide range of issues, insure that the regime earns a reputation for keeping its promises to all concerned. Those are some of the reasons why even authoritarian populist regimes can embrace many features of constitutionalism, as Müller and others argue.

Yet important as those judicial and administrative institutions and practices are, they do not mean that the promises advanced by an authoritarian regime, even a self-proclaimed populist authoritarian regime, will be the ones its people would choose if they could do so freely. Nor do they guarantee that authoritarian governors will comply with constitutional limitations when it threatens their power and purposes to do so. Important features of modern constitutionalism can therefore be adopted, and are being adopted, without any embrace of what proponents of liberal constitutionalism have long seen as the soul of the enterprise: constitutional democracy and a rule of law that applies to all.

Through a vigorous analysis that continues her extraordinary scholarly and political engagement with post-Soviet Hungary, legal sociologist Kim Scheppele provides a grimly compelling reminder that both the "constitutional" and the "democracy" do matter if morally acceptable legal rule is to be achieved. Just as there can be constitutionalism without democracy—indeed, there can be authoritarian constitutionalism that is hostile to democracy—there can also be populist democracy without any genuine commitment to constitutionalism. In opposition to proponents of unbridled legal positivism, Scheppele argues that even though Hungary's currently ruling Fidesz Party came to power in 2010 with a two-thirds parliamentary majority, and hence substantial claims to democratic authority, it has since enacted a set of policies and constitutional amendments that have moved Hungary sharply toward a totalitarian system that does not merit the designation "constitutional." Even as American scholars like Levinson question whether the U.S. Constitution is adequately democratic, Scheppele, a leading voice among modern critics of authoritarian populism, revives the case for rejecting democracy alone as the ultimate standard of governing legitimacy—especially when it is used against democratic institutions by shutting down the opportunities for political participation and political change of the ruling party's opponents. Her analysis shows why many are now suggesting, against voices like Levinson's, that at least some of the undemocratic features of the U.S. Constitution, and of constitutionalism more generally, may well be elements that deserve to be globally influential insofar as they work to preserve rather than to obstruct the realization of basic democratic and human rights.

Although the rise of authoritarian forms of populism appears to be the chief alternative to liberal democratic constitutionalism today, it remains true that much of the world still displays legacies of the preceding major alternative, Communism. The Soviet-style system that preceded the current Hungarian regime and many others is commonly seen today as one that was constitutional and democratic only in form, never in content or practice. But moving beyond those familiar critiques, comparative politics scholar Valerie

Bunce highlights a central and yet less discussed feature of Soviet constitutionalism: its explicit recognition of different nationalities and ethnocultural groups as distinctive members of the Soviet Socialist Republic, a recognition echoed, Bunce shows, in various other Soviet-era Communist constitutions. From many political points of view in many parts of the world, these features of Soviet constitutionalism might be regarded as desirable parts of a "politics of recognition" that respects valued social identities, even as it seeks to join them in common political and economic institutions that can benefit all. Recognition of group identities, particularly for long-discriminated-against and disadvantaged communities, forms a feature of many modern "transformative" constitutions, beginning with India's influential example and including many modern Latin American and African constitutions.

Yet Bunce demonstrates that not only is it true that, in the Soviet era, these recognitions fell far short of providing truly equal status to all nations and groups. They have since that time often become lines of fracture and antagonism that have worked against the achievement of healthy and stable political communities in the wake of Communism's dramatic decline. Her arguments reinforce a long and distinguished line of comparative politics scholarship that warns against undue accommodation of the aspirations of ethnic and national minorities and in favor of an emphasis on more universalistic forms of citizenship within constitutional democracies—civic forms that this scholarship attributes to American constitutionalism at its best, with reservations about apparent departures such as race-conscious aid policies (e.g., Horwitz 1985). In this regard, too, the U.S. Constitution, as amended after the Civil War, is gaining renewed credibility as a model of civic universalism, though at some risk of minimizing the history of ongoing racial and ethnic discrimination that the nation has displayed.

Vividly aware of how "universalism" has often meant compulsory conformity in many nations, comparative politics and legal scholar Jaime Lluch provides a different perspective. Lluch contends that experiences in North America and Europe offer evidence that constitutional democracies are often better off providing a significant measure of accommodation and recognition to those within their bounds who see themselves as minority nationalities. If these sorts of minorities, like the Catalonians in Spain and the Francophone residents of Quebec in Canada, are not given a significant measure of regional and cultural autonomy, Lluch suggests, the results over time are far less likely to display voluntary assimilation to a shared national identity than a more militant separatism, of the sort that Catalonians in particular are now displaying. That outcome is far from inevitable. A range of economic considerations, strategic judgments, and successes or failures in political mobilization can all contribute to determinations of whether strong separatist movements will emerge. But Lluch's analysis makes a forceful case that in many circumstances constitutional democracies are likely to be more stable and successful if they give a measure of acceptance to the claims for distinctive legal and political statuses of national minorities. This argument counters in some ways the lessons that many draw from post-Communist societies, and so it also casts doubts on whether the U.S. Constitution is a good model in this regard. As a native and current resident of Puerto Rico, another national minority community that has long struggled for appropriate recognition and autonomous authority and is in crisis today, Lluch is well positioned to judge the pertinent limitations of the U.S. model.

Law professor Heinz Klug's analysis of postapartheid South Africa provides another native's-eye view of modern constitution-making. His arguments blend elements of all the foregoing analyses. Persuaded in part by international boycotts, some leading adherents of the preceding authoritarian and racist South African regime came to accept the notion that some transition to a more genuinely constitutional, rule-of-law, indeed democratic system was necessary to achieve national security and prosperity. But rather than relying on any directly democratic processes of constitution-making, South Africa's transition was carefully negotiated between representatives of the nation's different racial and ethnocultural groups, among others. It also involved using the South African constitutional court to guarantee that the new constitution would not unduly threaten core economic and security interests of the long-ruling white minority. Subsequently in South African constitutional jurisprudence, values of human dignity have come to be almost universally espoused, fitting with the patterns McCrudden depicts. But in South Africa as elsewhere, human dignity is understood by partisans of different causes to mean very different things, from a focus on individual rights that is hostile to policies of racial reparations to vigorous efforts to promote more sweeping forms of economic, racial, gender, sexual, and cultural equality. Despite these efforts, severe inequalities continue to persist in South Africa today, along with profound political discontents that threaten the future of this still-new constitutional democracy.

Yet Klug finds some basis for cautious optimism that the negotiated, far less than fully democratic processes of South African constitution-making, including still-contentious forms of recognition for the rights of the white minority and the aspirations of long-excluded coloreds and blacks, may yet be on a longer historic track to greater democracy with a firmer constitutional rule of law. If so, its institutions and norms will almost certainly confirm the Law and Versteeg argument that constitutional democracy in many parts of the world does not closely resemble any of the main particulars of America's seminal Constitution of 1787. But they will provide further confirmation of the contentions of Akhil Amar and others that the world after the American Constitution is one in which aspirations to create and sustain some form of constitutional democracy are far more prevalent than they were before—or, perhaps, might otherwise have been.

The essays collected here cannot claim to encompass the full range of modern constitutions that have emerged in recent decades, much less the whole arc of modern constitutional experience since the late eighteenth century. Although the arguments of these scholars are informed by and reference constitution-making on every inhabited continent, they are weighted toward North American and European examples. Even so, they provide confirmation both that the making of modern constitutions inescapably involves responses to all of the six tasks of constitutional formation that we have identified and that, as Law and Versteeg contend, no uniform responses to any of them are emerging, even among this necessarily restricted sample. Yet the chapters that follow collectively identify some patterns, reviewed in the volume's conclusion, that provide a measure of guidance for the challenges and prospects of modern constitutions in the rapidly changing political world of the twenty-first century.

Notes

1. "Constitute: The World's Constitutions to Read, Search, and Compare," https://www.constituteproject.org/#/search.

2. "Constitution of the Republic of Ecuador," *Political Database of the Americas*, http://pdba.georgetown.edu/Constitutions/Ecuador/english08.html.

References

Amar, Akhil. 2006. *America's Constitution: A Biography*. New York: Random House.

———. 2012a. *America's Unwritten Constitution: The Precedents and Principles We Live By*. New York: Basic Books.

——. 2012b. "Why "'We the People" Loses Appeal' Misses the Point." *Constitution Daily*, February 10, 2012. http://blog.constitutioncenter.org/2012/02/why-"'we-the-people'-loses-appeal"-misses-the-point/.

Armitage, David. 2007. *The Declaration of Independence: A Global History*. Cambridge, MA: Harvard University Press.

Armstrong, Arthur Hilary. 1981. *An Introduction to Ancient Philosophy*. Lanham, MD: Rowman & Littlefield.

Dinghra, Alisha. 2014. "Indian Constitutionalism: A Case of Transformative Constitutionalism." *Asian Journal of Multidisciplinary Studies* 2 (7): 135–139.

Ford, Henry Jones. 1920. "Present Tendencies in American Politics." *American Political Science Review* 14 (1): 1–13.

Gargarella, Roberto. 2018. "Constitutional Changes and Judicial Power in Latin America." In *Latin America Since the Left Turn*, edited by Tulia G. Falleti and Emilio A. Parrado, 189–213. Philadelphia: University of Pennsylvania Press.

Graber, Mark A., Sanford Levinson, and Mark Tushnet, eds. 2018. *Constitutional Democracy in Crisis?* New York: Oxford University Press.

Horwitz, Donald L. 1985. *Ethnic Groups in Conflict*. Berkeley: University of California Press.

Law, David S., and Mila Versteeg. 2012. "The Declining Influence of the U.S. Constitution." *New York University Law Review* 87 (3): 762–858.

Levinson, Sanford V. 2006. *Our Undemocratic Constitution: Where the Constitution Goes Wrong (and How We the People Can Correct It)*. New York: Oxford University Press.

——. 2012. *Framed: America's 51 Constitutions and the Crisis of Governance*. New York: Oxford University Press.

Müller, Jan-Werner. 2016. *What Is Populism?* Philadelphia: University of Pennsylvania Press.

Pipes, Richard. 1990. *The Russian Revolution*. New York: Alfred A. Knopf.

PART I

The Example of American Constitutionalism

CHAPTER 1

Is the Influence of the U.S. Constitution Declining?

David S. Law and Mila Versteeg

> I would not look to the U.S. Constitution if I were drafting a constitution in the year 2012.
>
> —Justice Ruth Bader Ginsburg

In 1987, to mark the bicentennial of the U.S. Constitution, *Time* magazine released a special issue in which it called the Constitution "a gift to all nations" and proclaimed proudly that 160 of the 170 nations then in existence had modeled their constitutions upon our own (Greenwald 1987, 92). As boastful as the claim may be, the editors of *Time* were not entirely without reason. Over its two centuries of history, the U.S. Constitution has had an immense impact on the development of constitutionalism around the world.[1] Constitutional law has been called one of the "great exports" of the United States (Liptak 2008, quoting Anne-Marie Slaughter). In a number of countries, constitutional drafters have copied extensively, and at times verbatim, from the text of the U.S. Constitution.[2] Countless more foreign constitutions have been characterized as this country's "constitutional offspring."[3]

It is widely assumed among scholars and the general public alike that the United States remains "the hegemonic model" for constitutionalism in other countries (Klug 2000, 597). There can be no denying the popularity of the Constitution's most important innovations, such as judicial review, entrenchment against legislative change, and the very idea of "a written, single-document constitution" (Klug 2000, 605).[4] Today, almost 90 percent of all countries possess written constitutional documents backed by some kind of judicial enforcement (see Law and Versteeg 2012, fig. 9). As a result, what Alexis de Tocqueville once described as an American peculiarity is now a basic feature of almost every state.[5]

There are growing suspicions, however, that America's status as a constitutional hegemon is under attack from all directions.[6] At one end of the spectrum, it is often said that the United States is losing constitutional influence because it is increasingly out of sync with an evolving global consensus on issues of human rights.[7] At the other end of the spectrum, a small but conspicuous number of so-called "populist" regimes have been openly and unapologetically revising their constitutions in ways that are hostile to human rights and pursuing "illiberal democracy" rather than the type of liberal constitutional democracy traditionally associated with the United States (see, e.g., Ginsburg and Huq 2018; Graber, Levinson and Tushnet 2018).[8] Indeed, to the extent that other countries still look to the United States as an example, their goal may be less to imitate American constitutionalism than to avoid its perceived flaws and mistakes.[9] The reluctance of the U.S. Supreme Court to pay "decent respect to the opinions of mankind"[10] by participating in an ongoing "global judicial dialogue" (Law and Chang 2011; see also Slaughter 2004, 74, 243) has been said to diminish the global appeal and influence of American constitutional jurisprudence.[11] Studies conducted by scholars in other countries offer tentative empirical evidence that citation to U.S. Supreme Court decisions by foreign courts is in fact on the decline.[12] But these studies do not address the extent to which the U.S. Constitution itself continues to influence the adoption and revision of constitutions in other countries.

Our empirical analysis of all national constitutions from World War II into the twenty-first century shows that the U.S. Constitution has become increasingly out of sync with the global mainstream, and that other countries have been increasingly unlikely to model their own constitutions on the U.S. Constitution. This chapter begins by introducing the data and methods that we use to quantify constitutional content and measure constitutional similarity. Next, we describe the global mainstream of constitution-writing over this period. Specifically, we define a hypothetical *generic bill of rights* that exemplifies current trends, and we pinpoint the ways in which the rights-related provisions of the U.S. Constitution depart from this generic model. We then document the growing divergence of the U.S. Constitution from the global mainstream. The chapter concludes with a discussion of possible explanations for the declining influence of the U.S. Constitution.

Methods for Measuring Constitutional Similarity

Our primary data set covers a total of 729 constitutions adopted by 188 different countries from 1946 to 2006.[13] Each constitution is represented by a string of sixty binary variables, where each variable corresponds to a particular rights-related constitutional provision: a zero indicates that the constitution in question lacks the provision in question, while a one indicates that it contains the provision. We call this string of variables the *rights index*. The appendix lists all of the components of the index.

We next used this index to calculate a measure of the similarity between constitutions. To be specific, the similarity score for constitutions A and B measures the correlation between the rights index for constitution A and the rights index for constitution B. The measure that we compute is Pearson's phi,[14] which is a correlation coefficient for binary variables. Calculation of Pearson's phi for every possible pairing of constitutions in each year of our data yields a total of 648,429 similarity scores, each of which ranges from −1 to 1. A similarity score of −1 means that the two constitutions have precisely the opposite content, while a score of 1 means that they have identical content, as measured by the index. The actual similarity scores ranged from −0.41 to 1, while the average similarity score across all pairs of constitutions over the entire period was 0.35.

The Rights Content of a Typical Constitution

If constitution-makers do in fact copy from prominent models, that emulation ought to manifest itself in the existence of discernible patterns of similarity among constitutions. In this section, we explore whether and to what extent there is a standard or generic way of writing constitutions. Is there a generic model of constitutionalism to which actual constitutions tend to conform? If so, what are the elements of this generic model and which constitutions correspond most closely to it?

Generic Constitutional Rights

A significant number of constitutional provisions are so ubiquitous that they might fairly be called generic. This fact is immediately evident from Table 1.1, which ranks the components of the rights index according to their global popularity in 2006 and documents the growth in their popularity over the last six decades. The most popular, or generic, rights in the world are freedom of religion, freedom of expression, the right to private property, and equality guarantees. Each of these rights can be found in no less than 97 percent of all constitutions in force as of 2006. Nor are these the only rights that might fairly be described as generic: each of the twenty-five most popular constitutional provisions appears in over 70 percent of all constitutions. The existence of a corpus of constitutional provisions that are shared by a wide majority of the world's constitutions can fairly be said to define a shared, or generic, global practice of rights constitutionalism (see Law 2005, 662–726). In other words, over 40 percent of the components of our rights index are relatively generic.

It is also evident from Table 1.1 that the trend toward adoption of a generic set of constitutional rights is gaining momentum. The adoption rate for most components of the rights index is increasing over time: an increasing number of rights are becoming generic, while those that can already be described as generic are becoming even more ubiquitous over time. The proportion of constitutions that contain women's rights, for example, has more than doubled over the last six decades, from just 35 percent to 91.

At the same time, very few of the components of the index are declining in popularity. For the most part, even relatively unpopular rights appear to be growing somewhat more common. The only two components of the index that are less prevalent now than they were sixty years ago are provisions specifying an official state religion, which once appeared in nearly 40 percent of the world's constitutions but now appear in less than 25 percent, and the right to bear arms. Even as the U.S. Supreme Court lurches toward a more expansive reading of the Second Amendment,[15] the global popularity of this right is in a nosedive: the percentage of constitutions that contain a right to bear arms has declined over the last sixty years from an already scant 8 percent to a mere 2 percent.

Table 1.1. Global Popularity of Rights Index Components by Decade

Type of provision	*Percentage of constitutions that include provision by decade*						
	1946	*1956*	*1966*	*1976*	*1986*	*1996*	*2006*
	n=63	*n=75*	*n=120*	*n=138*	*n=156*	*n=182*	*n=188*
1. Freedom of religion	81	88	87	88	92	95	97
2. Freedom of the press and/or expression	87	88	84	86	87	95	97
3. Equality guarantee	71	77	85	88	92	95	97
4. Private property rights	81	85	81	83	87	95	97
5. Privacy rights	83	83	78	81	83	94	95
6. Prohibition of arbitrary arrest and detention	76	81	81	79	81	92	94
7. Right of assembly	73	77	73	75	81	90	94
8. Right of association	72	74	78	77	80	91	93
9. Women's rights	35	51	62	70	77	90	91
10. Freedom of movement	50	55	58	58	64	84	88
11. Right of access to court	68	68	64	62	64	85	86
12. Prohibition of torture	37	37	41	45	56	80	84
13. Voting rights	63	74	73	69	74	82	84
14. Right to work	55	65	59	67	65	80	82
15. Education right (positive)	65	72	59	65	65	78	82
16. Judicial review	25	32	53	51	58	80	82
17. Prohibition of ex post facto laws	41	51	57	60	67	77	80
18. Physical needs rights	44	60	52	57	61	75	79
19. Right to life	33	33	38	41	51	71	78
20. Presumption of innocence	8	12	31	37	49	69	74
21. Right not to be expelled from home territory	30	33	38	44	48	70	73
22. Limits on property rights	51	63	58	68	70	70	73
23. Right to present a defense	30	37	52	57	64	69	72
24. Right to unionize and/or strike	25	35	49	50	50	69	72
25. Right to counsel	10	17	31	38	47	66	70
26. Right to public trial	43	47	46	48	53	65	69
27. Family rights	28	28	38	43	46	62	67
28. Right to form political parties	9	16	28	26	31	63	65
29. Children's rights	25	35	30	35	40	59	65
30. Citizen duties	53	62	52	59	56	63	65
31. Right to a healthy environment	0	0	1	8	20	52	63

(continued)

Table 1.1. (continued)

	Percentage of constitutions that include provision by decade						
	1946	*1956*	*1966*	*1976*	*1986*	*1996*	*2006*
Type of provision	*n=63*	*n=75*	*n=120*	*n=138*	*n=156*	*n=182*	*n=188*
32. Other workers' rights	32	45	38	42	46	57	59
33. Education right (negative)	57	56	44	38	35	52	55
34. Minority rights	16	24	20	20	26	43	51
35. Prohibition of double jeopardy	16	19	26	31	37	46	50
36. Right against self-incrimination	29	29	32	31	38	47	49
37. Right to a timely trial	8	11	18	22	31	40	47
38. Artistic freedom	10	16	13	17	23	42	45
39. Handicapped people's rights	0	1	3	5	13	30	43
40. Ombudsman or human rights commission	5	5	4	9	15	27	37
41. Marriage rights	18	31	30	28	26	32	35
42. Right to asylum	11	21	18	21	21	32	35
43. Reference to international human rights treaties	0	1	18	17	15	30	35
44. Elderly people's rights	3	3	3	7	12	26	34
45. Right to information about government	2	4	3	5	8	25	34
46. Separation of church and state	20	25	28	25	25	36	34
47. Right to protection of one's reputation or honor	13	11	8	10	17	29	32
48. Affirmative action	3	9	17	20	26	27	30
49. Natural resources for benefit of all	8	7	8	15	19	27	29
50. Right to appeal to higher court	8	8	7	7	8	20	25
51. Prohibition of death penalty	10	9	8	9	12	20	24
52. Official state religion	39	39	32	27	26	24	22
53. Prisoners' rights	10	12	9	12	10	15	18
54. Consumer rights	0	0	0	1	6	12	16
55. Right to resist when rights are violated	8	7	4	4	4	15	16
56. Substantive principles for education	11	16	10	15	15	14	14

(continued)

Table 1.1. (continued)

	Percentage of constitutions that include provision by decade						
	1946	*1956*	*1966*	*1976*	*1986*	*1996*	*2006*
Type of provision	*n=63*	*n=75*	*n=120*	*n=138*	*n=156*	*n=182*	*n=188*
57. Prohibition of genocide/ crimes against humanity	0	0	0	1	2	6	12
58. Crime victims' rights	0	0	0	0	1	7	10
59. Protection of fetuses	0	0	1	1	6	7	8
60. Right to bear arms	8	6	4	4	3	3	2

A Generic Bill of Rights

Because we know what constitutional content is generic, we can also define a hypothetical generic constitution. As noted above, the twenty-five most common components of our rights index appear in over 70 percent of the world's constitutions and thus can fairly be called generic. By coincidence, the average constitution has, over the last sixty years, contained exactly twenty-five of the sixty components in our index. Accordingly, by selecting the twenty-five most common provisions, we can construct a hypothetical bill of rights that expresses the mainstream of global constitution-writing. This generic bill of rights contains both the average *number* of rights provisions and the most *common* rights provisions over the last six decades. Its content consists of all twenty-five rights above the horizontal dividing line in Table 1.1.

Needless to say, not all constitutions are equally (or increasingly) generic. Table 1.2 lists the real-world constitutions that are most and least similar to our hypothetical "generic constitution" as of 2006. The list of the most generic or mainstream constitutions is dominated by Commonwealth countries, with a handful of former French colonies interspersed among them. The constitutions of former British colonies were often drafted under strong British influence at the time of independence and, as a result, tend to share a common blueprint.[16] Over time, a number of Commonwealth members, such as Canada, New Zealand, and the United Kingdom itself, have adopted rights provisions that have rendered their constitutions more generic.[17] A notable exception to the trend among Commonwealth countries,

Table 1.2. Most and Least Generic Constitutions as of 2006

Rank	*Most generic constitutions (as of 2006)*	*Similarity to generic constitution*
1.	Djibouti	0.76
2.	St. Lucia	0.74
3.	Botswana	0.73
4.	Grenada	0.73
5.	Mali	0.71
6.	Antigua & Barbuda	0.70
7.	Kenya	0.70
8.	St. Kitts & Nevis	0.70
9.	St. Vincent & Grenadines	0.70
10.	Solomon Islands	0.70
Rank	*Least generic constitutions (as of 2006)*	*Similarity to generic constitution*
1.	Saudi Arabia	0.09
2.	Brunei	0.12
3.	Australia	0.12
4.	Argentina	0.16
5.	Norway	0.18
6.	China	0.20
7.	Indonesia	0.23
8.	Turkmenistan	0.28
9.	Armenia	0.29
10.	Colombia	0.29

however, is Australia, which instead possesses one of the world's *least* mainstream constitutions. With a constitution that contains only a scattering of rights, Australia now enjoys the dubious distinction of being "the only western nation without any form of Bill of Rights at any level of government" (Williams 2004, 305).[18]

The absence of the U.S. Constitution from Table 1.2 is revealing. Although the U.S. Constitution is not one of the world's least generic constitutions, it is not on the list of the world's most mainstream constitutions either. Table 1.3 identifies the dissimilarities between the "generic bill of rights" described above and the U.S. Constitution. The fact that the U.S. Constitution departs in so many ways from the global mainstream hints strongly at the possibility that the U.S. Constitution is not widely emulated. It is this possibility that we explore at length in the next section.

Table 1.3. Itemized Comparison of the U.S. Constitution and Generic Bill of Rights

Provisions found in both documents	*Provisions found only in the generic bill of rights*	*Provisions found only in the U.S. Constitution*
Right to life	Freedom of movement	Right to bear arms
Prohibition of torture	Right not to be expelled from home territory	Separation of church and state
Prohibition of arbitrary arrest or detention	Presumption of innocence	Right to public trial
Right of access to court/ impartial tribunal	Right of association	Right to timely trial
Right to present a defense	Establishment of judicial review	Right against self-incrimination
Prohibition of ex post facto laws	Right to work	Prohibition of double jeopardy
Right to counsel	Right to unionize and/ or strike	
Freedom of religion	Physical needs rights	
Right of assembly	Right to education	
Right to vote	Women's rights	
Right to private property	Limits on property rights	
Equality guarantee		
Right to privacy*		
Freedom of expression		

* The prohibition of "unreasonable searches and seizures" in the Fourth Amendment to the U.S. Constitution is coded as a provision that protects privacy.

The Declining Influence of the U.S. Constitution

Constitutional Similarity as an Indicator of Constitutional Influence

The existence of this generic core of constitutional content raises the question of whether there are particular countries that play an especially significant role in driving its popularity or shaping its content. Are there specific constitutions that define this core and serve as models for rights constitutionalism in other countries? And if so, is the U.S. Constitution such a model?

Much can be learned about the influence of various constitutions simply by analyzing the extent to which constitutions resemble one another or typify global practice. If two constitutions are becoming increasingly dissimilar, it stands to reason that neither is following the example of the other. Likewise, an increasingly atypical constitution is almost certainly not serving as a model for global constitutionalism. To the extent that a particular constitution is increasingly out of sync with global trends, we can rule out the possibility that it is leading those trends. And it is in precisely this manner that the declining influence of the U.S. Constitution can be shown.

Declining Similarity to the U.S. Constitution in the Area of Constitutional Rights

If the components of the rights index are used as the benchmark, the world's constitutions have on average become less similar to the U.S. Constitution over the last sixty years. As Figure 1.1 reveals, average similarity to the U.S. Constitution was higher in 1946 than in 2006.[19] Although the 1990s were a period of intense constitution-making activity[20] during which American victory in the Cold War might have been expected to translate into American constitutional influence, this decade actually saw a noticeable decline in average similarity to the U.S. Constitution. During this time, dozens of Central and Eastern European countries overhauled their Soviet-era constitutions (see Elster 1995, 368–369), while countries in Africa and Asia underwent a contemporaneous wave of constitutional reforms.[21] Whatever constitutional script prevailed amid the ostensible triumph of liberal democracy,[22] however, it was not that of the venerable U.S. Constitution.

Which constitutions have shown the most extreme similarity—or dissimilarity—to the U.S. Constitution over the last six decades? Table 1.4 sets forth the answer. Most similar to the U.S. Constitution, for many years, was the constitution of Liberia, which is unsurprising given the degree to which the histories of the two countries are intertwined. Not only was Liberia founded by freed slaves from the United States, but the first Liberian constitutions were drafted with the help of the American Colonialization Society, the organization that arranged the settlement of the former slaves.[23] Likewise, the fact that the Philippines was a colony of the United States readily explains the proximity of its postwar constitution to the American model.[24]

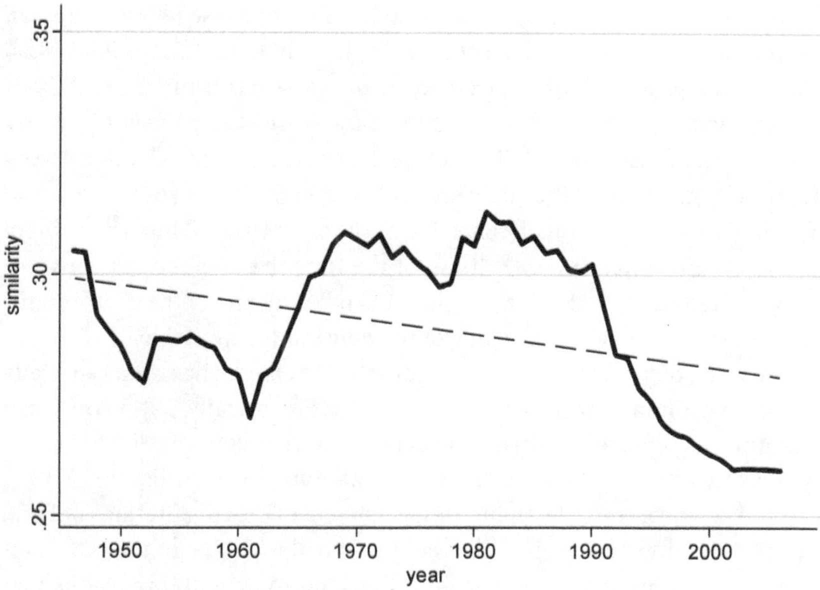

Figure 1.1. Average Similarity to the U.S. Constitution

Table 1.4. Constitutions That Are Most Similar and Dissimilar to the U.S. Constitution

The five constitutions most similar to the U.S. Constitution	
Liberia (through 1983)	0.82
Tonga (through 2006)	0.75
Uganda (1967–1994)	0.70
Philippines (through 1972)	0.70
Kiribati (1979–2006)	0.70
The five constitutions least similar to the U.S. Constitution	
Burkina Faso (1988–1990)	−0.18
Ghana (1991)	−0.17
New Zealand (1962–1970)	−0.13
Venezuela (1948–1952)	−0.13
Indonesia (2001–2006)	−0.13

By contrast, the reasons for the close and continuing resemblance between the American and Tongan constitutions are less obvious.[25] Tonga is a British colony that is governed through a mixture of Western institutions and chieftainship, with a polity divided into three classes—the king, the nobility, and the commoners (see Powles 2009, 140–141). Perhaps the crucial link between the two constitutions is that they are both very old: At 134 years of age and counting, the constitution of Tonga is by now older than all but a handful of the constitutions in our data.[26] Thus, at the time that the Tongan constitution was drafted, the U.S. Constitution was not only one of the most prominent models available, but also one of the *only* models available.

The trend of growing divergence from the U.S. model has been especially pronounced among Latin American countries. Historically, Latin American constitutions reflected American hegemony in the region in the form of a high degree of resemblance to the U.S. Constitution (see Billias 2009, 124–141). Today, by contrast, the rights-related content of the constitutions of Peru, Argentina, and Venezuela is negatively correlated with that of the U.S. Constitution, meaning that these constitutions tend to contain provisions that the U.S. Constitution lacks, while at the same time omitting provisions that can be found in the U.S. Constitution. Many of today's Latin American constitutions were adopted during the early twenty-first-century "left turn" in Latin American politics that has since reversed, but that ideological reversal has not been accompanied by constitutional revisions back in the direction of the American model (see generally Falleti and Parrado 2017).

The Flagging Popularity of the Structural Constitution

Our analysis thus far offers strong evidence that the U.S. Constitution is losing popularity as a model for constitution-makers, at least as far as the enumeration of rights is concerned. But what of the structural and institutional innovations for which the U.S. Constitution is also renowned? There are three features of what has come to be known as the "structural constitution"[27] that are closely associated with American constitutionalism: federalism,[28] presidentialism,[29] and judicial review.[30] Is it merely the particular rights guarantees found in the U.S. Constitution that fail to inspire today's constitution-makers, or is the global popularity of the structural constitution also in decline? The answer appears to be that the most distinctive and celebrated structural features of the U.S. Constitution have also fallen out of vogue.

Figure 1.2. Percentage of Countries with Federal Systems

Federalism

Federalism held considerable appeal to constitution-makers in the early nineteenth century, and nowhere more so than in Latin America, where it was embraced by Argentina, Brazil, Chile, Uruguay, Venezuela, and Mexico, among others (see, e.g., Billias, 2009, 106, 124–140; Horowitz 2009, 506). Even at the peak of its popularity in the early twentieth century, however, only 22 percent of the world's nations employed some form of federalism.[31] Since that time, federalism has diminished in popularity.[32] Following a significant decline in the interwar period, the proportion of countries with a federal system recovered somewhat to about 18 percent in the immediate aftermath of World War II but has since stabilized at a mere 12 percent. These developments are depicted in Figure 1.2, which graphs the proportion of countries with a federal system over the last two centuries.[33]

Presidentialism

A similar fate has befallen another famous American constitutional innovation, that of presidentialism. Like federalism, presidentialism enjoyed early popularity

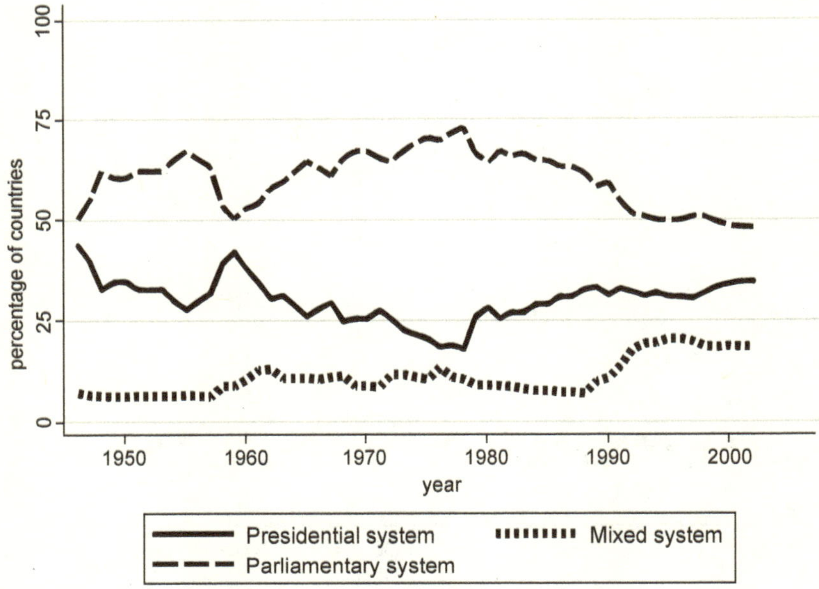

Figure 1.3. Popularity of Presidential, Parliamentary, and Mixed Systems

in Latin America.[34] Many of these early Latin American experiments with presidentialism degenerated into dictatorial rule,[35] however, and these failures helped to give presidentialism itself a bad name[36] and to discourage other nations from adopting similar systems.[37] Figure 1.3 depicts the prevalence of presidential, semi-presidential (or mixed), and parliamentary systems among the world's democracies over the last six decades.[38] In absolute terms, the parliamentary model has consistently been the most popular of the three and is at present the choice of roughly half of the world's democracies. By contrast, although presidentialism has enjoyed a slight resurgence since its nadir in the 1970s, it remains less widespread now than it was in the immediate aftermath of World War II. What has gained popularity over time, mainly at the expense of parliamentarism, is the mixed, or semi-presidential, model, which was widely adopted among the former Soviet bloc countries that emerged from Communism in the 1990s.[39]

Judicial Review

It is perhaps ironic that the most popular innovation of American constitutionalism has been judicial review,[40] given that this celebrated institution is nowhere mentioned in the U.S. Constitution itself. Today, the majority of the world's constitutions mandate judicial review in some form. In 1946, only 25 percent of all constitutions explicitly provided for judicial review; by 2006, that proportion had increased to 82 percent.

The particular form of judicial review that has proven most popular, however, is not the form that was pioneered by the United States.[41] Under the American model, the power of judicial review is vested in courts of general jurisdiction, which rule upon the constitutionality of government action as the need arises in the course of ordinary litigation.[42] Under the European model, by contrast, the power to decide constitutional questions is exercised exclusively by a specialized constitutional court that stands apart from the regular judiciary.[43] A further distinction is routinely drawn between concrete review, which characterizes the American model, and abstract review, which typifies the European model. In a system of concrete review, courts decide constitutional questions in the course of ordinary litigation, as part of what Americans would call a case or controversy,[44] whereas in a system of abstract review, the constitutionality of a law can be decided in the absence of a concrete, adversarial dispute and, indeed, before the law has even gone into effect.[45]

Over the last six decades, a growing proportion of constitutions have adopted the European model of abstract review by specialized courts, as opposed to the American model of concrete review by ordinary courts. At the close of World War II, the American model enjoyed a commanding lead over the European model as the choice of over 80 percent of constitution-makers, but its popularity began to erode in the 1970s. By the mid-1990s, the European model had overtaken the American model as the choice of over half the world's constitutions. Figure 1.4 illustrates these global trends. The creation of specialized constitutional courts of the European variety has proven especially popular among newly democratic states, where distrust of existing judicial institutions associated with the old regime is often widespread.[46] Thus, although the U.S. Constitution may have pioneered the idea of binding judicial enforcement of individual rights—an idea that now enjoys nearly universal acceptance—it is no longer the leading source of inspiration for how such enforcement is to be institutionalized. The form of judicial review that other countries tend to adopt has a more European than American flavor.

To the extent that there is a trend toward "illiberal democracy"—which is debatable (see Law and Lin 2018)—any such trend would only heighten

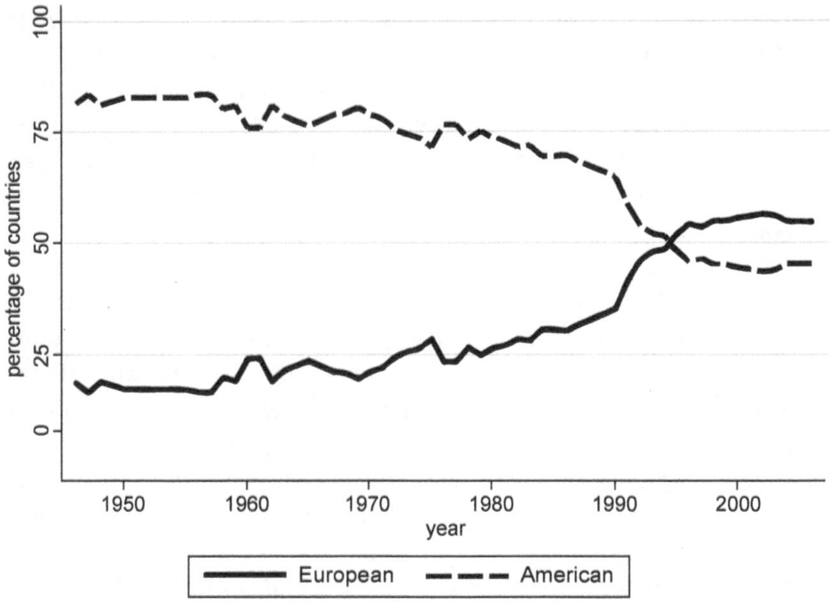

Figure 1.4. Popularity of American-Style Versus European-Style Judicial Review

constitutional divergence from the U.S. model. Countries like Hungary, Poland, and Turkey are attracting concern for centralizing power, rather than embracing federalism; consolidating the authority of strongman leaders who control their respective parliamentary parties; and actively curtailing the role of independent judicial review (Furtak 2017).

Friends But Not Followers: Constitutionalism Among American Allies

It is plausible to think that the influence of the U.S. Constitution is declining only among certain groups of countries and not others. One possibility, for example, is that the decline of similarity to the U.S. Constitution might track polarization of the global community into pro- and anti-American contingents. As a superpower, the United States has inevitably alienated some countries while attracting and influencing others. Might it be the case, therefore, that some countries have chosen to resist American hegemony by repudiating American-style constitutionalism, while others that remain aligned with the

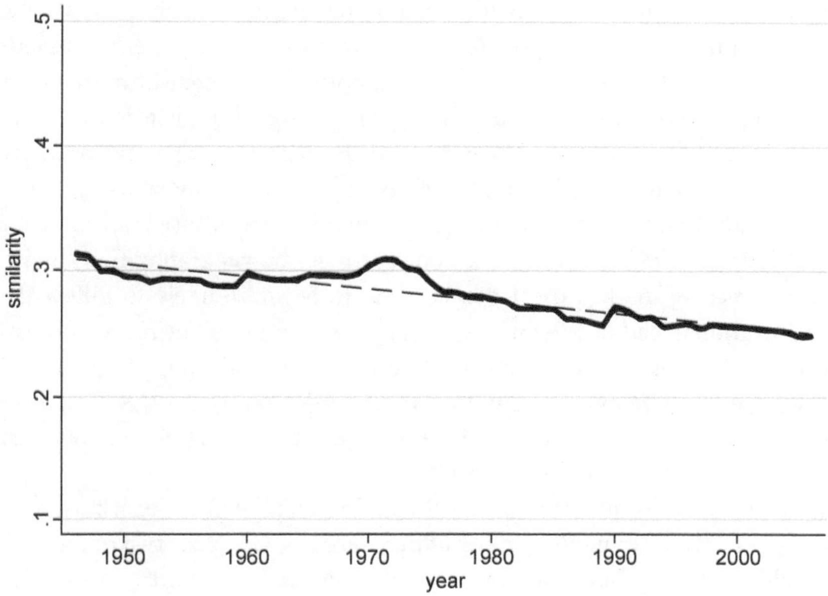

Figure 1.5. Average Similarity to the U.S. Constitution Among U.S. Allies

United States or within its sphere of geopolitical influence have remained faithful to the American constitutional model?

Examination of our data on the rights-related content of the relevant constitutions suggests that the answer is no. Figure 1.5 above depicts the average level of similarity to the U.S. Constitution among allies of the United States, defined as those countries that deployed troops either to Afghanistan in 2001 or to Iraq in 2003 (see Goderis and Versteeg 2012, 143, table 2). The graph offers little support for the notion that the U.S. Constitution remains an attractive model for America's allies. If anything, the American example is being rejected to an even greater extent by America's allies than by the global community at large.

Other Spheres of American Influence: Regional, Political, and Legal

Of course, a country's military alliances may not capture the scope or extent of its constitutional influence. It may be that the countries most likely to follow the American constitutional model are not merely sympathetic to the United States, but also *similar* to it in relevant ways. Relevant similarities might be geographic, historical, political, or legal in nature. For example, Western Europe and Latin America have close historical and political ties to the United States and have been within the American sphere of influence. Countries in those regions might thus be more likely to adhere to an American model of constitutionalism than those elsewhere. Or perhaps the relevant peer group is defined less by geography than by regime type: we might expect democracies to be more likely to follow the constitutional lead of a fellow democracy. Yet another plausible hypothesis is that countries with the same legal heritage and traditions as the United States ought to be more receptive to the example set by the U.S. Constitution, which is itself rooted in the common law tradition (see, e.g., Schauer 2005, 917; D. Strauss 1996, 877–890).

Our data offer little support for the notion that the U.S. Constitution remains an attractive model for any of these groups. Consider two of the geographic regions where the U.S. Constitution might be expected to enjoy enduring influence, Latin America and Western Europe. After decades of slow and irregular movement away from the American model, Latin American constitutions began to differentiate themselves quite sharply from the U.S. Constitution in the 1980s, and that trend continues through the present. Likewise, Western European constitutions are less similar to the U.S. Constitution now than at any point over the last sixty years, although the extent of the decline in similarity has been less dramatic. Figure 1.6 graphs the trends in both Latin America and Western Europe.

The trend among common law countries is also negative. Although common law countries converged strongly on the American model over the 1960s, they have been drifting in the opposite direction since the mid-1980s. It is among the world's democracies, however, that constitutional similarity to the United States has declined most dramatically. Over the 1960s and 1970s, democratic constitutions as a whole became more similar to the U.S. Constitution, only to reverse course in the 1980s and 1990s. The turn of the twenty-first century, however, saw the beginning of a steep plunge that continues through the most recent years for which we have data, to the point that the constitutions of the world's democracies are, on average, less similar to the U.S. Constitution now than they were at the end of World War II. Figure 1.7 illustrates this drift away from the American model among both democracies and common law countries.

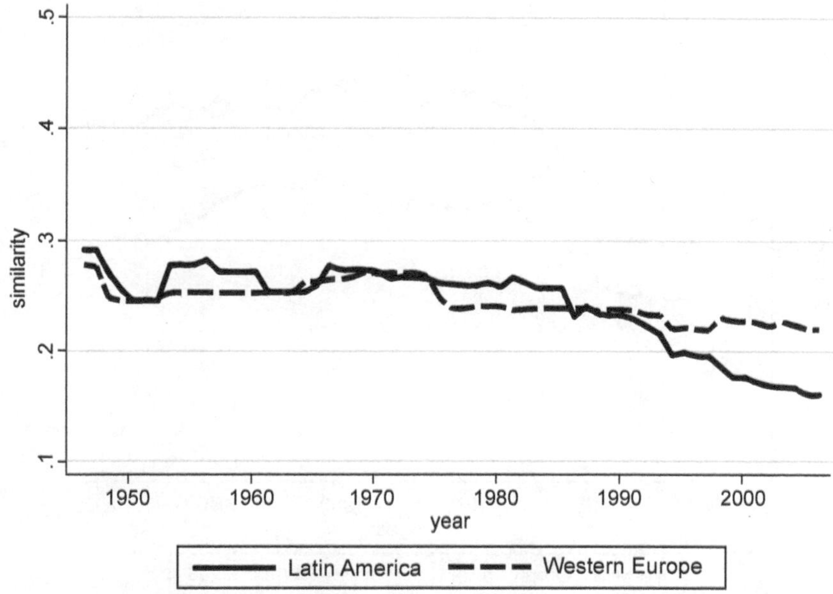

Figure 1.6. Average Similarity to the U.S. Constitution in Latin America and Western Europe

What Variables Predict Similarity to the U.S. Constitution?

Regression analysis can be used to identify variables that predict constitutional similarity to the United States.[47] The results largely confirm the impressions conveyed by the figures above. The specific variables that we test are: (1) whether the country that adopted the constitution is located in Western Europe; (2) whether the country is located in Latin America; (3) whether the country has a common law system; (4) whether the country is militarily allied with the United States, as measured by whether it sent troops to either Afghanistan in 2001 or Iraq in 2003; and (5) the country's level of democracy, as measured numerically in the political science literature.[48] To evaluate the possibility that older or less frequently updated constitutions may bear a greater resemblance to the U.S. Constitution than newer or more frequently updated constitutions, we also include (6) the number of years since the constitution was adopted or last revised with respect to any of the sixty provisions in the rights index.[49]

Temporal and spatial variables require special attention from a methodological perspective. Given how infrequently constitutions are amended

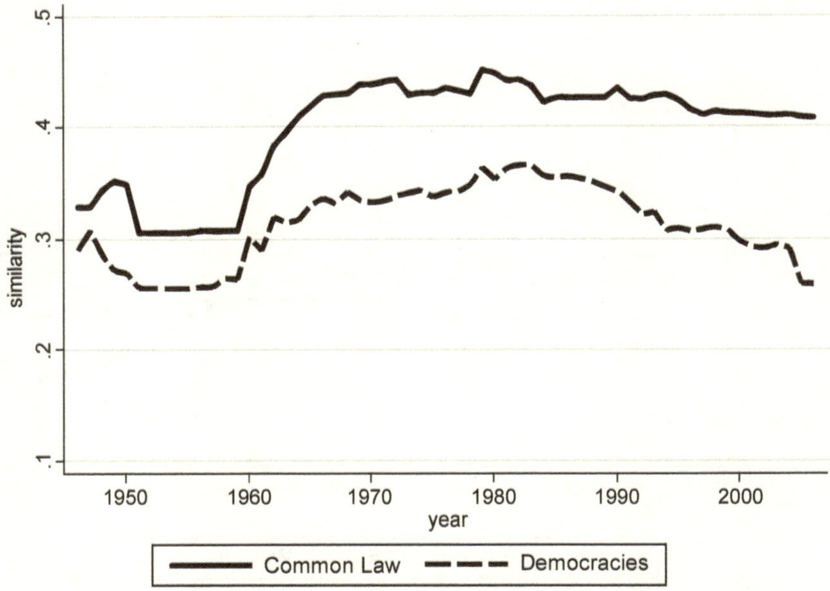

Figure 1.7. Average Similarity to the U.S. Constitution Among Democracies and Common Law Countries

or replaced, the strongest predictor of a constitution's similarity to the U.S. Constitution in any given year is likely to be its similarity to the U.S. Constitution in the preceding year. To prevent the relatively static nature of many constitutions from distorting our results, we include as a predictor (7) similarity to the U.S. Constitution over the *preceding* decade.[50] The regression model further includes (8) decade-specific predictor variables that enable us to determine which decades, if any, were characterized by distinctive trends.[51] Finally, we tested the possibility that similarity to the U.S. Constitution might correspond to sheer physical proximity to the United States by estimating an alternative version of the model in which we replaced the two existing geographically based variables—namely, the indicators of whether a country is part of Latin America or Western Europe—with a single variable that measures the physical distance between the country's capital and New York City.[52]

Although the model as a whole does a fairly good job of predicting constitutional similarity,[53] only a handful of specific variables proved to be statistically meaningful predictors of similarity to the U.S. Constitution. There is no statistically significant relationship between a country's level of democracy and the extent to which its constitution resembles the U.S. Constitution. Likewise, neither the fact that a country is militarily allied with the United States nor the fact that it is located inside or outside of Western Europe appears to make a difference. Nor does mere physical proximity to the United States, by itself, predict increased constitutional similarity to the United States. On the contrary, the fact that a country is located in nearby Latin America predicts *decreased* similarity to the American model. Notwithstanding Latin America's reputation for being highly receptive to American constitutional ideas in the nineteenth century, the region has on the whole exhibited the opposite tendency over the second half of the twentieth century.[54]

Common law countries as a group exhibit constitutional similarity to the U.S. Constitution, but this tendency is fairly muted and has diminished since the 1980s.[55] As expected, constitutions that are older or less frequently updated exhibit greater similarity to the U.S. Constitution than do recently drafted or amended ones.[56] Finally, the results of the regression confirm that the steep decline in average similarity to the U.S. Constitution over the last two decades pictured in Figure 1.1 is statistically significant.[57]

Why Is the U.S. Constitution Increasingly Atypical?

There are undoubtedly many reasons for which the U.S. Constitution, notwithstanding its long reputation for being exceedingly influential, is becoming increasingly atypical by global standards, but a handful of quantitative and qualitative differences between the U.S. Constitution and other constitutions deserve particular attention. First, the U.S. Constitution is increasingly atypical in the purely quantitative sense that it offers relatively few enumerated rights.[58] While the catalog of rights found in other constitutions has steadily grown (see Law and Versteeg 2011, 1194–1198, on this "rights creep"), the laconic U.S. Constitution has not added any rights at all over the last century. As a result, it contains only twenty-one of the sixty provisions in our rights index, whereas the average constitution currently contains thirty-four.

Second, among the relatively few rights that the U.S. Constitution does contain are provisions that happen to be rare at a global level. One is the Establishment Clause: today, only about one-third of the world's constitutions provide expressly for a separation of church and state (see Table 1.1). Another is a right that is now so rare that it has become practically sui generis—namely, the right to bear arms. The only other constitutions in the world today that still feature such a right are those of Guatemala, Mexico, and arguably Haiti,[59] while the Argentinean constitution contains a somewhat different duty to bear arms in defense of the fatherland.[60]

Third, the U.S. Constitution omits a number of the generic building blocks of global rights constitutionalism. Women's rights, for example, can currently be found in over 90 percent of the world's constitutions, but they do not appear anywhere in the text of the U.S. Constitution (see Table 1.1). The same is true for physical needs rights, such as the right to social security, the right to health care, and the right to food, which appear in some form in roughly 80 percent of the world's constitutions but have never attained constitutional status in the United States (see Table 1.1).[61] The U.S. Constitution is, instead, rooted in a libertarian constitutional tradition that is inherently antithetical to the notion of positive rights.[62]

Fourth, the fact that the U.S. Constitution is both old—older, indeed, than any other constitution currently in force[63]—and extremely difficult to amend[64] raises the possibility that it is simply becoming obsolete. Whereas the average constitution has a 38 percent chance of being revised in any given year and is replaced every nineteen years (Elkins, Ginsburg, and Melton 2009, 101, 129), the U.S. Constitution has survived over two centuries and has been amended only once in the last forty years.[65] Critics have thus argued that the U.S. Constitution is in many respects dysfunctional, antiquated, and sorely in need of repair.[66] Indeed, the older a constitution becomes, the more dysfunctional it may be. A constitution is likely to become increasingly obsolete over time, but efforts to update it may be thwarted by the fact that the costs involved in switching to a new set of arrangements are likely to increase as well.[67]

Even if continued use of an old constitution with little or no amendment makes sense for a particular country, constitutional drafters elsewhere working with a relatively clean slate, the benefit of hindsight, and contemporary needs and circumstances in mind may be unlikely to adopt that constitution as a template for their own efforts. And to the extent that they do look to the old system for inspiration, they may look not to its ancient core, but to the subsequent engineering efforts that have kept it viable. With respect to the U.S. Constitution, some of these efforts have been statutory, as in the case of the Civil Rights Act of 1964,[68] the Administrative Procedure Act,[69] or even the Social Security Act.[70] Others have been the handiwork of judges: many of the most famous and important features of American constitutional law, such as substantive due process[71] and judicial review,[72] are not to be found in the text of the Constitution at all, but have instead been fashioned by the Supreme Court, which Woodrow Wilson justifiably dubbed a "constitutional convention in continuous session" (quoted in Peltason 1997, 191).

Conclusion: Why Is the U.S. Constitution Not a Model for Other Countries?

The content of the U.S. Constitution is becoming increasingly atypical by global standards. Over the last three decades, other countries have become less likely to model the rights-related provisions of their own constitutions upon those found in the U.S. Constitution. Meanwhile, global adoption of key structural features of the Constitution, such as federalism, presidentialism, and a decentralized model of judicial review, is at best stable and at worst declining. The idea of adopting a formal constitution still owes much to the United States, but the manner in which constitutions are written increasingly does not.

If the U.S. Constitution is indeed losing popularity as a model for other countries, what—or who—is to blame? A conclusive answer is elusive, but five possibilities suggest themselves: (1) the advent of a superior or more attractive competitor; (2) a general decline in American hegemony; (3) judicial parochialism; (4) a creed of American exceptionalism; and (5) constitutional obsolescence.

Superior Competitor

There is little indication that the U.S. Constitution has been displaced by any specific competitor. Indeed, it is doubtful that any particular constitution can currently be described as a dominant model for other countries. There is an increasingly clear and broad consensus on the types of rights that a constitution should include, to the point that one can articulate the content of a generic bill of rights with considerable precision (see Table 1.1).

Yet it is difficult to pinpoint a specific constitution[73]—or regional or international human rights instrument[74]—that is clearly the driving force behind this emerging paradigm. Our findings suggest, instead, that the development of global constitutionalism is a polycentric and multipolar process that is not dominated by any particular country.[75] The result is the constitutional equivalent of Esperanto, a synthesis of many languages that does not imitate any specific language.

Declining American Hegemony

Another possibility is that America's capacity for constitutional leadership is at least partly a function of American "soft power" more generally.[76] It is reasonable to suspect that the overall influence and appeal of the United States and its institutions have a powerful spillover effect into the constitutional arena. The popularity of American culture, the prestige of American universities, and the efficacy of American diplomacy can all be expected to affect the appeal of American constitutionalism, and vice versa. All are elements of an overall American brand, and the strength of that brand helps to determine the strength of each of its elements. Thus, any erosion of the American brand may also diminish the appeal of the Constitution for reasons that have little or nothing to do with the Constitution itself. Likewise, a decline in American constitutional influence of the type documented in this chapter is potentially indicative of a broader decline in American soft power.

Judicial Parochialism

Critics suggest that the Supreme Court has undermined the global appeal of its own jurisprudence by failing to acknowledge the relevant intellectual contributions of foreign courts on questions of common concern and by pursuing interpretive approaches that lack acceptance elsewhere.[77] On this view, the Supreme Court may bear some responsibility for the declining influence of not only its own jurisprudence, but also the actual U.S. Constitution. One might argue that the Court's approach to constitutional issues has undermined the appeal of American constitutionalism more generally, to the point that other countries have become unwilling to look either to American constitutional jurisprudence or to the U.S. Constitution itself for inspiration.[78]

It could instead be the case, however, that the U.S. Constitution undermines the global appeal of the Supreme Court's jurisprudence, rather than the other way around. As the oldest formal constitution still in force and one of the most rarely amended constitutions in the world, the U.S. Constitution contains relatively few of the rights that have become popular in recent decades. There is little reason for the Korean Constitutional Court, for example, to look to American jurisprudence when interpreting the numerous social or economic rights of the Korean Constitution, for the simple reason that the U.S. Constitution itself lacks comparable provisions.[79] At the same time, some of the provisions that the U.S. Constitution does contain may appear increasingly problematic, unnecessary, or even undesirable with the benefit of two hundred years of hindsight.[80] A body of jurisprudence focused on the interpretation of a constitutional document widely regarded as out of date and out of line with global practice could suffer from guilt by association.

Moreover, even if the Supreme Court were committed to interpreting the Constitution in line with global trends, it would still lack the power to update the actual text of the document. Indeed, efforts by the C ourt to update the Constitution via interpretation may actually reduce the likelihood of formal amendment by rendering such amendment unnecessary as a practical matter.[81] Such efforts might render the Court's jurisprudence more attractive to foreign audiences, but they would not necessarily make the U.S. Constitution itself a more attractive template for other countries.

American Exceptionalism

A more forgiving explanation for the U.S. Constitution's increasingly outlier status would emphasize its role in articulating and defining a unique national identity. It is frequently suggested that formal constitutions serve an expressive function as statements of national identity.[82] This view finds little support in our own empirical findings, which suggest instead that constitutions tend to contain relatively standardized packages of rights (see Law and Versteeg 2011, 1243; and above), and that even the most expressive parts of a constitution recycle familiar elements and narratives (Law 2016). Nevertheless, to the extent that constitutions do serve such a function, the distinctiveness of the U.S. Constitution may reflect the uniqueness of America's national identity. In this vein, some have argued that the U.S. Constitution lies at the heart of an "American creed of exceptionalism" (Calabresi 2006), which combines a belief that the United States occupies a unique position in the world with a commitment to the qualities that set the United States apart from other countries.[83] If the U.S. Constitution is indeed a statement of unique national identity, other countries cannot be expected to treat it as a template for their own constitutions.

It is doubtful that the declining influence of American constitutionalism can be explained simply as a consequence of American exceptionalism. Historically, American exceptionalism did not prevent other countries from following the example set by American constitutionalism.[84] The disinclination of other countries to model their own constitutions upon the U.S. Constitution since the 1980s has not been for lack of opportunity. The collapse of the Soviet Union simultaneously elevated the United States to the position of lone superpower and generated a wave of constitution-making, the combination of which ought to have created ample opportunities for the spread of American constitutionalism. But this did not come to pass.

Constitutional Obsolescence

Any account of the declining global appeal of the U.S. Constitution must contend with the static character of the Constitution itself. A consequence of our collective reluctance to revise or rewrite the U.S. Constitution[85] is a constitution that is out of touch not only with the global mainstream, but also with the United States itself. Our constitution simultaneously fails to reflect well-accepted realities of American governance (such as the party system and the administrative state)[86] and prescribes institutional arrangements that are unwanted, superfluous, or even profoundly antidemocratic (such as an electoral college with ultimate responsibility for selecting the president and an upper house that assigns the same number of seats to Delaware as to California).[87]

Even Americans seem to find it necessary to employ something more up-to-date than the U.S. Constitution as a template for other countries. Japan's 1946 constitution was initially drafted by U.S. military personnel pursuant to guidelines issued by General MacArthur (see Law 2013a, 242–244). Far from being a copy of the U.S. Constitution, however, the Nihonkoku Kenpō includes a much wider and more progressive array of rights and remains much more in sync with the global constitutional mainstream, even though it has never been amended.[88] In other words, an American-drafted constitution that has remained unchanged for generations manages to make the U.S. Constitution look obsolete. How surprising can it be that other countries are increasingly reluctant to copy the U.S. Constitution when Americans themselves decline to use it as a model for other countries?

It is a matter of opinion whether Americans should care if the U.S. Constitution is regarded by the rest of the world as a curio or antiquity unworthy of imitation. Empirical analysis can establish whether the United States supplies the constitutional template for the rest of the world; it cannot establish whether the rest of the world supplies a constitutional template that the United States ought to follow. What can be said, however, is that America's chronic reluctance to revise or update its constitution represents a failing by America's own standards. In adopting the Constitution, the United States simultaneously pioneered the act of constitution-writing and defined that act as a fundamental part of self-government and self-determination. It is a terrible irony that the United States has become exceptionally reluctant to practice what it pioneered and what remains its greatest contribution to constitutionalism. Refusal to revise the Constitution in the light of experience runs counter to the Enlightenment ideals of rational self-improvement and self-determination that spawned the Constitution in the first place.[89] Nothing could be more true to the spirit of the Constitution than to update it in light of both the lessons learned over the nineteenth and twentieth centuries and the challenges of the twenty-first century. To do so would be to renew our commitment to constitutionalism and self-government, and to honor the role and function of the Constitution rather than its text.

If the United States were to revise its formal constitution today—with the benefit of over two centuries of experience, and in a manner that addresses contemporary challenges while remaining faithful to the nation's best traditions—there is no guarantee that other countries would follow its lead. But the world would surely pay close attention.

Appendix: Components of the Rights Index

Abortion restrictions and/or protection of fetuses
Affirmative action provision authorizing or requiring compensatory action in favor of disadvantaged groups

Artistic and/or scientific freedom
Children's rights (including the prohibition of child labor)
Citizen duties, affirmatively imposed
Consumer rights
Crime victims' rights
Education right, negative (including freedom of education and right to establish private schools)
Education right, positive (right to receive an education)
Elderly people's rights (including equality regardless of age)
Establishment of a human rights commission or ombudsman
Establishment of judicial review (judicial invalidation of unconstitutional laws)
Establishment of substantive principles to be taught in schools (including religious, Communist, nationalist, internationalist, or democratic principles)
Express limitations on property rights (including limitations through regulation, substantive limits (for example, property may be limited by its social function), restriction of land rights, or mandate of land reform)
Express reference to international human rights treaty obligations
Family rights
Freedom of expression and/or freedom of the press
Freedom of movement
Freedom of religion
Guarantee of equality (including both blanket equality provisions and enumerated guarantees of equality without respect to race, place of origin, ethnicity, education, social status, caste, tribe, religion, belief or philosophical conviction, political preference or opinion, economic status or property ownership, ancestry, nationality, disability, age, sexual orientation, language, and/or HIV/AIDS status)
Handicapped people's rights (including equality regardless of disability)
Marriage rights
Minority rights (including special protection of minorities, protection of minority language, right to preserve traditional ways of life or culture, right for minority groups to establish their own schooling, right to minority representation in national government, right to use traditional lands, and right to some degree of autonomy for minority communities)

Physical needs rights or subsistence rights (including the right to social security, right to adequate standard of living, right to food, right to housing, right to water, and right to health)
Presumption of innocence
Prisoners' rights
Privacy rights (including personal privacy, inviolability of the home, protection of personal data, privacy of family life, and inviolability of communication)
Private property rights
Proclamation of an official state religion
Prohibition of arbitrary arrest or detention
Prohibition of death penalty
Prohibition of double jeopardy
Prohibition of ex post facto laws (retroactive laws)
Prohibition of genocide and/or crimes against humanity
Prohibition of torture
Requirement that the government use natural resources effectively and/or for the benefit of all citizens
Right of access to court or impartial tribunal
Right of assembly
Right of association
Right to appeal to higher court
Right to asylum
Right to bear arms
Right to counsel
Right to form political parties
Right to a healthy environment (including the duty to protect the environment, civil or criminal liability for damaging the environment, right to information about the environment, right to compensation when living environment is damaged, and right to participate in environmental planning)
Right to information about government
Right to life
Right to not be expelled from home territory
Right to present a defense
Right to protection of one's reputation or honor
Right to a public trial
Right to resist the government when rights are violated

Right to work (including the freedom to choose one's occupation and freedom of enterprise)
Right against self-incrimination
Right to strike and/or form a trade union
Right to a timely trial
Separation of church and state
Voting rights
Women's rights (including gender equality, women's empowerment in labor relations (e.g., equal pay for equal work), equality of spouses within the family, special protection of women (e.g., special conditions at work), right to maternity leave and special protection of mothers)
Workers' rights (including the right to work, right to favorable working conditions, right to rest, and right to minimum wage)

Notes

This chapter is a revised and abridged version of an article entitled "The Declining Influence of the United States Constitution," which was first published in the June 2012 issue of the *New York University Law Review* (Law and Versteeg 2012). The New York University School of Law furnished Professor Law with invaluable support and hospitality during the authorship of the original article. Collaboration between the authors was made possible by a grant from the Center for Empirical Research in the Law at Washington University in St. Louis.

Note to epigraph: Video clip of an interview with Justice Ginsburg, originally broadcast by the Egyptian television station Al-Hayat TV on January 30, 2012 (MEMRI 2012).

1. A considerable body of scholarship has sought to document the influence of the U.S. Constitution abroad (see, e.g., Billias 1990, 2009; Beer 1979; Henkin and Rosenthal 1990). Although some of these studies are more restrained in their conclusions than others, they have generally concluded that "the influence of American constitutionalism abroad was profound in the past and remains a remarkable contribution to humankind's search for freedom under a system of laws" (Billias 2009, xv).

2. Billias (2009, 105) notes that "few [regions] made greater use of North American constitutionalism" than Latin America and that "huge sections of two constitutions—Argentina's in 1853 and Brazil's in 1891—were copied word for word from the U.S. Constitution"; Horowitz (2009, 505) describes what Simon Bolivar dubbed a "craze for imitation" among Latin American constitutional drafters in the nineteenth century.

3. United States v. Then, 56 F.3d 464, 469 (2d Cir. 1995) (Calabresi, J., concurring) ("Since World War II, many countries have adopted forms of judicial review,

which—though different from ours in many particulars—unmistakably draw their origin and inspiration from American constitutional theory and practice. . . . These countries are our 'constitutional offspring'").

4. See Elkins, Ginsburg, and Melton (2009, 48–50), observing that "formal constitutions are the norm" for most countries, and deeming every country in the world from 1789 to 2006 to have possessed a formal constitution with the sole exception of the United Kingdom; Gardbaum (2008, 393, 411), identifying the United States as "the inventor of modern constitutional supremacy" in the form of "a constitution containing a bill of rights that is entrenched, the supreme law of the land, and enforced by the power of judicial review," and observing that these "constitutional fundamentals" have become so prevalent that "countries which continue to reject one or all of them . . . are now truly exceptional."

5. See Tocqueville ([1835] 2001, 72–77), deeming "the right of judges to found their decisions on the *Constitution* rather than on the *laws*" a form of "immense political power" that is "peculiar to the American magistrate" (emphasis in original).

6. See, e.g., Klug (2000, 598), arguing that "instead of enjoying an unassailable, dominant status," advocates of the American model now face "open competition from advocates of the German, Canadian, Indian, or other constitutional experiences"; Osiatynsky (2003, 260), noting that in post–Cold War Eastern Europe, the American constitutional model was "rejected almost out of hand because of the drastic difference in U.S. and postcommunist traditions and social conditions"; Schauer (2000, 260), commenting that "in some political quarters, avoiding American influence just because it is American often appears to be a driving force"; Stone Sweet (2008, 231), deeming "the American experience" "increasingly irrelevant to global constitutionalism"; Weinrib (2006, 84), stating that "the Constitution of the United States provided the inspiration for the rights-protecting constitutions of liberal democracies across the world. Yet the constitutional systems developed or newly established since the Second World War now differ from their U.S. precursor"; Schor, (2010, 157), noting that "the once predominant position of the United States within the Western constitutional tradition is under challenge by constitutional seeds planted immediately after the Second World War, such as the Universal Declaration of Human Rights (1948) and the German Basic Law (1949)."

7. See, e.g., Allan and Huscroft (2006, 2): "The U.S. Bill of Rights looks old and deficient compared to modern bills of rights." See also Schauer (2000, 258), arguing that constitution-makers are increasingly less likely to borrow from the U.S. Constitution, because "on issues of freedom of speech, freedom of the press, and equality, for example, the United States is seen as representing an extreme position." See generally Ignatieff (2005), documenting different aspects of "American exceptionalism" in the realm of human rights.

8. Whether these developments amount to a genuinely worldwide turn or trend against liberal constitutional democracy is, however, open to question. See Law and Lin (2018, 423–428), arguing that Asia is characterized not by antidemocratic or illiberal contagion but rather by a high degree of inertia.

9. See, e.g., Choudhry (2004, 15–24), discussing the lengths to which Canadian constitutional drafters went to "avoid substantive due process altogether, not merely its economic limb" (23); Klug (2000, 605–606), noting India's rejection of the phrase "due process of law" for fear of inviting *Lochner*-style jurisprudence, and raising the possibility that the U.S. Constitution may now serve as an "anti-model." See generally Scheppele (2003), discussing the phenomenon of "aversive constitutionalism," wherein certain countries serve as negative models that other countries consciously strive not to emulate.

10. Knight v. Florida, 528 U.S. 990, 997 (1999) (Breyer, J., dissenting from denial of certiorari), quoting Declaration of Independence, para. 1.

11. See, e.g., Slaughter (2004, 74), arguing that courts that are adept at "captur[ing] and crystalliz[ing] the work of their fellow constitutional judges around the world" enjoy disproportionate influence; Aharon Barak (Barak and Fried 2002, 16, 27, 114), arguing that the Supreme Court is "losing the central role it once had among courts in modern democracies," whereas "the Supreme Court of Canada is particularly noteworthy for its frequent and fruitful use of comparative law," with the result that "Canadian law serves as a source of inspiration for many countries around the world"; Law and Chang (2011, 568–74), contrasting the U.S. Supreme Court's relatively rare use of foreign law in constitutional cases with the Taiwanese Constitutional Court's nearly automatic consideration of foreign law; Liptak (2008), suggesting that the influence of the Supreme Court is waning in part because it does not engage in open intellectual exchange with foreign courts.

12. See, e.g., L'Heureux-Dubé (1998, 29): "An informal analysis of Canadian Supreme Court decisions since 1986 revealed that the Rehnquist Court was cited in fewer than one-half as many cases as the Warren Court, and in just under one-third the number of Burger Court cases." See also Smyth (2008, 425, table 1), reporting a decline in citations to U.S. federal court decisions by Australian state supreme courts from 1905 to 2005; also, e.g., Allan, Huscroft, and Lynch (2007, 437), finding that courts and litigants involved in rights litigation in New Zealand cite Canadian Supreme Court decisions more often than U.S. Supreme Court decisions. Michael Kirby (2001, 291) observes, with the benefit of personal experience as a High Court judge, that the High Court of Australia often turns for inspiration to "the Supreme Court of India, or the Court of Appeal of New Zealand, or the Constitutional Court of South Africa" instead of the U.S. Supreme Court. But cf. Law and Chang (2011, 558), observing that the Taiwanese Constitutional Court's citation of U.S. jurisprudence has fluctuated with the number of U.S.-educated justices on the court; Law (2015, 963–964, 979–980), reporting that both the Korean Constitutional Court and the Taiwanese Constitutional Court make a habit of researching and analyzing U.S. jurisprudence in the course of their deliberations. See generally Groppi and Ponthoreau (2013) for studies of the extent to which constitutional judges in various countries cite foreign jurisprudence, including that of the U.S. Supreme Court.

13. This data set was first introduced in Goderis and Versteeg (2011); it is also analyzed in Law and Versteeg (2011).

14. Compare Elkins, Ginsburg, and Melton (2008, 1155), using Pearson's phi to measure constitutional similarity, with Elkins, Ginsburg, and Melton (2009), using raw percentages in lieu of Pearson's phi as a measure of constitutional similarity. We employ Pearson's phi because it captures the fact that constitutional similarity is a function of what constitutions omit as well as what they affirmatively contain. Suppose, for example, that two constitutions do not affirmatively share any rights in common, but both happen to omit certain rights. In percentage terms, the similarity between the two constitutions is zero. A similarity score of zero is misleading in this case, however, because it fails to reflect the fact that the two constitutions share certain omissions in common. By contrast, the manner in which Pearson's phi is calculated incorporates both inclusions and omissions.

15. See McDonald v. City of Chicago, 130 S. Ct. 3020, 3026 (2010), holding the Second Amendment applicable to states; District of Columbia v. Heller, 554 U.S. 570, 629 (2008), invalidating a federal ban on handguns in the District of Columbia on Second Amendment grounds.

16. See Parkinson (2007, 1–19), describing the United Kingdom's involvement in the drafting of the independence constitutions of its (former) colonies in Africa and the Caribbean, and its insistence upon bills of rights modeled upon the European Convention on Human Rights; Franck and Thiruvengadam (2003, 500–504), describing a "transformation in British attitudes towards written constitutions with Bills of Rights" that ultimately led to the inclusion of bills of rights "heavily influenced by the provisions of the [European Convention on Human Rights]" in the constitutions of Nigeria, Kenya, and Uganda.

17. See Erdos (2010, 47–125), documenting the rise of bills of rights in Canada, New Zealand, and the United Kingdom; Gardbaum (2001, 708–709), outlining the features of the new rights-protection mechanisms in Canada, New Zealand, and the United Kingdom.

18. Williams (2004) notes that Australia became the last holdout among Western nations following Britain's enactment of the Human Rights Act 1998 (305); and reviews the six "important, but scattered, freedoms" found in the Australian Constitution (313–317).

19. Because the content of the U.S. Constitution did not change at all over this time frame with respect to the components of the rights index, the decrease in the average level of similarity necessarily reflects the evolution of other constitutions away from the U.S. Constitution, rather than evolution of the U.S. Constitution away from other constitutions.

20. See Elkins, Ginsburg, and Melton (2008, 113 fig. 5.2), documenting a global surge in the number of new constitutions circa the early 1990s; Elster (1995, 368–369), identifying "at least seven . . . waves" of constitution-making, the most recent of which followed the fall of Communism in 1989.

21. See, e.g., Alston (1999, 1–2), noting the "prolonged fit of 'constitutional fever'" that took hold in Africa following the Cold War; Davis (2010, 433), describing the East

Asian landscape in recent decades as "riddled with constitution-making exercises"; Go (2003, 78), noting that "many of the postcolonial constitutions in existence in 2000 were written in the 1990s"; Le Vine, (1997, 198), pointing to a proliferation of "re-democratized regimes and constitutions" as evidence of a "democratic revival in West Africa" between 1989 and 1997.

22. See Fukuyama (1992, xi), suggesting that the triumph of liberal democracy in the 1990s was so complete that it marked "the end of history."

23. See Dippel (2005, 168), observing that the Liberian Constitution of 1847 embraced the principles of the Virginia Declaration of Rights; Horowitz (2009, 507), identifying Harvard Law School professor Simon Greenleaf as the author of Liberia's 1847 constitution and noting that its 1983 revision was also modeled on the U.S. Constitution.

24. See Billias (2009, 229–33), describing U.S. influence on the drafting of the constitution of the Philippines; Horowitz (2009, 507), characterizing the 1935 Philippine constitution as an "American-style document."

25. Historical evidence suggests that the Tongan constitution-making process was influenced more by the Kingdom of Hawaii than the United States. See Parkinson (2007, 32), noting that Tonga's bill of rights was influenced by the Hawaiian constitutions of 1825 and 1864.

26. Among the few national constitutions currently in force that predate that of Tonga are those of Belgium, New Zealand, Norway, and the United States. Unlike the U.S. Constitution, however, the constitutions of Belgium, New Zealand, and Norway have been amended multiple times in recent decades. See Siaroff (2000, 186), counting four sets of revisions to the Belgian constitution from 1970 through 1993; Harris (2004, 279–280), listing thirty new constitutional statutes passed in New Zealand from 1972 to 2003; Rasch and Congleton (2006, 337 fig.12.2), reporting that, from 1989 to 1993 alone, the Norwegian Constitution was amended five times.

27. See, e.g., Wilkinson (2004, 1688), defining as "structural" "those provisions that appear to direct responsibility for a decision to a particular branch of the federal government or to the states" and arguing that such provisions are as integral to safeguarding individual liberty as those that explicitly concern individual rights.

28. See Beyme (1987, 71), attributing "the modern idea of federalism" to the United States and arguing that "of all the institutions within the American constitutional structure, it is federalism that has had the greatest influence in the world."

29. See Billias (2009, 34, 35), noting that "presidentialism was largely the invention of the framers" and that the U.S. president was "quite unlike any other chief executive existing in any nation at the time."

30. See, e.g., Billias (2009, 4), identifying "three important institutions incorporated in the U.S. Constitution: presidentialism, federalism, and judicial review"; Horowitz (2009, 503), noting that "federalism, presidentialism and judicial review are widely known and adopted, albeit in varying frequencies, around the world."

31. Our data on the prevalence of federalism is drawn from the "cent" variable in the Polity III data set (Jaggers and Gurr 1996), which covers 177 countries from 1800 to 1994. (Although there exists a more recent "Polity IV" iteration of this data set, the newer iteration lacks the data on federalism analyzed here.) The coding of this variable divides countries into the following three categories: (1) a "Unitary State" category, in which regional units have little or no independent decision-making authority; (2) an "Intermediate" category; and (3) a "Federal State" category, in which most or all regional units have substantial decision-making authority.

32. See Watts (2008, 4), noting that, from 1960 through the late 1980s, federalism suffered declining popularity and many "post-war federal experiments . . . were temporarily suspended or abandoned outright," but there was a "revival of interest" in federal systems in the 1990s; Horowitz (2009, 503, 518), noting that "federalism proved particularly attractive in the first decades of the nineteenth century" but is at present "relatively unpopular."

33. Figure 1.2 depicts the percentage of nations with a value of "3" on the "cent" variable from the Polity III data set—namely, those nations that are identified as "Federal States."

34. See Billias (2009, 363–364), noting that the countries "that tried the purely presidential system were few in number" and mainly confined to nineteenth-century Latin America; Loewenstein (1949, 447), describing Latin America as the "primary area of adoption" of the presidential system.

35. See Cheibub (2007, 150–51, 154), noting that, after an initial period of stability under presidential constitutions in the late nineteenth century, numerous Latin American countries in the 1920s and 1930s experienced "democratic breakdowns" and transitions to military dictatorship.

36. See Mainwaring (1990, 163), pointing to an entire body of scholarship that "excoriated presidentialism" in reaction to early experiments with presidentialism in Latin America.

37. See Horowitz (2009, 516), observing that presidentialism "remains a minority taste."

38. See Cheibub, Gandhi, and Vreeland (2010, 79), noting the "general consensus" that democratic governments can be divided into "presidential," "parliamentary," and "mixed" or "semi-presidential" systems. The data underlying Figure 1.3 is derived from the variable "Hinst" coded by José Cheibub and Jennifer Gandhi. This variable is coded 0 for a "Parliamentary Democracy," 1 for a "Mixed Democracy," 2 for a "Presidential Democracy," 3 for a "Civilian Dictatorship," 4 for a "Military Dictatorship," and 5 for a "Monarchic Dictatorship." See Cheibub, Gandhi, and Vreeland (2010, 68), describing the "six-fold regime classification"; Norris (2009). Figure 1.3 is a graph of the percentage of countries in each of the first three categories.

39. See Skach (2005, 120), describing "semi-presidentialism" as the "modal type" of government adopted by former Soviet bloc countries; Stepan and Skach (1993, 4), noting

that "of the approximately twenty-five countries that now constitute Eastern Europe and the former Soviet Union, only three . . . have chosen pure parliamentarianism."

40. See Billias (2009, 321, 365), describing judicial review as "the fastest-growing American institution abroad" as of 1989 and characterizing judicial review as "America's most important export" (quoting Beyme 1987, 85).

41. See Stone Sweet (2008, 223 and table 9.1), reporting that countries that have adopted the "European model" outnumber those that have adopted the "American model" by a count of eighty-five to fifty-three, with another thirty-six countries that employ a mixture of the two models or some other unique and unclassifiable mechanism.

42. See Gardbaum (2008, 412–413) for a summary of the differences between the American and European models); see also Stone Sweet (2008, 222, 223, and table 9.1).

43. See Stone Sweet (2002, 79), discussing Kelsen's invention of the "modern European constitutional court," which "enjoy[s] exclusive and final constitutional jurisdiction," as well as its adoption by "most of Central and Eastern Europe."

44. See U.S. Const. art. III, § 2 (providing that the "judicial Power shall extend" to specified categories of "Cases" and "Controversies").

45. See Gardbaum (2008, 412–13), reviewing the distinguishing features of the American and European models; Stone Sweet (2008, 224–25), defining and distinguishing "abstract review" and "concrete review," and the European and American models of judicial review. The possibility that courts can engage in constitutional review of laws before they have even been promulgated introduces yet another twist on the institution of judicial review—namely, the distinction between ex ante and ex post review. Ex ante or pre-enactment review refers to judicial review of laws that have not yet gone into effect. Ex ante review is closely identified with the European model.

46. See Ginsburg (2003, 9–10), discussing the possibility that new democracies may distrust the judiciary because it "was typically trained, selected, and promoted under the previous regime."

47. To be specific, we estimated an ordinary least squares regression model with robust standard errors that are both corrected for problems of heteroscedasticity that are common to panel data and clustered at the state level to allow for serial correlation over time. To address the serial correlation of standard errors that tends to characterize time-series data, the model includes, as an additional predictor variable, a lagged version of the dependent variable—namely, the constitution's similarity to the U.S. Constitution over the *preceding* decade. Finally, because constitutions tend to change infrequently, our model predicts changes in similarity not from year to year, but instead from decade to decade.

48. Our measure of a country's level of democracy is the "polity2" variable from the Polity IV data set, which ranges from +10 (strongly democratic) to −10 (strongly autocratic). For purposes of this chapter, countries with a score of 6 or higher are classified as "democracies." See Marshall and Jaggers (2007, 15–16).

49. We did not attempt to distinguish between substantial and insubstantial (or important and unimportant) amendments. See Elkins, Ginsburg, and Melton (2009,

55–59), discussing the difficulties of arbitrariness and subjectivity involved in drawing such distinctions.

50. See Beck and Katz (1996, 8–9), explaining that inclusion of a lagged version of the dependent variable is a standard technique for addressing the problem of serial correlation in time-series data.

51. To be specific, the model included a separate dummy variable for each decade, with similarity levels in the 1940s serving as the baseline for comparison.

52. The alternative version of the model was the same in all respects save for the replacement of the two regional dummy variables with a continuous variable that measures the distance between New York City and each country's capital city in kilometers.

53. The r-squared associated with the regression is 0.835.

54. The fact that a country is located in Latin America is a statistically significant predictor of decreased similarity to the U.S. Constitution at a 5 percent confidence level ($p = 0.04$).

55. In this case, the fact that a country has a common law system is a statistically significant predictor of increased similarity at the 5 percent confidence level ($p = 0.016$). However, statistical significance must not be confused with substantive significance. A measure of statistical significance, such as a p-value, captures the likelihood that the relationship observed between two variables is more than a mere fluke of the data, but it does not measure the magnitude of the relationship. On a scale from −1 to 1, where −1 is perfect dissimilarity and 1 is perfect similarity, the fact that a country has a common law system increases the predicted similarity of its constitution to that of the United States by only 0.02, holding all other variables constant.

56. Like the presence or absence of a common law system, the age of a constitution is a statistically significant predictor of increased similarity ($p < 0.01$), but the size of this effect is modest. On a scale from −1 (representing perfect dissimilarity) to 1 (representing perfect similarity), the addition of one year to a constitution's lifespan increases its predicted similarity to the U.S. Constitution by only 0.001.

57. The dummy variables for the 1990s and the 2000s are statistically significant predictors of decreased similarity at a 1 percent confidence level (with p-values of 0.004 and 0.006, respectively).

58. See, e.g., Gardbaum (2008, 395), deeming it a distinguishing feature of the U.S. Constitution that it contains "comparatively few enumerated rights."

59. Constitución Política de los Estados Unidos Mexicanos, as amended, art. 10, Diario Oficial de la Federación, February 5, 1917 (guaranteeing inhabitants of Mexico "the right to possess arms in their homes for their security and legitimate defense," subject to the qualification that "federal law shall determine the cases, conditions, requirements and places in which inhabitants may be authorized to carry arms"); Constitución Política de la Republica de Guatemala, as amended, art. 38, Diario de Centro América, June 3, 1985 (recognizing Guatemalans' "right to own weapons for personal use, not prohibited by the law, in the place of inhabitation," and "the right to

bear arms . . . regulated by the law"). The Haitian constitution contains a right to armed self-defense within one's home but also provides that the right cannot be exercised without the express authorization of law enforcement. Constitution de La République D'Haïti, as amended, June 20, 2012, art. 268-1 ("Tout citoyen a droit à l'auto-défense armée, dans les limites de son domicile mais n'a pas droit au port d'armes sans l'autorisation expresse et motivée du Chef de la Police"). For purposes of the statistical analyses in this chapter, Haiti was not counted as having a constitutional right to bear arms.

60. Constitución Nacional (Arg.), art. 21 ("Every Argentine citizen is obliged to bear arms in defense of his country and of this Constitution, in accordance with such laws as the Congress may enact for the purpose and with decrees of the National Executive"; translated in Blaustein and Flanz 1983, 6).

61. See also Ignatieff (2005, 10): "The U.S. Constitution makes no reference to socioeconomic and welfare rights—entitlements to food, shelter, health care, and unemployment insurance—that are standard features of both international rights regimes and the constitutions of European states."

62. See Hartz (1991, 9), arguing that the U.S. Constitution is rooted in a deeply and persistently Lockean intellectual tradition.

63. See Pildes (2011, 254), identifying the U.S. Constitution as the oldest of its kind; MEMRI (2012), quoting Justice Ginsburg's observation that the United States has "the oldest written constitution still in force in the world."

64. See S. Levinson (2006, 21), identifying the U.S. Constitution as "the most difficult to amend of any constitution currently existing in the world today"; Law and McGowan (2007, 93), observing that "the nationwide supermajoritarian action needed to adopt a constitutional amendment is notoriously difficult and costly" to secure, and noting by way of illustration that ratification of the uncontroversial Twenty-Seventh Amendment was delayed by over two hundred years.

65. First proposed in 1789, the Twenty-Seventh Amendment was not ratified until 1992 (see S. Levinson 1994, 102).

66. See, e.g., S. Levinson (2006, 9), arguing that the U.S. Constitution is "significantly dysfunctional" to the point of warranting a constitutional convention; Sabato (2007, 4–5), bemoaning the "political ossification" and "grotesque" inequities that have resulted from failure to engage in more than "insufficient tinkering" with the Constitution over the last two centuries; Ignatieff (2005, 11), dubbing the U.S. Bill of Rights "a late eighteenth-century constitution surrounded by twenty-first century ones, a grandfather clock in a shop window full of digital timepieces."

67. See, e.g., Elkins, Ginsburg, and Melton (2009 20), observing that "a large institutional infrastructure has developed alongside the U.S. Constitution and the investment in these institutions has been considerable," and that "political life has grown around [the Constitution] and adapted to its idiosyncratic edicts"; D. Levinson (2011, 714–715), describing various mechanisms that ensure "systems of constitutional law will tend to be self-entrenching, accumulating greater political support over time."

68. See Eskridge and Ferejohn (2001, 1237), dubbing the Civil Rights Act of 1964 a "super-statute" that has "pervasively affected federal statutes and constitutional law" alike.

69. See Shapiro and Stone Sweet (2002, 138), characterizing both the Civil Rights Act of 1964 and the Administrative Procedure Act as "constitution-like" in the sense that both are "entangled with constitutions" and "treated as overarching norms applied in judicial review of a wide range of government—and often private—actions."

70. See Young (2007, 427, 446, 461), observing that the Social Security Act is "*functionally* more entrenched, at least right now, than the First Amendment's prohibition on flag burning," and describing it as the "sort of extracanonical supplementation . . . by which a Constitution that is very old and hard to amend manages to serve the needs of a modern and highly complex society").

71. See, e.g., Roe v. Wade, 410 U.S. 113 (1973), recognizing a constitutional right to abortion; Griswold v. Connecticut, 381 U.S. 479 (1965), establishing a constitutional right of married couples to use contraception; Lochner v. New York, 198 U.S. 45 (1905), invoking a constitutionally protected liberty of contract to invalidate state workplace regulations.

72. See, e.g., Marbury v. Madison, 5 U.S. (1 Cranch) 137 (1803), establishing the power of judicial review; Cooper v. Aaron, 358 U.S. 1 (1958), asserting judicial supremacy in the area of constitutional interpretation; City of Boerne v. Flores, 521 U.S. 507 (1997), reiterating that the judiciary possesses final say over the meaning of the Constitution, notwithstanding the enforcement powers expressly given to Congress by section 5 of the Fourteenth Amendment.

73. See Law and Versteeg (2012, 809–833), examining patterns of global similarity to the constitutions of Canada, South Africa, Germany, and India. Although Canada in particular does appear to exercise a quantifiable degree of constitutional influence or leadership, that influence is not uniform and global but instead appears to reflect a model of constitutionalism that is somewhat distinctive to common law countries (814–821).

74. See Law and Versteeg (2012, 833–50), examining patterns of global similarity to a variety of international and regional human rights instruments.

75. See Law and Versteeg (2011, 1164), documenting empirically the simultaneous growth of "generic rights constitutionalism" and emergence of increasingly distinct "libertarian" and "statist" constitutional paradigms.

76. See Nye (2004, x), defining "soft power" as "the ability to get what you want through attraction" without resort to "sticks and carrots" or "coercion or payments," and citing the construction by Chinese student protesters in Tiananmen Square of a replica of the Statue of Liberty as an example of American soft power.

77. See note 11 above and accompanying text discussing possible consequences of the U.S. Supreme Court's comparatively sparing use of foreign law; Jackson and Greene (2011, 607), acknowledging that originalism is not a "made-only-in-the-USA phenomenon," but observing that the U.S. Supreme Court is nevertheless "more concerned with

original understandings than are their counterparts in many other jurisdictions"; L'Heureux-Dubé (1998, 33), observing that decisions focused on the intent of eighteenth-century constitutional framers are "unhelpful to those who are interpreting constitutions or human rights provisions drafted in the latter half of the twentieth century," and that originalism "is usually simply not the focus, or even a topic, of debate elsewhere."

78. See, e.g., Klug (2000, 598) arguing that, "although historically the United States Constitution provided an inspiration to many, the recent direction of United States constitutional jurisprudence has led most constitution-makers to seek alternative models."

79. See Law (2015, 963, 970), noting that the "lack of social and economic rights in the U.S. Constitution . . . limits the relevance of U.S. jurisprudence to the Korean Constitutional Court," and quoting the observation of an official at the Korean Constitutional Court that U.S. jurisprudence is not a focus of research in cases involving social welfare rights "because we know the U.S. Constitution doesn't have social rights provisions."

80. See, e.g., Gardbaum (2008, 395), observing that the distinguishing features of the U.S. Constitution include its sheer age and consequent attention to "anachronistic concerns"; Law and Versteeg (2011, 1200–1202, table 2), reporting that, by contrast with the U.S. Constitution, nearly three-quarters of the world's constitutions contain express restrictions on property rights, while only 2 percent contain a right to bear arms; and see above, notes 9 (and accompanying text noting efforts by constitutional drafters in other countries to steer clear of language that could open the door to *Lochner*-style substantive due process jurisprudence) and 70 (and accompanying text reviewing various criticisms of the U.S. Constitution voiced by American scholars).

81. See, e.g., Sunstein (2005, 98), suggesting that the Equal Rights Amendment failed to secure ratification in part because the Supreme Court had already interpreted the Equal Protection Clause to reach sex discrimination.

82. See Law and Versteeg (2011, 1167, 1170), surveying the literature to the effect that constitutions are "unique and defining statements of national aspiration and identity," but concluding as an empirical matter that the rights-related content of the world's constitutions is relatively standardized and tends to vary in predictable ways; Tushnet (1999, 1270–1271), discussing the long-held view among many comparative legal scholars that "constitutions emerge out of each nation's distinctive history and express its distinctive character."

83. Calabresi (2006, 1335, 1340, 1397) argues that other scholars are "dead right" to characterize the Constitution as the "focal point" of an "American creed of exceptionalism"; see, e.g., S. Levinson (1988, 5, 96), quoting the views of Samuel Huntington and others that the Constitution is the "central covenant of the community," the "supreme symbol and manifestation" "of the American nation," the "central sacred text" of the United States as a "faith community," the "conscious political act" to which

the United States owes its very existence, and so forth (internal quotation marks omitted); Gardbaum (2008, 392–393), noting the "widespread" view of "both American and comparative legal scholars" that American constitutional law is a defining element of American exceptionalism; Rahdert (2007, 589–602), observing that negative reactions to the U.S. Supreme Court's use of foreign precedent "tap into a longstanding tradition of exceptionalism and particularism in American attitudes toward foreign law."

84. See, e.g., Rosenkrantz (2003, 271–277), describing Argentina's extensive borrowing of both constitutional text and constitutional jurisprudence from the United States during the nineteenth century.

85. See Sabato (2007, 196), reporting the results of a 2006 public opinion poll in which 52 percent strongly opposed and another 14 percent somewhat opposed the holding of a new constitutional convention to "bring our Constitution up to date after the passage of more than 200 years."

86. The fiasco of the election of 1800, in which party-line voting caused a tie in the electoral college between the presidential and vice presidential candidates of the same party, led to adoption of the Twelfth Amendment. Even the Twelfth Amendment, however, declined to endorse or even acknowledge the existence of political parties but instead adopted the narrow procedural solution of separate ballots for president and vice president. See Levinson and Young (2001, 926–32). And see, e.g., P. Strauss (1984, 575, 578), noting that the existence of administrative agencies "is barely hinted at in the Constitution," and that independent regulatory agencies are widely viewed as a "headless 'fourth branch' of government" that does not fall neatly within the three-branch structure ordained by the Constitution.

87. U.S. Const. amend. XII; art. I, § 3.

88. See Law (2013b, 10–11), noting that "the Kenpō contains nineteen of the twenty most popular constitutional rights in the world," whereas "the U.S. Constitution contains only twelve," and that "progressive Americans can only dream of a constitution" that guarantees "minimum standards of wholesome and cultured living" (art. 25), the right to education (art. 26), and "the right of workers to organize and to bargain and act collectively" (art. 28), to name only a few of the rights that are found in the Kenpō but absent from the U.S. Constitution.

89. See, e.g., Wojtyczek (2012, 286), observing that constitutionalism was "initially invented as an instrument for putting the Enlightenment Project into practice."

References

Allan, James, and Grant Huscroft. 2006. "Constitutional Rights Coming Home to Roost? Rights Internationalism in American Courts." *San Diego Law Review* 43 (1): 1–59.

Allan, James, Grant Huscroft, and Nessa Lynch. 2007. "The Citation of Overseas Authority in Rights Litigation in New Zealand: How Much Bark? How Much Bite?" *Otago Law Review* 11 (3): 433–467.

Alston, Philip. 1999. "A Framework for the Comparative Analysis of Bills of Rights." In *Promoting Human Rights Through Bills of Rights: Comparative Perspectives*, edited by Philip Alston, chapter 1. Oxford: Clarendon Press.

Barak, Aharon, and Charles Fried. 2002. "The Supreme Court, 2001 Term." *Harvard Law Review* 116 (1): 13–198, 200–464.

Beck, Nathaniel, and Jonathan N. Katz. 1996. "Nuisance vs. Substance: Specifying and Estimating Time–Series–Cross-Section Models." *Political Analysis* 6: 1–36.

Beer, Lawrence W., ed. 1979. *Constitutionalism in Asia: Asian Views of the American Influence*. Berkeley: University of California Press.

Beyme, Klaus von. 1987. *America as a Model: The Impact of American Democracy in the World*. New York: St. Martin's.

Billias, George Athan, ed. 1990. *American Constitutionalism Abroad: Selected Essays in Comparative Constitutional History*. Santa Barbara, CA: Praeger.

———. 2009. *American Constitutionalism Heard Round the World, 1776–1989: A Global Perspective*. New York: New York University Press.

Blaustein, Albert P., and Gisbert H. Flanz, eds. 1983. "Argentina." In *Constitutions of the Countries of the World*, vol. 1. Dobbs Ferry, NY: Oceana.

Calabresi, Steven G. 2006. "'A Shining City on a Hill': American Exceptionalism and the Supreme Court's Practice of Relying on Foreign Law." *Boston University Law Review* 86 (5): 1335–1416.

Cheibub, José Antonio. 2007. *Presidentialism, Parliamentarism, and Democracy*. New York: Cambridge University Press.

Cheibub, José Antonio, Jennifer Gandhi, and James Raymond Vreeland. 2010. "Democracy and Dictatorship Revisited." *Public Choice* 143 (1–2): 67–101.

Choudhry, Sujit. 2004. "The *Lochner* Era and Comparative Constitutionalism." *International Journal of Constitutional Law* 2 (1): 1–55.

Davis, Michael C. 2010. "The Political Economy and Culture of Human Rights in East Asia." In *Research Handbook on International Human Rights Law*, edited by Sarah Joseph and Adam McBeth, 414–439. Northampton, MA: Edward Elgar.

Dippel, Horst. 2005. "Modern Constitutionalism: An Introduction to a History in Need of Writing." *Legal History Review* 73 (1–2): 153–169.

Elkins, Zachary, Tom Ginsburg, and James Melton. 2008. "Baghdad, Tokyo, Kabul . . . : Constitution Making in Occupied States." *William and Mary Law Review* 49 (4): 1139–1178.

———. 2009. *The Endurance of National Constitutions*. New York: Cambridge University Press.

Elster, Jon. 1995. "Forces and Mechanisms in the Constitution-Making Process." *Duke Law Journal* 45 (2): 364–396.

Epstein, Lee, and Gary King. 2002. "The Rules of Inference." *University of Chicago Law Review* 69 (1): 1–133.

Erdos, David. 2010. *Delegating Rights Protection: The Rise of Bills of Rights in the Westminster World.* New York: Oxford University Press.

Eskridge, William N., Jr., and John Ferejohn. 2001. "Super-Statutes." *Duke Law Journal* 50: 1215–1276.

Falleti, Tulia G., and Emilio A. Parrado, eds. 2017. *Latin America Since the Left Turn.* Philadelphia: University of Pennsylvania Press.

Franck, Thomas M., and Arun K. Thiruvengadam. 2003. "International Law and Constitution-Making." *Chinese Journal of International Law* 2 (2): 467–518.

Fukuyama, Francis. 1992. *The End of History and the Last Man.* New York: Free Press.

Furtak, Florian T. 2017. "Democracy Under Pressure: The Case of Poland, Hungary and Turkey." *Journal of Civil and Legal Sciences* 6 (2): 1000e119.

Gardbaum Stephen. 2001. "The New Commonwealth Model of Constitutionalism." *American Journal of Comparative Law* 49 (4): 707–760.

———. 2008. "The Myth and the Reality of American Constitutional Exceptionalism." *Michigan Law Review* 107 (3): 391–466.

Ginsburg, Tom. 2003. *Judicial Review in New Democracies: Constitutional Courts in Asian Cases.* New York: Cambridge University Press.

Ginsburg, Tom, and Aziz Z. Huq. 2018. *How to Save a Constitutional Democracy.* Chicago: University of Chicago Press.

Go, Julian. 2003. "A Globalizing Constitutionalism? Views from the Postcolony, 1945–2000." *International Sociology* 18 (1): 71–95.

Goderis, Benedikt, and Mila Versteeg. 2011. "The Transnational Origins of Constitutions: An Empirical Analysis, Sixth Annual Conference on Empirical Legal Studies." November 4, 2011. Manuscript on file with the *New York University Law Review.*

———. 2012. "Human Rights Violations After 9/11 and the Role of Constitutional Constraints." *Journal of Legal Studies* 41 (1): 131–164.

Graber, Mark A., Sanford Levinson, and Mark Tushnet. Introduction to *Constitutional Democracy in Crisis?*, edited by Mark A. Graber, Sanford Levinson, and Mark Tushnet. New York: Oxford University Press.

Greenwald, John. 1987. "A Gift to All Nations." *Time*, July 6, 1987, 92.

Groppi, Tania, and Marie-Claire Ponthoreau, eds. 2013. *The Use of Foreign Precedents by Constitutional Judges.* Oxford: Hart Publishing.

Harris, B. V. 2004. "The Constitutional Future of New Zealand." *New Zealand Law Review* 2: 269–312.

Hartz, Louis. 1991. *The Liberal Tradition in America.* 2nd ed. New York: Harcourt Brace.

Henkin, Louis, and Albert J. Rosenthal, eds. 1990. *Constitutionalism and Rights: The Influence of the United States Constitution Abroad.* New York: Columbia University Press.

Horowitz, Donald L. 2009. "*The Federalist* Abroad in the World." In *The Federalist Papers: Alexander Hamilton, James Madison, John Jay*, edited by Ian Shapiro, 502–532. New Haven, CT: Yale University Press.

Ignatieff, Michael, ed. 2005. *American Exceptionalism and Human Rights*. Princeton, NJ: Princeton University Press.

Jackson, Vicki C., and Jamal Greene. 2011. "Constitutional Interpretation in Comparative Perspective: Comparing Judges or Courts?" In *Comparative Constitutional Law*, edited by Tom Ginsburg and Rosalind Dixon, 599–623. Northampton, MA: Edward Elgar.

Jaggers, Keith, and Ted Robert Gurr. 1996. "Polity III: Regime Type and Political Authority, 1800–1994." Ann Arbor, MI: Inter-University Consortium for Political and Social Science Research. Available at icpsr.umich.edu/icpsrweb/ICPSR/studies/6695.

Kirby, Michael. 2001. "Think Globally." *Green Bag*, 2nd ser., 4 (3): 287–296.

Klug, Heinz. 2000. "Model and Anti-Model: The United States Constitution and the 'Rise of World Constitutionalism.'" *Wisconsin Law Review* 2000 (3): 597–616.

L'Heureux-Dubé, Claire. 1998. "The Importance of Dialogue: Globalization and the International Impact of the Rehnquist Court." *Tulsa Law Journal* 34 (1): 15–40.

Law, David S. 2005. "Generic Constitutional Law." *Minnesota Law Review* 89 (3): 652–751.

———. 2013a. "The Myth of the Imposed Constitution." In *Social and Political Foundations of Constitutions*, edited by Denis Galligan and Mila Versteeg, 239–268. New York: Cambridge University Press.

———. 2013b. *Nihon no saikosai wo kaibou suru* [The Japanese Supreme Court and Judicial Review]. Translated by Shin-ichi Nishikawa. Tokyo: Gendaijinbunsha.

———. 2015. "Judicial Comparativism and Judicial Diplomacy." *University of Pennsylvania Law Review* 163 (4): 927–1036.

———. 2016. "Constitutional Archetypes." *University of Texas Law Review* 95 (1): 153–243.

Law, David S., and Wen-Chen Chang. 2011. "The Limits of Global Judicial Dialogue." *Washington Law Review* 86 (3): 523–577.

Law, David S., and Chien-Chih Lin. 2018. "Constitutional Inertia and Regime Pluralism in Asia." In *Constitutional Democracy in Crisis?*, edited by Mark A. Graber, Sanford Levinson, and Mark Tushnet, 423–441. New York: Oxford University Press.

Law David S., and David McGowan. 2007. "There Is Nothing Pragmatic About Originalism." *Northwestern University Law Review Colloquy* 102: 86–101.

Law, David S., and Mila Versteeg. 2011. "The Evolution and Ideology of Global Constitutionalism." *California Law Review* 99 (5): 1163–1253.

———. 2012. "The Declining Influence of the United States Constitution." *New York University Law Review* 87 (3): 762–858.

Le Vine, Victor T. 1997. "The Fall and Rise of Constitutionalism in West Africa." *Journal of Modern African Studies* 35 (2): 181–206.

Levinson, Daryl J. 2011. "Parchment and Politics: The Positive Puzzle of Constitutional Commitment." *Harvard Law Review* 124 (3): 657–746.

Levinson, Sanford. 1988. *Constitutional Faith*. Princeton, NJ: Princeton University Press.

———. 1994. "Authorizing Constitutional Text: On the Purported Twenty-Seventh Amendment." *Constitutional Commentary* 11: 101–113.

———. 2006. *Our Undemocratic Constitution*. New York: Oxford University Press.

Levinson, Sanford, and Ernest A. Young. 2001. "Who's Afraid of the Twelfth Amendment?" *Florida State University Law Review* 29: 925–973.

L'Heureux-Dubé, Claire. 1998. "The Importance of Dialogue: Globalization and the International Impact of the Rehnquist Court." *Tulsa Law Journal* 34 (1): 15–40.

Liptak, Adam. 2008. "U.S. Court, a Longtime Beacon, Is Now Guiding Fewer Nations." *New York Times*, September 18, 2008.

Loewenstein, Karl. 1949. "The Presidency Outside the United States: A Study in Comparative Political Institutions." *Journal of Politics* 11 (3): 447–496.

Mainwaring, Scott. 1990. "Presidentialism in Latin America." *Latin American Research Review* 25 (1): 157–179.

Marshall, Monty G., and Keith Jaggers. 2007. "Polity IV Project: Dataset Users' Manual." Center for Systemic Peace. https://home.bi.no/ a0110709/PolityIV_manual.pdf. The 2016 data set is available at www.systemicpeace.org/inscr/p4manualv2016.pdf.

MEMRI (Middle East Media Research Institute). 2012. TV Monitor Project. "U.S. Supreme Court Justice Ruth Bader Ginsburg to Egyptians: Look to the Constitutions of South Africa or Canada, Not to the U.S. Constitution" (video clip of an interview with Justice Ginsburg, originally broadcast by the Egyptian television station Al-Hayat TV, January 30, 2012). http://www.memritv.org/clip/en/3295.htm.

Norris, Pippa. 2009. *Democracy Cross-National Dataset, Release 3.0*. Pippa Norris Data. www.pippanorris.com/data.

Nye, Joseph S., Jr. 2004. *Soft Power: The Means to Success in World Politics*. New York: Public Affairs.

Osiatynski, Wiktor. 2003. "Paradoxes of Constitutional Borrowing." *International Journal of Constitutional Law* 1: 244–268.

Parkinson, Charles O. H. 2007. *Bills of Rights and Decolonization: The Emergence of Domestic Human Rights Instruments in Britain's Overseas Territories*. New York: Oxford University Press.

Peltason, J. W. 1997. *Corwin and Peltason's Understanding the Constitution*. 14th ed. New York: Harcourt Brace College Publishers.

Pildes, Richard H. 2011. "Political Parties and Constitutionalism." In *Comparative Constitutional Law*, edited by Tom Ginsburg and Rosalind Dixon, 254–264. Northampton, MA: Edward Elgar.

Powles, Guy. 2009. "Accommodating Monarchy and Representative Government: Tonga's Political Reform Process." *Pacific Economic Bulletin* 24 (3): 140–147.

Rahdert, Mark C. 2007. "Comparative Constitutional Advocacy." *American University Law Review* 56 (3): 553–665.

Rasch, Bjørn Erik, and Roger D. Congleton. 2006. "Amendment Procedures and Constitutional Stability." In *Democratic Constitutional Design and Public Policy: Analysis and Evidence*, edited by Roger D. Congleton and Birgitta Swedenborg, 319–342. Cambridge, MA: MIT Press.

Rosenkrantz, Carlos F. 2003. "Against Borrowings and Other Nonauthoritative Uses of Foreign Law." *International Journal of Constitutional Law* 1 (2): 269–295.

Sabato, Larry J. 2007. *A More Perfect Constitution: Ideas to Inspire a New Generation.* New York: Walker.

Schauer, Frederick. 2000. "The Politics and Incentives of Legal Transplantation." In *Governance in a Globalizing World*, edited by Joseph S. Nye Jr. and John D. Donahue, 253–270. Cambridge, Mass.: Visions of Governance for the 21st Century.

———. 2005. "On the Migration of Constitutional Ideas." *Connecticut Law Review* 37 (4): 907–920.

Scheppele, Kim Lane. 2003. "Aspirational and Aversive Constitutionalism: The Case for Studying Cross-Constitutional Influence Through Negative Models." *International Journal of Constitutional Law* 1 (2): 296–324.

Schor, Miguel. 2010. Review of *American Constitutionalism Heard Around the World, 1789–1989: A Global Perspective*, by George Athan Billias. *Law and Politics Book Review* 20 (5): 155–157. Available at http://www.lpbr.net/2010/05/american-constitutionalism-heard-around.html.

Shapiro, Martin, and Alec Stone Sweet. 2002. *On Law, Politics, and Judicialization.* New York: Oxford University Press.

Siaroff, Alan. 2000. *Comparative European Party Systems: An Analysis of Parliamentary Elections Since 1945.* New York: Garland.

Skach, Cindy. 2005. *Borrowing Constitutional Designs: Constitutional Law in Weimar Germany and the French Fifth Republic.* Princeton, NJ: Princeton University Press.

Slaughter, Anne-Marie. 2004. *A New World Order.* Princeton, NJ: Princeton University Press.

Smyth, Russell. 2008. "Citations of Foreign Decisions in Australian State Supreme Courts over the Course of the Twentieth Century: An Empirical Analysis." *Temple International and Comparative Law Journal* 22 (2): 409–436.

Stepan, Alfred, and Cindy Skach. 1993. "Constitutional Frameworks and Democratic Consolidation: Parliamentarianism Versus Presidentialism." *World Politics* 46 (1): 1–22.

Stone Sweet, Alec. 2002. "Constitutional Courts and Parliamentary Democracy." *West European Politics* 25 (1): 77–100

———. 2008. "Constitutions and Judicial Power." In *Comparative Politics*, edited by Daniele Caramani, 217–239. New York: Oxford University Press.

Strauss, David A. 1996. "Common Law Constitutional Interpretation." *University of Chicago Law Review* 63 (3): 877–935.

Strauss, Peter A. 1984. "The Place of Agencies in the Government: Separation of Powers and the Fourth Branch." *Columbia Law Review* 84 (3): 573–669.

Sunstein, Cass R. 2005. "Why Does the American Constitution Lack Social and Economic Guarantees?" In *American Exceptionalism and Human Rights*, edited by Michael Ignatieff, 90–110. Princeton, NJ: Princeton University Press.

Tocqueville, Alexis de. (1835) 2001. *Democracy in America*. Edited and translated by Richard D. Heffner. Signet Classic Edition. New York: New American Library.

Tushnet, Mark. 1999. "The Possibilities of Comparative Constitutional Law." *Yale Law Journal* 108 (6): 1225–1309.

Watts, Ronald L. 2008. *Comparing Federal Systems*. 3rd ed. Montreal: McGill-Queen's University Press.

Weinrib, Lorraine E. 2006. "The Postwar Paradigm and American Exceptionalism." In *The Migration of Constitutional Ideas*, edited by Sujit Choudhry, 83–113. New York: Cambridge University Press.

Wilkinson, J. Harvie, III. 2004. "Our Structural Constitution." *Columbia Law Review* 104 (6): 1687–1709.

Williams, George. 2004. "Human Rights and Judicial Review in a Nation Without a Bill of Rights: The Australian Experience." In *Constitutionalism in the Charter Era*, edited by Grant Huscroft and Ian Ross Brodie, 305–334. Markham, ON: LexisNexis.

Wojtyczek, Krzysztof. 2012. "Toward a Global Constitutional Space?" In *Public Law: Twenty Years After*, edited by Krzysztof Wojtyczek, chapter 8. Athens, Greece: EPLO.

Young, Ernest A. 2007. "The Constitution Outside the Constitution." *Yale Law Journal* 117 (3): 408–473.

CHAPTER 2

Is the U.S. Constitution Sufficiently Democratic?: How Would We Know and Do We Really Care?

Sanford Levinson

I have been writing now for more than a decade on the insufficiently democratic nature of the United States Constitution, including a book published in 2006 with the explicit title *Our Undemocratic Constitution: Where the Constitution Goes Wrong (and How We the People Can Correct It)*. A later book, published in 2012, continued the argument, though as indicated by the title, *Framed: America's 51 Constitutions and the Crisis of Governance*, I have also become interested in America's *state* constitutions. It is, I believe, clear beyond reasonable doubt that each and every one of the fifty state constitutions is considerably more democratic than is the U.S. Constitution, even as amended, albeit infrequently and insufficiently, over the past 225 years. At the same time, I have focused on the increasing discontents expressed by Americans across the political spectrum about the actual operation of our political system—discontents dramatically expressed in the election of 2016, without leading to their decline.

An obvious question, however, concerns the metrics by which one assesses the extent to which the U.S. Constitution merits the designation "democratic" *or* "undemocratic." The words have become almost textbook examples of what political philosophers call "essentially contested concepts," meaning not only that reasonable people can and have for a very long time disagreed about the metrics, but also, and just as important, that the terms have taken on a *normative* as well as more detached *analytic* valence. At least since the mid-nineteenth century, "democracy" and "democratic" have, with some exceptions, been thought to be complimentary terms, whereas "undemocratic"—or, even more obviously, "oligarchic" or "tyrannical"—has been a term of opprobrium. There is a reason, after all, that some notable tyrannies in the past century have styled themselves "democratic" or "people's'" republics.

Earlier ages were distinctly less taken by the notion of "democracy," however defined. As I noted at some length in *Framed*, there is a reason that the 1787 Constitution guarantees to states a "republican form of government" and not a "democratic" one. Though there were some notable exceptions among the framers—such as Philadelphia's James Wilson—few of them would have described themselves as "democrats." As Morton Horwitz has noted, the Supreme Court did not begin using the term to describe the American experiment until the twentieth century (Horwitz 1993, 57–58). Still, there can be little doubt that in our own time "democracy" is thought to be desirable. Almost a century ago, Woodrow Wilson defined American entrance into World War I as an effort to "make the world safe for democracy," and, since then, American presidents of both parties have committed the United States to what I have called "the democracy project" (Levinson 2010). In one of his first trips abroad after becoming president in January 2009, President Obama told a student in Strasbourg, France, that "we should be promoting democracy everywhere we can" (White House Office of the Press Secretary 2009). Subsequently he was criticized more often for being insufficiently militant in that project, especially following the "Arab Spring," rather than for potentially dangerous delusions of grandeur. Donald Trump has since set a different tone, but he still claims to be the true champion of the people, not antidemocratic.

In any event, agreeing on the metrics by which we determine whether a given country is or is not "democratic" is no easy task. Even more delicate than simply a binary opposition of "democratic" and "undemocratic" is an ordinal ranking by which we compare the extent of one presumptively "democratic" country's democracy with that of another also "democratic" polity country, as is done regularly by the *Economist* magazine. In 2018, it counted 20 "full democracies, beginning with Norway at 9.27 and ending with Costa Rica with 8.07. Then followed a number of "flawed democracies," including the United States with a score of 7.90, which placed it at number 25, behind Estonia and Chile, the latter of which, of course, had been notably autocratic through 1990 (Economist Intelligence Unit 2018 Democracy, 2019). At this writing, protestors are pressing the government to alter the constitution written under the Pinochet dictatorship. And the United States increasingly appears as part of the subject matter in books dealing with the decline or even "death" of democracies. (Levitsky and Ziblatt, 2018).

Let me begin, though, with what surely has to be one tempting, even if not necessarily overriding, metric, the actual ability of voting majorities—or of majorities of the entire population, which may of course generate quite different conclusions—to translate their policy preferences into laws passed and enforced by government. For anyone fully conscious of the 1960s, the current second decade of the twenty-first century is rich with golden anniversaries. For example, 2013 was the fiftieth anniversary of the Supreme Court's enunciation in the 1963 case *Wesberry v. Sanders* of the "one-person/one-vote" doctrine that, for better and perhaps for worse, transformed the way we elect all state legislative institutions and the U.S. House of Representatives. *Wesberry*, which concerned congressional districts, was succeeded the following year by *Reynolds v. Sims*,[1] which struck down malapportioned state legislatures throughout the American states. It is worth a brief look at the terms used by Chief Justice Earl Warren in *Reynolds*, which he believed to be the single most important one of his tenure as chief justice, including *Brown v. Board of Education.*

For the court, Warren defined "representative government" as "grounded" on the notion that "a majority of the people of a State could elect a majority of that State's legislators." He refers as well to "the democratic ideals of equality and majority rule, which," he asserts, have "served this Nation so well in the past." There is something more than a bit odd about this assertion, inasmuch as the case before him instantiates the extent to which the American political system up to that time, at both the national and state levels, had rather systematically *resisted* the notions of "equality and majority rule" in the name of other values—and political interests—that were thought to be more important. (We shall presently look at the most spectacular deviation from these ostensible "democratic ideals," the U.S. Senate.) Be that as it may, he also writes of the Constitution as requiring "self-government through the medium of elected representatives of the people, and each and every citizen has an inalienable right *to full and effective participation* in the political processes of his State's legislative bodies" (italics added).

In a political order predicated on the affiliation of otherwise isolated individuals with social movements or political parties, it is certainly plausible to identify "effective participation" with the belief, and reality, that one will win an election if one's party gains a majority of the vote. It cannot suffice, for example, to be told only that one has an individual vote that counts "equally" with all other individual votes. Among other things, that restricted notion of voting equality would make the outcome of an election almost literally irrelevant, since the "democratic ideals" would be defined only by the ability to cast an "equal vote" that is in fact counted. We must also decide what it means to "win an election."

That, too, is no easy task. Surely winning an election must means something more than the ability of the ostensible winners to occupy seats in some political institution. As anyone who has ever participated in an election for high-school student council or, indeed, student or even faculty government within university settings, becoming a member does not in the least mean that one is gaining as well any genuine decision-making authority with regard to the kinds of issues that matter most to students or faculty. Retained powers of principals, deans, provosts, presidents, and regents limit any "self-governance" by the elected representatives. This suggests that we should include in our standard for "winning elections" the actual probabilities that the result will be visible and important changes in public policy presumptively supported by the relevant electorate or the people elected to office in their name.

This emphasis on majority rule was central to Warren's explanation of his rejection of what was once known as "little federalism," by which states emulated the U.S. Senate by, for example, giving each county the same representation in the state senate. This was true, for example, in North Carolina, where I grew up in Henderson County, which, with approximately 30,000 people, had the same one senator as did Mecklenburg County, where Charlotte is located, which at that time had a population of around 200,000. One would be surprised if Warren, a former governor of California, was enamored of any analogy to the U.S. Senate. Although California had "only" somewhat more than ten million people in 1950 (receiving thirty seats in the House of Representatives), its voting power in the Senate was equal to that of Wyoming, with its approximately 290,000 population, a ratio of almost 35–1 (which has more than doubled since).

Warren, one suspects, would have agreed with James Madison's description of equal voting power in the Senate, in *Federalist* 62, as a "lesser evil," the greater evil being the breakdown of the effort to achieve a new constitutional order should the small states like Delaware carry out their well-articulated threat to walk out of the 1787 Constitutional Convention in Philadelphia—and perhaps even seek alliance with another country in the international system—should their extortionate demands to equal voting power not be met. As Warren put it, "a compromise between the larger and smaller States on this matter averted a deadlock in the Constitutional Convention which had threatened to abort the birth of our Nation." Perhaps this is an instance where avoiding an abortion was worth it, but a "lesser evil" is still an "evil." It scarcely provides an inspiration for later constitutional designers, save for the broader issue about the necessity to make unattractive—even what Israeli philosopher Avishai Margalit (2009) calls "rotten"—compromises in order to achieve the end of gaining acquiescence to a particular constitution.

"The right of a citizen to equal representation and to have his vote weighted equally with those of all other citizens," wrote Warren, would, if confined to only one house of a bicameral state legislature, "amount to little if States could effectively submerge the equal population principle in the apportionment of seats in the other house." Warren, with his deep experience in California politics, well knew that in "little federalism" states, political majorities, whatever their apparent statewide success with regard, say, to electing a governor and a majority of the "lower house," "might be almost as effectively thwarted as if neither house were apportioned on a population basis. Deadlock between the two bodies might result in compromise and concession on some issues. But, in all too many cases, the more probable result would be *frustration of the majority will* through minority veto in the house not apportioned on a population basis, stemming directly from the failure to accord adequate overall legislative representation to all of the State's citizens on a nondiscriminatory basis" (emphasis added). It should be obvious, incidentally, that the "compromise[s] and concession[s]" that might be elicited almost undoubtedly differ from what would be the case if the minority benefiting from malapportionment did not have the degree of power assigned them by the apportionment rules. This, after all, is exactly what happened in the Philadelphia convention, to Madison's intense dismay.

So one way of determining the degree to which the U.S. Constitution is "democratic" or not is simply to assess the extent to which it systematically sets up veto points in the way of a majority's achieving its policy goals. Another way of putting this is to ask if elections "really matter" with regard to moving the dinosaur that is the national government, especially if we compare the American national election systems—and I use the plural advisedly—with not only a host of possible foreign countries who have wisely rejected our reliance on a byzantine system of separated institutions and multiple checks and balances, but also many American states, even if none has chosen a parliamentary model. Though most celebrants of the U.S. Constitution prefer to emphasize the degree to which it offers direct protection of certain rights, in keeping with the post–World War II linkage between "constitutionalism" and "rights protection," it is absolutely crucial to recognize that at least as important—I am strongly tempted to argue *more* important—is the set of institutions established by constitutions to structure the basic conduct of politics and, therefore, to determine, as a practical matter, the prospects for success of any given political agendas.

From my current perspective, the most significant feature of the U.S. Constitution is its establishment of multiple veto points that function as often fatal roadblocks to any proposed changes in the polity. This begins, as Warren suggests, with the specific form of national-level bicameralism; thanks to *Reynolds*, that is altogether different from the bicameralism found in forty-nine of the fifty states, even if one wishes, as I do, that more of these states would emulate Nebraska by adopting unicameralism. After all, one might well answer in the negative to the question posed by Alan Tarr, perhaps the most distinguished scholar of American state constitutions, in his 2010 testimony to the Pennsylvania legislators: Are there "good reasons, other than tradition and familiarity, for bicameralism in the American states?"

As it happens, I personally think the answer is yes, especially in states at least as large as Pennsylvania, though I think there is no good reason for a bicameralism in which the so-called upper houses mimic so closely, when all is said and done, the lower ones in terms of mechanisms of election. Imagine, for example, that the second house is chosen through a robust system of proportional representation, while the first one is selected by conventional single-member districts, or, my own favorite notion these days, the members of the second house were chosen by an Athenian or Venetian-style lottery system, thus omitting election entirely and relying on statistics to provide at least as "representative" cross section of the public as is generated by the contemporary electoral process. But, of course, I digress, and I should return to the subject at hand, the U.S. Constitution. We all know that it isn't enough to prevail in both the U.S. House of Representatives and the U.S. Senate, as happened, say, in the 2006 elections with regard to the Democratic Party. There is still the hurdle of the presidential veto, especially if the president is a member of the other party, as was most certainly the case between 2007 and 2009 and then again during the last years of the Obama Administration.

The most dramatic form of the veto, of course, is the actual negation of legislation supported by majorities of both houses. But the very existence of the presidential veto gives presidents significant bargaining power in the shaping of legislation itself. I now regularly refer to the United States as having a *tricameral* legislature, precisely because of the power of presidents in this regard. One reason for the president's power is the presumptive ability of the president to prevail against legislative opposition, given the requirement established by the 1787 Constitution that each of the two houses present two-thirds majorities to override a veto. Even among presidential (or gubernatorial) systems throughout the world and within the United States, the presidential veto is unusually strong because of the barriers to a successful override.

A common justification of the presidential veto is that the president is entitled to speak for the nation because of his having been nationally elected. That is often a tendentious claim, given that any assessment requires grappling with the egregious electoral college. All of us are familiar with the fact that, as in 2000 and 2016, the electoral college may crown the candidate who comes in second in the national popular vote, which, as a constitutional matter, is utterly irrelevant. This is the major explanation of the fact that candidates of both parties pay basically no attention to getting out the vote in what have come to be called "non-battleground" states. As someone who splits his time between Massachusetts and Texas, I can bear witness to the fact that residents of those states had far less direct knowledge that the United States was electing a president in 2012 and 2016 than did residents of Pennsylvania, Ohio, or Florida. In 2016, of course, narrow Trump victories in Wisconsin, Michigan, and Pennsylvania quite literally more than offset significant Clinton margins in New York, Illinois, and California. It made no difference that Clinton received almost three million more popular votes than did Trump.

The continuing possibility of such electoral vote losses by popular vote front-runners is certainly not a plus of the electoral college. However, I regard as equally problematic the fact that it regularly sends to the White House persons who, even if they came in first past the post in the popular vote, received far short of a majority of the vote. The most important example in our history is surely the man often considered Trump's antipode, Abraham Lincoln, who gained office with 39.8 percent of the national vote—with the conflagration of war as the consequence. Those who condemn secessionists because they rejected the "democratic process" that chose Lincoln have, I want to suggest, a peculiar definition of "democracy." Less freighted, but worth bookending, were the 1968 and 1992 elections of Richard Nixon and Bill Clinton, respectively, each of whom gained office with approximately 43 percent of the popular vote. We do not even have to go outside the United States—say, to France—to discover that many modern political systems avoid this possibility by having runoffs between the two top candidates, so that the winner can always make a plausible argument to have been chosen by "the majority." Georgia, for example, has runoffs to select its public officials, including governors and senators. Interestingly enough, though Texas has no such system in general elections, so that Rick Perry was reelected in 2006 with 39 percent of the vote (Texas Office of the Secretary of State 2006), runoff systems *are* used in party primaries, which helps to explain why Ted Cruz is now the U.S. senator from Texas. It may be worth noting that Maine has recently adopted the so-called Alternative Transferrable Vote system—sometimes called an "instant runoff"—that assures that the winner of the election will in fact have received majority support by virtue of counting the "second preferences" of those who vote for the candidates coming in behind the first two "winners" in the popular vote (assuming, of course, that neither of them received a majority in the initial balloting).

There is at least one other distinction worth noting between the U.S. Constitution and many state constitutions in our quest to apply the majoritarian metric. The national constitution was created by men who were, to put it gently, skeptical about the capacity of ordinary Americans to engage in what some might define as genuine "self-governance," that is, making decisions about important political matters themselves rather than through representatives designated to do the job. Whatever the proclamation of the Constitution's being "ordained" by "We the People," the national government, almost uniquely among the fifty-one constitutional systems within the United States—Delaware is the one exception—is committed to the exclusivity of *representative democracy* and therefore excludes the slightest scintilla of *direct democracy*, with significant consequences for the national polity.

Consider just two implications of the rejection of direct democracy. As everyone knows, if one objects to legislation passed by Congress and signed by the president, or perhaps passed by override of the president's veto, there are only two basic responses (beyond, of course, hoping for implicit "civil disobedience" by relevant public officials who will simply ignore the legislation in question). One response is to begin organizing for the next election in an effort to vote the rascals out and hope that their replacements will repeal the offending legislation. Aside from already-mentioned problems of apportionment of voting power, an additional issue even in impeccably designed districts is that a voter will almost invariably have to choose among less-than-perfect candidates. Some will have "wrong" views on some issues that one cares about even while holding "correct" views about others. What if, for example, one hopes for the repeal of *two* pieces of legislation, one supported and the other opposed by each of two candidates?

Whomever one votes for may proclaim a misleading "mandate" upon election by claiming that his or her supporters approve even the most prominently discussed positions of the candidate, let alone all of the ones that garnered relatively little public attention. Only the fanatical "single-issue" voter brackets out all but the one overwhelmingly salient issue, but even in that case, one has to find many other such fanatics in order to assure that an elected representative will really care. As many political scientists have demonstrated, "interpreting" the meaning of elections, whether for individual candidates or the candidates as an aggregate, is often little more reliable, if at all, than careful study of tea leaves.

But, of course, even if single-issue voters are unusually successful, they often discover that it is as difficult to *repeal* legislation as it is to pass it in the first place. Imagine, for example, that Republicans regained the Senate in 2012, as many observers expected them to do prior to certain disastrous nominations that led to the Democrats actually picking up seats. So long as President Obama would have won anyway, one can be absolutely confident that he would have successfully vetoed any Republican attempts to repeal the Affordable Care Act. This is why elections have limited impact at the national level, at least so long as one aspires either to the passage or repeal of legislation. The only people entitled to be optimistic—perhaps they are the roughly 18 percent of the populace who describe themselves as "approving" of Congress (Lardieri 2019)—are those who prefer maintaining the status quo to taking the risk that legislation of any kind might in fact be adopted.

If one gives up on elections as a mechanism guaranteeing, save in relatively unusual circumstances, the ability to repeal objectionable legislation that managed to survive the veto points in the way of passage, then the other response, especially in the United States, is to race off to the nearest courthouse and to complain that the legislation in question is unconstitutional. I will not take up your valuable time by discussing the extent to which judicial review is "counter-majoritarian," the well-known term coined by the late Alexander Bickel (1962) that has itself been subjected to withering criticism, much of which I'm sympathetic with. But it has always been especially problematic to figure out why the judiciary should be able to set aside *national* legislation, in contrast to *state* legislation, save for a very limited set of occasions. Justice Oliver Wendell Holmes (1920) notably declared that the nation could well survive the elimination of judicial review of national legislation even as he thought it important that the Supreme Court could continue to monitor state legislation. Even if one disagrees with Holmes—and I confess I am uncertain about my own views on the matter—it is important to realize that, as an empirical matter, the court has only rarely invalidated significant national legislation.

One reason I do not teach *Marbury v. Madison* and spend a perhaps inordinate amount of time on *McCulloch v. Maryland* is that the latter is, in every way, more important. The Supreme Court played its essential function of legitimizing what many at the time viewed as questionable acts by the national government and, of course, equally delegitimated Maryland's attempt to engage in what Jessica Bulman-Pozen and Heather Gerken (2009, 1258) have aptly labeled "uncooperative federalism." It is true, of course, that the contemporary conservative majority of the Supreme Court has been far more prone to invalidate national legislation than were earlier courts, though even Chief Justice John Roberts ultimately flinched at the prospect of negating the most important piece of federal social legislation in the past four decades. Still, assume that the law one doesn't like is simply stupid, even pernicious in many ways, albeit not unconstitutional, whether measured by existing judicial doctrine or even by one's favorite constitutional theory.

After all, no one, liberal *or* conservative, believes that it is enough to identify a law as stupid or even pernicious in order to know that it is unconstitutional. George Mason, speaking to his colleagues in the Philadelphia convention on July 21, 1787, assumed that judges would have the power to "declare an unconstitutional law void." But he also reminded his colleagues that "with regard to every law however unjust oppressive or pernicious, which did not come plainly under this description, they would be under the necessity, as Judges to give it a free course" (2 Records of the Federal Convention, Volume 2, July 21, 1787, available at https://oll.libertyfund.org/titles/f Farrand arrand-the-records-of-the-federal-convention-of-1787-vol-2). This simply echoed the like statement of Pennsylvania's own James Wilson that same day: "Laws may be unjust, may be unwise, may be dangerous, may be destructive, and yet may not be so unconstitutional as to justify the Judges in refusal to give them effect" (Id.). We should always remember, in this context, that

Oliver Wendell Holmes helped to form the constitutional consciousness of many Progressives and New Dealers when he wrote, in his canonical *Lochner* dissent, that "it is settled by various decisions of this court that state constitutions and state laws may regulate life in many ways which we, as legislators, might think as injudicious, or, if you like, as tyrannical."[2]

So there is good reason to be wary of either elections *or* judicial review to protect Americans against the consequences of unwise legislation that is on the books. This is why I have become a fan of what I have to call "citizen review" as an alternative to "judicial review" or to the election process as a mechanism for relieving us of unwanted legislation (Levinson 1979). This process has been manifested recently in Maine and Ohio. Section 17 of Article IV of the Maine Constitution, aptly titled "Proceedings for people's veto," provides that petitions signed by no fewer than 10 percent of the number of voters in the previous gubernatorial election trigger a referendum by the general electorate as to whether a bill passed by the legislature (and, almost certainly, signed by the governor) will in fact take effect.[3] A similar provision in the Ohio Constitution allows appeal to the electorate. In 2009, 53 percent of the Maine electorate overrode a law legalizing same-sex marriage that had received both legislative and gubernatorial approval (although Maine voters later reversed course, by a similar margin, and approved same-sex marriage in a 2012 referendum) (Goodnough 2009; *New York Times* 2012). Two years later, in 2011, a majority voted to override a law widely viewed as making it more difficult for people to vote in Maine elections (*New York Times* 2011). In Ohio, a law restricting the power of public employee unions was successfully overturned by popular referendum (Tavernise and Greenhouse 2011). Given my own politics, I am tempted to say that two out of three isn't bad!

I invite you to consider whether we would have been better off, all things considered, in 2011–2012 had "Obamacare" been subjected to a national referendum, deciding whether the bill would live or die, instead of being taken before the federal judiciary. Instead, we were treated to the spectacle of lawyers shouting at one another and changing almost no minds in the process, with the ultimate result being the 5–4 decision upholding the central aspect of the legislation, the so-called "mandate." I am quite confident that Chief Justice Roberts's opinion upholding the mandate on "tax clause" grounds while rejecting its legitimacy under the Commerce Clause is treated with disdain by at least 75 percent of those who study constitutional law for a living. After all, it was, in effect, rejected by eight of his nine colleagues.

My real point, though, is that many states, because of their adoption of procedures allowing "direct democracy," have a "safety valve" against the particular kinds of veto points generated by representative democracy, whether one focuses either on initial passage of legislation or the repeal of such legislation as does pass. It is worth mentioning the special problem posed by the almost certain opposition of representatives to particular changes that would challenge their entrenched power, as with proposals at the state level to eliminate bicameralism. I have on more than one occasion quoted the emendation by political scientist John P. Roche of Lord Acton's famous comment about power and corruption. "Power corrupts," said Roche, "and the prospect of losing power corrupts absolutely" (Levinson and Blake 2016, 229). Former Minnesota governor Jesse Ventura sensibly urged Minnesotans to eliminate their senate, because it both hindered the passage of necessary legislation and simply cost the state a considerable amount of money for no good reason (Ayres 1999). Not surprisingly Ventura, almost always described as a "maverick" inasmuch as he won his office with a minority of the total vote by running as an independent in a multicandidate election that did not allow a runoff, failed in his efforts. Perhaps one explanation, in addition to Ventura's lack of political skills, is the simple fact that Minnesota, unlike Nebraska and seventeen other states, has no provision for citizen initiatives and referenda that would have allowed Ventura and his supporters to do an end run around recalcitrant state senators, as ultimately happened in Nebraska.

I will not detail further the undemocratic features of the U.S. Constitution, not least because I have devoted two books to this task. Those books have emphasized the likely consequences—I use that adjective in order to recognize that complex problems of causal analysis are involved—of the formal structures drafted in Philadelphia, ratified in 1787–1788, and left remarkably unchanged thereafter. I will conclude this section by mentioning one final clause that I find particularly egregious, Article V, which sets out the procedures for amending the Constitution. It is not only that these procedures add up to making the U.S. Constitution perhaps the most difficult to amend constitution in the entire world. The only reason for the "perhaps," incidentally, is that some states, such as Iowa, require that amendments be proposed by successive legislatures before being submitted to the voters for popular ratification. This makes impossible the rapid proposal and approval found with regard to several national amendments, including, for example, the Seventeenth Amendment ending legislative election for senators and the Twenty-First Amendment repealing prohibition, both proposed and ratified within approximately a single year. And some constitutions, most famously Germany's, have so-called "eternity" clauses that prohibit certain specific kinds of amendments and, therefore, apparently license constitutional courts to invalidate even constitutional amendments themselves should they run afoul of such clauses.

So let me review the bidding, as it were: I think it is beyond argument not only that the U.S. Constitution fails a primary test of twentieth- and twenty-first-century "democracy," but also, and just as important, that that is far less the case with regard to America's state constitutions and the systems of government they establish (or "constitute"). I have become insistent—perhaps even crankish—in arguing that we must stop identifying "American constitutionalism" exclusively with the atypical U.S. Constitution. I am a big fan of John Dinan's book *The American State Constitutional Tradition* (2006), which draws on the constitutional developments of America's state constitutions and the significant differences between and among them, on the one hand, and the 1787 Constitution, on the other. (I have, for example, not discussed the implications of the fact that most state judges are, in one way or another, accountable to state electorates.)

We are left with two primary questions, though. Does it really matter to most Americans that the U.S. Constitution is so strikingly undemocratic? I have come to the conclusion that the answer is no. A common reaction to my earlier book—recall its title, *Our Undemocratic Constitution*—was to be told, sometimes quite condescendingly, that I simply misunderstood American constitutionalism (at least when it is defined by the U.S. Constitution). The demigods who framed the Constitution explicitly established, I was told, a "republic," not a "democracy," and we should keep it that way. I have no doubt that few, if any, of these respondents could even identify the John Birch Society or its founder Robert Welch, but they adopted its motto, developed during the 1950s as part of a broader argument that Dwight Eisenhower was a Communist sympathizer inasmuch as he basically accepted the legitimacy of the New Deal. Indeed, I have come to the further conclusion that most Americans, whatever their use of the term "republican" in this context, are far from "civic republicans" with regard to the importance of actually turning aside from one's private pursuits to participate in politics. I suspect that a "benevolent despotism" that genuinely "delivered the requisite material goods" would garner far more approval than does the present Congress.

It is well beyond the scope of this essay to offer a full analysis of the rejection of a participation-oriented civic republicanism. We might, however, ask ourselves if we today share Hamilton's and Madison's seeming confidence in 1787 of a perhaps endlessly "extended republic." The Constitution was drafted, and defended, to establish a national polity of approximately four to five million persons, most of whom were denied any participatory role in national politics. And the country extended only to the east bank of the Mississippi River and from what is now Maine to the present southern border of Georgia. California alone has approximately eight times the entire population of the original United States—and it is only about 12 percent of the total population today, which is at least sixty times the initial population at its origin, not to mention the expansion of the country into the mid-Pacific and, depending on one's view of Puerto Rico, the mid-Caribbean. Economists relish pointing out that it is basically irrational for any given individual to vote, let alone to expend even further energies in civic governance. Free riding is the "rational choice."

My second remaining question, however, is entirely relevant to this essay: How do we account for the fact that what Dinan calls the "American state constitutional tradition" has had so little impact on the "tradition" linked with the national constitution? Federalism is often praised as offering "little laboratories of experimentation," which, presumably, the rest of the country could learn from. Why, apparently, has so little been learned from the development and history of American state government?

One response, of course, is simply to say that they are such fundamentally different enterprises that there is just nothing to be learned from state practices. (Is the same true with regard to learning in the other direction?) From this perspective, it is foolish to ask students, as I often do, to compare, say, the California or Texas constitutions, on the one hand, with the U.S. Constitution, on the other, and then to indicate which they prefer, with regard to some specific issues of constitutional design, and why. Perhaps this is like asking them to compare even their favorite piece of music with their favorite food. They are two radically different domains of life. I confess I find this answer wholly unpersuasive. Even if one concedes that there are some significant differences in the purposes and domains of the U.S. Constitution and that of a particular state—think, for example, of the particular "national security" responsibilities of the national government, with its plethora of armed forces, or the unique ability of the national government to inflate the currency by printing money—that scarcely explains, without more, the fact that forty-eight of the fifty states have rejected the "unitary executive," particularly with regard to giving state governors the power to appoint attorneys general. Only in those two states would we go through the *sturm und drang* similar to that experienced in the United States between 2017 and 2019 with regard to whether or not President Trump would in fact fire Robert Mueller (and, for that matter, Attorney General Jeff Sessions or Deputy Attorney General Ron Rosenstein). And I have already indicted my own willingness at least to contemplate the possibility that we would be better off with at least milder forms of direct democracy, such as that found in Maine, than with the exclusive reliance on representative democracy foisted upon us by the delegates to the Philadelphia convention.

Let me conclude, then, by offering two other hypotheses for discussion. One involves popular *consciousness*; the other, our inadequate public *education*. As to the first, I return to a central theme of my first book, *Constitutional Faith*, which emphasized the singular role that the U.S. Constitution plays in American civil religion (Levinson 1988). As one might well expect with religious symbols, it is often treated with the "veneration" that James Madison notably called for in *Federalist* 49, devoted to rebutting the arguments made by Thomas Jefferson in favor of frequent conventions that might subject the Constitution to continuing scrutiny and assessment by "We the People." Alexander Hamilton, in the very first paragraph of *Federalist* 1, emphasizes that "it seems to have been reserved to the people of this country, by their conduct and example, to decide the important question, whether *societies of men are really capable or not of establishing good government from reflection and choice, or whether they are forever destined to depend for their political constitutions on accident and force*" (italics added).

In a lecture I gave at the University of Nebraska titled "'Reflection and Choice': A One-Time Experience?" (Levinson 2013), I asked if we treat the initial *Federalist* merely as an historical document, interesting to us, if at all, as an artifact of late eighteenth-century political thought, as against its being a text that genuinely speaks to us today in 2019 (see also Levinson, 2015, 9–12). Do *we* see ourselves as capable of judging how to achieve good government? Do *we* view ourselves as empowered to engage in genuine "reflection" about the adequacy of our Constitution and the possible relationship between its proclivity to establish so many veto points and the malaise about our political system that seems so endemic to contemporary American politics, regardless of one's place on the political spectrum? And, if one agrees with my "reflections" about the dysfunctionalities of our constitutional order, do we feel empowered as well to engage in a genuine "choice" about reforming it and emulating those who acted in Independence Hall? Both Hamilton and Madison spoke of the necessity of paying due attention to the "lessons of experience," even if they required rejecting "tradition" and established ways of doing things. Do *we* pay suitable attention to such lessons, or do we settle instead for what I am sometimes tempted to describe as mindless veneration of the framers' handiwork?

Whatever else may be said of America's state constitutions, one can be quite confident that few, if any, are treated even with great respect, let alone veneration. The one exception may be Massachusetts, explained perhaps by the fact that the 1780 Massachusetts Constitution, the oldest continuing constitution in the United States, was substantially drafted by John Adams. I am confident, though, that the trigger for the copious literature on Adams, like the other founding fathers, has almost nothing to do with that particular aspect of his remarkable career. Most Americans, I suspect, are ignorant of the fact that their states even have constitutions of their own. Indeed, far more to the point, I don't have to engage in sheer speculation in order to note that almost no "leading" law school makes its students aware of the fact that the American constitutional tradition is in fact far more complex than one would think, at least if one takes our state constitutions and their history into account. Instead, "American constitutionalism" is identified exclusively with the national constitution, and students can graduate and embark on careers of distinction—perhaps even becoming presidents or chief justices—without once engaging in systematic reflection on the differences among our various constitutions.

Consciousness is, at least to some extent, a function of education. Much has been written recently about the absolutely dismal status of what used to be called "civic education" in America. Let me suggest, though, that the "solution" is not simply to intensify the presentation of material about the national constitution. I have, in recent years, offered "reading courses" at the Harvard Law School on comparative national and state constitutions in the United States, and I have discovered that almost no students were ever properly introduced to their state constitutions in the course of their education. "Comparative constitutional law," in most law schools and, I suspect, political science departments, is synonymous with the placement of *national* constitutions, whether France's or South Africa's, next to one another, including that of the United States, with concomitant attention to what similarities and differences one might find. Moreover, in law schools,

I regret to say, comparisons or contrasts most often involve *rights* and not the different *structures*, which I fear are treated as far less interesting. One must also concede that there are extraordinarily important, and difficult, questions of causality linked to structural analysis that may be absent if one looks only at the debates about different political and social values surrounding, say, hate speech, abortion, or affirmative action in various countries.

When comparing different countries, and even states, it is always tempting to rely simply on "culturalist" assumptions that diminish perhaps to the vanishing point the relevance of institutions. In the half century since I arrived at graduate school, political science has remained divided between those who emphasize "political culture" or economic resources and those they dismiss as "epiphenomenal" on the "other side," who believe that formal institutions genuinely matter, that the outcomes of the debates in Philadelphia were of enduring importance in explaining subsequent American history, for good and, all too often, for ill. I certainly do not want to be interpreted as arguing that institutions explain 100 percent of the variance between any given polities. That would be extraordinarily foolish. Perhaps institutions explain only 10 percent. But there are times when that may be enough, given other factors admittedly traceable to cultural or economic aspects of the polity, to explain why one system will "go over the cliff," fiscal or otherwise, while another manages to veer toward a safer outcome.

In any event, I remain willing to continue playing my self-assigned role of critic of the U.S. Constitution. I would like to think that I am Paul Revere, telling my fellow Americans that it is time to confront the potential menace posed to us by the deficiencies in the Constitution that, left unexamined and unchanged, will increasingly prove to be a clear and present danger to our own future and that of our ancestors (not to mention people around the world who are necessarily affected by decisions made and unmade by those who claim to govern the United States). It is, of course, possible, even if one grants the possibility that I am correct in my analysis, that I am Cassandra, the truth of whose prophecies was entirely irrelevant, whether one explains this by the consciousness of her audience or the whimsy of Greek gods who took malign pleasure in making sure that no one listened to her. The final possibility, of course, is that I am Chicken Little, whose warnings are simply the result of an excited, perhaps hysterical, consciousness of my own, so that the correct response is simply to lighten up, stop worrying, and be happy, secure in the knowledge, after all, that God does indeed take care of children and the United States. Would that were true!

Notes

1. Reynolds v. Sims, 377 U.S. 533 (1964).
2. Lochner v. New York, 198 U.S. 45 (1905).
3. See https://ballotpedia.org/Article_IV-Part_Third,_Maine_Constitution.

References

Ayres, B. Drummond, Jr. 1999. "Ventura's Mission: Turning Two into One." Political Briefing. *New York Times*, August 22, 1999, 32.

Bickel, Alexander M. 1962. *The Least Dangerous Branch: The Supreme Court at the Bar of Politics*. New York: Bobbs-Merrill Company.

Bulman-Pozen, Jessica, and Heather K. Gerken. 2009. "Uncooperative Federalism." *Yale Law Review* 118 (7): 1256–1310.

Dinan, John J. 2006. *The American State Constitutional Tradition*. Lawrence: University Press of Kansas.

Economist Intelligence Unit 2018 Democracy Index. Available at https://www.abc.net.au/news/2019-01-10/democracy-index-economist-intelligence-unit-2018/10703184.

Farrand, Max. *2 Records of the Federal Convention*. Available at https://oll.libertyfund.org/titles/f Farrand arrand-the-records-of-the-federal-convention-of-1787-vol-2.

The Federalist Papers: Alexander Hamilton, James Madison, John Jay. 2009. Edited by Ian Shapiro, 502–532. New Haven, CT: Yale University Press.

Goodnough, Abby. 2009. "Gay Rights Rebuke May Result in a Change in Tactics." *New York Times*, November 5, 2009, A25.

Holmes, Oliver Wendell. 1920. *Collected Legal Papers*. New York: Harcourt, Brace and Howe.

Horwitz, Morton J. 1993. "The Supreme Court, 1992 Term." *Harvard Law Review* 107 (1): 27–142.

Lardieri, Alexa. 2019. "Americans Don't Like the Congressional Leadership." *U.S. News and World Report*, January 3, 2019. Available at usnews.com/news/politics/articles/2019-01-03/americans-dont-like-the-congressional-leadership.

Levinson, Sanford. 1979. "'The Constitution' in American Civil Religion." *Supreme Court Review* 1979: 123–151.

———. 1988. *Constitutional Faith*. Princeton, NJ: Princeton University Press.

———. 2006. *Our Undemocratic Constitution: Where the Constitution Goes Wrong (and How We the People Can Correct It)*. New York: Oxford University Press.

———. 2010. "Democracy and the Extended Republic: Reflections on the Fishkinian Project." *Good Society* 19 (1): 63–67.

———. 2012. *Framed: America's 51 Constitutions and the Crisis of Governance*. New York: Oxford University Press.

———. 2013. "'Reflection and Choice': A One-Time Experience?" *Nebraska Law Review* 92 (2): 239–258.

———. 2015. *An Argument Open to All: Reading the Federalist in the 21st Century*. New Haven: Yale University Press.

Levinson, Sanford V., and William D. Blake. 2016. "When Americans Think About Constitutional Reform: Some Data and Reflections." *Ohio State Law Journal* 77 (2): 211–236.

Levitsky, Steven and Daniel Ziblatt. 2018. *How Democracies Die*. New York: Crown Publishers.

Margalit, Avishai. 2009. *On Compromise and Rotten Compromise*. Princeton, NJ: Princeton University Press.

New York Times. 2011. "Back to Common Sense at the Polls." November 10, 2011, A34.

———. 2012. "A Festive Mood in Maine as Same-Sex Marriage Becomes Legal." December 30, 2012, 20.

Tarr, G. Alan. 2010. "Bicameralism or Unicameralism? Testimony Before the Majority Policy Committee, Pennsylvania Legislature, April, 2010." Available at statecon.camden.rutgers.edu/sites/statecon/files/publications/bicameralism.pdf.

Tavernise, Sabrina, and Steven Greenhouse. 2011. "Ohio Vote on Labor Is Parsed for Omens." *New York Times*, November 10, 2011, A16.

Texas Office of the Secretary of State. 2006. "Race Summary Report: 2006 General Election." Available at elections.sos.state.tx.us/elchist127_state.htm.

White House Office of the Press Secretary. 2009. "Remarks by President Obama at Strasbourg Town Hall." Available at obamawhitehouse.archives.gov/the-press-office/remarks-president-obama-strasbourg-town-hall.

CHAPTER 3

State Constitutional Details and America's Positive Rights

Emily Zackin

As David Law and Mila Versteeg note in Chapter 1 of this volume, assertions about America's constitutional exceptionalism are commonplace.[1] For instance, noted law professor Cass Sunstein (2005, 4) has declared that "the constitutions of most nations create social and economic rights, whether or not they are enforceable. But the American Constitution does nothing of the kind." He goes on to ask, "Why is this? What makes the American Constitution so distinctive in this regard?" Many scholars have answered this question with classically exceptionalist tropes, particularly with reference to America's unique political culture.[2] For instance, prominent constitutional scholar Frederick Schauer (2005, 46) writes: "American distrust of government is a contributing factor to a strongly libertarian approach to constitutional rights. The Constitution of the United States is a strongly negative constitution, and viewing a constitution as the vehicle for ensuring social rights, community rights, or positive citizen entitlements of any kind is . . . highly disfavored." Other theorists have followed suit, opining that "the constitutionalization of positive rights will not occur absent a shift in America's classically liberal political culture" (Bentley 2007, 1723). Andrew Moravcsik (2005) has written that, while he doubts that such abstract cultural differences can, on their own, explain divergent policy outcomes, "Americans [do] tend to shy away from state intervention to redress social inequality—now established in most advanced industrial democracies as the primary fiscal task of the state. The aversion to state intervention is a distinctively American trait as compared to the political cultures of other advanced industrial democracies."

Studies of state and local politics have played a key role in undermining the notion of American exceptionalism. When we expand our examination of American governance beyond the federal level, even nineteenth-century America no longer appears to lack regulatory, protective government. On the contrary, it is quite clear that state governments regulated social life in a variety of arenas and established interventionist policies to promote social welfare well before the New Deal (see, e.g., Mink 1995). Historian William Novak has been particularly influential in establishing that, even during the supposedly stateless nineteenth century, governmental regulation was a pervasive feature of American politics. Americans' everyday lives, Novak demonstrates, were permeated by the assumption that government's proper function was to continually intervene, regulate, and perfect community life. It was simply state and local governments that played this interventionist role (Novak 1996, 42). Even the federal government itself now appears to have been far more interventionist during the nineteenth century than was once believed. Building on existing norms of state and local governance, the federal government of the nineteenth century worked in partnership with state, local, and private intermediaries to meet social and economic needs (Balogh 2009; Johnson 2007). As a result of this research, few would continue to defend assertions of American exceptionalism in their strongest form. However, many continue to describe America's constitutional tradition as exceptional. Constitutional exceptionalism has thus outlived the dogma from which it was derived.

I have argued for some time that we must apply our knowledge of American political development to our assessment of America's constitutional rights. Just as it is a mistake to take the measure of the American state by looking only at the federal government, it is misleading to assess America's rights tradition exclusively with reference to the United States Constitution. The study of state and local governance has discredited claims about America's exceptional political development. Similarly, the study of state constitutions challenges assertions about the exceptional nature of America's constitutional rights.

When you read America's state constitutions, however, it can sometimes seem that the people who wrote them must have failed to grasp the purpose and the nature of constitutional law. State constitutions do contain declarations of guiding principles and outline the basic structures of state government, but in most cases, these recognizably constitutional features are surrounded, even engulfed, by hundreds of mundane administrative details. As the *New York Times* put it, for example, the "great phrases [of New York's constitution] all but drown in the fine print." For example, the article pointed out, the state constitution even concerns itself with the construction of ski trails (MacKenzie 1987). In fact, New York's "ski trails" provision has become emblematic of the outlandish level of detail in most state constitutions (Adams 1970, 73; Bamberger 2000, 17; Benjamin and Dullea 1997, 16; Jewell and Patterson 1966, 138; Reed 2001, 89; Schapiro 1998, 391; Tarr 1998, 2).

The fact that so many state constitutions contain provisions about policy choices as detailed as the construction of ski trails has cast doubt on whether these constitutions are really constitutional at all. James Gardner, for example, argues that provisions like this one discredit the entire enterprise of state constitution writing. "What can one say about the character of a people who enshrine these types of provisions in their constitutions . . . ?" he asks. "Can one say of New Yorkers . . . that they are a people who cherish their liberty to ski?" (Gardner 1992, 819). Because the sovereign body that drafted the state constitution was petty enough to enshrine details like the width of ski trails in its fundamental law, Gardner tells us, he finds it difficult to credit that body with a comprehensive vision or "a meaningful history of purposeful debate" (820). If the framers of New York's constitution could not be bothered to take seriously their own fundamental law, surely it would seem that *we* should not waste our time in the attempt.

Before we accept state constitutions as a meaningful component of the American constitutional tradition, then, it seems we must first address this nagging "ski trails" problem. In other words, we must consider whether these odd-looking documents are a legitimate element of American constitutionalism, and whether we should really revise our conception of American constitutional rights based solely on their (highly detailed) contents. In order to answer these questions, it is necessary to explore why the detailed nature of state constitutions strikes so many observers as so problematic.

I believe that state constitutional details seem disturbingly unconstitutional for four related reasons. First, these details can appear idiosyncratic and parochial. Thus, they seem to reflect unique local anxieties and interests rather than national political concerns. Second, these details appear to be an extension of politics as usual, rather than a product of detached, disinterested, and visionary planning. Third, state constitutions' details appear to focus on mundane and trivial policy decisions, instead of enshrining weighty commitments or fundamental guarantees. Finally, detailed state constitutional provisions have been accused of hobbling the states they created, rather than facilitating their fruitful development. At the heart of each of these concerns over detail lies the conviction that state constitution-making is not appropriately or sufficiently principled to create true constitutions. As a result, the critics of state constitutions sometimes argue and regularly imply that these documents (and particularly their details) can lay only questionable claim to the title of "constitution."

After exploring each of these critiques of state constitutionalism, I argue that state constitutions, even their very detailed provisions, can and do reflect nationwide, principled commitments. Not only do these details often address issues of national salience, but their origins, while in some ways different from those of the federal Constitution, are not inherently less elevated. Indeed, the origins of these provisions highlight the ways in which state constitutions reflect their champions' principled (and quite familiar) use of constitutions and constitutional politics. As we will see, even the notorious ski trails provision reflects quintessentially constitutional aims. To recognize the principled nature of state constitutionalism, however, we must reconsider the ubiquitous assumptions about "higher lawmaking" and states' idiosyncrasies that have animated their critics.

Do State Constitutions Reflect Idiosyncratic Anxieties or National Concerns?

If one is primarily familiar with the U.S. Constitution, it can be quite jarring to learn that Florida's current constitution bans the use of a particular kind of fishing net, or that Oklahoma's constitution currently includes a provision relating to the operation of grain elevators.[3] If one hears only these examples or reads only a single constitution that contains them, one might well conclude that state constitutions reflect narrow, local concerns and particularistic interests as much as or more than they reflect any kind of nationwide commitments. It would seem that such documents could hardly serve as an adequate foundation for any argument about the character of American constitutional law or its national rights tradition.

However, when one examines contemporaneous constitutions together, the regional and national problems and controversies that shaped them become wholly unmistakable. In fact, scholars of state constitutionalism are generally quick to note that these detailed provisions reflect larger trends in constitution writing in other American states that today extend around the world (Tarr 1998; Dinan 2006; Williams 2009). Constitutions have over time become more elaborate almost everywhere except at the national level in the United States (Tsebelis 2017, 832). The "particularistic" interests that seem to have shaped state constitutions, moreover, have rarely been unique to their own states. The study of state constitutions at higher levels of aggregation quickly brings their commonalities into focus. Although state governments are often described as isolated "laboratories" in which new policies can be tested without danger to the nation as a whole,[4] it is mistaken to imagine states as a disorganized array of isolated decision-makers. While it is certainly possible to find idiosyncratic provisions in more than one state constitution, most address a similar set of policy problems. What may appear as an odd and misplaced detail in a single state constitution is therefore very likely to appear in many other contemporaneous constitutions as well.

This coordination between American state constitutions is, in part, a result of the efforts of their framers to study the latest state constitutional practices and to apply the lessons that other states offered as they designed their own fundamental laws. Throughout the nineteenth and twentieth centuries, constitutional conventions and advisory commissions on constitutional revision have engaged in broad comparative studies of constitutional law and borrowed heavily from one another. Constitutional conventions' delegates not only discussed the situations and constitutions of neighboring states, but also conducted comparative surveys that were national in scope. As Christian Fritz (1994, 976) has demonstrated, the delegates to nineteenth-century state constitutional conventions regularly consulted compilations of America's state constitutions, many of which were even published in pocket-sized editions for easy reference. They also discussed the social problems that other states faced and the success or failure of their constitutional solutions. Delegates often defended the provisions they supported with reference to the other states that had adopted similar constitutional mechanisms.[5]

Constitutional similarities were not only the product of their framers' studies but also the products of the coordinated efforts of national social movements, working through states. Well before constitutional conventions' first meetings, the leaders of these movements typically attempted to ensure that the convention would consider their demands. Thus, the similarities between state constitutions can be explained in large part by the work of nationwide interest groups, like farmers' organizations, labor unions, and women's groups, which promoted their agendas through and across individual states (Clemens 1997).

As early as the first decades of the nineteenth century, state-level organizations within the same broad movement communicated and coordinated across vast geographic distances, reporting on both legislative and constitutional developments in other states and sharing experiences about the most successful tactics. As we will see, publications like labor newspapers, teachers' journals, and environmental magazines all informed their readers about constitutional developments of even far-flung states and urged their readers to fight for similar provisions in their own state constitutions. In the run-up to New Mexico's constitutional convention, for example, the *New Mexico Journal of Education* asked existing state superintendents of education to recommend the most desirable constitutional provisions. It then printed the advice for the benefit of the state's own constitutional convention. Similarly, in her work on behalf of protective labor legislation, Florence Kelley (Illinois's first state factory inspector) published a book reviewing the status of maximum hours laws in states across the country and recommending that proponents of labor regulation follow Utah's example in pursuing the constitutional right to an eight-hour day, especially for those laboring under particularly dangerous conditions (Kelley 1905). Twentieth-century environmental activists also shared ideas for common constitutional rights. In 1968, for example, *Audubon* magazine published the text of New York's "environmental bill of rights," recommending that its readers consider supporting the inclusion of a similar provision in their own state constitutions. Indeed, nationwide efforts to influence the development of state constitutions have been so vigorous and long-lived that the study of changing details in state constitutions is, to a large extent, also the study of American social movements. Many of these movements have had ties to international counterparts who have worked for constitutional changes in other countries as well (see, e.g., Keck and Sikkink 1998, 48–49, 74, 194).

Are State Constitutions Products of Pluralistic Competition or Disinterested Judgment?

Of course, it is entirely possible to recognize international trends in constitution writing but still view American state constitutions (in all their trendy detail) as anathema to legitimate constitutional endeavors. Thus, many who have noted that state constitutions include a predictable set of details still see those details as extremely troubling. Their objection is premised, in part, on the idea that proper constitutional drafting is conducted not through competition between interest groups but through detached and reasoned judgments. Thus, the framers of the U.S. Constitution are regularly described as disinterested political theorists of the highest order. At times Indian constitutionalism, shaped by the contrasting visions of Mohandas Gandhi and especially B. R. Ambedkar, is described in equally elevated terms (e.g., Cabrera 2017). By contrast, state constitutions appear to be bloated with the demands of many narrow interest groups and polluted by the bargains they have struck (Friedman 2005, 74–75).

The details in state constitutions appear to be evidence that these documents reflect pluralistic competition rather than principled judgments about how to frame a government.[6] After all, state constitutions often specify particular projects to which the state's monetary resources must be committed, and many even include details about how this money should be raised and distributed. In other words, since state constitutions appear to enshrine the detailed outcomes of petty bargains, they appear to lack sufficiently lofty origins. Thus, like many others, James Gardner (1992, 822) has explained that upon examination, "we find state constitutions wanting. . . . The stories to which they lend themselves are not stories of principle and integrity, but stories of expediency and compromise at best, foolishness and inconstancy at worst."

It is true that state constitutions are so detailed in large part because these documents provide so many points of entry for the direct participation of citizens and citizen groups. Unlike the amendment procedures specified in the federal Constitution, the amendment procedures for state constitutions promote broad popular involvement in their development. For instance, while the U.S. Constitution may be revised through convention, Congress must establish such a convention, and a two-thirds majority of the states' legislatures is required to force Congress into convening one. This is a rigorous amendment procedure, and the U.S. Constitution has never been amended through this process. At the state level, constitutional conventions can typically be convened through either a majoritarian or supermajoritarian vote of the legislature and approved directly by voters. Fourteen states even allow citizens to vote at regular intervals on whether to call a convention without a prior legislative proposal. As a result, the "persistent demands of reform-oriented interest groups" have frequently been sufficient to bring state constitutional conventions into being (Cornwell, Goodman, and Swanson 1970, 107). Once a convention is called, its delegates are generally elected through a direct vote of the citizenry, and these elections offer further opportunities for citizen participation and for the influence of organized groups. Furthermore, amendments to the U.S. Constitution (introduced through a supermajoritarian vote of both houses of Congress) must be ratified by three-quarters of the states, typically through state legislatures. By contrast, state constitutional amendments (while frequently introduced through supermajoritarian legislative procedures) are generally ratified through a direct vote of the state's electorate. These statewide plebiscites offer yet another opportunity for direct popular participation in state constitutional change. Of course, the initiative and referendum procedure for amending state constitutions (introduced in Oregon in 1902 and since adopted by seventeen other states) is particularly remarkable in this respect, enabling citizens to amend state constitutions through petitions and popular votes alone. As of 2005, there had been 233 state constitutional conventions and only one federal convention (Williams 2009, 95). Furthermore, as of 1996, an average of 120 amendments per state had been added to state constitutions, while the federal constitution has only been amended twenty-seven times (Tarr 1998, 24).

Because the U.S. Constitution is so hard to amend formally, its meaning has, for the most part, evolved through changes in judicial doctrine (Griffin 1996). While popular movements have clearly influenced the Constitution's meaning, therefore, they have generally pursued constitutional change through litigation. As a result, the short and ambiguous provisions of the U.S. Constitution have remained largely unchanged at the level of their text, lending the Constitution an air of stability and changelessness. In addition, even for those who recognize that the meaning of the Constitution has changed through litigation, this particular mode of change appears to lift constitutional questions above the competition and bargaining that characterize other forms of political decision-making and to replace it with a principled and reasoned method of resolving disputes.

While the text of the U.S. Constitution is quite difficult to revise, it is relatively easy to change the text of state constitutions through popular pressure. Consequently, activists seeking to influence the meaning of state constitutions have often engaged in a form of politics closely associated with electoral and legislative competition.[7] For instance, interest groups often sought to ensure that candidates for membership in constitutional conventions vowed to promote the agenda of their organization. Montana's League of Conservation Voters even circulated a questionnaire to all of the candidates in elections for the state's 1971 constitutional convention, asking about their position on environmental rights in the constitution (Montana Legislature 1982, 1229). Labor unions used similar tactics, extracting promises of cooperation from candidates in exchange for their electoral support. Several labor groups even decided to try to staff constitutional conventions with their own members (see, e.g., *Michigan Union Advocate* 1907; *New York Times* 1893). The advocates of state constitutional change also published pamphlets, staged rallies, organized speaking tours, and campaigned in elections and statewide referenda. They circulated proposed articles for inclusion in the constitution and hired lobbyists to attend constitutional conventions in order to promote those articles. These tactics are neither separate from nor elevated above popular pressure and electoral competition in the way that the judicial process often appears to be. As a result, the provisions they generated have often been characterized as catalogs of interest groups' contests and bargains over state resources, rather than the products of disinterested and far-sighted deliberation.

It is a mistake to dismiss state constitutional politics as mere horse-trading simply because its form appears to differ from the federal model of detached and principled judging. First of all, this charge fails to distinguish the tactics of constitutional movements from the content of their demands. Pluralistic politics may center on groups' bids for a bigger piece of some pie, but pluralistic competition may also focus on the pursuit of fundamental values. Thus, sustained public interest in the content of state constitutions and democratic competition to shape their meaning should hardly be deemed unprincipled on its face. Furthermore, the allocation of a polity's resources is a decision in which fundamental values are often (perhaps always) implicated. Although the distribution of the state's resources was often at stake in state constitutional controversies, popular constitutional activism was hardly confined to petty squabbling. As we will see, many of the popular movements to influence state constitutions invoked broad principles as they engaged in a competition for voters' support and delegates' obedience.

Not only did popular movements outline broad principles of governance in their efforts to shape state constitutions, but the politics surrounding the federal Constitution are not as different from the state model as state constitutions' critics would have us believe. For example, both bargaining and elections played a significant role in shaping the federal Constitution, not just those of the states. In fact, several provisions of the U.S. Constitution were famously the result of bargains between particular interests, including America's bicameral legislature and its notorious three-fifths clause. In addition, the meaning of the federal Constitution is, like that of state constitutions, shaped through electoral competition. Although the U.S. Constitution is interpreted by Supreme Court justices with life tenure, rather than revised by popular amendments, Supreme Court justices are nonetheless selected and confirmed by elected officials. While the Supreme Court may lag behind public opinion and political change, therefore, it is by no means severed from them (Dahl 1957).[8] The Court is also discouraged from rendering widely unpopular decisions by the fact that it lacks the budgetary and police powers to enforce its own decisions and must rely on elected officials for this function. It is further constrained by the fact that Congress may attempt to curb judicial power in the face of unpopular decisions and in the hope of reaping electoral gains (Clark 2010). Consequently, the U.S. Constitution's meaning has dramatically changed over time as political winds shifted and new policy preferences have come to dominate the political landscape (Kersch 2004).

In what has become an extremely influential argument, Bruce Ackerman (1998) posits the existence of rare historical moments in which the views of the entire electorate foment and then legitimate changes in the meaning of the Constitution. These "constitutional moments" are so rare, Ackerman tells us, because, most of the time, most of the people are largely indifferent to debates about constitutional meaning. Once in a great while, however, disagreements about the Constitution create such a political crisis that the entire citizenry is forced to pay attention and voice an opinion. At such moments, Ackerman argues, the citizenry has effectively amended the Constitution by deciding on new constitutional meanings, which the Supreme Court will then enforce. Like state constitutions, the U.S. Constitution is neither above nor immune from popular pressure. However, popular pressure at the federal level is typically seen to have legitimated shifts in the Constitution's meaning. At the state level, where we witness the existence of sustained constitutional movements rather than ephemeral constitutional moments, this popular involvement is widely viewed with suspicion.

If democratic constitutions must mediate the tension between the competing goals of minority rights and majority rule (Eisgruber 2001), then we might say that state constitutions have simply struck a more majoritarian balance than their federal counterpart.[9] Indeed, the impressive degree of popular involvement in shaping state constitutions might well convince us to take state constitutions more, not less, seriously as a mirror of Americans' political commitments (Dinan 2006). In any case, we should not mistake constitutional provisions shaped through grassroots organizing and electoral competition as inherently unprincipled. To be sure, responsiveness to popular pressure is not an unmitigated virtue. A constitutional system capable of resisting popular pressure may also be more capable of protecting important principles in the face of public outrage than one that cannot.[10] However, it is important to remember that popular pressure and pluralistic competition may arise from principled commitments, and we cannot infer a lack of principle simply because state constitutions were shaped through pluralistic competition.

Are State Constitutions Trivial or Weighty?

Of course, most critiques of state constitutions not only cite concerns about the political tactics through which their detailed provisions were added but also chafe at their seemingly trivial content. Despite its different emphasis, this objection also stems from the conviction that real constitutions are defined, at least in part, by their elevated, higher-lawmaking origins. Proper constitution-making, we are told, must transcend not only the competition that characterizes ordinary politics but also the mundane particulars with which ordinary politics is occupied. In other words, constitutional lawmaking ought to address only the framework and principles of good government, not muck about in the minutia of everyday policies. Here again, we learn that state constitutions should look more like the U.S. Constitution, which establishes governing institutions, endows them with broad powers, and then places principled limits on their purview and discretion.

Like its fellows, this critique of state constitutionalism trades on an idealized and largely inaccurate picture of the federal constitutional endeavor. After all, the practical meaning of the federal Constitution's majestic statements of principle has been worked out in the context of specific policy battles (Whittington 1999). Thus, while the U.S. Constitution's text may be less detailed than those of the states, its law and meaning is equally bound up in detail. Furthermore, as Richard Primus (1999) has demonstrated, even the rights originally chosen for inclusion in the federal Constitution were not (or at least not only) statements of timeless and universal values, but reflections of very timely and specific dissatisfactions with the British colonial system.

The Third Amendment's prohibition on quartering soldiers in any house without the consent of its owner during peacetime, for instance, can hardly escape characterization as a detailed policy provision.

The critique of state constitutional detail as embarrassingly trivial has an even larger problem than its idealized view of the federal Constitution. The standard critique assumes a clear distinction between specific policy details (which belong only in statutes) and statements of fundamental values or frameworks for government (which belong in constitutions). However, these two categories are not necessarily distinct and certainly not mutually exclusive. Many, if not all, of the details in state constitutions simultaneously describe highly specific policies and reflect the important principles of governance that these policies were created to advance. In fact, even the infamous ski trails provision exhibits this dual character. It is both a highly detailed policy mandate and the recognition of a fundamental value.

Since the ski trails provision is such a ubiquitous emblem of state constitutional failure, it may be instructive to inquire about its real origins. When we do so, it is immediately obvious that the drafters of the ski trails provision were neither overwhelmed by their devotion to snow sports nor confused about the difference between constitutions and statutes. Instead, they promoted the amendment only so that the state legislature could construct ski trails in an area designated as protected wilderness. In 1941, when the ski trails provision was created, this construction project was widely understood to require special authorization in the constitution itself because another, older provision mandated that the state's forest preserve be "forever kept as wild forest land," and further specified that no timber could ever be removed from the protected area. Since the construction of ski trails required the removal of timber, the state could not build them without first revising the constitution. Thus, the advocates of the ski trails provision were attempting to create a narrow exception to a countervailing constitutional mandate.

It is not immediately clear, however, that this history helps to defend state constitutional detail against the charge of triviality. Indeed, detractors of state constitution writing note that high levels of detail have, over time, given rise to even higher levels of minutia.[11] Though less detailed than the ski-related amendment, the "Forever Wild" provision exemplifies the complications associated with "freezing" specific policy details in a constitution. Once a specific rule about the disposition of forestland was inscribed and rigidified in the constitution, even a trivial change to that rule necessitated the creation of an equally trivial constitutional amendment. Again, therefore, it seems that those who drafted New York's constitution must simply have lacked the foresight to do it properly. By placing this detailed policy in their constitution, they invited even further cluttering of their fundamental law.

We cannot ask the nineteenth-century framers of the Forever Wild provision whether, in hindsight, they wish they had omitted this detailed policy mandate.[12] However, we do know that, placed in the same position, and with time on their side, their successors celebrated this constitutional provision, despite the even more detailed amendments that had been required to modify it. At New York's constitutional convention of 1967, for instance, convention delegates supported the Forever Wild provision in force. Notwithstanding the thirteen amendments (including the ski trails amendment) that had been passed to carve out narrow exceptions to the Forever Wild provision, they praised it lavishly.[13] The president of the constitutional convention even declared, "I believe that the 1967 Constitutional Convention should not go down in history as the one which abridged the right of the people of the State to the protection of one of the State's greatest natural resources" (New York State Office of Legislative Research 1967, 20). This description of the Forever Wild provision as a right of the people to the protection of the state's resources echoed the arguments of its earliest champions.

The framers of the original Forever Wild provision included details about the management of the state forest in order to establish and safeguard the state's natural environment and the people who depended on it. By the 1890s, it was clear that irresponsible logging practices could denude forests, and many worried that if the forest were destroyed, its streams would cease to flow, and that this outcome would threaten the viability of commercial waterways like the Hudson River and Erie Canal (Graham and Graham 1978, 99). The state legislature had, by this time, created several different commissions to oversee and protect the state's forest. However, in the years leading up to the state's constitutional convention of 1894, widespread concern emerged about whether the forest commission could or would provide adequate protection for the state's wilderness. One installment of an eleven-part series in the *New York Times* on the continued irresponsibility of logging in the protected forestland announced "Shameful Work Going on in Adirondacks—Everything Being Ruined by the Rapacious Lumberman—State Employees Engaged in the Business" (cited in Terrie 1981, 277). To make matters worse, the appointed chair of the forest committee, Theodore Basselin, was actually a lumber baron.[14]

Not only did the forest commission seem untrustworthy, but even the legislature itself appeared to be unduly sympathetic to lumbering interests. Only a year before the constitutional convention was scheduled to begin, the legislature passed a "cutting bill," authorizing the forest commission to sell timber from any part of the forest preserve to private logging interests (Graham and Graham 1978, 124). In his subsequent report to the state land office, the state engineer and surveyor predicted that lumbering under this law would seriously damage the Adirondack forest. At this same time, the northern part of the state was suffering from a drought, and forest fires were raging throughout the Adirondacks. In the midst of these fires, the popular press raised the specter of the forest's total destruction at the hands of loggers (Terrie 1981, 283–284). Several decades after the constitutional convention, one scholar described the situation this way: "There was unhampered legislative control . . . that played for the most part into the greedy hands of the lumber interests. The net result was to convince all true friends of the forests, and a majority of the voters, that the guarding of the woods could not safely be left to a free-handed legislature" (Donaldson 1921, 167–168).

To many who worried about the health of the forest preserve, the competence of the forest commission, and the character of the legislature, the constitutional convention of 1894 seemed to offer a solution. Since the legislature (and its forest commission) could not be trusted to make decisions about the use or health of the state's wilderness, they hoped that protection for the state's forests could be secured directly through constitutional amendment. In order to ensure that the legislature and the forest commission would be unable to make irresponsible decisions about the use of the state forest, the convention adopted a constitutional provision that deprived the commission and even the legislature of discretion over the management of this land. The provision not only mandated that the area in question be "forever kept as wild forest land" but also permanently forbade the removal of any timber.[15]

The Forever Wild provision is, like its ski trails amendment, highly detailed. After all, it specifies that no timber can be removed from a particular part of the state. However, as the history and legacy of this provision illustrate, it is not only a meticulous set of instructions about the precise policy the legislature had to adopt but also a constitutional commitment to the broad principle of responsible treatment of the environment. The reason that it attempted to realize this broad principle by constitutionalizing a detailed policy is that the constitutional convention did not trust the legislature or its forest commission to implement ambiguous instructions about political values. In order to keep the legislature in check, to ensure that it would govern in accordance with their broad values, they drafted exhaustive policy instructions.

In the years after the adoption of the Forever Wild provision, a preservationist organization known as the Association for Protection of the Adirondacks litigated under the Forever Wild provision when it perceived encroachment on the wilderness. Even when the state legislature authorized the forest commission to build a bobsled track for the 1932 Olympics (to be held in Lake Placid), the association sued the conservation commissioner, arguing that the construction of a bobsled track would violate the Forever Wild provision of the state constitution by requiring the removal of timber. Two courts agreed,[16] and the Court of Appeals explained: "However tempting it may be to yield to the seductive influences of outdoor sports and international contests, we must not overlook the fact that constitutional provisions cannot always adjust themselves to the nice relationships of life." The decision then described the framers' intention to protect the state's wilderness from any possible abuses, and continued "this plea in behalf of sport is a plea for an open door through which abuses as well as benefits may pass. The Constitution intends to take no more chances with abuses, and, therefore, says the door must be kept shut."[17] Eleven years after the bobsled case, when the forest commission wanted to build ski trails in the forest preserve, it was widely understood that a constitutional amendment would be necessary to authorize their construction.

The history of New York's ski trails amendment demonstrates that the seemingly mundane details in state constitutions do not reflect the lack of principle in state constitutional politics. Out of context, it may seem obvious that ski trails (or bobsled tracks) are an appropriate topic for statutory law alone, and that they are not deserving of constitutional treatment. However, it should now be clear how fundamental values were centrally implicated in the issue of ski trails. The value of wilderness as well as the significant challenges in preserving it help to explain why reasonable and serious people felt the need to address ski trails in their constitutions. Gardner (1992, 819) is correct that New Yorkers did not value ski trails so highly that they felt the "need to place them beyond the reach of temporary majorities and transient passions, and to permit their alteration only by future direct action of the people themselves." However, the ski trails amendment is, nevertheless, the direct result of New Yorkers' attempts to protect the state's wilderness in just that way.[18] The state constitution includes details about the management of the state forest precisely because it embodies such a firm commitment to the broad principle of environmental preservation. Many recently written national constitutions express similar commitments as matters of what their proponents regard as high principles (Daly 2012).

Thus, the ski trails provision is an emblem of the supposedly inappropriate detail and the apparently petty concerns that have debased state constitutions. Yet, upon closer inspection, even this provision appears purposeful, sensible, and principled. It is not alone. State constitutions do contain many detailed policies, but these policy instructions do not necessarily represent a departure from recognizable constitutional practices. On the contrary, many reflect a familiar use of constitutional politics. Like the ski trails provision, these state constitutional details typically circumscribe governmental discretion, offering a solution when the governing institutions they established could not be trusted to handle a particular kind of policy. State constitutions' specificity, therefore, is not an indication of their triviality, but a mechanism through which their framers hoped to limit government's choices in order to ensure that its officials would act in accordance with principled commitments. The detailed provisions that these movements championed were products not of their petty squabbles and narrow visions but of their practical concerns about legislative compliance. Properly understood, as a check on the discretion of the state and its officers, these detailed provisions and the movements to create them are recognizable as quintessentially constitutional in nature. They limit the discretion of particular branches of government over particular types of policies, and thus fulfill one of the central and most recognizable roles of constitutional law.

Limiting Government's Discretion Without Limiting Its Scope

The detailed provisions in state constitutions, like the Forever Wild provision, were often crafted as checks on legislative discretion, and this history has engendered one further critique. The details in state constitutions have been accused of hobbling the very governments they establish. For instance, Kermit Hall (1991) has argued that, as state constitutions grew more detailed, they "became antigovernment, stripping from political officials the legal authority they needed to govern" (401). According to Hall, the framers of state constitutions hampered their governments on purpose, because they were fearful that government would become too effective and expansive. Thus, Hall tells us, "the assumptions underlying state constitutions were not just laissez-faire; they were positively hostile, save in a few limited areas, to the exercise of government power" (401). He continues, "State constitutions since the mid-nineteenth century have reflected the persistent localism and anti-governmentalism that underlie much of American political culture" (410). The detailed provisions in state constitutions are often interpreted in this way, as anti-statist measures and reflections of Americans' deep suspicion of government power.

It is certainly the case that misgivings about state legislatures have driven constitutional conventions to place limits on legislatures. This practice is particularly conspicuous in nineteenth-century constitutions, many of which placed restrictions on the gifts and benefits that legislators could receive from corporations, established relatively low caps on state indebtedness, and forbade the state from financing internal improvement projects (Tarr 1998, 112–116). These measures were responses to a disastrous history of states' efforts to attract industry and promote economic development, efforts that bankrupted or nearly bankrupted many state governments. During the national economic boom of the 1830s, states participated in what one historian has described as a "headlong venture in deficit spending" (Meyers 1957, 85). State legislatures issued bonds to finance the creation of canals, railroads, and banks, often dispensing significant benefits to these enterprises, including the grant of monopoly charters (Meyers 1957, 85; Tarr 1998, 110). Following the economic collapse of 1839, these policies plunged state governments into crisis, causing many to question their legislatures' competence. Constitutional conventions, which were often called in direct response to the states' economic crises, moved quickly and decisively to place limits on legislatures in the hopes that these restrictions would prevent them from being drawn back into risky speculation, or worse yet, corrupted by wealthy corporate interests (Tarr 1998, 112). Many of the provisions that resulted, like anti-corruption measures and limits on state indebtedness, were indeed designed to prevent government from intervening in the ways that it had before. However, other limits on legislative discretion had an entirely different purpose.

It is easy to assume that any restriction on the legislature must be a move toward smaller, more limited government. However, we should not confuse the desire to limit legislative choices with the goal of limiting the role of government. Similarly, we should not conflate the curtailment of the state's discretion with the reduction of its scope. Constitutional provisions may limit legislative discretion not only by restraining the state, but also by telling government that it must actively intervene in the state's social and economic life. Many of the provisions in state constitutions were not only aimed at telling state legislatures what they could no longer do, but also telling them what they had to do. In other words, state constitutions not only contain prohibitions on particular types of legislative activity, but also include mandates for legislative action.

Positive Rights

While certain kinds of legislative participation in economic activities were understood by many nineteenth-century constitution-makers to be risky and undesirable, a total lack of legislative involvement in markets was also seen to pose unacceptable risks. Thus, constitutional drafters not only required legislatures to refrain from speculative participation in the market, they also drafted positive constitutional rights, requiring legislatures to intervene in the state's economic life in order to mitigate some of the undesirable effects of the capitalist system. For example, the widespread anger at the "wildcat" banks and monopolistic railroads of the 1830s resulted in many constitutional mandates that the state create particular banking regulations and engage in legislative action to protect the railroads' employees and customers (Tarr 1998, 115). Several constitutions even included protections for debtors, requiring legislatures to ensure that homesteads under a certain value would be protected from forced sale to meet the demands of creditors.[19] One delegate to the Michigan constitutional convention of 1850 explained that the purpose of these constitutional provisions was to "throw around every homestead, every fireside, every hearth-stone, the shield of its protection—to stay the proud waves of wealth, capital, and usury, from carrying over the homes of suffering, crushed, bleeding humanity" (cited in Hershock 1995, 47). As this explanation attests, nineteenth-century movements for greater state intervention and protection used state constitutions in their attempts to establish social safety nets. The detailed provisions they drafted were intended not only to restrain the state but also to force their legislatures into an expanded and protective role.

The creation of detailed constitutional mandates for an interventionist welfare state was not limited to the nineteenth century. In the face of ongoing resistance to public schooling and redistributive taxation to fund it, education activists throughout the nineteenth and twentieth centuries have resorted to the creation of detailed constitutional instructions. Similarly, labor activists of the Gilded Age and Progressive Era wanted constitutions to mandate that government protect them from corporations' use of blacklists and private, strike-breaking armies, using constitutional provisions to establish the regulatory programs that legislatures had been reluctant to establish and courts reluctant to endorse. Environmental activists continued this tradition even into the late twentieth century, using state constitutions to place cleanup funds beyond the use of legislatures and to ban specific practices that threatened the natural environment (Zackin 2013, chaps. 5–7). All of these provisions are detailed, but they are not idiosyncratic, petty, or trivial. On the contrary, they reflect considered and widespread attempts to realize important principles in the face of recalcitrant legislatures and/or hostile courts.

The advocates of these positive rights consistently argued that, for a certain segment of the population, intrusive government and the risks such government posed to private property and individual liberty were not the most salient or urgent threats to the well-being of every citizen. For at least certain groups of people, restrictions on government and protections for private property would mean little unless government also provided protection from other, even more immediate dangers—like poverty, dangerous working conditions, and environmental catastrophe. Furthermore, the advocates of these provisions insisted that protections against these nongovernmental threats were too fundamental to be left in the hands of legislatures. In other words, the movements on behalf of positive rights at the state level sought to weave a social safety net of heartier stuff than mere statutes. Statutory law would certainly compose much of the protection they sought, but they insisted that it must be reinforced by constitutional mandates. These crucial safeguards could not be a matter of legislative choice, these movements declared, but must instead be secured as obligations on the state, and must therefore be placed in the state's highest law. Different political movements over different centuries and across many states made this argument, and many of them succeeded in having protective guarantees added to state constitutions.

It may seem difficult to believe that highly salient commitments on issues of national importance could be reflected only in state constitutions, while omitted from the federal document. However, the federal government played a far smaller role than state and local governments in crafting social policy throughout much of American history. This is arguably the case even today, but it is entirely clear in the case of pre–New Deal politics. Before the 1930s, state governments were primarily responsible for regulating working conditions and employment relationships, for establishing public education, protecting the public health, supervising the management of natural resources like land and water, and caring for the aged, indigent, and insane. In fact, under the dominant interpretation of the U.S. Constitution's Commerce Clause, Congress wasn't even thought to possess the authority to regulate in many of these areas. This is not to say that the federal government had no role in shaping America's social policies. However, states were primarily responsible for enacting the laws that governed these realms of social and economic life. Since states were the primary sources of law in most areas of social policy, their fundamental laws were the natural targets for activist groups seeking a more interventionist and protective state. Throughout the nineteenth and early twentieth centuries, Americans understood themselves to be living simultaneously under (at least) two governments of consequence (the state and federal governments), and under two meaningful constitutions (their state and federal constitutions). Even well into the twentieth century, the policies of state governments were significant enough that some organizations continued to devote resources to shaping America's state constitutions.

One final reason that we might expect to find positive rights in state constitutions, even if they are absent from the Bill of Rights, is that the Bill of Rights was added to the federal Constitution in order to satisfy Anti-Federalists that the new national government would not impinge too dramatically on the sovereignty of the existing state governments. The Bill of Rights was not written to apply to state governments, but was created primarily to ensure that the new national government would not replicate the recent, unwanted intrusions of the British colonial system. It is no wonder, then, that the U.S. Constitution's Bill of Rights seems (at least at first blush) to devote itself almost entirely to limiting government. Thus, while the Bill of Rights may reflect a suspicion of the federal government, we cannot infer from this document that even its drafters were suspicious of all government.

State constitutions reveal positive rights to be very much a part of America's constitutional politics and belie the claim that the United States is exceptional in its lack of positive rights. In fact, some of these constitutional provisions closely resemble the positive rights in constitutions all over the world. For instance, Article 24 of the Belgian constitution of 1970 states, "Everyone has the right to education. . . . Access to education is free until the end of mandatory schooling." The Missouri Constitution of 1865 declared, "The general assembly shall establish and maintain free schools for the gratuitous instruction of all persons . . . between the ages of five and twenty-one years." Article 24 of the 1993 Peruvian constitution states that "the worker is entitled to a fair and adequate remuneration enabling him to provide for himself and his family," and the Wyoming Constitution of 1889 says, "The rights of labor shall have just protection through laws calculated to secure to the laborer proper rewards for his service." These U.S. constitutional mandates, created in the nineteenth century, are still in place today. While the kinds of socioeconomic protections in the Peruvian and Belgian constitutions are often thought to be missing from American constitutional law, the texts of America's state constitutions have contained virtually identical guarantees for well over a century.

Notes

This essay builds on chapters 1 and 2 of *Looking for Rights in All the Wrong Places* (Zackin 2013).

1. For instance, one constitutional scholar has opined that "by limiting political authority and the very scope of politics itself, the American system aims to allow maximum opportunity for individual flourishing . . . *fairness* rather than *justice* is the hallmark of our legal aspirations and our cherished rights" (Abraham 1996, 3). Another scholar described the scholarly consensus this way: "One common and influential view of the [U.S.] Constitution suggests that it creates, almost exclusively, negative obligations of government and negative rights" (Sklansky 2002, 1233).

2. Sunstein himself does not believe this cultural explanation is correct and argues instead that America's lack of positive constitutional rights is the result of historical contingency. He attributes America's lack of positive rights to Nixon's (narrow) electoral win and to his conservative Supreme Court appointments. If so, few if any would predict that the court appointments of President Trump will alter that picture.

3. See Florida Constitution of 1968, Article 10, Section 16; and Oklahoma Constitution of 1907, Article 9, Section 33.

4. This metaphor is often attributed to Justice Louis Brandeis. In a dissenting opinion, Brandeis wrote, "It is one of the happy incidents of the federal system that a single courageous state may, if its citizens choose, serve as a laboratory; and try novel social and economic experiments without risk to the rest of the country." New State Ice Co. v. Liebmann, 285 U.S. 262, 311 (1932).

5. In 1921, the National Municipal League even began publishing a "model state constitution" with the hope of further standardizing these documents through the provision of a template (Graves 1941).

6. Alan Tarr (1998, 58) describes this view of state constitutions this way: "Given this understanding of state constitution-making, one would not expect the products of this process to embody a coherent design or overarching perspective on politics any more than one would expect it of a collection of state statutes."

7. Of course, the meaning of state constitutions can and does change through informal mechanisms as well (see, e.g., Besso 2005).

8. Consider how Senate Republicans refused to consider the nomination of Merrick Garland during President Barack Obama's last year in office, insisting that a nominee should come only after the verdict of the next election, which produced Donald Trump and Neil Gorsuch.

9. As John Dinan (2000) has demonstrated, the drafters of many state constitutions designed flexible constitutions precisely so that ordinary citizens might wrest control of the state from entrenched economic elites.

10. Indeed, litigation is often celebrated as a mode of constitutional change precisely because it allows Supreme Court justices to consider principled arguments and protect unpopular minorities, rather than bending to popular whims (Ely 1980).

11. For instance, legal historian James Willard Hurst (1950, 203) has written: "Not only did the practice [of adding details to a constitution] depart from the general notion of the dignity of constitutions; it also violated the proved practical wisdom of not freezing detailed policy into a form hard to change."

12. The Forever Wild provision was created as part of the 1894 state constitution.

13. One delegate to the convention argued that the Forever Wild provision allowed the state to address its changing needs without placing the forest at too great a risk. He explained that "the power and speed with which men and machines can radically change the face of the Forest Preserve has multiplied a 'hundredfold' since 1894." In the face of increasingly powerful and efficient means of deforestation and development, he argued, "the constitutional amendment procedure [had] worked to permit slow, conservative change" (New York State Office of Legislative Research 1967, 25).

14. The *New York Herald* quipped that the forest commission ought to change its motto from "protect the forests" to "protect the forests from Basselin" (Graham and Graham 1978, 123).

15. The specific terms and wording of this provision were actually drafted by the New York Board of Trade and Transportation, which was concerned about the viability of the state's waterways (Graham and Graham 1978, 127).

16. See Association for the Protection of the Adirondacks v. Alexander MacDonald, 288 A. D. 73 (1930); and Association for the Protection of the Adirondacks v. Alexander MacDonald, 253 N.Y. 234 (1930).

17. Association for the Protection of the Adirondacks, 253 N.Y. at 242.

18. In 1877, for example, one plea for the state to preserve the Adirondack forests read, "Nature herself has here formed a park that only needs preserving. . . . Let the state preserve that which Nature has so kindly bestowed with a lavish hand" (cited in Simpson 1992, 570). When the constitutional convention of 1915 reexamined the wisdom of the forest provision, many delegates expressed a similar sentiment. One declared: "There is twenty million dollars' worth of timber [in the forest preserve], but the question for you to decide is, what are we to do with that timber? Shall we treat it as we should if it belonged to you and me as a purely commercial proposition, or shall we handle and keep it for the other greater reasons that outweigh a hundred times the commercial side" (cited in Terrie 1989, 269–270).

19. Between 1845 and 1860, Texas, Wisconsin, California, Michigan, Indiana, Maryland, and Minnesota all added homestead exemptions to their constitutions (London 1948).

References

Abraham, David. 1996. "Liberty Without Equality: The Property-Rights Connection in a 'Negative Citizenship' Regime." *Law and Social Inquiry: Journal of the American Bar Foundation* 21 (1): 1–65.

Ackerman, Bruce. 1998. *We the People*. Vol. 2, *Transformations*. Cambridge, MA: Belknap Press of Harvard University Press.

Adams, John Clarke. 1970. *The Quest for Democratic Law: The Role of Parliament in the Legislative Process*. New York: Crowell.

Balogh, Brian. 2009. *A Government Out of Sight: The Mystery of National Authority in Nineteenth-Century America*. Cambridge: Cambridge University Press.

Bamberger, Michael A. 2000. *Reckless Legislation: How Lawmakers Ignore the Constitution*. New Brunswick, NJ: Rutgers University Press.

Benjamin, Gerald, and Henrik N. Dullea. 1997. *Decision 1997: Constitutional Change in New York*. Albany, NY: Rockefeller Institute Press.

Bentley, Curt. 2007. "Constrained by the Liberal Tradition: Why the Supreme Court Has Not Found Positive Rights in the American Constitution." *Brigham Young University Law Review* 2007 (6): 1721–1765.

Besso, Michael. 2005. "Constitutional Amendment Procedures and the Informal Political Construction of Constitutions." *Journal of Politics* 67 (1): 69–87.

Cabrera, Luis. 2017. "Gandhiji, I Have No Homeland: Cosmopolitan Insights from BR Ambedkar, India's Anti-Caste Campaigner and Constitutional Architect." *Political Studies* 65 (3): 576–593.

Clark, Tom S. 2010. *The Limits of Judicial Independence: Political Economy of Institutions and Decisions*. New York: Cambridge University Press.

Clemens, Elisabeth Stephanie. 1997. *The People's Lobby: Organizational Innovation and the Rise of Interest Group Politics in the United States, 1890–1925.* Chicago: University of Chicago Press.

Cornwell, Elmer E., Jr., Jay S. Goodman, and Wayne R. Swanson. 1970. "State Constitutional Conventions: Delegates, Roll Calls, and Issues." *Midwest Journal of Political Science* 14 (1): 105–130.

Dahl, Robert. 1957. "Decision-Making in a Democracy: The Supreme Court as a National Policy-Maker." *Journal of Public Law* 6 (2): 279–295.

Daly, Erin. 2012. "Constitutional Protection for Environmental Rights: The Benefits of Environmental Process." *International Journal of Peace Studies* 17 (2): 71–80.

Dinan, John J. 2000. "The Earth Belongs Always to the Living Generation: The Development of State Constitutional Amendment and Revision Procedures." *Review of Politics* 62 (4): 645–674.

———. 2006. *The American State Constitutional Tradition.* Lawrence: University Press of Kansas.

Donaldson, Alfred L. 1921. *A History of the Adirondacks.* New York: Century.

Eisgruber, Christopher L. 2001. *Constitutional Self-Government.* Cambridge, MA: Harvard University Press.

Ely, John Hart. 1980. *Democracy and Distrust: A Theory of Judicial Review.* Cambridge, MA: Harvard University Press.

Friedman, Lawrence M. 2005. *A History of American Law.* 3rd ed. New York: Simon & Schuster.

Fritz, Christian G. 1994. "The American Constitutional Tradition Revisited: Preliminary Observations on State Constitution-Making in the Nineteenth-Century West." *Rutgers Law Journal* 25 (4): 945–998.

Gardner, James A. 1992. "The Failed Discourse of State Constitutionalism." *Michigan Law Review* 90 (4): 761–837.

Graham, Frank, and Ada Graham. 1978. *The Adirondack Park: A Political History.* New York: Knopf; distributed by Random House.

Graves, W. Brooke. 1941. "Fourth Edition of the Model State Constitution." *American Political Science Review* 35 (5): 916–919.

Griffin, Stephen M. 1996. *American Constitutionalism: From Theory to Politics.* Princeton, NJ: Princeton University Press.

Hall, Kermit L. 1991. "Mostly Anchor and Little Sail: The Evolution of American State Constitutions." In *Toward a Usable Past: Liberty Under State Constitutions,* edited by Paul Finkelman and Stephen E. Gottlieb, 388–418. Athens: University of Georgia Press.

Hershock, Martin. 1995. "To Shield a Bleeding Humanity: Conflict and Consensus in Mid-Nineteenth-Century Michigan Political Culture." *Mid-America: An Historical Review* 77 (1): 33–50b.

Hurst, James Willard. 1950. *The Growth of American Law: The Law Makers.* Boston: Little, Brown and Company.

Jewell, Malcolm E., and Samuel C. Patterson. 1966. *The Legislative Process in the United States.* New York: Random House.

Johnson, Kimberley S. 2007. *Governing the American State: Congress and the New Federalism, 1877–1929.* Princeton Studies in American Politics. Princeton, NJ: Princeton University Press.

Keck, Margaret E., and Kathryn Sikkink. 1998. *Activists Beyond Borders: Advocacy Networks in International Politics.* Ithaca, NY: Cornell University Press.

Kelley, Florence. 1905. *Some Ethical Gains Through Legislation.* New York: Macmillan.

Kersch, Kenneth Ira. 2004. *Constructing Civil Liberties: Discontinuities in the Development of American Constitutional Law.* Cambridge: Cambridge University Press.

London, Lena. 1948. "Homestead Exemption in the Wisconsin Constitution." *Wisconsin Magazine of History* 32 (2): 176–184.

MacKenzie, John P. 1987. "New York's Old, and Fat, Constitution." *New York Times,* April 20, 1987.

Meyers, Marvin. 1957. *The Jacksonian Persuasion Politics and Belief.* Stanford, CA: Stanford University Press.

Michigan Union Advocate. 1907. "Labor Unionists Have Put Candidates in the Field." July 19, 1907.

Mink, Gwendolyn. 1995. *The Wages of Motherhood: Inequality in the Welfare State, 1917–1942.* Ithaca, NY: Cornell University Press.

Montana Legislature. 1982. *Montana Constitutional Convention, 1971–1972.* Helena: Montana Legislature in cooperation with the Montana Legislative Convention Editing and Publishing Committee.

Moravcsik, Andrew. 2005. "The Paradox of U.S. Human Rights Policy." In *American Exceptionalism and Human Rights,* edited by Michael Ignatieff, 147–197. Princeton, NJ: Princeton University Press.

New York State Office of Legislative Research. 1967. *Constitutional Protection of the Forest Preserve.* Albany, NY.

New York Times. 1893. "Workingmen and the Convention." October 24, 1893.

Novak, William J. 1996. *The People's Welfare: Law and Regulation in Nineteenth-Century America.* Studies in Legal History. Chapel Hill: University of North Carolina Press.

Primus, Richard A. 1999. *The American Language of Rights.* Ideas in Context. Cambridge: Cambridge University Press.

Reed, Douglas S. 2001. *On Equal Terms: The Constitutional Politics of Educational Opportunity.* Princeton, NJ: Princeton University Press.

Schapiro, Robert A. 1998. "Identity and Interpretation in State Constitutional Law." *Virginia Law Review* 84 (3): 389–457.

Schauer, Frederick. 2005. "The Exceptional First Amendment." In *American Exceptionalism and Human Rights,* edited by Michael Ignatieff, 29–56. Princeton, NJ: Princeton University Press.

Simpson, Charles R. 1992. "The Wilderness in American Capitalism: The Sacralization of Nature." *International Journal of Politics, Culture, and Society* 5 (4): 555–576.

Sklansky, David A. 2002. "Quasi-Affirmative Rights in Constitutional Criminal Procedure." *Virginia Law Review* 88 (6): 1229–1300.

Sunstein, Cass R. 2005. "Why Does the American Constitution Lack Social and Economic Guarantees?" *Syracuse Law Review* 56 (1): 1–25.

Tarr, G. Alan. 1998. *Understanding State Constitutions.* Princeton, NJ: Princeton University Press.

Terrie, Philip G. 1981. "The Adirondack Forest Preserve: The Irony of Forever Wild." *New York History* 62 (3): 261–288.

———. 1989. "Forever Wild Forever: The Forest Preserve Debate at the New York State Constitutional Convention of 1915." *New York History* 70 (3): 251–275.

Tsebelis, George. 2017. "The Time Inconsistency of Long Constitutions: Evidence from the World." *European Journal of Political Research* 56 (4): 820–845.

Whittington, Keith E. 1999. *Constitutional Construction: Divided Powers and Constitutional Meaning.* Cambridge, MA: Harvard University Press.

Williams, Robert F. 2009. *The Law of American State Constitutions.* New York: Oxford University Press.

Zackin, Emily. 2013. *Looking for Rights in All the Wrong Places: Why State Constitutions Contain America's Positive Rights.* Princeton, NJ: Princeton University Press.

PART II

Global Patterns and Problems in Modern Constitution-Making

CHAPTER 4

Dignity, Rights, and the Comparative Method

Christopher McCrudden

In this chapter, I single out for more extensive discussion one of the constitutional challenges identified in the Introduction to this volume: what should the purposes of a constitution be? It is well known that one answer to this, an answer that post–World War II constitution-makers have increasingly given, is that their constitutions should reflect and incorporate the fundamental values of their society, often in the form of constitutional rights.

I have suggested in a previous article that there is also a growing trend to understand these constitutional rights as designed to secure a fundamental meta-principle, frequently framed as "human dignity" (McCrudden 2008). This feature of modern global constitutionalism can reasonably be seen as, at least in part, deriving from the duty of government to secure natural rights, such as those instantiated in late eighteenth- and early nineteenth-century European and American constitutions. Its intellectual ancestry certainly includes the American revolutionaries' 1776 Declaration of Independence and its assertion that governments are instituted to secure certain inalienable rights—an assertion that, as David Armitage's (2008) work suggests, may have been more influential in global political history than any feature of the text of the U.S. Constitution. Nonetheless, the growth of dignity talk in the modern era has an additional, more diverse range of sources. These include Catholic traditions, Social Democratic thought, and reactions against the horrors of the Second World War (McCrudden 2013a). In this respect, I suggested that we may be seeing a degree of convergence in world constitutionalism and in the interpretation of human rights. I argued, however, that the rhetoric of human dignity is far more widely shared than are understandings of what tasks and limits dignity actually sets for governments.

In this chapter, I try to make further sense of the role that dignity plays by considering in more detail how the emergence of dignity coincides with two other common phenomena in rights interpretation: the use of the comparative method and the slow collapse of the distinction between international human rights and constitutional rights. Though the recent authoritarian turn in the governance of many societies is making that collapse even more gradual, it is too soon to tell whether this longer-term trend is ending or even being reversed.

The crux of my argument is that we need to incorporate into our normative understanding of rights in modern constitutions these three features of human rights discourse: the close interrelationship between constitutional and human rights; the extensive use of experience from other jurisdictions in the development and interpretation of constitutional and human rights norms; and, especially, the resort to "human dignity" as an overall justificatory meta-principle. I shall suggest that the phenomenon of comparison and borrowing in human rights discourse tells us something fundamental about the different ways in which we view the nature of "human rights" and "human dignity," about where they have come from, and (possibly) what their trajectory is, and therefore something important about modern constitutional development.

Before seeing how they combine together, however, we need to examine, in somewhat more detail, the comparative method, and the slow merging of international and constitutional rights, beginning with the latter.

International and Constitutional Rights

The distinction that some have sought to emphasize between "constitutional" rights and "human" rights has become fuzzy and indistinct, at least in those jurisdictions that enacted their constitutional rights protections after World War II (which is the bulk of states). Since 1945, "domestic constitutional orders [are] shaped in part by demands that state reconstruction be negotiated within a framework that recognizes and implements particular forms of the range of available transnational human rights" (Klug 2005, 93). At least in these states, it is clearly envisaged that the first port of call, as it were, for effective implementation of international human rights norms is to be at the domestic level. In several human rights treaties, such as the International Covenant on Civil and Political Rights (Article 2), there are provisions that require the ratifying state to implement the treaty effectively in the country's domestic law. Also, while some human rights treaties provide for independent international supervisory mechanisms and procedures for ruling on complaints, as a general rule those complaining that their rights have been violated must have exhausted domestic remedies before being able to complain successfully.

Increasingly, too, in several jurisdictions, courts have regard to international legal norms that have not even passed the test of formal validity for that legal system (McCrudden 2014). That is, even courts in dualist systems are having regard to the treaty norms where the treaty is not "incorporated" into domestic law. There are several different ways in which this may happen. There may be a requirement in that legal system that the courts should presume that the executive and/or the legislature did not intend to act contrary to legal obligations that bind that state in international law. This is often important in influencing the interpretation that is given to domestic legal requirements. Where, for example, more than one interpretation is possible, the interpretation is adopted that would enable that state to remain in conformity with its international legal obligations. Even more radically, some courts in some jurisdictions use international obligations in domestic litigation when the state has neither incorporated that norm, nor even ratified the treaty concerned. Some courts have taken the existence of these norms as evidence of customary international law. Others go even further, regarding the existence of the treaty norm as being relevant for the interpretation of national constitutional principles, in particular domestic bills of rights.

This subtle change in the relationship between constitutional rights and international human rights has percolated into some recent accounts of human rights by philosophers. Unlike Joseph Raz and John Rawls, Charles Beitz sets out in detail the "most important features of [human rights] practice" (Beitz 2009, 13), and, unlike Raz and Rawls, he does not seek radically to distinguish the domestic practice of rights creation and interpretation from the global practice of human rights. "The discursive community in which the practice resides," he writes, "consists of a heterogeneous group of agents, including the governments of states, international organizations, participants in the processes of international law, *economic actors such as business firms, members of nongovernmental organizations, and participants in domestic and transnational political networks and social movements*" (Beitz 2009, 8; emphasis added). He quotes, with approval, Sally Merry's observation that "instead of viewing human rights as a form of global law that imposes rules, it is better imagined as a cultural practice, as a means of producing new cultural understandings and actions" (Beitz, 2009, 38; quoting Merry 2009). Note, too, that the international dimension is softened: what Raz identified as a key feature of what can count as a human right as that which "justif[ies] international action" if it is violated (Raz 2010b, 329) becomes Beitz's "object of legitimate international concern" (Beitz 2009, 137).

Comparative Method

One of the methods used in identifying and interpreting human rights norms is comparison, to which we now turn. In an article published two decades ago (McCrudden 2000), I argued that it was then commonplace in several jurisdictions for judges to refer to the decisions of the courts of foreign jurisdictions when interpreting domestic human rights guarantees, but that there had also been a persistent undercurrent of skepticism about this trend and the emergence of a growing debate about its appropriateness. The article raised for debate the meaning and significance of national judges' citation of judgments from other jurisdictions as part of their reasoning in cases with a significant human (or constitutional) rights aspect. Several questions were identified and explored in an attempt to consider various aspects of the general phenomenon. These included empirical questions (how far does it happen and where?), jurisprudential questions (can we identify criteria that help explain why it does or does not happen?), and normative questions (is it legitimate?). After a review of the existing literature was undertaken with a view to determining how far scholars had succeeded in answering these questions, the article concluded that significant gaps existed in our understanding of the phenomenon and raised for discussion the methodologies that might be appropriate for addressing the phenomenon in the future.

After that, the phenomenon of judicial borrowing continued apace and the use by justices of the United States Supreme Court of foreign jurisprudence in several high-profile cases further intensified the debate (particularly in the United States) (McCrudden 2007c). Due in particular to extensive research in the area, we now have a lot more information about global use of comparisons in the human and constitutional rights context than was available at the end of the last century.

Quite a lot of this further research concerns the issue of *judicial* borrowing, unsurprisingly. Numerous examples have been uncovered where the courts in one jurisdiction have examined and cited the approaches adopted in a different jurisdiction, with a view to considering how the foreign approach might help in deciding the case before it. Over time, we can see the development in some jurisdictions of a view that international human rights provisions illustrate a set of shared values and that it is part of the function of the national judiciary to put flesh on the bones of these provisions; to take part, in effect, in a common interpretative enterprise with judges in other jurisdictions. As one author has put it, some courts have "construed human rights as part of an international public policy," the expression of a "higher law" thinking (Francioni 1997, 32).

More recently, however (and significantly because of recent historical and political science research on human rights), we are now much more aware of the extensive nature of borrowing in *nonjudicial* human and constitutional rights contexts, both historically and currently. At the national level, we see the use of comparison in the development of different systems of fundamental or constitutional or human rights, in particular from the perspective of the drafters of constitutional-type documents like bills of rights. There are some prime examples to draw on, such as Germany, Ireland, the United States, and India, which illustrate how the drafting of modern constitutions drew extensively on comparison even at a time when there was no clearly articulated international human rights document.

At the international level, the use of comparison in the drafting of international human rights treaties, such as the European Convention on Human Rights and the UN covenants, is now well known. The use of comparison in the development of customary international human rights law has also been extensively considered. Comparison is also used extensively in the interpretation of international and regional human rights texts by authoritative bodies. This may involve not only the use of domestic comparisons by international and regional bodies, but also the use of comparisons by one body of other international and regional bodies. For example, the Inter-American Court of Human Rights now regularly cites the jurisprudence of the European Court of Human Rights, and vice versa (McCrudden 2013b). Human rights activists such as nongovernmental organizations (NGOs) also extensively use comparisons transnationally (McCrudden 2015). So too, other major social actors use comparisons extensively, in particular in the context of the development of "nonstate" law, such as in developing codes of corporate practice.

I am not particularly concerned in this chapter to document more extensively than this my claim that the popularity of the comparative method in the drafting and interpretation of constitutional rights is a significant part of human rights discourse, at least outside the United States.[1] To do this systematically would require much greater space than I have available for current purposes. I have no doubt, however, that it is possible to provide extensive evidence that this trend is both sufficiently significant and widespread for it to be regarded as part of current human rights practice. The issue I am interested in exploring is what, if anything, this phenomenon says about the nature of human rights.

My focus in this chapter, in contrast to the analysis of Jeremy Waldron (2012), is (1) to address the normative role of the use of comparison primarily as a *human and constitutional rights issue* rather than the use of the borrowing in other areas of law and policy more generally; (2) to consider the normative implications of the use of comparison *generally*, including in the political identification of constitutional rights, rather than primarily in the judicial context; and (3) to focus on the use of borrowing globally, rather than primarily in the United States context. This focus is adopted because I am interested in exploring the implications of the use of the comparative method for, and in particular the normativity of the comparative method in, *human rights theory*, rather than *jurisprudential* theory.

Descriptive Versus Normative Methodologies for Understanding Human Rights

How are we to determine what "human rights" are? Several different methodologies have been proposed to answer that question. One approach is descriptive; the other is normative (although the distinction is perhaps questionable). A descriptive approach attempts to answer the question by describing, for example, how the term has come to be used historically and how it may have changed over time. The development of human rights thinking in Western thought has moved through various phases. In the eighteenth century the view of human rights involved limited government, with negative duties against the state, and concentrated on liberty rights and, particularly, property rights. It was essentially a pessimistic view of the state and an optimistic view of the individual: if left alone, the individual would flourish. In the nineteenth century came the rise of political and civil rights, with the emphasis being placed on civic participation and formal equality between citizens. The state was something that growing numbers saw themselves as having the right to exercise a degree of control over, and human rights thinking was closely associated with democratic thinking. In the twentieth century, we see the growth of social and economic rights, which depend on government for their realization; human rights moves from essentially being concerned with negative rights to embracing positive rights; government has the role of protecting people from misfortune and guaranteeing a degree of distributive justice. Later still, we have the growth of further generations of rights, particularly those concerned with the environment and with minorities as such.

Another type of "descriptive" approach to the issue of how best to understand human rights is that which lawyers often adopt. We say that human rights are those rights designated as such by law, whether domestic law or international law. So, to the question, "what are human rights?" one response is to say: look at the Universal Declaration of Human Rights, or look at the International Covenant on Civil and Political Rights, or look at the German Basic Law. The way to avoid getting into the deeper theoretical problems is to retreat to the texts. There are, however, at least two problems with this approach. The first is that the apparent consensus surrounding the international texts is largely illusory, even at the level of formal commitment. It wasn't until 1992 that the United States ratified the 1966 International Covenant on Civil and Political Rights, for example, and only then after depositing an extensive array of reservations and declarations essentially limiting its obligations to those already recognized in U.S. federal constitutional law. More problematic still, the texts are so open-ended, and drafted at such a level of generality, that the really hard questions of interpretation are not at all clearly addressed, and we must (either explicitly or implicitly) adopt a theoretical approach to the meaning of human rights in order to interpret them.

The alternative to "descriptive" approaches (if, indeed, they are simply descriptive) is to adopt a more explicitly "normative" approach to the idea of human rights. By this I mean that there is some attempt to reason through to the position that a particular claim is a human rights claim from a moral or ethical position. In the seventeenth and eighteenth centuries, advocates of rights derived them from God, or from what was "natural." In our own day, there has been no shortage of moral or ethical explanations of the normative underpinnings of human rights, but little consensus.

The familiar story is that when the Universal Declaration of Human Rights was being drafted in 1948, the participants were able to agree on what they were against, but not on *why* they were against these violations. Since the 1970s at least, the human rights enterprise has become both more powerful and more controversial, legally, politically, and ethically, and this absence of a clear agreement on the foundations has threatened to undermine the project. As practical use of concrete rights proceeds, nagging questions about foundations come to the surface and beg for further discussion. Some have argued that human rights derive from the concept of "equal concern and respect," some from notions of distributive justice, some from ideas of what is necessary to satisfy basic social needs, and some from "human dignity," with the last emerging as a global front-runner (though, again, the recent resurgence of nationalist movements may well be slowing its pace).

Human Rights Theory

In this chapter, I am concerned to explore the implications of the three features of human rights practice I have identified (comparison, the merging of constitutional and human rights, and resort to "dignity") for attempts to develop a normative theory of human rights. But what should such a theory consist of? Joseph Raz (2010b) has identified the task of a theory of human rights in an analysis that seems generally convincing. It is, he says, "(a) to establish the essential features which contemporary human rights practice attributes to the rights it acknowledges to be human rights; and (b) to identify the moral standards which qualify anything to be so acknowledged" (Raz 2010b, 327). I shall proceed on the basis of this general approach.

Comparative Method Revisited

We can return now to think a little more about the role of the comparative method in this context. When judicial practice is set alongside nonjudicial practice in human rights identification and interpretation, a complex pattern emerges. I shall be able to do little more than sketch what appears to me to be the outlines of this pattern, leaving the evidence needed to justify this outline to be taken on trust in the interests of space and time. The evidence seems to me to indicate clearly a significant use of the comparative method, but one in which the *reasons* for the comparative method being adopted are varied in the extreme.

Such information as we now have discussing the broader political contexts in which such comparisons take place show how significantly the use of the comparative method may vary over time and place. One example must suffice. After the fall of the Berlin Wall, we saw a developing global "market" in liberal ideologies, where states competed with each other to try to influence how far their own particular liberalism won out over other competing liberalisms. With the fall of the Soviet Union, liberal constitutionalism was the only game in town, and the main question was which version would emerge as dominant. There was a significant development in what might be called "human rights tourism" (which I admit to taking part in), where different countries and organizations sent representatives to emerging democracies to sell *their* brand of human rights protection. Is this use of the comparative method similar to the use of the comparative method in the construction of the Irish Constitution in 1922 or 1937? Or the use of the comparative method in the drawing up of the EU Charter of Fundamental Rights? Or the use of the comparative method in Cuba when Castro was embarking on a new constitution? Or the use of the comparative method by the judges of the European Court of Human Rights compared to the use of that method by the judges of the U.S. Supreme Court?

We should distinguish initially between two different ways in which the comparative method is related to the normativity of human rights. We can identify the comparative method as normative in the sense that when, for example, a court interpreting the meaning of some human rights provision thinks that it should look to how other courts have interpreted this right, then the comparative method may become what James Griffin (2010, 351) identifies as part of the rule of recognition by which human rights are recognized legally. Waldron (2012, 55) also sees "no particular reason . . . that modern [legal] positivism, defined in terms of the tools and methodology of [H. L. A.] Hart's [positivistic] jurisprudence, should preclude the idea of ius gentium, defined as positive law." Although he tackles this issue in a more detailed and sophisticated manner, this is, essentially, what Waldron is concerned to explore in much of his book on judicial borrowing from other jurisdictions, and his primary concern, therefore, is what may make foreign law normatively relevant in this sense in the judicial context.

When Raz identifies the task of a theory of human rights as including the identification of the "moral standards which qualify anything to be so acknowledged," I understand him not to be interested in identifying normative elements in human rights practice in this "rule of recognition" sense (*legal* normativity), but rather in identifying what moral standards provide good reasons for anything being identified as a human right, independently of being included as law within the rule of recognition. Can we say that the comparative method provides a good *moral* reason for identifying a particular norm or value as a human right in the political sphere, or in the context of drafting a new bill of rights, for example? This second way of considering the normativity of a human rights comparative method is my primary focus in this chapter.

The two ways of considering the issue of normativity may be linked, of course, where "legal normativity" incorporates considerations of "moral normativity." One of Waldron's (2012, 35) concerns is to explore how far that is so, concluding (à la Ronald Dworkin) that "ius gentium consists of a body of *principles*, discerned interpretively from the commonalities that exist among the positive laws of various countries, by a legal sensibility that is both lawyerly and moralized" (emphasis in original). Waldron's argument, therefore, raises some of the philosophical issues explored below, but primarily insofar as they are relevant in determining the legal normativity in the judicial context, and in the context of the use of comparative method generally, not in the human rights context specifically. The modesty of his primary arguments in support of transnational judicial borrowing (that we should learn from others and that like cases should be treated alike) is explainable, perhaps, by his attempt to generate normative reasons to justify the use of the comparative across all legal categories and not just human rights. This imposes significant limits, therefore, on how far Waldron can help us identify the normative role of the comparative method in the human rights context specifically and in the making of human rights as well as in their interpretation.

Charles Beitz's *The Idea of Human Rights*

Other philosophers are more helpful in this regard. Although Charles Beitz does not, specifically, address the role of the comparative method, it is not particularly challenging to see how it would fit within his account. We have seen earlier that, in his discussion of the "normativity" of human rights (in the second sense identified above), Beitz (2009, 137) develops a schema for justifying claims about the contents of human rights doctrine, including the contention that the interest should be such that a failure by a state to protect it "would be a suitable object of international concern." Importantly, he suggests that to be seen to be such, "the account should not depend exclusively on beliefs and norms that are specific to a single culture or way of life" (137). In an important passage (137–138), he indicates that this requirement that the beliefs and norms transcend the parochial can be satisfied in several ways:

> For example, some interests are sufficiently generic that it would be reasonable to expect anyone to recognize their importance (e.g. the interests in physical security and adequate nutrition). In other cases, although the interest when specifically described might not be widely shared, it may be able to be brought under a more abstract description that enables its importance to be recognized even by those who do not share it (e.g. "being able to follow one's religion"). In still other cases, the importance of the interest may be derivative: for example, it may be that under contingent but currently prevalent historical circumstances, the satisfaction of the interest would be instrumental to the satisfaction of other interests already identified as important (e.g. perhaps, interests in political participation or in the nondiscriminatory application of the law).

In each of these ways of satisfying the requirement that the interest is not simply a parochial one, the comparative method is likely to be well to the fore. A potentially extensive comparative practice thus seems to fit well with Beitz, but it requires not insignificant variations of Beitz's model for it to be able to be as fully integrated as our earlier description of human rights borrowing indicates that it should.

Juridical and Political Paradigms

First, Beitz draws too sharp a line between what he calls a "juridical paradigm of implementation" of human rights and a "political" paradigm. The former is said to be characterized by two features: an "aspiration for juridical human rights institutions at the global level," and an "expectation that to the extent possible individual states would carry out their obligations under human rights agreements by incorporating human rights protections in their constitutions and laws on the model of a 'bill of rights'" (Beitz 2009, 41). Most "international and transnational efforts to promote and defend human rights are more accurately understood as political rather than legal," in this sense, according to Beitz (2009, 40).

There are two problems with this. The first is that Beitz, as most political philosophers appear to do, focuses essentially on a United Nations human rights paradigm, rather than one that encompasses the regional arrangements, which in many countries are considerably more important in practice and fit much more closely his juridical paradigm's second feature. The second, more important, problem is that the bodies acting under his juridical paradigm demonstrate many of the same features as those acting under Beitz's political paradigm. In particular, (juridical) human rights supply reasons for action not only to other legal actors but also "to other kinds of agents as well, frequently acting without specific legal authority" (Beitz 2009, 41; see also McCrudden and O'Leary 2013, on the role of the Venice Commission; McCrudden 2007b, on the role of the OSCE High Commissioner on National Minorities). Beitz's account needs to be modified in this respect, because without such a change the different roles that the comparative method plays in different contexts (including the legal and judicial) will be insufficiently appreciated.

Intersubjectivity

Second, Beitz appears to place insufficient weight on the extent to which global human rights practice has drawn and continues to draw from bottom-up social movements fighting to have their own and others' interests recognized as worthy of inclusion as an object of international concern (Raz 2010a, 41). Such movements use the banner of human rights as a portmanteau moral basis for their specific claims. They are if anything doing so all the more fiercely in countries where regimes have recently become more authoritarian (Rodrígo-Garavito and Gomez 2018). They seek to use human rights as a moral umbrella to strengthen the normative weight of a specific claimed right, hence their desire to be seen as part of a human rights movement. Beitz's description of human rights practice, despite his explicit denial that this is so, appears too statist to fully encompass this dimension.

My concern in this regard is heightened by Beitz's statement that "human rights do not appear as a fundamental moral category" as such. Rather, he suggests, we should seek explanations of the normativity of human rights in each particular human right. "The reasons we have to care about them vary with the content of the right in question and the nature of our relationship, if any, with various classes of potential victims of abuse" (Beitz 2009, 128). This seems to me not to capture adequately the moral connections between those norms that we consider human rights.

Beitz himself appears to accept that what holds human rights practice together is the idea that the interests encompassed by human rights are ones "intersubjectively recognizable as [sufficiently] important or urgent" (139) to become "a suitable object of international concern," (140) but does not follow the logic of this intuition sufficiently far. Beitz is clear that he rejects the idea that human rights should be interpreted as "deriving their authority from a single, more basic value or interest such as those of human dignity, personhood, or membership" (128). But while we can agree that they may not "derive their *authority*" from such values as dignity, that does not mean that dignity (or some other value) is not in some way centrally *involved* in human rights practice (including the making of constitutional rights), and not just in the context of particular individual human rights, which is as far as Beitz is willing to accept may be the case (138n10).

For an approach that appears to recognize more clearly the extent to which the category of human rights may have greater normative coherence than Beitz is willing to accept, we can turn to James Griffin. Griffin argues that we need to get beyond a purely functional approach to our understanding of what human rights are, such as that which hangs over Beitz (and even more Raz and Rawls). For Griffin, "we need to know how to attach moral weight . . . to rights." We must "have a sufficiently rich understanding of the value that rights represent" (Griffin 2010, 341). For Griffin "a rich understanding of the dignity, or worth of the human person" is required (342). He asks, rhetorically: "Do not human rights have their own intrinsically valuable purpose: the protection of human dignity? What more point do human rights need than that?" (352). The second rhetorical question goes too far (we need an understanding of human rights practice as well, I think). We do not need to transcend a functional approach entirely in order to incorporate his insight. My suggestion is that Beitz's "practical" approach should be supplemented by greater attention to the idea of intersubjectivity in our understanding of how human rights practice works *in practice.*

Human Dignity as Meta-Principle

How does this produce a richer description of human rights practice? A useful framing for the inclusion of intersubjectivity as an element in the practice of human rights is suggested by the work of Lynn Hunt (2007). Hunt's argument is that the spread of human rights thinking depends on the increasing incorporation of others within a circle of "empathy" (27). One of the ways in which claims of empathy were successfully made in the past was by appealing to universalistic rights language. "Rights questions," according to Hunt (147), "revealed a tendency to cascade" and escape their original confines, leading to claims from a variety of individuals who came from groups previously outside the circle of empathy, such as slaves. But Hunt does not fully explain how the move from empathy to legal rights protection took place.

One suggestion, with support from work by Jürgen Habermas (2010), is that "dignity" may provide the language in which empathy is conceptualized. Habermas's argument is, essentially, that human dignity provided the mechanism for bringing universalistic moral ideas into the nation-state. "Universalistic moral notions," he writes, "have long since gained entry into the human and civil rights of democratic constitutions through the . . . idea of human dignity" (Habermas 2010, 479). He describes the "catalytic role" (466) of the concept of human dignity in developing human rights as we currently understand them. Human dignity served as a "conceptual hinge" that made possible the "improbable synthesis" between, on the one hand, a morality of equal respect and, on the other hand, individually enforceable rights established by law, and a "portal" through which it could be achieved (Habermas 2010, 469–470). This is essentially a functional explanation but one that is able to incorporate the moral dimension on which actors within human rights practice heavily rely.

Michael Ignatieff's (1999) approach is helpful at this point. He sees human rights as part of "the argument about what we can, and cannot, should and should not do to other human beings." In calling for an end to "rights inflation," he urges the adoption of a minimalism based on "the ground we share." This has, in the past, been based on the intuitions that derive from our own experiences, and our capacity (which he terms a "natural fact about human beings") to empathize with others: "we possess the faculty of imagining the pain and degradation done to other human beings as if it were our own." This "secular" defense of human rights is based, then, "on practical historical experience and a minimalist anthropology." What the substance of this "common ground" may be is likely to change over time, with the possibility that what we consider unacceptable will become acceptable, and vice versa. Our "agreed ends" are thus, potentially at least, in constant flux and depend on historical experience interacting with our capacity for empathy, leading us to articulate a moral principle that some act is or is not acceptable, is or is not required, so far as other human beings are concerned. We might, and some do, describe the end sought as achieving the dignity of human beings, with what that requires being in a state of flux.

"Dignity" and the Comparative Method

Ignatieff's argument is particularly useful in helping us to identify how comparison becomes potentially relevant at three different stages: at the stage of identifying "practical historical experience"; at the stage of testing and developing our intuitions of empathy; and at the stage of determining whether (and how far) rights are an appropriate way of delivering the required end of protecting and fulfilling human dignity. This is not to say that the rights (or dignity) *depend* on legal or political recognition. On the contrary (and here they share a similarity with older ideas of natural rights going back to the American Declaration of Independence and beyond), they "provide an independent standard or measure for judging the success or legitimacy" of any particular political society (Baynes 2009, 2).

We are repeatedly told in human rights practice that dignity provides a good moral reason for identifying a standard as a human right (and many actors in human rights practice appear to believe this), but we know that "dignity" is extraordinarily vague and indeterminate. Those who are committed to this position may be able to identify a basic minimum core to the idea, but deriving any particular standards or principles or rights in any particular context is subject to considerable debate and dispute (McCrudden 2008). The comparative method now enters the picture, in helping those actors in human rights practice to identify how this basic minimum core may be understood, both over time and in other contemporary societies. Essentially what is happening here is the use of an inductive method, based on experience, as a way of understanding the contemporary idea of the use of dignity and of human rights.

The Limits of "Agreement-Based" Theory

We need to be careful, however, not to slip into an agreement-based theory of human rights. David Hollenbach (2013), for example, uses an inductive method to identify where there appears to be a consensus, and then wants to rely on that consensus as a basis for arguing that this provides grounds for generating a normative obligation to further that consensus. This is similar to approaches that have sought to find ways of resolving fundamental political disputes by searching for an "overlapping consensus" among the disputing parties. I do *not* suggest that this is primarily what is happening when comparison is resorted to in human rights practice.

Nor is it desirable normatively. The idea of an "overlapping consensus," most clearly identified with John Rawls (although not in the international human rights context), has come in for convincing criticism, much of which need not detain us here. Insofar as Hollenbach's strategy does share a family resemblance with Rawls, it is subject to similar criticisms, particularly if one sees consensus as fully formed and not open to further development or refinement. Kenneth Baynes (2009, 9) objects to any approach that "seeks to gain wide support by looking for an empirical or de facto consensus on rights among the dominant traditions." This strategy, Baynes argues, "is not likely to succeed as there is no guarantee that such a consensus exists or that its content would be especially compelling" (2009, 9). For Baynes, an agreement-based approach also "reflects a compromise to existing political powers" (2009, 9).[2] Why would a given consensus be seen as a powerful basis for deciding what dignity requires, given that there may be a sexist consensus or a homophobic consensus, and we would not think that this should generate the norms required by dignity? But if we say we should only take into account "enlightened" opinion, is that not assuming the very concept we are seeking to identify?

Paolo Carozza (2013) is also skeptical of a consensus approach in the sense identified. He accepts that it has operated to some degree in the past. He considers, for example, that the practical or overlapping consensus method that Jacques Maritain advocated in drafting the Universal Declaration of Human Rights was highly successful in many ways. He queries, however, whether we can follow the same path today, relying on a practical consensus around human rights to achieve similarly positive results. Constructing the human rights project solely on the grounds of a practical overlapping consensus, he argues, has contributed to several serious problems over six decades: problems of institutional weakness, problems of noncompliance, problems of ideological capture, the masking of fundamental differences, and heavy bureaucratization and proceduralization. All of these, he believes, are, in one way or another, related to the original structure of the discourse. In this, he appears to agree with Beitz that "actual agreement is, in general, too strong a condition to impose on critical standards, and therefore on human rights" (Beitz 2009, 87).

Comparative Method and Human Rights Theory

That said, we can usefully distinguish a requirement of *substantive* moral agreement on dignity or rights from a *methodological* agreement on how to discuss our substantive moral disagreements on rights and dignity. The comparative method plays an important *methodological* role in the construction and interpretation of rights, as a descriptive matter. But it does more than that; it also appears to play an important normative role as well. If it has become a central part of human and constitutional rights practice, this is because it forms part of an emerging overlapping *methodological* consensus on the identification and interpretation of human rights, whether that is at the stage of constitutional drafting or human rights interpretation and political debate. When we combine this practice with other, predominantly functional approaches to the determination of human rights, such as the role of dignity, we are close to being able to identify an overlapping consensus on *method*, even when the consensus on substance seems further away than ever.

There are several functions that the comparative method appears to serve in human rights practice, none of them unproblematic. We can say, uncontroversially, that one of the central and abiding issues in discussions about human rights is the continual tension between the universal and the local. Comparison in the human rights context seems to play an intriguing role in dealing with this tension. On the one hand, comparison recognizes the local because it is dependent on a concept of the "foreign," the "other," and this seems to play into a way of thinking about human rights that emphasizes the state-based nature of where the drama of human rights is played out. On the other hand, the assumption of comparison is also that there is something sufficiently similar in the phenomenon of rights protection in different countries for the comparison to be at least relevant, appearing to strengthen a more universalistic view of rights. Comparison thus seems to play a deeply ambiguous role in the discourse of human rights, one that is linked closely to both universality and localism. At the moment this ambiguity is a strength not a weakness because it provides a bridge for both to be considered.

An integrated theory of human rights and constitutional rights must also explain another central feature of human rights practice—namely, the extent to which rights are balanced against other rights (e.g., freedom of religion versus equality) and against other values (e.g., due process versus national security). I suggested previously (McCrudden 2007a, 617), quoting Ignatieff (2003, 95), that we should "stop thinking of human rights as trumps and begin thinking of them as a language that creates the basis for deliberation," and that the role of human rights is to "reconcile moral ends to concrete situations and [in doing so] to make painful compromises not only between means and ends, but between ends themselves" (Ignatieff 2003, 22). There are significantly differing ways and means by which deliberation is conducted, and compromises are made, but they all depend on the contending parties being willing to engage with each other.

Another possible good of the comparative method in this context, and one particularly valuable in an era of resurgent assertive nationalisms, therefore, might be to keep "agonists"[3] in conversation with each other, rather than to supply technical directions about how conflicting values and rights are to be accommodated (as may also be the case with "dignity"; see Siegel 2013). Observing the structure of struggle around the comparative method, we might argue that a conversation among agonists involves a common fidelity to the comparative method, even as they profoundly disagree about its entailments and about the forms of human flourishing they may prefer. So, on that view, the virtue of the comparative method is not that it provides answers but that it may create the conditions for the task of trying to look for an answer to, or at least an accommodation of, conflicting values and rights. Whether the comparative method in practice serves this integrative function, whether it actually does do any work in terms of helping us keep in respectful conversation, is a question of empirical judgment.

Finally, we may seek to rely on a strategy of incorporating the comparative method if, as Carozza (2013) argues, we understand that in the original human rights project its use was not meant to be an end point, but was intended only to be the starting point for a reasoned reflection and dialogue about the requirements of justice and the protection of the human. Carozza suggests, and I agree, that human rights theory needs to incorporate an understanding that human rights practice involves fundamental reflections on human experience that go to the origin of our understanding of our own humanity. Such reflection is all the more important because at least some involved in human rights practice consider that there is something irreducible about the human person that cannot be fully captured. This means that there is always going to be a need for discussion, the likelihood of disagreement, and a certain underdetermination. The very nature of what we are talking about—the human person—means that we should never presume to be able to specify human dignity (or human rights) beyond contestation. The comparative method invites openness to the posing of the question of what it is to be human in our public and communal discourse and a method for structuring that discussion.

Conclusion

In conclusion, I have suggested that to achieve an understanding of the nature of human rights practice we need to keep in mind three features of human rights discourse that are well documented empirically. The first is the past and present interrelationship between constitutional rights at the domestic level and human rights at the international and regional levels. The second is the past and present popularity of comparative methodology in identifying and interpreting both domestic constitutional rights and international human rights. The third is the extensive use of "human dignity" in order to explain why human rights are important. Understanding these three elements in human rights practice in combination is important if we are to grasp the extent to which the identification and interpretation of human rights globally, and constitutional interpretation of constitutional rights nationally, is converging and diverging. That question is all the more urgent today as the globalizing trends of the second half of the twentieth century confront sharp opposition movements in the twenty-first.

Notes

1. To American readers, claims that these aspects have become important elements of human rights discourse may be greeted with some skepticism. After all, the relationship

between constitutional rights and international human rights in U.S. law has long been somewhat distant both in theory and in practice, and the use of comparative methodology in the interpretation of U.S. federal constitutional rights is highly controversial. I do not want here to enter into the debate about American exceptionalism or about trends in American constitutional practice; suffice it to say that all I want to suggest for the purposes of this chapter is that readers should not reject my claims about what constitutes "human rights practice," based on U.S. constitutional practice—how U.S. practice fits within human rights theory is for another day.

2. Baynes attributes these problems to Ignatieff. I disagree, however, with Baynes's reading of Ignatieff on this point. When discussing Rawls, Baynes distinguishes between "what is feasible given human nature as we know it" and a "compromise with existing power relations," but the former describes Ignatieff as accurately as it does Rawls; both rely, to that extent, on a minimal anthropology (2009, 9).

3. "Agonists" refers, in brief, to those who are skeptical about the likelihood that politics can surmount the most basic societal divisions and that the principal issue is how to manage such divisions.

References

Armitage, David. 2008. *The Declaration of Independence: A Global History*. Cambridge, MA: Harvard University Press.

Baynes, Kenneth. 2009. "Discourse Ethics and the Political Conception of Human Rights." *Ethics and Global Politics* 2 (1): 1–21.

Beitz, Charles. 2009. *The Idea of Human Rights*. Oxford: Oxford University Press.

Carozza, Paolo. 2013. "Human Rights, Human Dignity, and Human Experience." In *Understanding Human Dignity*, edited by Christopher McCrudden, 615–629. Proceedings of the British Academy 192. Oxford: Oxford University Press.

Francioni, Francesco. 1997. "The Jurisprudence of International Human Rights Enforcement: Reflections on the Italian Experience." In *Enforcing International Human Rights in Domestic Courts*, edited by Benedetto Conforti and Francesco Francioni, 15–34. The Hague: Martinus Nijhoff.

Griffin, James. 2010. "Human Rights and the Autonomy of International Law." In *The Philosophy of International Law*, edited by Samantha Besson and John Tasioulas, 339–355. Oxford: Oxford University Press.

Habermas, Jürgen. 2010. "The Concept of Human Dignity and the Realistic Utopia of Human Rights." *Metaphilosophy* 41 (4): 464–480.

Hollenbach, David. 2013. "Human Dignity: Experience and History, Practical Reason, and Faith." In *Understanding Human Dignity*, edited by Christopher McCrudden, 123–140. Proceedings of the British Academy 192. Oxford: Oxford University Press.

Hunt, Lynn. 2007. *Inventing Human Rights: A History*. New York: W. W. Norton.
Ignatieff, Michael. 1999. "Human Rights: The Midlife Crisis." *New York Review of Books*, May 20, 1999.
———. 2003. "Human Rights as Politics and Idolatry." In Michael Ignatieff, *Human Rights as Politics and Idolatry*, edited by Amy Gutmann, 3–98. Princeton, NJ: Princeton University Press.
Klug, Heinz. 2005. "Transnational Human Rights: Exploring the Persistence and Globalization of Human Rights." *Annual Review of Law and Social Science* 1: 85–103.
McCrudden, Christopher. 2000. "A Common Law of Human Rights? Transnational Judicial Conversations on Constitutional Rights." *Oxford Journal of Legal Studies* 10 (4): 499–532.
———. 2007a. *Buying Social Justice*. Oxford: Oxford University Press.
———. 2007b. "Consociationalism, Equality, and Minorities in the Northern Ireland Bill of Rights Debate: The Role of the OSCE High Commissioner on National Minorities." In *Judges, Transition, and Human Rights*, edited by John Morison, Kieran McEvoy, and Gordon Anthony, 315–354. Oxford: Oxford University Press.
———. 2007c. "Judicial Comparativism and Human Rights." In *Comparative Law: A Handbook*, edited by Esin Örucü and David Nelken, 71–398. Oxford: Hart.
———. 2008. "Human Dignity and Judicial Interpretation of Human Rights." *European Journal of International Law* 19 (4): 655–724.
———. 2013a. "In Pursuit of Human Dignity: An Introduction to Current Debates." In *Understanding Human Dignity*, edited by Christopher McCrudden, 1–58. Proceedings of the British Academy 192. Oxford: Oxford University Press.
———. 2013b. "Using Comparative Reasoning in Human Rights Adjudication: The Court of Justice of the European Union and the European Court of Human Rights Compared." *Cambridge Yearbook of European Legal Studies* 15:383–415.
———. 2014. "The Pluralism of Human Rights Adjudication." In *Reasoning Rights: Comparative Judicial Engagement*, edited by Liora Lazarus, Christopher McCrudden, and Nigel Bowles, 3–27. Oxford: Hart.
———. 2015. "Transnational Culture Wars." *International Journal of Constitutional Law* 13 (2): 434–462.
McCrudden, Christopher, and Brendan O'Leary. 2013. *Courts and Consociations*. Oxford: Oxford University Press.
Merry, Sally Engle. 2009. *Mobilizing for Human Rights: International Law in Domestic Politics*. New York: Cambridge University Press.
Raz, Joseph. 2010a. "Human Rights in the Emerging World Order." *Transnational Legal Theory* 1: 31–47.
———. 2010b. "Human Rights Without Foundations." In *The Philosophy of International Law*, edited by Samantha Besson and John Tasioulas, 321–337. Oxford: Oxford University Press.

Rodrígo-Garavito, César, and Krizna Gomez, eds. 2018. *Rising to the Populist Challenge: A New Playbook for Human Rights Activists.* Bogotá, Colombia: Dejusticia.

Siegel, Reva. 2013. "Dignity and the Duty to Protect Unborn Life." In *Understanding Human Dignity*, edited by Christopher McCrudden, 509–523. Proceedings of the British Academy 192. Oxford: Oxford University Press.

Waldron, Jeremy. 2012. *"Partly Laws Common to All Mankind": Foreign Law in American Courts.* New Haven, CT: Yale University Press.

CHAPTER 5

Beyond Window Dressing: Constitutions in Authoritarian Regimes

Tom Ginsburg

It is common to characterize constitutions in dictatorships as mere shams (Murphy 1993; Elster 2013, 212; Law and Versteeg 2013), constitutions without constitutionalism (Okoth-Ogendo 1993), or window dressing (e.g., Lutz 1994). This view is rooted in the idea that constitutionalism is an inherently democratic phenomenon, and so constitutions, properly considered, are only found in democracies. Authoritarian constitutions, it is argued, are epiphenomenal (Sartori 1962). Today, even as a wave of new authoritarian regimes labeled "populists" are rewriting their constitutions, analysts argue that those constitutions provide no meaningful checks on the powers of populist nationalist leaders (Müller 2016).

This widely held view is understandable but also provokes an obvious question. Why would authoritarians bother to write constitutions? Since the emergence of the modern written constitution as a technology of governance in the late eighteenth century, the vast majority of such documents have been drafted by regimes that we would call authoritarian. And although at least until recently commentators proclaimed that we are in an "age of democracy," the Comparative Constitutions Project data shows that more than half of constitutions in force today were drafted by dictators (Elkins, Ginsburg, and Melton 2014, 145–146). Furthermore, we have many examples of dictators who spent significant time and energy on the production of constitutions. Stalin himself devoted significant direct attention to the drafting of the Soviet Constitution of 1936, sometimes considered the poster child of a "sham" constitution (Getty 1991). Again, why would he spend political energy on a useless project?

A common answer is that authoritarian constitutions are simply designed to serve as a kind of window dressing, to obfuscate the real functioning of the political system. This answer, though, raises another question: who would possibly be fooled by such a project (Przeworski 2014)? If the analyst is able to identify the constitution as a sham, why are citizens, the international community, or other audiences so easily fooled? The question bears no simple answer.

It behooves us, then, to think about the other possible functions that constitutions might play for authoritarians. This is in keeping with a recent trend in political science of trying to understand the institutions of authoritarian regimes, which exhibit significant internal variation and complexity (Gandhi 2008; Levitsky and Way 2010; Svolik 2013; Schedler 2013). A general finding of this literature is that institutions can serve to extend the life and efficacy of authoritarian regimes. Semi-competitive elections, for example, transmit information to the leaders about issues that the public is interested in. They can also allow the regime to identify potential opponents who can then be repressed or co-opted. Semi-independent courts can play a number of functions for authoritarians, allowing them to attract foreign investment or discipline bureaucracies through administrative law regimes (Moustafa 2007). In short, institutions matter, for authoritarians as well as democrats.

Constitutions are especially important institutions by virtue of their status as the highest normative acts of a state and their role in identifying (at least some of) the other institutional structures involved in wielding power. In trying to understand the various roles that constitutions can play, I will draw on a framework introduced with my colleague Alberto Simpser (2014). We characterized constitutional provisions as serving either as operating manuals, billboards, blueprints, or window dressing. The categories are fairly intuitive. An operating manual is a text that lays out how a machine is to function: follow the instructions and the system will operate. A billboard is an advertisement, designed to communicate information about the intentions and capacities of drafters. The audience may be the subjects of the constitutional order, or perhaps external actors, whose behavior drafters seek to influence. A blueprint, in turn, is a plan. It does not describe a machine that is currently operating; it describes one that is to be built in the future. The blueprint articulates goals and lays out how to get to an aspirational future. Finally, window dressing, as the name suggests, is designed to obfuscate.

These four categories of operating manuals, billboards, blueprints, and window dressing capture a range of roles that might potentially be played by texts. In principle they apply to both dictatorships and democracies. But the particular character or mix of roles might be different as between dictatorships and democracies. Let us discuss each of these roles in further depth to try to understand this question.

Operating Manuals

All regimes need institutions, and they need to coordinate on what institutions will play what role. A written constitutional text can minimize conflict over basic institutions for any regime. Constitutions set up legislatures, courts, and executives, and provide for basic rules including eligibility for office, meeting dates, and voting rules. Laying out the structures of government facilitates their operation because it prevents continuous renegotiation over their features. Following the instructions provided in the operating manual minimizes conflict. Indeed, there is a hopeful suggestion in the literature that under certain circumstances constitutional systems can be "self-enforcing" (Ordeshook 1992; Weingast 1997), meaning that they will work on their own accord in certain ways—from James Russell Lowell's phrase, "a machine that would go of itself" (Kammen 1986). Constitutional operating manuals can facilitate constitutionalist functions of precommiting rulers to abide by certain rules and controlling their subordinates.

Roger Myerson's (2008) work on the emergence of constitutionalism illustrates the utility of this logic to authoritarians. As Myerson describes, the early kings of England needed mechanisms to ensure that taxes were collected and that agents were properly motivated to do so. Absolute power is unlikely to motivate lower-level agents sufficiently, for each agent will fear arbitrary discipline by the monarch-principal. The table of the Exchequer, in Myerson's account, provides a constitutional solution to the problem. Taxes are laid out on the table and verified by an independent agent of the king, the Exchequer. The table generates common knowledge among the agents of the king, so that all can observe the amounts of taxes each agent is providing. When an agent does not deliver a sufficient amount of taxes, every other agent will observe that fact and so will not fear arbitrary punishment by the king, so long as the agents act honestly. Common knowledge and the constitutional commitment by the king only to punish agents whose malfeasance has been publicly verified help to make government more effective. "Without such an institutionalized check on the leader," Myerson writes, "he could not credibly raise the support he needs to compete for power" (2008, 130). Windsor Castle could not have been built without this simple constitutional solution to the agency problem.

In the modern era, the internal coordination function of authoritarian constitutions is the focus of Robert Barros's (2002) study of the Chilean Constitution under Augusto Pinochet. Barros argues that the constitutional tribunal, in particular, facilitated coordination among the various military branches that composed the junta. These branches were in competition with each other for relative power, even as they needed to maintain cohesion vis-à-vis outsiders. The tribunal helped them coordinate and enforced patterns that prevented any one individual from dominating all the others. Even Augusto Pinochet, whose name is eponymous with the dictatorship, was forced to submit to the tribunal's dictates. This theme of internal tension and external cohesion is a central feature of authoritarian regimes and one whose management is a crucial function for constitutional institutions (see generally Negretto 2013).

Another example of an operating manual function comes from Egypt, as recounted by Kristen Stilt (2014). In the face of American pressure to move toward democracy, President Hosni Mubarak of Egypt decided to amend the constitution to allow for multiparty elections in 2005. But the particular amendment that was adopted turned out to be a very clever provision to sustain his dictatorship (Stilt 2014, 123–124). The revised article on presidential elections allowed political parties that had been in existence for five years and achieved certain seat thresholds to nominate candidates. But it turned out that only Mubarak's party met these facially neutral criteria. Other independent candidates were allowed to run if they met a complex formula of demonstrated support from the various legislative bodies of the country. The article also allowed a waiver for candidates of other political parties in the initial election after the amendment, but this waiver did not apply to independent candidates.

The complex article was perfectly designed to ensure the maintenance of the regime. The Muslim Brotherhood was the largest political force but had been banned as a political party and so could not meet the waiver provision. Although the Brotherhood could in principle run independent candidates, they would not meet the complex formula of having support in the existing assemblies. In short, the system was designed to maintain authoritarian rule, while relieving the regime of pressure from Washington. There was nothing hidden about this, in the sense that the text could be perfectly implemented without artifice. But it also reflected a sophisticated political logic that made it less than clear to outsiders. No wonder the Egyptian Constitution has been described as "the joke that turned serious" (El-Ghobashy 2008)

In short, operating manuals can serve to help the regime coordinate internally, while dominating externally. Constitutional texts can facilitate both, if players follow the rules and the game itself is rigged against challengers. The primary distinction between democratic and authoritarian operating manuals is apparent on its face and concerns the openness of the political process to challengers.

Billboards

Billboards are communicative devices. When the insiders come to agreement about certain ideological matters, they may want to enshrine these agreements in the written constitution so as to communicate with outsiders. These outsiders might be the citizens within a country, or perhaps international actors, such as investors, donors, and foreign powers. Enshrining an ideological position in the constitution provides an authoritative statement about the boundaries of what is or is not acceptable in political discourse.

Andreas Schedler (2013) argues that this function is particularly important for authoritarians, who are inherently "theatrical." Because ordinary political communication is suppressed, authoritarians need to create their own empirical realities and shape perceptions through their performances. Constitutional texts, by virtue of their status as the highest set of norms in the state, play a special role here. They provide a kind of advertisement and often contain long preambles that articulate a litany of policies and history. Indeed, preambles of authoritarian constitutions are systematically longer than those found in democracies.[1]

The billboard function seems to be particularly important for Communist regimes and their constitutions. In contemporary China and Vietnam, for example, there is intense internal debate over the direction of policy, but it takes place within the relatively closed venues of the party-state system. Constitutional changes can be useful to help announce new political discourses and clarify the boundaries of debate. In recent years, for example, old discourses of Marxist-Leninism and Maoism have become hollow but have not been replaced. Instead they have been supplemented, sometimes through constitutional amendments. The Chinese Constitution, for example, was amended in 2004 to include the notion of private property rights, alongside state and collective property. Furthermore, the "advanced productive forces" in society are now represented; this euphemism for capitalists signals the consolidation of Deng Xiaoping's notion that "to get rich is glorious." These constitutional changes provide signals about the overall nature of the regime, making it more difficult to revert to earlier configurations.

Constitutional "billboards" also play a role in internal transitions within authoritarian regimes. The enshrinement of a new leader or generation of leadership is often accompanied by a constitutional amendment or even replacement. This can be seen as a confirmation of a new direction or the maintenance of the old language and also an act demonstrating that the new leader has power over the ultimate symbols of state authority.

Authoritarian constitutions also serve as foreign policy statements. In 2012, for example, North Korea amended the preamble to its constitution to declare that the country had become "an undefeated country with a strong ideology, a nuclear power state, and invincible military power." Adopted in the wake of a failed rocket launch, the statement seems partly designed to reassure locals of the regime's self-confidence, but also to indicate that the controversial international nuclear stance is here to stay. So far, the North Koreans' limited receptivity to Donald Trump's "denuclearization" overtures have not extended to any effort to alter this constitutional declaration. Since 1975, China's preamble has said that Taiwan is part of the country's "sacred territory" going on to provide that "it is the lofty duty of the entire Chinese people, including our compatriots in Taiwan, to accomplish the great task of reunifying the motherland." Another example is the preamble to Syria's constitution of 1973, which speaks of pan-Arab nationalism and the need to fight Zionism. The 2012 version, adopted in the face of a serious challenge to the regime, reflects substantial continuity, self-consciously asserting, "Syria has occupied an important political position as it is the beating heart of Arabism, the forefront of confrontation with the Zionist enemy and the bedrock of resistance against colonial hegemony on the Arab world and its capabilities and wealth."[2]

This billboard function can work in tandem with the operating manual function. But authoritarian regimes, by virtue of their theatricality noted above, seem to place greater emphasis on the former than on the latter. Indeed, in many cases, the former is the dominant role for the constitutional text. In the case of China, for example, the constitution is not judicially enforceable, and at this writing there is a serious ideological purge of those who argue for its enforceability.

Blueprints

Blueprints are plans for the future, and constitutions can be aspirational documents as well as operating manuals (Dorf 2009). Aspirational rhetoric can be used to justify a "temporary" period of authoritarian rule, perhaps after a military coup in which a return to democracy is promised, or as an affirmative substantive vision for the future.

To take one important example of the latter, Mexico's 1917 constitution included a large number of economic and social rights, promising land, education, and work to the citizenry. These provisions were not mere window dressing for a totalitarian party, as might be said of equivalent promises in Stalin's constitution of 1936, but instead were aspirations. It took several decades before the land reform promises articulated there could be realized, but by the 1940s a policy emerged and land reform began in earnest. And it is likely that the blueprint was part of the reason that the policy was eventually effectuated. Blueprints orient the leadership and citizenry toward certain defined goals, increasing the costs of ignoring them and rewarding mobilization around them.

Window Dressing

Although the title of this chapter indicates some skepticism toward window dressing as the primary or sole motive of authoritarian constitution-makers, there is no denying that obfuscation may sometimes serve useful purposes. We thus see frequent references to democracy and human rights, even in countries that make little to no effort to advance these projects. For example, North Korea's constitution guarantees its citizens "democratic rights and liberties" (Article 64). The extensive lists of rights found in many totalitarian constitutions are hardly meant to provide for meaningful constraint on the state. As David Law and Mila Versteeg (2013, 165) argue, there are few costs that can be imposed on authoritarian states that violate human rights but perhaps some benefits to declaring that rights exist. Such declarations may give the regime a small measure of international legitimacy, allowing the continued flow of foreign aid, for example.

In our recent writing (Ginsburg and Simpser 2014), Alberto Simpser and I noted that window dressing might be designed not only to keep outsiders from looking in but also to keep insiders from looking out: a systematic gap between paper and practice tends to cheapen the value of paper. So, for example, one might think that by including a long set of rights in the Soviet Constitution of 1936, Stalin sought to instruct his people that constitutions in the West as well as in the socialist world had nothing to do with protection from government. This too might enhance regime power.

Finally, constitutions may simply be works of fiction. Consider the regimes under the thumb of the Soviet Union during the long Cold War. Surely leaders in such countries had little scope for genuine policy deliberation. Maybe decisions such as that to leave the leading role of the Communist Party unmentioned in Poland in 1952 (Przeworski 2014), while neighboring countries did so declare, reflect purely aesthetic choices, not designed to have any consequence or reflect any particular position.

Whatever the rationale, there is a common assumption that democracies do not engage in "window dressing" as much as do authoritarians. While there are sometimes large gaps between paper and practice in democracies, it tends to be in the direction of overperformance, so the paper constitution doesn't reflect the full state of actual protections. For example, the Nineteenth Amendment to the U.S. Constitution guarantees women the right to vote, but in practice constitutional protection of women's equality has extended to many realms not explicitly identified in the constitutional text (Dorf 2009). In contrast, dictatorships tend to overpromise relative to their actual level of constitutional practice (Law and Versteeg 2013).

Distinguishing the Functions

This typology of operating manual, billboard, blueprint, or window dressing is designed to indicate that there are various roles constitutions can play beyond a binary of "perfectly implemented" and "sham." The particular mix of roles will vary across time and space, and even across different provisions of the same constitution. The roles may exist to varying degrees in

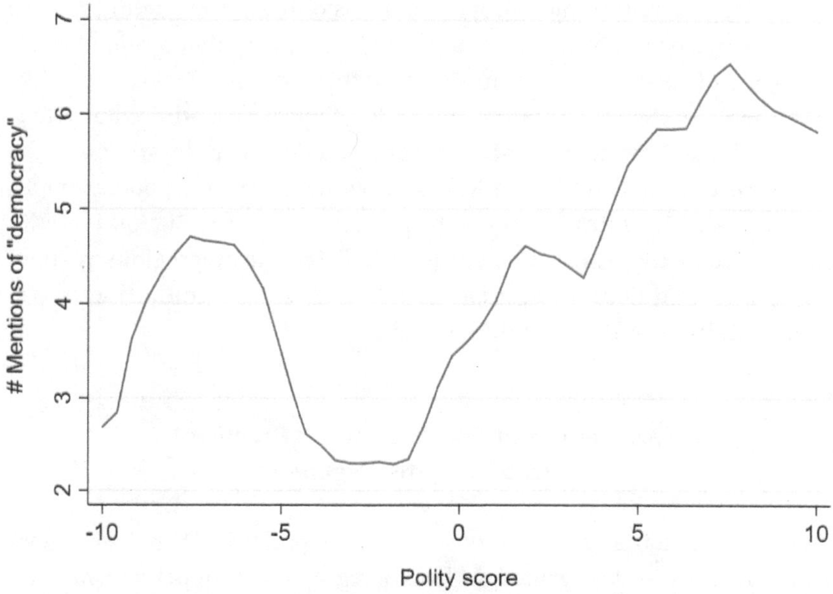

Figure 5.1. Average number of mentions of Democracy in Constitutions by Polity Score, 1789–2015

all constitutional orders, but we suspect that authoritarians tend toward billboard and window dressing roles more than do democracies.

In practice, it may sometimes be difficult to distinguish between window dressing and blueprints, since such a distinction relies on understanding the inscrutable motives of an authoritarian regime. Consider Figure 5.1, showing the average number of mentions of the word "democracy" in national constitutions written from 1789 through 2015, by the Polity index of democracy. (Note that Polity is a continuous index, and in many analyses, a cutoff of 6 or 7 on the Polity scale is used to indicate countries that are "democracies.")

Figure 5.1 indicates that, interestingly, countries at the bottom end of the scale tend to talk a good deal about democracy—the window dressing dynamic. But countries in the middle of the scale (which might include many countries that are categorized as "illiberal democracies" or "electoral authoritarians") tend to talk about democracy at levels that are correlated with their actual democracy score, perhaps reflecting a combination of the operating manual and blueprint dynamics. At the very highest end of the scale, there is a slight dropoff in terms of rhetorical commitment to democracy. One might think about this as suggesting that strong democracies do not need to talk very much about their commitment to the political system, as their institutions speak for themselves; while many true dictatorships seem to pretend they are something they are not. The *Democratic* Republic of North Korea (seven mentions) is a good example. This analysis illustrates that the same provisions can play different roles in different contexts. And it also suggests that the most egregious regimes may use constitutions in different ways than the lesser authoritarian regimes (Elkins, Ginsburg, and Melton 2014).

Authoritarian Constitutions in Practice: Stabilizing the Regime

How do authoritarian constitutions function in practice? There is some evidence that constitutions extend the lives of regimes that adopt them. Michael Albertus and Victor Menaldo (2014) argue that constitutions contribute to regime endurance by facilitating the consolidation of political power and the internal coordination of the governing coalition. Constitutional commitments can also facilitate investment and growth, which in turn may extend the lives of regimes. Drawing on large-N data on Latin American dictatorships from 1950 to 2002, they find empirical support for the proposition that authoritarian constitutions significantly extend the life expectancy of dictatorships and enhance investment and economic growth.

The drafting of constitutions is itself a political project that can serve certain purposes, such as engaging in an important project that can serve both to distract and also to gain information about social concerns. The processes of authoritarian constitution-making are often hidden to us, and, as Adam Przeworski (2014) notes, this prevents us from understanding the internal conflicts and motives of drafters (see also Barros 2002). No doubt there is more than meets the eye.

J. Arch Getty's (1991) archival research into the drafting and early implementation of the 1936 Soviet Constitution showed that the constitution-making process was important for generating information on the preferences of the population. At Stalin's direction Moscow demanded that local officials initiate broad discussions of the document among the populace, and Soviet citizens contributed many thousands of comments about the proposed text.

Many of the Soviet comments complained about the constitutional guarantee of free social benefits to workers but not to peasants (Getty 1991, 24–27), while others focused on the need to further punish members of the former clergy. The process of soliciting information allowed the regime to gauge what issues were important to the public, even if it chose to ignore them in the final analysis.

Ginsburg and Simpser (2014) recount the creation of the 1998 Constitution of the Maldives, which took seventeen years. Soon after taking office in 1978, President Maumoon Gayoom set up a special majlis, composed of a mix of elected and appointed persons, to undertake the process of constitutional reform. The process of constitution-making culminated in a new document in 1998, consolidating presidential rule. The constitution-making process was itself a discrete political project with its own logic: it allowed Gayoom a set of governmental positions that facilitated patronage as well as an ability to gain information on new political talent through the electoral process. The point of the process was not necessarily the final product, which could surely have been produced much more quickly.

Constitutions also provide arenas for political contestation within the narrow elite that lead authoritarian regimes (Schedler 2013). Constitutional provisions may therefore matter as vehicles for channeling conflict. Consider the Constitution of the Islamic Republic of Iran, recently analyzed in depth by Mirjam Künkler (n.d.). Künkler argues that the Iranian constitution, while certainly used by an autocratic and authoritarian government, was not a facade. Instead the constitution functioned as the primary arena for a battle over political power between the supreme leader and his opponents. In this case, the constitutional structure has served to facilitate a conservative backlash against claims of popular sovereignty, even under a regime that came to power through revolution.

The first 1979 draft of the Iranian constitution, which came very close to being ratified, was modeled largely on the French constitution of 1958. It granted men and women full equality, and while it set up institutions of clerical oversight of legislation, it did not grant complete clerical control. Ayatollah Khomeini largely agreed with the constitutional draft and proposed to put it to a popular referendum. However, others asked for a constituent assembly. In the end, a forty-member Assembly of Experts, largely dominated by Khomeini's confidants, was established to finalize the text.

By the time the final 1979 draft of the constitution was approved, the hierarchy of secular or republican versus Islamic power in the governmental structure had been radically reversed. A new article was introduced, making invalid all legislation and regulations that did not adhere to "Islamic precepts," and establishing *velayat-e faqih*, "guardianship of the jurist," which placed a senior Islamic jurist of exemplary qualities as a supreme leader above the three branches of government, with direct control of the military, media, and judiciary. While the intellectual basis of this maneuver had developed over many years in Shia political thought, the enormous amount of governmental power given to the faqih had no institutional precedent (Ansari and Shadmehr n.d.). For centuries, jurists had debated whether the ulema were in some sense the source of legitimate temporal authority exercised by rulers, but the idea of direct rule by a supreme jurist-leader was an innovation. Furthermore, the Assembly of Experts took out the amendment clause of the constitution and added that legislation by the parliament (majlis) had to be approved by a Guardian Council. The constitution was officially Islamized.

A series of deadlocks over labor law and land reform between the parliament (representing the secular part of government) and the Guardian Council (religious) each time propelled controversial reinterpretation of the relationship between Islamic and state law. The first time, the minister of labor successfully proposed a new legal principle of "obligatory conditions," an extension of Shia contract law, which basically gave the state (as a third party) power to intervene and override sharia when the public interest so required (Kunkler n.d). But subsequent conflicts led to gridlock with the ulema-dominated Guardian Council. This led Khomeini to turn to the old idea of "expediency," or *maslahat*, and he created an Expediency Council appointed by the supreme leader. This body had the power to resolve disputes between the Guardian Council and the parliament.

The next major change came in 1989 when the 1979 constitution, promulgated without an amendment clause, had to be amended to allow President Khamenei to become Ayatollah Khomeini's successor as supreme leader, despite his lack of qualifications as an Islamic jurist. The constitution became much more streamlined as an effect of this amendment, eliminating the requirement that the supreme leader be the *marja'* (highest religious authority), centralizing power in the office of the supreme leader (declaring it "absolute"), and formally establishing the recently created Expediency Council.

As Künkler convincingly demonstrates, the Iranian constitution was not a facade, but in fact a primary site of political and legal struggle. The next few decades saw expansion of the powers granted to the supreme leader but also reformist attempts by the office of the president to limit the autocratic rule of the supreme leader. The constitution remains at the center of political struggle in Iran.

Authoritarian Constitutions and Regime Transition

There is, of course, the possibility that the provisions of an authoritarian constitution can be used against the regime, and this is a risk that the dictator must consider (Law and Versteeg 2014). Tamir Moustafa (2007) makes the related point that empowering courts is a "two-edged" sword for dictators, who must sometimes pay the cost of pushing back on institutions they themselves created. In extreme cases, constitutional institutions can provide triggers for democratic transition. As Alexei Trochev (2013) shows, the bills of rights and judicial institutions adopted by authoritarians in Georgia, Ukraine, and Kyrgyzstan ultimately invalidated key elections, and led to the downfall of the regime itself.

In addition, there are a small number of constitutions adopted by authoritarians in which transition is part of the institutional design, so the constitution provides both a blueprint and an operating manual to effectuate a return to democracy. These might be called "transformational authoritarian constitutions" (Ginsburg 2014). Examples include the constitutions of Chile of 1980; Indonesia of 1945; Turkey of 1982; Portugal of 1974; and Taiwan's constitution, drafted on the mainland of China in 1947. Less well-known examples include Panama's military-drafted document of 1972 and Guyana's of 1980.

Why would new democrats retain a constitution of dictators? As an initial matter, one might think about this category of countries as being examples of those in which formal constitutional replacement is not correlated with actual "small-c" constitutional change. In some countries, shifts between democracy and dictatorship tend to be marked by formal constitutional revision and replacement. In others, the two are less tightly linked. My colleagues and I use this observation to argue that constitutional change is a distinct phenomenon from regime change (Elkins, Ginsburg, and Melton 2009). Chile, for example, is a country whose history is marked by constitutional stability along with political fluctuation. As such, the 1980 constitution shares something in common with its predecessors of 1832 and 1925: it has governed until now over a period of great political change.

There are other possible reasons a country would retain an authoritarian constitution after a return to democracy. One possibility is that the old constitution must be retained for political reasons—either because it enjoys some legitimacy among the general population, or because its erstwhile proponents still retain enough power to block any attempt at replacements. The Mexican and Indonesian cases seem like examples of the former dynamic. In both cases, the constitution was associated with a significant event—a revolution or a moment of independence—and so retains legitimacy notwithstanding its use by authoritarians. Chile, on the other hand, is a case of retained veto over major change. Political forces associated with the erstwhile military regime play a potential spoiler role and continue to benefit from a set of institutions—the binomial legislative system, supermajority requirements over certain rules, and ex ante review by a constitutional tribunal—that remain important today though changes are now being considered.

Assuming that this group forms a coherent category, what are the criteria that distinguish a transformational authoritarian constitution? As an ideal type, the following seem to be essential criteria: (1) the constitution is explicitly framed as helping to structure a return to electoral democracy, after a period that may or may not be specified; (2) the constitution reflects certain policy goals designed to be permanent, that is, to constrain the future democratic regime; and (3) the constitution provides for an enforcement mechanism to ensure that both these goals are met. In other words, the transformational authoritarian constitution acknowledges the superiority of popular sovereignty and seeks to transfer power to democrats, but only subject to certain limitations. Further, there is some institutional mechanism guaranteeing these limits.

The 1982 Constitution of Turkey provides a nice paradigmatic example (Goldenziel 2013, 36–37; Isiksel 2013). Turkey has a long tradition of electoral politics but has also experienced periodic bouts of military rule. As Jill Goldenziel (2013, 35) notes, the Venice Commission calls Turkey a "tutelary democracy," in which democracy is bounded by an alliance of the military, bureaucracy, and courts. In the 1960s, the Kemalist elite that had run Turkey for decades established a constitutional court, in part to protect the core values of secularism from reversal by religious parties. As those parties increased in popularity, the court repeatedly disbanded them and also engaged in a long series of battles with the elected branches of government.

The 1982 constitution, adopted during one of the periods of direct military rule, illustrates many of the themes of transformational authoritarianism. It is in form a democratic document, calling for elections. Like many military-adopted documents, it speaks of the essential role of the military in saving the nation, but it also speaks in a democratic register: democracy is mentioned five times. It reaffirms the values of republicanism and secularism as foundational principles that are unamendable. But it also sets up clear mechanisms to limit democratic politics. These included the National Security Council, which served as a check on and supplement to the civilian cabinet (Isiksel 2013, 717). Furthermore, the constitution featured a low threshold to declaring a state of exception that could be extended indefinitely. Most prominently, the Turkish Constitutional Court plays an important role in enforcing the strictures of the 1982 constitution, providing a strict boundary on democratic politics. The court, and the judiciary more broadly, has served to slow down Turkey's democratic transition at several crucial junctures (Bali 2013). To provide only one example, in 2008, the Constitutional Court ruled that properly enacted constitutional amendments overturning the ban on wearing a headscarf at state universities were themselves unconstitutional. It also sought to ban the country's ruling political party, the Justice and Development Party (AKP), for violating principles of secularism.

Beginning in 2003, a series of amendments have been passed to try to reform the constitution to reflect the rise of the new populist Islamist party, the AKP. Although these efforts have been increasingly successful, especially with the expansion of presidential powers via amendments written in 2017 and upheld in elections in 2018, the legacy of the document is turning out to be difficult to escape. Many believe the AKP under its leader Recep Tayyib Erdogan has replaced one form of authoritarianism with another and has used some of the very same instrumentalities as the military. As Turkuler Isiksel (2013, 725) notes, in some circumstances "authoritarian constitutionalism encourages challengers to develop the same bad habits as the old guard."

Other examples of transformational authoritarian constitutions might include several of Thailand's twenty constitutions adopted since 1932, including the current one, ratified in 2017. Thailand has been a uniquely unstable constitutional environment, as government has oscillated between corrupt civilians and military authoritarians. Military governments in Thailand, at least since the 1970s, have as a formal matter accepted the moral superiority of democracy, but have occasionally stepped in to remove particular leaders or clear a situation of gridlock. After a coup, the military now seems to routinely promise a return to civilian rule but also has drafted constitutions that differ on one crucial point from their civilian counterparts: ensuring a nonelected upper house (Ginsburg 2009). This reflects the military-bureaucratic distrust of elected politicians and allows a veto on change by ensuring that some appointed actors will have a say on policy.

Myanmar's current document, adopted after a seventeen-year drafting process in 2008, surprised many observers by providing a mechanism for political liberalization. Although the complex structure of the political system ensures a continued veto for ex-military officers, the pace of liberalization allowed the release and subsequent parliamentary election of dissident leader Aung San Suu Kyi. At the same time, many political prisoners remain, and freedom of expression has been limited. Aung San Suu Kyi herself, now state counselor, an office akin to prime minister, has been criticized for complicity in the repression of minorities. The constitutional document is a kind of operating manual for both limited exercise of popular power and the maintenance of a veto by the military. While the first years of the system saw rapid evolution in the political situation, the current configuration looks a lot like a stable equilibrium of power sharing between the military and a dominant political party.

Closer to home the Panama Constitution of 1972, promulgated by General Torrijos following his 1968 coup, designated him as "Maximum Leader of the Panamanian Revolution," with extraordinary powers to last for six years (Article 277). These powers expired in 1978, and, under U.S. pressure, the National Assembly passed a series of amendments calling for a return to democratic processes over the next several years. Formally, the constitution remains in force today, having survived the rise and fall of strongman Manuel Noriega.

Chile seems to fit the paradigm of a transformational authoritarian constitution quite well. General Pinochet's junta passed the 1980 constitution with an eye to returning power to democratic forces through an orderly transition. This constitution entrenched property rights (a major concern of the Chilean right), banned Communist parties, gave the military a de facto veto through the power to appoint senators, and set up, among other institutions, a constitutional tribunal with power to engage in pre-promulgation review of legislation as a check on the conduct of future actors. But besides these veto points, the Chilean Constitution seems fairly democratic in form. It contains a relatively large number of rights, certainly more than its predecessor constitution of 1925. It provides for elections after a period of time. And it provides for judicial independence, among other features associated with electoral democracy. The distinguishing features of the 1980 constitution are those that regulate time and process rather substance.

Transformational authoritarian constitutions bear some relation to the species of transitional constitutionalism, as described by Ruti Teitel (2000). But they differ in that, unlike those documents that focus on reckoning with the past, transformational authoritarian constitutions are typically designed to insulate the designers from any future justice. Hence the various mechanisms of immunity found in the 1980 constitution in Chile provided a paradigm example: the category of *leyes*, requiring a four-sevenths majority; the Constitutional Court; the binomial election system; and the guarantees of impunity, all served to insulate the former rulers for a generation.

Transformational authoritarian documents may be transformational with regard to regime type but not with regard to accountability for past crimes. While transitional constitutionalism as explored by Teitel focuses on coming to terms with the past, the transformational authoritarian document obfuscates the past. As the English-language expression goes, one must break a few eggs to make an omelet, and we don't want to examine that process too carefully. The logic is that without guarantees of a future role and some immunity for the transformational authoritarian, democratic transition is impossible in the first place. In this sense transformational authoritarian constitutions form a kind of counter-category to Teitel's transitional constitutionalism.

From a normative point of view, transformational authoritarian constitutions remind us that entrenchment is a two-edged sword. While democratic theorists celebrate entrenchment as helping to make democratic self-rule possible, it may also serve to limit the scope of that self-rule in situations when one must bargain with an old regime. Entrenchment, as Professor Isiksel (2013, 708) puts it, can "foreclose institutional innovation, adaptation, and learning, magnifying the inadequacies, imperfections, and even injustices of the norm in question." The idea that the technology of constitutionalism slows down political processes goes back at least to the American founding fathers, but the ends to which this tool is deployed are as myriad as constitution-making circumstances.

In this regard, it is worth noting that authoritarians are increasingly facile at manipulating democratic institutions. We have now witnessed, in Turkey, Hungary, and Venezuela, to name just three examples, constitutional democracies that have suffered major reversals. In each case, the end came not through a coup d'état or revolution, but through a series of incremental changes, enacted in constitutionally legitimate ways, that ended up entrenching a single party or leader for the foreseeable future (Huq and Ginsburg 2018). This kind of constitutional backsliding involves the manipulation of the form of democracy to consolidate autocratic power. Such erosion can take frontal form, through formal amendment of the constitution, or use more subtle modalities of manipulating institutions of accountability, or capturing the electoral administration. Constitutions can slow these processes, but they can also facilitate them. The new phenomenon of backsliding serves as a reminder that institutions are fallible, and constitutions only provide, at best, speed bumps rather than infallible barriers against tyranny. Perhaps more interestingly, the phenomenon suggests that the transformational authoritarian constitution may be a thing of the past, and the new authoritarian style will involve the perversion of democratic constitutions.

The Lessons of Authoritarian Constitutions

Simpser and I consider the lessons of authoritarian constitutions both for our understanding of authoritarian regimes and for the study of constitutions (Ginsburg and Simpser 2014). A first point is that rules matter and are worthy of study, even when there is a good deal of discretion at the top of the political system. Many of our ideas about institutions have been developed in the context of democratic regimes, but there is good reason to assume that authoritarian institutions matter as well, even if they have their own logic (Svolik 2013). Constitutions without constitutionalism cannot be dismissed completely, although they may have very different functions.

A related point is that constitutions provide ideological clues and insights into the political idiom of authoritarian regimes. As our brief discussion of China indicated, constitutions can bound acceptable discourses and signal that certain ideas are accepted.

Authoritarian constitutions also call our attention away from the American fetish with judicial enforcement. As Stéphanie Balme and Michael W. Dowdle (2009) point out, "even in the most effective constitutional system, significant aspects of constitutional structure are invariably nonjusticiable." In dictatorships, constitutions can provide resources for political enforcement and so fit into the idea that we need to look at the authoritarian constitution outside the courts.

The categories offered in this chapter reflect the beginning of a research agenda, rather than its conclusion. But the myriad examples of authoritarian constitutions old and new, reinforced by the heightening efforts of authoritarians to rewrite constitutions in many parts of the world today, should collectively serve to make the case that it is time to take authoritarian constitutions seriously, as a category with much internal variation and much more to uncover.

Notes

1. For 605 constitutions that contain preambles, a simple correlation between the number of words and the level of democracy is –.10.

2. Const. Syria (2012), pmbl.

References

Albertus, Michael, and Victor Menaldo. 2014. "The Political Economy of Autocratic Constitutions." In *Constitutions in Authoritarian Regimes*, edited by Tom Ginsburg and Alberto Simpser, 53–82. New York: Cambridge University Press.

Ansari, Hassan Farhang and Mehdi Shadmehr. n.d. "The Jurisprudential Origins of the Iranian Revolution." Manuscript on file with author.

Bali, Asli. 2013. "The Perils of Judicial Independence: Constitutional Transition and the Turkish Example." *Virginia Journal of International Law* 52: 235–320.

Balme, Stéphanie, and Michael W. Dowdle. 2009. *Building Constitutionalism in China*. New York: Palgrave Macmillan.

Barros, Robert. 2002. *Constitutionalism and Dictatorship: Pinochet, the Junta, and the 1980 Constitution*. Cambridge: Cambridge University Press.

Brown, Nathan. n.d. "Constitutionalizing Authoritarianism and Democracy in Egypt and Tunisia." Manuscript on file with author.

Carey, John. 2000. "Parchment, Equilibria, and Institutions." *Comparative Political Studies* 33: 735–761.

Dorf, Michael. 2009. "The Aspirational Constitution." *George Washington University Law Review* 77 (5/6): 1631–1671.

El-Ghobashy, Mona. 2008. "Constitutional Contention in Contemporary Egypt." *American Behavioral Scientist* 51 (11): 1590–1610.

Elkins, Zachary, Tom Ginsburg, and James Melton. 2009. *The Endurance of National Constitutions*. Cambridge: Cambridge University Press.

———. 2014. "The Content of Authoritarian Constitutions." In *Constitutions in Authoritarian Regimes*, edited by Tom Ginsburg and Alberto Simpser, 141–164. New York: Cambridge University Press.

Elster, Jon. 2013. *Securities Against Misrule*. New York: Cambridge University Press.

Gandhi, Jennifer. 2008. *Political Institutions Under Dictatorship*. New York: Cambridge University Press.

———. 2014. "The Role of Presidential Power in Authoritarian Elections." In *Constitutions in Authoritarian Regimes*, edited by Tom Ginsburg and Alberto Simpser, 199–217. New York: Cambridge University Press.

Getty, J. Arch. 1991. "State and Society Under Stalin: Constitutions and Elections in the 1930s." *Slavic Review* 50 (1): 18–35.

Ginsburg, Tom. 2009. "Constitutional Afterlife: The Continuing Impact of Thailand's Postpolitical Constitution." *International Journal of Constitutional Law* 7 (1): 83–105.

———. 2014. "Fruit of the Poisoned Vine? Some Comparative Observations on Chile's Constitution." In Spanish. *Centro de Estudios Politicos.*

Ginsburg, Tom, and Alberto Simpser. 2014. Introduction to *Constitutions in Authoritarian Regimes*, edited by Tom Ginsburg and Alberto Simpser, 1–19. New York: Cambridge University Press.

Goldenziel, Jill. 2013. "Veiled Political Questions: Islamic Dress, Constitutionalism and the Ascendance of Courts." *American Journal of Comparative Law* 61 (1): 1–50.

Huq, Aziz, and Tom Ginsburg. 2018. "How to Lose a Constitutional Democracy." *UCLA Law Review* 65 (1): 78–169.

Isiksel, Turkulér. 2013. "Between Text and Context: Turkey's Tradition of Authoritarian Constitutionalism." *International Journal of Constitutional Law* 11 (3): 702–726.

Kammen, Michael. 1986. *A Machine That Would Go of Itself: The Constitution in American Culture*. New York: Alfred A. Knopf.

Künkler, Mirjam. n.d. "No Façade Constitution: Constitutional Law and Political Change in Post-1979 Iran." Manuscript on file with author.

Law, David S., and Mila Versteeg. 2013. "Sham Constitutions." *California Law Review* 101 (4): 863–952.

———. 2014. "Constitutional Variation Among Strains of Authoritarianism." In *Constitutions in Authoritarian Regimes*, edited by Tom Ginsburg and Alberto Simpser, 165–196. New York: Cambridge University Press.

Levitsky, Steven, and Lucan A. Way. 2010. *Competitive Authoritarianism: Hybrid Regimes After the Cold War*. New York: Cambridge University Press.

Lutz, Donald. 1994. "Toward a Theory of Constitutional Amendment." *American Political Science Review* 88 (2): 355–370.

Moustafa, Tamir. 2007. *The Struggle for Constitutional Power in Egypt*. New York: Cambridge University Press.

Müller, Jan-Werner. 2016. *What Is Populism?* Philadelphia: University of Pennsylvania Press.

Murphy, Walter F. 1993. "Constitutions, Constitutionalism, and Democracy." In *Constitutionalism and Democracy: Transitions in the Contemporary World*, edited by

Douglas Greenberg, Stanley N. Katz, Melanie Beth Oliviero, and Steven C. Wheatley, 3–25. New York: Oxford University Press.

Myerson, Roger B. 2008. "The Autocrat's Credibility Problem and Foundations of the Constitutional State." *American Political Science Review* 102 (1): 125–139.

Negretto, Gabriel. 2013. *Making Constitutions*. New York: Cambridge University Press.

Okoth-Ogendo, H. W. O. 1993. "Constitutions Without Constitutionalism: An African Political Paradox." In *Constitutionalism and Democracy: Transitions in the Contemporary World*, edited by Douglas Greenberg, Stanley N. Katz, Melanie Beth Oliviero, and Steven C. Wheatley, 65–82. New York: Oxford University Press.

Ordeshook, Peter C. 1992. "Constitutional Stability." *Constitutional Political Economy* 3 (2): 137–175.

Przeworski, Adam. 2014. "Ruling Against Rules." In *Constitutions in Authoritarian Regimes*, edited by Tom Ginsburg and Alberto Simpser, 21–35. New York: Cambridge University Press.

Sartori, Giovanni. 1962. "Constitutionalism: A Preliminary Discussion." *American Political Science Review* 56 (4): 853–863.

Schedler, Andreas. 2013. *The Politics of Uncertainty: Sustaining and Subverting Electoral Authoritarianism*. New York: Oxford University Press.

Stilt, Kristen. 2014. "Constitutions in Authoritarian Regimes: The Egyptian Constitution of 1971." In *Constitutions in Authoritarian Regimes*, edited by Tom Ginsburg and Alberto Simpser, 111–137. New York: Cambridge University Press.

Svolik, Milan. 2013. *The Politics of Authoritarian Rule*. New York: Cambridge University Press.

Teitel, Ruti. 2000. *Transitional Justice*. Oxford: Oxford University Press.

Trochev, Alexei. 2013. "Fragmentation? Defection? Legitimacy? Explaining Judicial Roles in Post-Communist 'Colored Revolutions.'" In *Consequential Courts: New Judicial Roles in Global Perspective*, edited by Diana Kapiszewski, Gordon Silverstein, and Robert A. Kagan, 67–92. Cambridge: Cambridge University Press.

Weingast, Barry. 1997. "The Political Foundations of Democracy and the Rule of Law." *American Political Science Review* 91 (2): 245–263.

CHAPTER 6

Unconstitutional Constituent Power

Kim Lane Scheppele

Can there be an unconstitutional constituent power? This may sound rather like that famous question about angels and heads of pins. But the question about constituent power matters rather more than one might think because not all powers that may claim to be constituent are. Extreme cases may help us see why.

Suppose I give myself the task of creating a new constitution for Idealaria. Since I have a lot of expertise in these matters of constitutional design (though no particular experience with Idealaria), I conjure up what the people of Idealaria should want, what kind of government they should have, and what sort of constitution they should adopt. I consult best practices and comparative constitutional history, design the most thoughtful of all possible constitutions, and then present the results to the population of Idealaria. Constituent power is pure reason, I tell the people of Idealaria. Here is your perfect constitution!

Well, the population of Idealaria might object, it might have been nice if you had consulted us!

They have a point—and that point bears on what is a legitimate constituent power. A constituent power can't just constitute itself as an exercise of reason; it has to be engaged with both the population for which the constitution would be written as well as with the specifics of the place.[1] Abstract constitutions won't do. Constitutions have to grow from the soil in which they are supposed to root.[2]

Take another country. Pandemonia,[3] let's call it. In Pandemonia, politics is highly polarized. Those of voting age have staked themselves out as Greens or Reds. Greens refuse to compromise with Reds, and Reds refuse to even talk to Greens. Nothing can get done in the government, which has a complex system of checks and balances, because the Greens veto everything that the Reds want to do and vice versa. The Greens, however, are constitutionally entrepreneurial—making the case to all who will listen that Pandemonia's key problem is the existing constitution because it routinely blocks the expression of true majoritarian preferences.[4] The Greens establish a constitutional convention that the Reds protest and boycott. The Greens meet, draft a new constitution for Pandemonia, and adopt it unanimously among themselves as the new constitution of the country. They then present the Reds with a fait accompli. As the constituent power of Pandemonia (because we were the only ones who showed up), they say, we now present the new constitution of Pandemonia under which we will all live. It just so happens, of course, that the rules are written to give the Greens an advantage and that the Reds will never again be able to veto their plans. Constituent power in action?

Well, no, you might rightly think. A group that controls a constitutional process to rig the rules to favor its members cannot call itself a constituent power. A constitutional drafting process has to be more representative. If parts of the population are systematically excluded or exclude themselves in protest, the resulting constitution cannot be considered legitimate.

If you agree that both of these constitutional drafting processes are problematic and give rise to an illegitimate constitution, then you probably also believe that a constitution must result from some process that systematically attempts to include all of the major players in its construction. A plan shouldn't be drafted for a theoretical people and a theoretical place. The process can't be rigged to exclude people who are then disadvantaged in the polity that results. In short, constituent power needs to embody meaningful consent of the actual population that is to be governed.

But how responsive does the process have to be—and how far must consent extend? And what counts as consent? Surely not every individual—or even every political faction—can exercise a veto!

A hypothetical country may help to show what is at stake here. So let us consider Freedonia.[5] In Freedonia, politics is very tempestuous. It is hard to keep a government standing for long because there are so many parties and the political spectrum is so wide that it is hard to form stable and enduring coalitions. Moreover, the parties of the right almost always have to bring the tiny group of fascists into the government in order to get a working majority, and the parties of the left almost always have to bring in the tiny group of communists to do the same, so politics is often torqued from extreme left to extreme right as governments change and the extremist parties hold their coalitions hostage to views that do not have widespread support. A coalition of civil society organizations organizes the parties of the middle, representing about 90 percent of the population, to draft a new constitution, in which parties that get less than 10 percent of the popular vote—the fascists and communists—have no representation in the constituent assembly. The fascists and the communists strenuously object, but the constitution is enacted over their objections, and the two parties are banned under the new constitution. Is the 90 percent group a legitimate constituent power?

And if you think that it is permissible for the 90 percent of the population to exclude the 10 percent, especially when that 10 percent consists of antiliberal groups, would it matter if the far right and the far left had formed 90 percent against the liberal 10 percent middle instead?

By now, you can see the problem. Our constitutional theory tells us that a constitution should be framed by a constituent power, but it turns out not to be terribly helpful at telling us how to find that constituent power or how to know, when some assemblage calls itself a constituent power, whether it has the right to do so. But as these three examples show, we may have strong intuitions that some sorts of constituent powers may be more legitimate than others—more *constitutional*, in a way. In this chapter, I want to try to try to explain why there *can* be an unconstitutional constituent power—first in theory and then with reference to the trouble case of Hungary.

Constitutional Theory and Constituent Power

Constitutional theory generally presupposes that the life of a constitution can be divided between the moment of its birth when the constituent power is summoned up to create a new constitution and the lifetime it has thereafter when a political community will live under this constitutional order. This distinction between the *pouvoir constituant* and the *pouvoir constitué* dates to the famous French revolutionary pamphlet of Emmanuel-Joseph Sieyès, "What Is the Third Estate?" Sieyès, of course, was attempting to justify the break in French politics caused by the refusal of the revolutionaries to honor the constitutional system they had inherited. No longer was the king to be the sole determinant of the constitutional system; instead, the "totality of citizens belonging to the common order" (Sieyès 2003, 99)—the Third

Estate—could claim the power, the *pouvoir constituant*, to make a constitution for the nation as a whole.

According to Sieyès, political revolutionaries could realize this power by convening a body of extraordinary representatives, tasked with speaking for the nation. What would bind these extraordinary representatives in the work of constitution-making? Sieyès (2003, 139) explained that the existing constitution could *not* be one of those constraints: "They are not to be subject to the constitutional forms on which they have to decide. In the first, place, this would be contradictory because these forms are in dispute, and it is up to them to settle them. Secondly, they have nothing to say about matters for which positive forms have been fixed. Thirdly, they have been put in the place of the Nation itself as if it was it that was settling the constitution. Like it [the nation], they are independent. . . . Their common will has the same worth as that of the nation itself."

For Sieyès, the freedom from prior constitutional understandings that liberated the constituent assembly did not mean that the *pouvoir constituant* was without constraint at all. He believed that an extraordinary representative assembly, convened for one purpose and one purpose only, could change the constitutional order only through the discovery and deployment of a common will, under which this new order must be constrained. The contours of this common will were defined by Sieyès as the sum of individual wills of the nation, determined by a majority in the case of disagreement. And this general will could—in fact, must—limit the creation of the constitution itself.

Sieyès's majoritarianism must be understood in the context in which he was arguing. Under the existing system of Estates General, the Third Estate could be outvoted by the other estates, even though the Third Estate constituted the numerical majority of the political community. In this context, majoritarianism was a revolutionary claim because the new political community was refusing to be governed by a minority allegedly acting on behalf of all. But in the context, where the Third Estate was being functionally excluded from having any part in determining the fate of the country because it would always be outnumbered by the First and Second Estates voting together, Sieyès might be interpreted as making a slightly different point: A constituent part of the political community cannot be spoken for by others.[6]

Elaborating a distinction that still animates most theories of constitution writing today, Sieyès argued that extraordinary representatives in the constituent moment are free of existing positive political forms, while still being deeply constrained by the common will of the nation in the exercise of the *pouvoir constituant*. By contrast, the ordinary representatives and daily government are bound in the exercise of the *pouvoir constitué* under the constitution that determines the positive political forms.

If the common will can constrain a constitution-making process, then it is important to understand what this common will is. The common—or general—will is a concept familiar to French constitutional theory not just from Sieyès's writing, but perhaps even more famously from the writings of Jean-Jacques Rousseau. Unlike Sieyès, Rousseau did not portray the general will as resulting from the summing up of the wills of individuals subject to the principle of majoritarianism. Instead, the general will for Rousseau is a collective property of a group and is not reducible to some one-step mathematical relationship of individual wills (like their mere addition or averaging). The general will's chief manifestation comes through the imagination of a common good in which all could share. The general will, in accomplishing this task, omits the partiality of individual and private wills and extracts from them only those elements that all share in common. Says Rousseau (2003, 203): "There is often a great deal of difference between the will of all and the general will. The latter looks only to the common interest; the former considers private interest and is only a sum of private wills. But take away from these same wills the pluses and minuses that cancel each other out, and the remaining sum of the differences is the general will."

Of course, as many have noted, the general will is far from an unambiguous and clear idea. It is an imagined unity that cannot be reduced to the sum of the parts. But the crucial element for our purposes is that some generally derived desire of the political self-governing group is a constraint on what the *pouvoir constituant* can do. The *pouvoir constituant* is not an unlimited power; it is simply not limited by prior political forms. It is subject to the constraint of the common good of the political community and is therefore not a roving idea that can be captured by anyone who pretends to speak in the community's name.

The idea that legitimate constitution-making is subject to no constraint other than a general will—but that it is in fact limited by that general will—can be found also in a theorist who, in many particulars, could not be more different from Rousseau. Writing in the turbulent years of the Weimar Republic, Carl Schmitt elaborated on these ideas of constituent power and its constraint in *Constitutional Theory*. According to Schmitt (2008, 75), "The constitution in the positive sense originates from an *act of the constitution-making power*. . . . This act *constitutes* the form and type of political unity, the existence of which is presupposed. It is not the case that political unity first arises during 'the establishment of a constitution.' The constitution in the positive sense entails only the conscious determination of the particular complete form, for which the political unity decides" (emphasis in original). For Schmitt, the political unity is a power that precedes any particular act of constitution-making and represents the decision by a political community that it will be self-governing, much as the general will served this purpose for Rousseau.

For Schmitt, a constitution is dependent on the existence of this political unity, which expresses itself in the foundational decision to make a constitution for itself. Through this political unity, the people bring a practical form of governance into existence in ways that cannot be changed by anything short of another overriding expression by this same political unity, or through a supplanting decision by another political unity occupying the same political space. Constitutional laws, the positive laws that elaborate what the legal constitution entails, may be changed in accordance with the rules for constitutional change given in a constitution itself. But the ability to change a constitutional law through an amendment to the constitution does not imply the ability to change the foundational principles of the constitution as a whole: "That 'the constitution' can be changed should not be taken to mean that the fundamental political decisions that constitute the substance of the constitution can be eliminated at any time by parliament and replaced through some other decision. The German Reich cannot be transformed into an absolute monarchy or into a Soviet republic through a two-thirds majority decision of the Reichstag" (Schmitt 2008, 79).[7] Instead, according to Schmitt (80), "constitution 'making' and constitutional 'change' [by constitutional amendment] are *qualitatively* different because in the first instance the word 'constitution' denotes the constitution as complete, total decision, while in the other instance, it denotes only the individual, constitutional *law*."

For Schmitt, a constituent assembly must be different from an ordinary parliament because only the constituent assembly can make a constitution. But also, for Schmitt, a constitution in the existential sense must not be confused with the specific written form that a particular constitution takes as it emerges from a constituent assembly. In any actual constitutional-drafting process, compromises among the different factions represented in the process are inevitable. Schmitt believed that one could and should see through these expedient political compromises to the more basic principles that grounded any existing constitution, principles so basic that they went without saying for all concerned when the constitutional text was written.

For example, Schmitt (2008, 90) found that the basic constitutional principles of the Weimar Constitution included: (1) the establishment of a bourgeois *Rechtsstaat* that put rights at the core of its existence, in which the principle of liberty was the "defining directive"; (2) the commitment to nonconcentration of political control, which found expression in the division of powers; and (3) the entrenchment of a basic political organization that could not be fundamentally altered by any particular set of temporary rulers, distilled in the idea of limited government. While specific features of the positive constitution could be changed or even suspended, this central creation—a rule-of-law state that put rights, division of powers, and the constitutional entrenchment of a political order at the core—could be modified not by any subsequent actual government in power but only by the political unity itself.

Schmitt's idea of the political unity is in many ways as compelling and also as mysterious as Rousseau's idea of the general will. But Schmitt gives this idea somewhat more concrete content when he describes this political unity as a historically changing force. In his account, this historically changing force is not abstract; it is different for each different political community, and it may be differently constituted at different moments for the same political community. As a result, the English constitution is different from the French, which is different in turn from the German—and each constitution has continually changing contours as the political community remakes itself over time. In each national tradition, the sequence of governmental forms—from absolute monarchy to constitutional monarchy to democratic republic, for example—is imagined by Schmitt to be the result of decisions of differently constituted political communities organizing themselves in successive waves across history. Each political community, considering its own history and its own aspirations, has the power to determine its own constitution by making a decision as to its own political form.

How does one know what the political unity is in order to understand the decision it has made? Schmitt (2008, 125), like Rousseau, locates this power in the idea of a political will:

> The constitution-making power is the political will, whose power or authority is capable of making the concrete comprehensive decision over the type and form of its political existence. The decision, therefore, defines the existence of the political unity in toto. . . .

> . . . In contrast to any dependence on a normative or abstract justice, the world "will" denotes the essentially existential character of this ground of validity.

For Schmitt, the constitution must therefore be understood as the decision by a political community to bring a certain form of political life into being. The constitution-making power that brings a constitution into existence "is unified and indivisible. It is not a coordinate additional authority (legislative, executive, judicial . . .) alongside other 'powers' and 'divisions of power'" (126). Instead, it is a foundational power that exists before and over all others (to borrow spatial metaphors). Building on Sieyès's formulation of the *pouvoir constituant*, Schmitt (128) concluded: "The people, the nation, remains the origin of all political action, the source of all power, which expresses itself in continually new forms, producing for itself these ever renewing forms and organizations. It does so, however, without ever subordinating itself, its political existence, to a conclusive formation."

According to Schmitt, while one constitution may succeed another in the same political space, such a succession may only be legitimately accomplished by a new decision made by the political unity, by the common will of the political community. From this understanding of the constituent power, one can discern the difference between a constitution-making power and a constitutional amendment in Schmitt's theory. Schmitt (2008, 150–151) argued that a constitutional amendment, determined by the ordinary representatives of a political community and not by the extraordinary representatives of the political unity, operates within a much more constrained political space than does the constitution-making process itself:

> The authority to "amend the constitution" granted by constitutional legislation means that other constitutional provisions can substitute for individual or multiple ones. They may do so, however, only under the presupposition that the identity and continuity of the constitution as an entirety is preserved. This means that the authority for constitutional amendment contains only the grant of authority to undertake changes, additions, extensions, deletions, etc., in constitutional provisions that preserve the constitution itself. . . .
>
> . . . *Constitutional amendment, therefore, is not constitutional annihilation*. . . . A constitution resting on the constitution-making

> power of the people cannot be transformed into a constitution of the monarchical principle by way of a constitutional "amendment."

This trajectory of political thought—from Sieyès inspired by Rousseau to Schmitt—emphasizes that constitutional change has limits. One sees these limits play themselves out differently in the three different phases of constitutional construction: constitution-making, constitutional amendment, and ordinary political life under a constitution. From this trajectory of ideas, one learns that there are limits to constitutional change, first and most clearly in the sense that a constitution can itself be created only as an expression of the general will of the political community. While constitution-making cannot be constrained by prior constitutions, it can be constrained by the requirement that a general will and not simply the will of a subset or a fraction of the political community underwrite the foundational elements of this new constitution.

Within any specific constitution-drafting process, however, some provisions of the positive constitution will emerge out of the inevitable political compromises that are made among those who are concretely sitting in the constituent assembly. Their different interests may lead to contingent but not foundational aspects of the new constitution.[8] These contingent provisions, traceable to some specific set of interests that are not general, can be changed by later amendment. But no later amendment can change the foundational elements of a constitution without transgressing the limits of a constituted power. Only the constituent power may make such fundamental changes; constituted power must stay within those limits. In daily constitutional life, of course, there may be contestation over the shape and meaning of the constitution as it applies to concrete political controversies. But as one moves from constitution-making to constitutional amendment to ordinary constitutional interpretation and contestation, the ability of ordinary participants to change the basic political order is ever more sharply constrained.

It follows from this analysis that a particular government that transgresses these limits on the constitution-making and constitutional amendment procedures will produce a breakdown in the existing constitutional order by creating a profound unconstitutionality of action. Such a breakdown can occur either if a government amends the constitution in a way that violates the basic principles of the constitution or if a government brings into being a new constitution without establishing that the will of the political community is unified on the need for and shape of this new constitution. Making amendments to constitutional fundamental principles and/or drafting a wholly new constitution without a political mandate to do so are both violations of the constitutional order that should call into question whether the new order is constitutional at all. There is, in other words, a possibility that a constituent power can itself be unconstitutional.

Democracy and Constituent Power in the Twenty-First Century

So far this discussion has been suitably abstract—about no particular political community and about no particular time. But both Sieyès and Schmitt were very much writing about particular communities in particular moments. Arguably, their theories are most clearly useful at such obvious junctures in history when a country changes course as the result of a violent break with its immediate autocratic past and attempts to set up a democratic government. Sieyès needed a new political vocabulary to describe political authority after the French Revolution; Schmitt created a new political vocabulary to legitimate the German constitutional order after World War I.

Necessity is the mother of invention, as the saying goes. In the realm of law, constitutional crises create a need for constitutional theory. Constitutional theory, however, easily forgets its roots. If one takes these ideas about constituent power out of their revolutionary context, then one might assume that all constituent power is as unbound as the examples that Sieyès and Schmitt used as the invisible empirical templates for their thinking. We need to recontextualize these ideas to see their limits.

Constituent power, in moments of political transition, becomes a sort of conjuring trick, a way of announcing that there is no break in legal authority since, at the revolutionary moment, people rise up to take state power into their own hands and create their own political future before they have managed to establish new institutions of self-governance. The idea of a constituent power, then, signals that there is never a political void and that the only sort of legitimate government formed from this point onward will be one with a democratic pedigree.

As this formulation makes clear, the very idea of constituent power builds in the role of "the people" at revolutionary moments; no other authority can stand in the place of the constituent power but the people themselves. In short, constituent power is, at its heart, a democratic idea.

The theory of constituent power rose with the establishment of written democratic constitutions and the idea of constituent power does no legitimating work without a theory of democracy. The legitimacy of a constitution does not rest on the connection between the fictive and actual authors of a constitutional text unless these fictive authors are imagined as democratically self-governing. The idea of constituent power is the prime mover in a system of democratic legitimacy because only "the people" can create a new regime with democratic aspirations that is justified by its own moral force. The people cannot be bound by what precedes this moment precisely because the prior governments were not bound by the people. Autocracies justified the rule of particular political leaders either through divine right or the valorization of force, or both. The appeal of the idea of constituent power lies precisely in the bridging role it plays between governments legitimated from the top down and governments legitimated from the bottom up because the bottom-up perspective is generalized as a force that lives through history and therefore is ever-present to rise to power when it can.

Practically speaking, the theory of constituent power has a special role at the moment when a country is shifting from an autocratic to a democratic form of government. Constituent power stands in relation to democracy the way that the divine right of kings stands with respect to monarchy. It is the legitimating ground on which this form of government stands and it marks the passage from autocratic into democratic rule.

This contextualization of the idea of constituent power suggests that an appeal to the democratic force of the people can only be used to expand and deepen a democratic order, and never to expand or limit it. The constituent power, as a revolutionary popular force, can only press for its own more perfect realization. A constituent power, given its democratic pedigree, cannot be used to justify a move from democracy to autocracy. It cannot be used to cast out those who were once included from the constitutional-democratic space absent their active consent.

Suppose, for example, that the white minority population in South Africa decided that it could not be self-governing in a polity where black voters were always guaranteed to have majority power. Suppose that these discontent whites in South African convened a constituent assembly, invoking constituent power, to draft a new constitution for South Africa that would allow whites to govern alone and would put the African and other minority populations into a kind of democratic receivership in which the white minority would make decisions for all.

Constituent power in action? One might recoil at the thought. But why, precisely?

The answer must be that constituent power as a legitimating concept cannot be used to deprive a segment of the population from its rightful ability to engage in self-governance. Practically speaking, this doesn't mean that all those who will be governed by a constitution necessarily have to be part of the process in which the constitution is created. But in its representative role, the constituent power cannot be sectarian; it cannot speak for some and not for others within its jurisdiction. It cannot put the interests of some in the political community above others. It must take the self-governing aspirations of all into account and attempt to represent them in the construction of common political community. Thus the actual historical invocation of constituent power to move from the white-dominant South African constitutional order to the multiracial and inclusive South African constitutional order was appropriate. Invoking constituent power to legitimate the move from an inclusive South Africa to a white-dominant South Africa is a category mistake.

A move from an inclusive democratic government to an exclusionary one cannot therefore not be justified in the name of a constituent power. A move from a flawed or partial constitutional democratic government to a more inclusive one can be. Hence the constituent power works as a one-way ratchet, justifying ever more inclusiveness, ever more democratic depth of participation, ever more enforcement of rights.

Or, so I contend, the abstract theory of constituent power must hold. But abstractions only get us so far. Let's examine a hard case where the identity and existence of a constituent power is a serious political question—repeatedly over a space of decades. Let us, then, turn to Hungary.

The "Rule-of-Law Revolution" of 1989–1990 and the Post-Communist Hungarian Constitution

After decades of living under a Soviet-imposed regime, Hungary went through dramatic political changes in 1989–1990 that resulted in a new constitution. The self-appointed democratic opposition in Hungary sought to negotiate a peaceful transition from Communism to democracy in 1989 and called upon the party in power to develop a new framework that would allow a multiparty election to occur and a new constitution to be written. The Hungarian National Roundtable of 1989 produced a new constitutional text that was adopted as a set of amendments to the existing Stalinist constitution, Law XX of 1949. At the National Roundtable, the democratic opposition groups negotiated directly with the Hungarian Socialist Workers Party (MSzMP) with the participation of a "third side" consisting of officially sanctioned organizations. The pacted transition of 1989–1990 that resulted from the National Roundtable allowed the country to move toward a system of multiparty elections, democratic transformation, rule of law, and general constitutional entrenchment.

Was the constitution produced through the Hungarian National Roundtable process the expression of a general will, as a constitution-making process requires? At one level, the situation was not promising. The Communist government was still operating in the shadow of the Soviet Union with the presence of Soviet troops in the country. It could not operate independently without considering whether its actions would be seen as having crossed invisible red lines drawn by Moscow. Even with what eventually turned out to be substantial political room to maneuver, the MSzMP government in 1989 did not have any democratic legitimacy of its own because it had been installed and maintained in power by a foreign force. The democratic opposition was self-appointed and hardly representative of the whole Hungarian population whose political views could not be fully probed at that time. The vast majority of the Hungarian population became mere spectators to the public part of the National Roundtable, which was a highly staged demonstration of the fact that negotiations were going on without revealing much about their substance. In fact, bargaining over the fundamental aspects of the constitution happened in subcommittees that were not visible to the public eye.[9] At first glance, the 1989 National Roundtable did not look like a will-forming or will-expressing constituent assembly.

That said, the situation was more ideal for constitution writing than one might imagine. It was clear that the winds of change were blowing through the region, but it was not at all clear what their effects would be. Prior to the National Roundtable, János Kádár had already been pushed out of office after thirty-two years as general secretary of the Communist Party (the MSzMP), and he died as the Roundtable process got underway. It was not just Kádár who left office; a whole generation of hard-liners associated with the worst of the communist abuses was displaced with him. Though there were still a few communists left in power who could still be associated with the horrors of the 1950s, the MSzMP was already changing because reformers were in the ascendancy. While the Communist Party went through these changes, opposition groups were forming (and were allowed to form) under a variety of rubrics ranging from trade unions to NGOs.

Perestroika provided an opening for political change throughout the Soviet bloc, and both the communists and the opposition groups agreed that Hungary would move toward a different form of government. They agreed the Hungarian people should be able to express their political views through an election with real choices, though neither the communists nor the opposition could know who would be the winners and who would be the losers in an election of a sort not held in nearly half a century.[10] Because of this uncertainty, no one could design new political institutions in such a way as to ensure that they would be able to gain and maintain power over the long run. As a result, everyone had the incentive going into the constitution-writing process to design a new system of government in which no one would be too badly off if the new politics went against their interests.

In this evolving situation, the new constitution guaranteed that power could not be captured indefinitely by whichever party emerged victorious in one particular election. The National Roundtable produced a constitution in which all would have the protection of rights under the watchful eye of a new and powerful Constitutional Court, and in which there were many safeguards to guarantee that there were limits to what any new government could do to those who lost out. The negotiations at the National Roundtable, then, were rather like deliberations behind a veil of ignorance, to use John Rawls's (1971, 118–123) term for a situation in which people decide on the shape of a basic political ordering not knowing what interests they would have in the political system that they designed.[11] Because the moment was fluid and all parties were aware of the potential dangers, the new Hungarian constitution was written in a way that aspired to constitute a general will much more than one might have imagined. The situation led all those at the Roundtable—and those watching them eagerly as history changed from one day to the next—to design the new constitution from a general point of view that was not dictated primarily by the short-term self-interest of any of the parties. How could one benefit one's own interests if it was not clear how to do so—or even what one's interests were?

Technically developed as a set of amendments to the existing communist constitution, the new Hungarian constitution was voted on piecemeal by the existing communist parliament over two weeks in mid-October 1989.[12] The Hungarian Republic was officially declared on October 23, 1989, two weeks before the fall of the Berlin Wall, with the adoption of this fundamentally new constitution. While the Hungarian parliament that passed this new constitution was itself neither representative nor legitimate, it largely deferred to the National Roundtable process and approved the constitution that the National Roundtable produced. It added a few amendments, for example, inserting a limitations clause on the rights provisions, permitting their restriction to defend public order, public security, public health, and public morality, as well as supplementing the list of agreed-upon rights with a provision about the right to social security (Arato and Miklósi 2010). The constitutional amendments were supplemented by a series of cardinal laws requiring a two-thirds vote of the parliament.[13] These laws were also agreed upon at the Roundtable, and they shaped crucial institutions in the new government, such as the Constitutional Court, the political parties, and the framework for elections (in particular expanding the number of individual constituencies). But otherwise, the parliament in 1989 agreed to exactly what had been negotiated at the National Roundtable.[14]

The 1989 constitution made a radical break with the 1949 constitution in substance, even as it was enacted using the amendment rules of that very constitution. Was the new 1989 constitution legitimate as a new constitution—and were these 1989 constitutional amendments legitimate amendments to the prior 1949 constitution? Insofar as the comprehensive amendments of 1989 completely changed the structure of Hungarian government from a party-state to a multiparty republic and from a state without guaranteed rights to a state that ensured rights for all, the changes of 1989 could not reasonably be thought of as mere constitutional amendments, though they took that form. The basic principles of the supremacy of the party-state and the guiding role of socialism could not be converted to principles of separation of powers and respect for liberal, bourgeois rights without fundamentally changing the 1949 constitution. Following from the theory of constitutional change elaborated in the first section of this essay, such radical change could only be accomplished by a constitutional founding rather than by an amendment of the old order. Making the changes formally as constitutional amendments does not settle their status from the standpoint of a theory of constituent power. For the changes to be legitimate under the conception of a constitutional order discussed above, a new constituent power had to be formed to make these amendments legitimate. But was such a constituent power present during this transition?

János Kis (1998), in a brilliant formulation of pacted transitions like the Hungarian one, explained that the old order in 1989 was already in the midst a legitimation crisis.[15] Such a crisis created the precondition for a new constitution that could be negotiated between those who held power and those who aspired to share that power. Unlike the revolutionary times through which Sieyès lived, when power was seized from one group by another, the "coordinated transition" of 1989 did not involve a public seizure of power or, for that matter, even a public repudiation of the old order. Instead, old and new orders cooperated so as not to leave a legal vacuum as the country moved from one political system into another. But the transition was no less radical for its cooperative nature. In a pacted transition,

> coordination cannot be maintained unless the holders of institutional power are ready and able to cooperate with the groups that belong to the extra-institutional opposition. Those in power do not have sufficient authority to secure compliance with the rule of the system during the transition period. They need additional authority and the opposition leaders are ready to lend it, provided there is an acceptable agreement on the changes that are to be implemented. . . . [This kind of political change] is marked by a conscious strategy to preserve coordination. (Kis 1998, 319)

The result, according to Kis, is "a transition scenario toward a new regime with a basis of legitimacy, which is incompatible with the belief that the old regime is legitimate as well" (320). In short, this structure of transition could constitute a constitution-founding moment because those who were designing the new constitutional order for themselves (and this included those who would be losing power as well as those who stood to gain) made a decision in this moment on the basic principles that would structure their new political life together. Those new principles represented a fundamental break with the old order even as elements of the old order helped the new order into existence. The agreement on the new order therefore extended to those members of the *ancien régime* who were themselves going to live in this new political order.

There is nothing in the idea of the *pouvoir constituant* that requires a radical break of political form in order to achieve a radical break in the underlying legitimacy of the system. True, a constituent power would not be *bound* by the prior political system; as a result, it was not strictly necessary for the 1989–1990 Hungarian constitution to have been achieved by constitutional amendment of the old system. But neither was it necessary to have a radical break in the underlying legitimating principle of the new constitution, creating formal legal discontinuity.

A constituent power may create a wholly new constitution, even if the new constitution has some structural elements in common with the previous one (and for that matter, even shares some of the same people in power). For example, the constitution that resulted from the French constituent assembly in 1789–1791 maintained the monarchy but put the king under constitutional constraint. There was a complete break in the legitimation of the two regimes, however, even though both shared not just the institution of the king, but also the same actual king. The new regime did not have to keep the king (either office or person), of course. The constituent power formed in that historical moment of the early French Revolution could have chosen a republic. But the fact that the revolutionaries at first created a constitutional monarchy did not mean that a constituent power had not been mobilized or that the new system failed to have a fundamentally different basis for legitimacy than had the *ancien régime*.[16]

The Hungarian transition in 1989–1990 was made possible by the fact that the Kádár government retained the support of virtually no one, not even those within the MSzMP who had, after all, deposed him and his circle before the transition began in earnest. Those from the MSzMP who took control of the government in 1988–1989 were largely (though not entirely) a group of reformers, already bent on changing the system. Even before convening the Roundtable, the new Communist government had passed a series of new laws that brought elements of liberalism to the state. Laws on the right of association, the right of assembly, and the right to strike passed the parliament in spring 1989, and a new draft constitution that would substantially liberalize the government was already being proposed by the new MSzMP justice minister and his staff months before that. The reformers within the MSzMP had already wanted to change the constitutional framework dramatically in 1988–1989. Not only had the appearances and reality of government in Hungary always been separated in the communist regime, but also they were increasingly and publicly *seen to have come apart* as opposition to the regime grew. And the reformers within the Communist Party wanted to fix this.

The communist constitution, Law XX of 1949, still had many pretty rights whose actual realization depended upon arbitrary decisions of state and party officials. A consistent enforcement of law was important to the legitimacy of the state, and yet those who lived under state socialism could never be certain that the law would be enforced as written. The legal system looked good in many respects on paper, but it was not real in daily life. The reformers from within the MSzMP were trying to bring the reality and promise of law together. A new constitution could hasten a transition to a more liberal government, or so the reformers thought.[17]

In the meantime, the political opposition had developed a highly legalistic view about how to lodge their protests to the arbitrariness of the communist system. Opposition members refused a strategy of violating the law to express their judgment that the regime was illegitimate. Instead, the political opposition urged everyone to *follow* the law in every particular:

> During periods of a legitimation crisis, disobedient behavior generally consists in breaking the law. In those countries of Eastern Europe where the democratic opposition was successful in laying down some kind of political tradition, the main form of disobedience was not violating the law, however, but sticking to it, practicing it publicly, challenging the power-holders to come to terms with the rules of a legal state in which citizens have rights. . . . Legalism was a highly relevant feature of the transition from communism to democracy in countries like Hungary. (Kis 1998, 335–336)

This strategy of compulsive adherence to legality on the part of the democratic opposition meant that their fundamental critique of the socialist system did not require a complete repudiation of prior law. Instead, the critique took the form that the regime should live up to the commitments that the law already promised. As a result, much of the law could remain the same in a political transition even as the basis for the political legitimacy of that law shifted underneath its unchanging surface. What did need to change, however, was the structure and, most important, the accountability of the government itself.

Both the reform communists and the democratic opposition came to the Roundtable agreed that the law should be made real and that a new government would be constituted after a multiparty election. This put a new constitution into focus, though at first differently for each side. While the reform communists wanted to enact a new constitution quickly, the democratic opposition thought that only an elected constituent assembly with public legitimacy should make such a fundamental change—and that would have to wait until after free elections occurred. In short, the reform Communists and the democratic opposition disagreed on how to constitute the constituent power.

The Roundtable negotiations arrived at the conclusion that the new political system would make as radical a break with the old system as the government in Moscow would permit. Convening a constituent assembly would have been provocative. But as 1989 went on and it became more and more clear that Moscow would not in fact intervene, the constitutional talks got bolder and bolder about the change that all thought was possible.

Both the MSzMP and the democratic opposition changed their positions as the Roundtable talks went on. The MSzMP agreed to put its fate before the Hungarian electorate without guarantees that it would control any of the key branches of power under a new constitution, and the democratic opposition agreed to more constitutional change than they had originally thought was wise before an election could legitimate (and perhaps amplify) their bargaining power. In fact, as the MSzMP Justice Ministry officials rolled out their constitutional proposals through the summer of 1989, the democratic opposition realized that the constitution that they could negotiate in the Roundtable subcommittees provide enough guarantees of political fairness for all sides that it became "worth defending."[18] In the end, both the MSzMP and the Opposition Roundtable agreed on a sweeping package of constitutional changes that not only guided the transition to a multiparty republic but also set up the key institutions of the new government, added a strong bill of rights, and created a Constitutional Court to defend the new constitution.[19]

The constitution that emerged from the Roundtable process in the fall of 1989 made many major alterations to the 1949 constitution. The governing party and the democratic opposition disagreed most intensely, however, over how the new president of the new republic would be selected. Since this issue could not be resolved within the Roundtable due to repeated deadlock, both the MSzMP and the democratic opposition agreed to put the question to the Hungarian public as a whole in a referendum, which was held in November 1989. The referendum determined that the new president was to be elected by the parliament rather than by general election, taking the democratic opposition's position in the debate, albeit with a very narrow majority.[20]

A list of some of the changes in the new constitution of 1989 will reveal how comprehensive the revision of the 1949 text was.[21] The new constitution provided that "parties shall not directly exercise public power and accordingly, no party shall direct any state organ" (Hungarian Constitution 1989, Article 3(3)). Parliament's power was strengthened so that it was the "supreme organ of state power and popular representation" with the power to "guarantee the constitutional order of society" and "determine the organization, direction and conditions of governmental activity" (Hungarian Constitution 1989, Article 19). As a rejection of the strong executive-ministerial powers during the Soviet period, the constitution mandated that the parliament was to meet during nine months of each year (Article 22).[22] But the 1989 constitution left the Soviet-style Council of Ministers largely unchanged, still possessing the power to issue decrees (Articles 33–40). In a significant addition to the constitutional framework, however, any minister or even the whole Council of Ministers could be subject to a vote of no confidence by the parliament (Article 39A), after which a new minister had to be named or a new council had to be formed. Through the revisions of 1989, the formerly supreme Council of Ministers became accountable to the parliament, which was itself about to change its party composition substantially.

The first multiparty elections in the late spring of 1990 put a center-right government composed of parties from the democratic opposition into power. The MDF (Hungarian Democratic Forum) formed a government with the conservative Smallholders and Christian Democratic parties. Shortly after the election, in which the Socialists (successor party to the MSzMP) won only 11 percent of the vote, a new set of major constitutional amendments was passed by the new parliament, rounding out the transition that had begun the year before.[23] In these constitutional changes, the Council of Ministers was finally abolished and replaced by a prime minister and ministerial government on a parliamentarist model (Hungarian Constitution 1989, as amended May 1990, Chapter VII). In addition, the general limitation clause on rights—that they could be legally infringed in the name of public order, public security, public health, and public morals—was removed.

The new center-right government could have decided to govern on its own. Instead, the largest party in the government entered into a power-limiting agreement[24] with the largest party in opposition. The Hungarian Democratic Forum (MDF) agreed with the opposition Free Democrats (SzDSz) that major governmental institutions and foundational areas of state policy would be decided upon not by a simple majority, but instead by a supermajority of two-thirds that would require the governing parties to consult and agree with the political opposition. This inclusive move,[25] which revealed both self-limitation of those in power and an agreement that crucial aspects of this new state would always be decided upon by a coalition of multiple political forces,[26] represented a commitment to govern as a political unity, as Schmitt might call it. As such, one may be warranted in concluding that the Hungarian transition, with its multiple multiparty pacts and its frequent consultation with the population as a whole (first through referendum and then through election), did in fact summon a *pouvoir constituant* to create a new constitution.

What were the foundational principles underlying this new constitution? While those involved in the constitutional drafting process never produced a list of these principles,[27] we can derive such principles from the most important elements of the various agreements from which no major faction dissented. While there was disagreement on specifics within the constitutional order, several principles were so taken for granted at the time that there were no serious proposals to the contrary under consideration.

First, consistent with Christopher McCrudden's argument elsewhere in this volume concerning trends in modern constitutionalism, the 1989–1990 constitution is centrally committed to human dignity, bolstered by a long list of constitutionally guaranteed rights. Rights had been hollow in the Soviet time; the transition enabled the rights that existed previously only on paper to become real. Moreover, the Roundtable process had brought Hungary into line with its international legal commitments by adding to the constitution virtually all of the rights the state had committed to defend through its ratification of international human rights treaties. The commitment to the legal enforceability of rights was realized through the creation of a powerful and independent Constitutional Court that could review all laws for their consistency with the new constitution, particularly the rights provisions. The realization of rights, centrally organized through the concept of human dignity, was a core element of the new constitution with which no political faction disagreed.

Second, the 1989–1990 constitution established the principle that Hungary would be a democratic, multiparty republic. The move from a communist state to a democratic republic was a key feature of the transition, signaled by the importance in the constitution of electoral mechanisms of political change. Moreover, given the history of the one-party state that preceded the new Hungarian republic, it was essential that this new democratic government retain its multiparty character. No single party could capture the government, as was evidenced in a crucial principle added in the 1989 constitutional changes: "No single social organization, state organ, or citizen shall . . . capture or exercise power by force or exclusive possession thereof. It shall be a right and a duty of everyone to take action under the law against such designs" (Hungarian Constitution, 1989, Article 2(3)).[28] But the new constitution never created a plebiscitary democracy, despite the use of a referendum in the process of constitutional creation. Instead, Hungary was firmly a republic, governing through representatives who were themselves democratically elected. These three elements—creating a democratic, multiparty, and republican state—marked the core agreement over the form of government Hungary would have under the new constitution. Again, there was no public challenge to this view at the time.

Finally, the 1989–1990 constitution distinguished itself from its predecessor in entrenching the principle of self-limiting power. The party-state had refused any limits on its own jurisdiction; the new Republic of Hungary would be characterized by a government that did not claim control over all of daily life. First, this was evidenced in the independence of individuals from the state, contained in the idea of fundamental rights. Second, this was evidenced in the withdrawal of the state from the economy and society, reflected in the constitutional protection of both free association and a free market. Finally, self-limitation of power was a founding principle because all major decisions in those crucial two years during which the constitution was created rejected simple majoritarianism as sufficient for the most crucial decisions that the state had to make.[29] These self-limitations were also enforced by the Constitutional Court, which had the power to scrutinize all laws in the light of the new constitution for their compatibility with these principles. Handing such power to the court was another act of the self-limitation even of democratically elected majorities.

If we take the basic principles of the 1989–1990 constitution to be (1) the protection of human dignity through the protection of rights, (2) the creation of a democratic, multiparty republic and (3) the self-limitation of state power, then the Constitutional Court's task was to elaborate and defend these principles as the guarantor of the constitution's integrity.

The Constitutional Court and the Invisible Constitution: Building the Constitutional Consensus

The new constitution created the new Hungarian Constitutional Court. The Constitutional Court was the first part of the new structure to operate when it opened on January 1, 1990, fully five months before the first election. The court immediately started to issue path-breaking decisions, indicating that it was going to take the new constitution seriously and create what the first court president László Sólyom (2000, 1, 38) would later call the "revolution under the rule of law." If the previous communist government had failed to take law seriously, the Constitutional Court would indicate its revolutionary break from the past by making the rule of law one of its key normative pillars. All laws consistent with the new constitution would begin to be enforced as written, starting immediately.

The Constitutional Court quickly stepped into the role of the guardian of this new constitution (Scheppele 2006) as it elaborated on what the new constitution meant. Nowhere was the role and operating theory of the new court more evident than in President Sólyom's concurring opinion in the death penalty case in late October 1990. In this opinion, Sólyom first proposed the idea of the "invisible constitution." The new invisible constitution had to stand above constant parliamentary attempts at revision, because a foundational principle of this new constitution was that it should be entrenched as a limit to state power. Sólyom's particular worry was that the new democratically elected parliament would keep amending the constitution to the point where its foundational elements would become blurry and its entrenchment would be under threat. Implicitly relying on the arc of constitutional theory we examined in the first part of this chapter, Sólyom created a distinction between the text of the constitution (what Schmitt would call the positive constitutional law) and the principles followed by the constituent power that had created the constitutional order (what Schmitt would call the foundational constitution). The invisible constitution was the set of crucial principles that made up the foundational constitution's commitments, which Sólyom called "the standard of constitutionality above the constitution." Being the result of an act of constituent power, the foundational principles of the constitutional order could not be changed by mere constitutional amendment. In forwarding this principle, Sólyom joined the distinguished set of constitutional theorists who believed it was crucial to distinguish between the *pouvoir constituant* and the *pouvoir constitué.*

The emergence of the idea of the invisible constitution in the death penalty case was highly symbolic. Less than one year into its work, the Constitutional Court heard this signature case, crucial because of the central role of the death penalty in the transformation of the Hungarian state. Under the communist government, the death penalty marked the absolute power of the state over the individual, and it was used for political crimes above all. After the 1956 uprising, about 230 people had been executed, most after trials before judges of questionable independence. Among those executed was Imre Nagy, prime minister during the temporary government established during the uprising. Nagy's symbolic reburial in June 1989 was the most visible sign that the communist monopoly on symbolic power had ended. In the new democratic and multiparty republic that followed, where human dignity was fundamental and the state was to come under constitutional control, the new constitution now marked the end of the communist claim to absolute power. But the death penalty remained on the books as one of its last remnants.

Ending the death penalty in 1990 was not politically controversial among political elites. The outgoing communist government, which had the option to defend the law before the court, refused to do so and even suggested that European legal development pushed Hungary in the direction of abolition. The chief state prosecutor, Kálmán Györgyi, who was also asked for his opinion by the Constitutional Court, also urged the death penalty's demise. Academic experts appointed by the court additionally found the death penalty to be indefensible under the country's new constitution. In its judgment, surprising no one, the court joined them all by finding the death penalty to be unconstitutional.[30] Only one dissent to the decision was filed; Justice Schmidt argued that the parliament and not the court should abolish the death penalty. But he certainly did not argue that the death penalty should stay.

Taking the opportunity in such a historic decision to mark what the case stood for in symbolic terms, President Sólyom's lengthy and theoretically ambitious concurring opinion went beyond the specific case to outline a particular theory of the new constitution and a particular role for the Constitutional Court in this new constitutional system. Pointing out that Hungary had gotten not just a new constitutional text, but a new constitutional order, Sólyom argued that Hungary now also had a new invisible constitution. In determining what the constitution was and what it meant, the Constitutional Court had a special role, according to Sólyom:

> The Constitutional Court must continue in its effort to explain the theoretical bases of the Constitution and of the rights included in it and to form a coherent system with its decisions, which as an "invisible Constitution" provides for a reliable standard of constitutionality beyond the Constitution, which nowadays is often amended out of current political interests; and therefore this coherent system will probably not conflict with the new Constitution to be established or with future Constitutions. The Constitutional Court enjoys freedom

> in this process as long as it remains within the framework of the concept of constitutionality. (Sólyom and Brunner 2000, 125–126)

With this analysis, Sólyom put the Constitutional Court in the position of a constituted power operating *under* the constitution's mandate. That said, the court was a privileged interpreter of the meaning of the constitution because it had the mandate to exclude "current political interests" in the course of making its decisions. Instead the task of the court was to be the expositor of a coherent system of legal values that would underwrite both this constitution and future constitutions[31] by referring back to what was decided by the constituent power mobilized at the time of constitutional drafting.

By the invisible constitution, President Sólyom identified a "principled coherence" to the constitution that could not be destroyed by amendments. The idea was both more and less powerful than its advocates wanted. It was less powerful than its advocates wished because the Constitutional Court never actually used the idea of an invisible constitution to ground any decisions or to limit amendments that could be made to the constitutional text. But it was more powerful than its detractors may have wanted because it began the process through which the Constitutional Court would elaborate the fundamental principles of the new constitutional order, beginning in the death penalty case with the centrality of human dignity.

President Sólyom's death penalty concurrence also implicitly acknowledged another fundamental principle of the new constitution: its self-limiting quality. No longer could the state assert primacy over all others in its territory; in the death penalty case, the dignity of the individual emerged as the untouchable core of the individual's relationship not only to the state but to others. With human dignity as a clear and unquestionable limit to state power, the new constitution had fundamentally transformed the state from one where the goals of the state dominated all other features of the society to one in which the state had limits. Abolishing the death penalty was one clear sign that things had changed—and had changed fundamentally.

President Sólyom's invocation of "constitutionality beyond the Constitution" was nonetheless disturbing to those not familiar with the arc of constitutional theory running from Emmanuel Sieyès through Carl Schmitt. Against that background, President Sólyom was simply asserting that neither the Constitutional Court nor any other configuration of state officials had the power to change the fundamental constitution created by the *pouvoir constituant*. Following this theoretical framework in which the constituent power and the constituted power were subject to different limits, Sólyom was merely stating the obvious to constitutional theorists, however shocking his pronouncement may have seemed at the time. Principles of the fundamental constitution could not be changed by the court or by the parliament, not even through the procedure of a constitutional amendment. Therefore, when the Constitutional Court explained that the unconstitutionality of the death penalty implicated the fundamental principle of human dignity, there was nothing the parliament could do to restore the death penalty again. The court was not writing a new constitution; it was explaining what the constituent power mobilized in the 1989–1990 constitutional drafting process had already decided.

As we can see from this account, the creation of a constituent power around the 1989 transition was not captured in a single constitutional assembly. Instead, it comprised a multistage process that started with the National Roundtable, followed by the amendment of the 1949 constitution by the last communist parliament, followed by the public referendum on the presidency, followed by the multiparty election, followed by the Paktum—and after January 1, 1990, the elaboration of the 1989–1990 multiparty agreements was coordinated by Constitutional Court (which was itself further certified by its high public approval). By the time all of those agreements and public certifications had occurred, Hungary had a constitutional system that was really taken for granted by all players in the system. In the 1989–1990 constitution, then, constituent power had expressed itself and created the framework for a new Hungarian constitutional system.

The 1989–1990 Constitution as Transitional

The 1989–1990 constitution had an Achilles' heel. Despite having successfully instantiated a constituent power, the new constitution always claimed that it was merely temporary. Given that it was written in a period of rapid political change, the various parties to the political transformation of 1989–1990 believed that they might, with reflection, do better once it was clear just what new state would emerge. As a result, the constitution was explicitly written as a transitional constitution, one to guide the new state until such time as the transition was complete. The preamble of the 1989–1990 constitution reflected this view: "In order to facilitate a peaceful political transition to a constitutional state, establish a multi-party system, parliamentary democracy and a social market economy, the Parliament of the Republic of Hungary hereby establishes the following text as the Constitution of the Republic of Hungary, until the country's new Constitution is adopted."[32]

That preamble raised a question that the text itself did not answer: When, then, was the transition over, so that a new constitution should replace the 1989–1990 one? Hungary had so quickly developed normal politics organized around a relatively stable six-party parliament that the transition seemed to be over before the first decade was out. Already in 1995, then, the government that was elected in the second free, multiparty election initiated a process to write a new constitution.

But the government of 1995 was no ordinary government. The election of 1994 brought the Socialists and the SzDSz together to form a *two-thirds* government.[33] The Socialists won an absolute majority of seats in the parliament and so could have governed alone; welcoming the SzDSz on board both broadened the coalition and relieved the anxieties of those who were nervous about the post–communist party running the government again so soon after its predecessor party had claimed a monopoly on power. But the coalition generated new worries: with two-thirds of the parliamentary mandates, the new government could theoretically do anything. One aspect of the 1949 constitution that had *not* been changed was the amendment rule that allowed a single two-thirds vote of the parliament to amend any provision of the text.

The constituent power that brought the 1989–1990 constitution into being agreed on three principles: that the new constitution required a commitment to the defense of individual rights, a multiparty democratic republic, and a self-limiting government. To change any one of these would require the mobilization of a new constituent power; amendments short of that could still be considered as amendments. Rather than challenge these constituent principles, however, Socialist-SzDSz government organized the new constitutional drafting process to realize those basic principles more fully. While the government could have changed the constitution by itself, the government used its two-thirds vote in the parliament to amend the constitution to require a *four-fifths* vote of the parliament to agree to a process through which a new constitution would be written. In short, as the first government possessed of the absolute constitution-changing power, the Socialist-SzDSz government of 1995 chose to put that power out of its reach.

In doing this, the government acknowledged both the centrality of a multiparty republic (requiring parties outside the government to participate in the constitutional drafting process) and also a self-limiting government (because the first supermajority put itself under even more onerous constraints).

Upon acquiring the four-fifths vote necessary to begin a new constitutional drafting process, the parliament charged a constitutional drafting committee composed of parliamentarians to come up with a new constitutional draft. Under the ground rules agreed by this super-supermajority of the parliament, the committee proceeded by starting with the 1989–1990 constitution, only changing any of its provisions if five of the six parliamentary parties agreed to the change. As a result of these ground rules, any two parties acting together—regardless of the size of their faction in the parliament—could block a change to the constitutional text.

In the end, as often happens with near-unanimity rules in complex political processes, the whole process foundered. The Smallholders Party, which had variously advocated a restoration of the monarchy and a return of the Holy Crown of St. Stephen to the center of the constitution, decided to boycott the process. The five remaining parties therefore had to agree all changes unanimously. While a number of changes were debated and received the approval of majorities of parliamentarians, no single change was able to clear the five-party threshold. As a result, the 1989–1990 constitution was left intact.

What did the failure of the 1995–1996 constitutional process signify? It is always hard to interpret a negative, but, at a minimum, it meant that there was no agreement on any other constitution besides the 1989–1990 constitution. While there were many proposals coming from different parts of the political spectrum to make changes big and small, none attracted the super-supermajorities required to actually refound the constitutional order. So Hungary's 1989–1990 constitution remained intact.

Perhaps more important for our purposes, however, the constituent power mobilized in 1989–1990 remained intact also. The values on which the constituent power agreed in the immediate post-communist transition guided the 1995–1996 constitutional drafting process so that those constitutional super-values were reinforced rather than rewritten. And then normal politics proceeded from there. No new constituent power was summoned or even attempted with the 1995–1996 constitutional drafting process. And so that constituent power—and that constitution—continued as the backbone of

Hungarian constitutionalism. For the next decade and a half, no more talk was heard about a new constitution.

The "Revolution of the Ballot Box" and Constitutional Change: What Are the Limits to Constitutional Amendment?

The election of 2010 produced a "revolution of the ballot box"[34] that soon resulted in the rapid adoption of a wholly new constitution. In the 2010 election, the center-right party Fidesz—in a joint party list with the Christian Democrats (KDNP)[35]—received 53 percent of the popular vote. In Hungary's complicated electoral system, that simple majority translated into 68 percent of the seats in the parliament.[36] With its two-thirds majority, the power to change everything in the constitutional order was in the hands of one political bloc. First through constitutional amendment and then through replacing the 1989–1990 constitution altogether, Fidesz claimed to exercise constituent power.

The 2010 election was run as a normal election, by contrast with the 1990 election, which had been run as a system-changing plebiscite. The campaign in 2010 did not feature pledges to change the constitutional order and voting did not carry the symbolic weight of choosing between an old and a new system of government. True, Hungarian politics in 2010 was spectacularly polarized. The Socialists were in disarray; the SzDSz had collapsed entirely; the far right was represented by a neo-fascist party called Jobbik and a new youth party of vaguely liberal and vaguely Green (but mostly vague) ideology called Politics Can Be Different (LMP) entered the scene. Only Fidesz remained a familiar and relatively untarnished alternative. But while Fidesz was eager to smear the Socialists and the Socialists returned the favor, nothing in the 2010 electoral campaign promised a radical system change. The election was a nasty version of politics as usual—but it was politics as usual.

That said, once the government headed by Fidesz leader Viktor Orbán took office, it claimed it had a mandate to change the constitutional order. Interpreting its two-thirds majority as the manifestation of a *pouvoir constituant*, Orbán announced his intention to create a new constitution, one that would finally and radically break from the Communist order of 1949–1989. Orbán denied that the 1989–1990 constitution had brought about a fundamental constitutional change and further denied that a legitimate constituent power had been summoned in those years. Instead, he and his party pledged to rewrite what they still called the "communist constitution."

At the time of the 2010 election, the constitution could still be amended by a single two-thirds vote of the parliament. But the constitution also said that a new constitutional drafting process could only be initiated by a four-fifths vote of the parliament.[37] As one of its first acts in power, the Fidesz parliament used its reliable two-thirds supermajority to amend the four-fifths rule, which paved the way for Fidesz to start a constitutional drafting process with only the votes of its own party. And so it did.

Before completing its own new constitution, the new Fidesz government amended the old constitution so frequently that the constitutional revolution occurred even before a new constitution was unveiled. Over the course of twelve constitutional amendments in its first year in office, the Fidesz government changed more than fifty different provisions in the 1989–1990 constitution (Bánkuti, Halmai, and Scheppele 2012).

While the Fidesz government eventually adopted a wholly new constitution in April 2011, one year after it took office, and has since continued to pursue constitutional changes, there is still an important question of how much a constitution can be changed by amendment within the limits of the prior authorizing constituent power. Were the constitutional changes of 2010–2011, including the new constitution itself, consistent with the principles that the constituent power had created and endorsed during the preceding twenty years? Or was this a new constitutional moment, in which a new constituent power was summoned up to change the basic principles of the new constitutional order?

Many of the constitutional amendments of 2010–2011 violated the core constitutional principles that the constituent power had established during and after the transition. The elimination of the four-fifths rule for agreement on the shape of a constitutional drafting process removed a crucial self-limitation on the power of two-thirds governments.[38] A constitutional amendment of June 5, 2010, changed the procedure for electing judges to the Constitutional Court, eliminating the first step of the process that had required a majority of parliamentary parties to agree to a nomination before a two-thirds vote could then elect that nominee to office.[39] Under the newly amended constitution, the votes of the governing party were alone enough to name constitutional judges, which removed another crucial self-limiting constraint on power. The government then amended the constitution again to remove crucial jurisdiction of the Constitutional Court in fiscal and tax matters, as retaliation against a Constitutional Court decision declaring a 98 percent retroactive tax unconstitutional.[40] Not only did this violate the principle of self-limiting power, but it also violated a basic human right present in all democratic constitutional systems worth the name, which is the right to be free of punitive ex post facto laws. The constitution was then amended again to increase the number of judges, which, together with retirements and other openings coming up in the normal scheme of things, gave the governing party the ability to name seven of the fifteen judges on the court in its first year in office. In a unicameral parliamentary system, which Hungary inherited from the Soviet period and did not revise in 1989–1990, the Constitutional Court was the primary check on power. With the amendments of 2010–2011, the independence of the Constitutional Court was sharply reduced.

The Fidesz government then passed a frenzy of subconstitutional laws to revamp the structure of many independent bodies. Virtually all of these laws had the effect of bringing formerly independent bodies, crucial to the enforcement of a self-limiting power, under the control of the government. The National Election Commission's composition was changed. All of the members elected for fixed terms of office before the 2010 election were unceremoniously booted off the commission and new members (all loyal to Fidesz) were elected in their place. This mattered not only for election supervision but also because any public referendum that might challenge the government first had to clear the hurdle of the electoral commission before it could be put to a popular vote. So the capture of the electoral commission functionally limited the ability of the public to challenge what was happening as the government prepared to rewrite the constitution.[41] This was yet another violation of the principle of self-limiting government.

Two new laws restructured the system of media regulation, so that a new Media Authority and a new Media Council appeared on the scene with the power to regulate public and private media in any medium (broadcast, internet, and print).[42] Among other things, the Media Council had the power to inflict bankrupting fines on any media organizations whose news operation failed to achieve political "balance" and the new Media Authority was responsible for awarding or renewing all broadcast frequencies. All of the seats on these crucial governing boards went to Fidesz supporters for terms that would run through three parliamentary election cycles, nine years. Not surprisingly, critics claimed that this chilled the robust debate that might have occurred over the constitutional revolution.

There was more, but we have already established enough to ask the key question: Was the constitutional-amendment process in the run-up to the drafting of the new constitution a *constitutional* constitutional-amendment process? If *constitutional* amendments are limited to matters that do not infringe the basic constitutional principles that a constituent power has established, as Schmitt would argue, then any amendment that transgresses the constituent power's red lines should be considered unconstitutional.

The Constitutional Court had a chance to rule on this question, but it failed to take the Schmittian route.[43] The reduction in the Constitutional Court's own jurisdiction was challenged before the Constitutional Court, but the court declined to find the constitutional amendment that did so unconstitutional. In fact, the majority of the court's justices argued that the court lacked jurisdiction to review the substance of the constitutional amendment or even the constitutionality of the procedure through which it was adopted. And the court said this even while pointing out that the constitutional amendment created a conflict with other provisions still in the constitution that ensured the rule of law and legal security. But, said the court, this was a matter for the constituent power and not for the court to resolve.

A dissenting opinion penned by Justice András Bragyova argued for reviewing both the procedure and substance of the amendment. He would have found the amendment limiting the court's jurisdiction unconstitutional for precisely the reasons that are by now familiar to readers of this chapter: Justice Bragyova found that the constitution embedded human rights, as well as a multiparty system, rule of law, parliamentary democracy, and social market economy, as principles that could not be modified by amendment. Those principles were unamendable, which is to say that they were created by a constituent power that could not be contradicted by anything less than a new constituent power, so the court had the power to declare the constitutional amendment unconstitutional. In a separate dissent, Justice László Kiss argued that the restriction on the jurisdiction of the court in matters affecting rights also violated unamendable principles, though his list was slightly different, including "the rule of law, the protection of the attained level of human rights, as well as the most important principles of voting rights, [and] the prohibition on obtaining or exercising power by violent means and on holding absolute power, and the norms regulating the right of resistance" (Halmai 2012, 198).

Even with the Constitutional Court's majority meekly accepting its constitutional fate, however, enough questions were raised about the amendments in the first year of the Fidesz government to cast doubt on whether these amendments continued the original constituent power. As I have argued here, these Fidesz amendments removed too many limitations on the power of the party to do anything it wanted, and the amendments also violated a basic principle established by the constituent power summoned in 1989–1990, the principle of self-limiting government. Moreover, since Fidesz repeatedly amended the constitution with the votes of only its own party, it also violated the constitutive principle that required that the post-1989 government remain a multiparty republic.

The Realization of the Existing Constituent Power? The New Hungarian Constitution of 2011–2012

While the Fidesz government was amending the constitution in 2010–2011 with the primary effect of bringing important independent institutions under its control, it also started the process of replacing the constitution altogether. At first, it appeared that the government would follow the track of "post-sovereign constitution-making" that Andrew Arato (2006/2007) has described.[44] The constitutional drafting process, as it was announced, would proceed in two interdependent steps: outlining principles first and then writing a full text afterward.

The constitutional committee of the parliament convened as a body that would develop constitutional principles for use in drafting a final text. The committee finished its work on March 7, 2011, when the committee published a seventeen-page document containing principles that, in the view of the committee, the new constitution should include. But by then, most of the democratic opposition[45] had walked out of the committee, complaining that none of their suggestions had been incorporated and arguing that they would no longer help to create the appearance that the draft principles had multiparty support.

On the day that the principles were reported out of committee to the floor of the parliament, the Fidesz supermajority then voted with its reliable two-thirds to call on any member of parliament to submit a proposed constitution to the parliament "with or without" following the principles on which the committee had agreed. The parliament gave all MPs one week—until March 14, 2011—to come up with a complete constitutional draft.

Notice what happened here. The government first announced that it would follow this two-stage process, with the newly elected parliament itself taking the lead on the first step. So far, so good. But the constitutional committee, with a majority of government members, simply vetoed any of the changes suggested by the opposition parties. So while that committee was formally representative of the parliament and generally mirrored the results of the recent election,[46] the proposals that emerged reflected only one party. And then even those proposed principles were ignored.

The democratic opposition might have thought it could make up for the disadvantage it had already suffered by engaging again in round two, in whatever process would draft the constitution. But that process and its ground rules were not specified until the day that the parliamentary committee's report was issued. Only then did the democratic opposition learn that it had one week to prepare a draft constitution—all without knowing before that day what the principles were that had to be followed. In the end, the principles turned out to be irrelevant, given that the parliament released any constitutional drafter from following them. (That was the last that was heard of the principles, which never made an appearance anywhere else in the process.) The crucial point was that the government gave everyone without inside knowledge about how the constitutional drafting process would proceed only one week to develop a constitutional draft.

In the end, two constitutional proposals were submitted to the parliament by the deadline: one offered by a collection of members of the Hungarian Parliament as well as members of the European Parliament from Fidesz and the other written by independent (former Socialist) MP Katalin Szilli. The Szilli draft was never discussed on the floor of the parliament. Only the Fidesz draft was considered, and it was introduced into the parliament as a "private member's bill" that could bypass the more rigorous parliamentary procedures required of a government bill.

In Hungarian parliamentary procedure, government bills must be introduced with a period of public consultation during which both opposition parties and civil society groups, as well as affected parties more generally, must be consulted. In addition, the ministries affected by a bill must have a chance to comment. An impact statement must be prepared that estimates the effects of the law on society before the parliament can take up the matter. With a private member's bill, however, none of these prior steps are required and a proposed law can go straight to the floor of the parliament for discussion. The proposed constitution, which had been drafted in secret in a close circle of party insiders, was introduced through a private member's bill, which eliminated the consultation round and allowed it to proceed on a fast track.

The Fidesz government set only one month for debate of the constitutional draft, which had been sprung out of the blue on an unprepared opposition and general public. While a few public debates were held, the by-now-Fidesz-controlled broadcast media said very little about the new constitution.[47] The general public, the NGO community, and the political opposition were caught off-balance. Foreign observers, including the Council of Europe[48] and the European Union,[49] had virtually no time to react.

Instead the government launched a "public consultation," which, the government said, was designed to take the public pulse on the new constitution. The public consultation was a questionnaire sent out to every voter in the country, and it consisted of twelve questions.[50] While many of the most crucial questions about the organization of government were never addressed in the questionnaire and a number of questions asked were puzzling (for example, should parliament sanction people who failed to show up before the parliament to testify at hearings?), the timing of the questionnaire meant that it could have no effect. The questionnaire was sent to households starting in February 2011, before the Fidesz draft became public, but the results were not due back until after the constitution was adopted in the parliament. The government claimed that 900,000 questionnaires were returned (out of roughly eight million voters). But the questionnaire could influence neither the draft nor the final constitution, and the government never published the results.[51]

The parliament itself scheduled only nine sessions to discuss the constitution, during which about 180 amendments were proposed. But the only alterations that had any chance were those offered by Fidesz. Democratic opposition parties, whose proposals were virtually all rejected, eventually walked out of the chamber and did not vote on the final constitution. Only the far-right Jobbik stayed and voted no. By the time that the final constitution came up for a vote in the parliament after these marathon sessions, neither observers nor the members of parliament knew which amendments had been added and which had not. There was no final draft text publicly available when the final vote was taken.

In a party-line vote, with all Fidesz members in favor and everyone else either boycotting or voting no, the new constitution passed parliament by the requisite two-thirds vote and was signed by the Fidesz-affiliated president on April 25, 2011. There was no public referendum to ratify the result. The new constitution went into effect on January 1, 2012, along with many of the "cardinal laws" that the constitution required to fill in the specifics.

If the new constitution honors the same constituent principles as the 1989–1990 constitution, then there was no need for the government to have summoned a new constituent power to underwrite it. A new constitution could then piggyback off the legitimation coming from the constitutional process of 1989–1990. So let us look at this new constitution to see whether it honors: (1) the protection of human dignity through the protection of rights; (2) the creation of a democratic, multiparty republic; and (3) the self-limitation of state power.

Let's begin with the self-limitation of state power. Already we saw that the constitutional amendments brought in by Fidesz in 2010–2011 violated this basic principle by removing many of the checks on its own power, making its power theoretically limitless. Unfortunately, the new constitution made that problem worse. Not only did the new constitution keep the institutional changes added by the amendments to the old constitution—the new system for electing judges to the Constitutional Court, the restriction in the court's jurisdiction, and the increased number of judges so that the votes of Fidesz alone were enough to name them all without multiparty input—but the new constitution went even further. Under its aegis, either in the constitution itself or in the cardinal laws that were required by the constitution as supplements, virtually all of the independent checking institutions were now occupied by Fidesz loyalists whose terms of office extended far beyond the current election cycle of four years. With terms of six, nine, and twelve years, Fidesz loyalists in key positions could hold power during the next two or sometimes three new parliaments down the road.

In addition, the new constitutional order severely limited the independence of the ordinary judiciary.[52] Under the old system, lower court judges were selected by panels of their fellow judges. Under the new system, the president of a newly created National Judicial Office has the power to select new judges, to promote and demote any judge, to begin disciplinary proceedings, and to select the leaders of each of the courts. The person actually chosen by parliament with its two-thirds majority as head of the National Judicial Office was both a close friend of Prime Minister Orbán and the wife of MEP József Szájer, the principal drafter of the new constitution. Moreover, under a new constitutional amendment to the new constitution, she had the power to assign any case to any court, overriding the usual procedural rules that specify jurisdiction in each case in a formal and rule-based fashion.[53] With one person possessed of so much power to shape the judiciary, especially one person so close to the governing party, it is hard to say that the judiciary is independent.

This structural dependence of the judiciary on a single person was compounded by the one-off trick that Fidesz pulled to get control of the judiciary even faster than the normal attrition rate would allow. Suddenly lowering the judicial retirement age from seventy to sixty-two meant that, overnight, Fidesz had 10 percent of the judicial seats in the country to fill. By firing people from the oldest age cohort, Fidesz ensured that the 10 percent of seats were not randomly distributed. Instead, they came disproportionately from the leadership stratum of the courts. The new retirement age eliminated 25 percent of the Supreme Court judges, nearly half of the appeals court presidents and two-fifths of the local court presidents (Scheppele 2012a). The new head of the National Judicial Office, then, got to remake the judiciary in the first year of the new constitution's existence with an appointment power that could not be second-guessed.[54]

In addition to the compromised independence of the judiciary, other independent institutions took a hit in the new constitutional order as well. The head of the state audit office was given additional powers to conduct investigations into the expenditures of state funds, and the public prosecutor, like the head of the National Judicial Office, was given the power to pick the court in which he could bring any criminal case. Both of these offices have extraordinary long terms—twelve years for the state audit office head and nine years for the public prosecutor. And both offices are now filled by people who are close to the governing party.

The ombudsmen's offices were also affected. Where the old constitution had three subject-matter-specific ombudsmen (for minorities, data protection, and the environment) *plus* an ombudsman with general jurisdiction, the new constitution has only one "parliamentary commissioner for human rights" with two deputies to do the same work. The office of the ombudsman for data protection was closed and his responsibilities were transferred to an office that is part of the government with a political appointee at its helm. The office, as a result, has lost its independence.

The dead-hand control of the current governing party could now extend over any other parliamentary majority that might be elected over the next several election cycles. A number of routes become available to it. For example, the new constitution established a Budget Council with the power to veto any budget produced by parliament that adds even a single forint to the national debt. The Budget Council consists of three officials, two elected by a two-thirds vote of parliament and one appointed by the president (thus far, always a Fidesz loyalist). All three members of the Budget Council have terms of office that exceed a normal parliamentary cycle—six years for two of the members and twelve for the other.

According to the new constitution, if parliament fails to agree on a budget by March 31 of each year, then the president may dissolve parliament and call new elections. Obviously, if the Budget Council, dominated by Fidesz loyalists, vetoes the budget on the eve of the deadline, the constitutional trigger can be pulled for new elections. As a result, if another party manages to gain power in a future election, this provision will always enable the remaining Fidesz party loyalists to spring a trap that generates new elections almost immediately after any new government takes office.

Under the new constitutional order, the governing party has managed to fill all of the major checking institutions with party loyalists who will be quite disinclined to limit the government's power. As a result, there are no constitutional guarantees any longer that this will be a self-limiting government. Of course, a government does not have to use all of the power that it has; it could in fact limit itself. But the point of a *constitutionally self-limiting government* is that one should not have to rely simply on the goodwill of a governing party. The new constitutional order therefore violates the first of the constituent principles established in the 1989–1990 summoning of constituent power.

What about the second principle—the guarantee of a multiparty democratic republic? This principle features three separate elements represented by each of the three words. Let's start with "multiparty." As our discussion has already pointed out, the constitution was brought in with the votes of only Fidesz, against opposition from all of the other parties. The new constitutional institutions were filled with the loyalists of only one party as well because the government removed all constraints on the power of their own two-thirds to name particular people to offices. Fidesz has since consistently refused the proposals, suggested amendments, and candidates of all of the other parties. This is a Fidesz constitution whose offices are filled by Fidesz loyalists and with devices that permit Fidesz to block multiparty appointments to key positions.

And "democratic"? In a democracy, power must be able to move back and forth between organized political factions, depending on the results of free and fair elections. But the election machinery set up by this system raises doubts about its fairness. Not only is the electoral commission filled entirely with Fidesz supporters,[55] but the electoral laws have proven to clearly favor Fidesz. In its constitution, Fidesz cut the size of the parliament in half, which required redistricting. (This move may have been the only one that actually had support across the political spectrum.) But the boundaries of the new electoral districts are now entrenched in a cardinal law that will require a two-thirds majority to change it. And these new districts were drawn in Fidesz's favor. Had all of the elections since 1998 been carried out under these new districts, Fidesz would have come to power in 1998 and would never have been voted out since, despite the fact that under the old system, Fidesz lost both the 2002 and 2006 elections, the latter by a large margin (Szigetvári, Tordai, and Vetô 2011).

Since the electoral districts were drawn, Fidesz introduced a constitutional amendment that required voter registration—and this in a country that has a complete and accurate civil list that registers everyone for the purposes of a national identification document. By some estimates, the voter registration requirement would have lowered the effective voting population by half. The voter registration scheme was struck down by the Constitutional Court twice: first on procedural grounds and then on substantive grounds because it interfered with the right of citizens to vote.[56] Fidesz did not further contest those rulings. But after once again winning two-thirds of the seats in parliament in April 2018, it has begun undertaking a series of further constitutional amendments, creating governmental powers and duties to preserve "Hungary's Christian culture," authorizing a new and Fidesz-favorable administrative high court, imposing a new ban on the resettlement of foreigners into Hungary, and more (*Daily News Hungary* 2018).

So is the new constitution committed to democracy? Observers have agreed for years that the Fidesz government consistently tries to rig the rules in its favor and to guarantee that it alone can win elections.[57] Add to this tricks like the potential Budget Council veto that can trigger new elections, and one can see that the ability of any other party to come to power and to stay in power is quite limited by current rules.

What, then, about "republic"? Hungary's official name used to be the Republic of Hungary. The new constitution changes the name merely to Hungary. But the constitution does formally guarantee (in Article B(2)) that the form of government is a republic. Can we take this constitutional provision at its word? We have already noted the lack of multiparty participation in the drafting of the constitution and lack of guarantees of multiparty participation in governance from here on out. Democratic government will be difficult to maintain under the rules, also, so the key elements of a republican form of government are under challenge. So is Hungary under the new constitution a multiparty democratic republic? The answer is not clearly yes. And it might even be no.

Finally, what about protection for basic rights? The new constitution impressively lists a variety of rights in its second major section. But as David Law and Mila Versteeg stress in their contribution to this volume, words on paper alone do not guarantee rights. Institutions must be established that respect rights; courts and other bodies must defend rights. As we have already seen, however, the independence of the ordinary judiciary has been severely compromised both by the politicization of judicial appointments and by the continued ability of elected officials to move any case to any court outside the usual legal rules about jurisdiction. In addition, the government of Hungary has created a new secret police, the anti-terrorism police, with the ability to bypass judicial warrants for many types of searches and the ability to engage in surveillance without having limits on how long and for what purposes the information so acquired can be used (for legal details, see Scheppele 2012c). In a context like this, it is hard to have faith that rights are or will be fairly protected.

The longer this government stays in power, however, the more clearly we can see that rights respected in most constitutional democracies are not respected in Hungary. One right whose realization deteriorated quickly has been freedom of religion. Under a new "cardinal law" on churches, the government of Hungary removed the legal status from more than three hundred religious organizations while establishing only thirty-three churches as official state-recognized religions. The rest have been cast into a legal no man's land, officially encouraged to register as secular organizations but denied this organizational status each time they have tried (see Baer 2012).

While Hungary has not yet become a country where human rights are subject to mass abuse, vulnerable populations are starting to leave. The emigration of Roma to Canada was so pronounced at one point that the government of Canada closed its borders by calling Hungary "safe" against all of the evidence.[58] Hungarian Jews have been leaving the country as well, citing anti-Semitism as a key reason (Liphshiz 2013). Vulnerable groups feel the lack of a rights culture first. The warning signs are clearly there. Hungarian institutions cannot be depended upon to defend the rights that are in the constitution.

From this evaluation, we can see that the three principles that the constituent power of 1989–1990 insisted upon are not guaranteed by the current constitution. Can this mean that Fidesz summoned a *new* constituent power to underwrite its constitution?

The Creation of a New Constituent Power?

If the constitution of 2012 was not authorized by the constituent power summoned in 1989–1990 because its constituent principles were violated, has Fidesz ever been able to mobilize a new constituent power? Given what we have seen of the process used to usher in the new constitution as well as the content of and public backing for this new constitutional order, the answer is no.

First, on process. By contrast with the constitutional drafting process of 1989–1990, which consisted of a Roundtable agreement, support by two successive parliaments (one before and one after a multiparty free election), a plebiscite, an election, and a multiparty pact that was reaffirmed despite an orderly process for changing it, the rushed constitutional drafting process of 2011 was attributable to one party and one party only. There was no attempt to get true consensus among the parliamentary parties. There was no meaningful public consultation to get input into the process. There was no referendum on the final constitution to certify public approval. There was just a hurried and secret constitutional process in which all those not in the governing party were left out.

Fidesz has always distrusted its co-parliamentarians, and it has insisted that it had a mandate resulting from the election to change everything. If Fidesz were acting on the basis of a public demand for a new constitution, one would expect popular support for its bold and aggressive moves. But opinion polls do not bear out the "mandate" theory. Instead, Fidesz lost more than half of its voters after it came to power in May 2010 (Scheppele, 2014).

Far from revealing that the public demanded constitutional change that Fidesz supplied, the polling data show that people were running away from Fidesz both in public opinion and in literally voting with their feet in the period when it imposed its changes—which have enabled it to consolidate power and insure electoral success ever since.[59]

Where was this constituent power that Fidesz invoked in creating its new constitution? The "revolution of the ballot box," if indeed such a revolution existed, dissipated as the content of the Fidesz constitutional plan was developed and publicized. The Fidesz constitution combines objectionable elements that we identified at the start of the paper. From the Idealaria scenario,

Fidesz borrowed the feature that the constitution was written behind closed doors by the brain trust of the party and presented without further debate or multiparty input as the ideal constitution for Hungary. From the Pandemonia scenario, Fidesz excluded the other parties from its constitutional-drafting process and presented its one-party constitution as if it were a constitution for the whole of the country. And from the Freedonia scenario, Fidesz declared itself the party of the middle and excluded the factions to either side of it. In the course of doing so (and contrary to the Freedonia example), Fidesz eliminated not 10 percent of the political spectrum but the majority.

Hungary has since been faced with a situation in which a new constitution was rammed through a stacked political process, in violation of the constituent power that accompanied the 1989–1990 process and without constituting a new constituent power to underwrite this new constitution. Fidesz claims to be a constitution-making power supported by the "revolution of the ballot box" but a closer analysis of what they have done demonstrates otherwise.

The idea of an unconstitutional constituent power may sound abstract, ideal, and irrelevant to any real-world constitutionalism, but we can see with the case of Hungary that it is important for constitutional theorists to elaborate when the claim to have established a constituent power is legitimate. The Hungarian case gives us many moments to analyze—from the 1989–1990 founding to the Constitutional Court's elaboration of the text, to the 1995–1996 constitutional drafting process, to the frenzy of amendments in 2010–2011, to the new constitution itself, and to the new amendments to the constitution after that. I have argued that there was a constituent power established in 1989–1990 that was not legitimately displaced by events after 2010. As a result, Hungary is currently operating under a government that has claimed an unconstitutional constituent power.

Notes

Pieces of this analysis can be found in an earlier form in the essay "On the Unconstitutionality of Constitutional Change" (Scheppele 2012d).

1. Jeremy Bentham's huge *Constitutional Code* was written as just such an abstract and ideal plan. He peddled it around various Latin American countries hoping for its acceptance somewhere, but, alas, for him, no country adopted it.

2. The image is Karl Llewellyn's (1960, 44): "Law, as against other disciplines, is like a tree. In its own soil it roots, and shades one spot alone."

3. The word "pandemonium" was coined by John Milton to describe a place where demons live (http://en.wiktionary.org/wiki/pandemonium). The plural might have more demons.

4. Any similarity between this argument and those of Sandy Levinson in his twin books *Our Democratic Constitution* (2006) and *Framed* (2012) is purely coincidental but perhaps not accidental.

5. Carrying on a long line of exemplary Freedonias; see http://en.wikipedia.org/wiki/Freedonia.

6. Sieyès did not address the question of whether majoritarianism would need to go "all the way down," so to speak. He assumed that the Third Estate itself would speak with one voice. But he never addressed what would happen if members of the Third Estate were divided so that no one portion of the "Third Estate" as a collectivity would represent a majority of those within it.

7. Of course, the Weimar Constitution did in fact become something else, as the state of exception authorized under Article 48 was used to undermine the system of constitutional checks on power, particularly after 1933. Once undermined through the invocation of its own exceptional provisions, the constitution collapsed in practice even as it remained formally in effect.

8. In this formulation, Schmitt almost seems to anticipate the later contributions of John Rawls, who argued that the basic constitution-writing process of any political order had to take place among people who were unaware of their specific interests and therefore who had to act on the basis of hypothetical interests they might have. Rawls then argued that the hypothetical interests such constitution-makers should assume were the interests of those who had the most to lose in the actual political community that resulted. Merely contingent interests were not to have a place in determining the basic elements of a constitution.

9. The proceedings of the National Roundtable, and in particular of the Opposition Roundtable that coordinated the views of the democratic opposition, were eventually published (Bozoki 1999–2000), but not until ten years after the fact.

10. In retrospect, it appears that everyone must have known that the anti-communists would win. But at the time, this was really not so clear. Among other things, the communist leaders were the only ones who were widely known; the challengers were new and untested. In addition, the communist leaders who were put forward in the election were the reformers who might have gotten the benefit of the doubt by being the ones to have opened up the process to constitutional change in the first place. Finally, Hungary in the 1980s was much less repressive than many of its neighbors, and the communists were not as widely hated as they were in other countries in the region. Plus, after Kádár and his immediate circle were pushed out, those who were left in the government did not have such a horrible track record.

11. Andrew Arato and Zoltán Miklósi (2010, 371), writing about this period, independently came to the conclusion that the Roundtable process approximated bargaining behind an "empirical veil of ignorance."

12. The 1989 constitution involved nearly one hundred separate amendments to the 1949 constitution.

13. The difference between a constitutional amendment, which requires a two-thirds vote, and a cardinal law, which also requires a two-thirds vote, can be found in the denominator of the fraction. A constitutional amendment requires a two-thirds vote of all of the members of parliament, while a cardinal law requires a two-thirds vote of any number of MPs above a quorum.

14. Throughout the National Roundtable process, the opposition groups met in the Opposition Roundtable, which itself had a complex inner dynamic that had to be navigated (see Arato and Miklósi 2010 for details).

15. János Kis is not only a distinguished philosopher, but in the years of the transition, he was the leader of the SzDSz (Free Democrats), a liberal political party that was the second-highest vote-getter in the 1990 elections.

16. The king, of course, eventually refused to hold up his end of the new constitutional deal and was executed as a new republic was declared.

17. These observations about the ideas of the reformers within the MSzMP are based on multiple interviews with those who had been the officials at the MSzMP Justice Ministry during this period, including fourteen hours of interviews I conducted in 1995 with former Justice Minister Kálmán Kulcsár himself. I also interviewed some the delegates from the MSzMP Justice Ministry to the Roundtable talks. The book *Democratic Changes in Hungary*, edited by Géza Kilényi (later a Constitutional Court judge) and Vanda Lamm (1990), gives voice to some of those who were involved in those negotiations on the Justice Ministry side, as does Kulcsár's (1994) book.

18. This phrase came up often in interviews I did in 1994–1995 with those who were deeply involved with the constitution-negotiating process at the time. In particular, Péter Tölgyessy used this phrase repeatedly. Tölgyessy had been the key Opposition Roundtable delegate to the three-person subcommittee that drafted the legal language of the new constitution. Interview with Péter Tölgyessy, White House (parliamentary office building), spring 1995.

19. This paragraph is based on a set of interviews I did in 1994–1995 with a number of the people who were involved in the constitutional drafting process at the Roundtable, including but not limited to those mentioned by name above.

20. The communists wanted the new president to be elected by popular vote, as their candidates were nationally known already. By contrast, the democratic opposition, consisting largely of self-appointed figures without broad recognition, wanted the new president to be elected by the parliament because they believed that they could win a majority there (Kis 1998, 350–355). The solution—to put the choice to the people themselves—fits Schmitt's general view that only a decision of the political unity can settle foundational questions. Though the referendum settled the issue by a very small margin, the narrow majority voted to limit its own power by deciding to not preserve its own power to elect the president and to permit the parliament to elect the president instead.

21. Because the 1989 constitution passed as a series of formal amendments to the 1949 constitution, the constitution retained its formal designation as Law XX of 1949, as amended. It was this absence of a name change that caused the Fidesz government elected in 2010 to claim that the communist constitution survived, despite the fundamental change described here. Compare Hungarian Constitution 1949, Law XX of 1949, https://lapa.princeton.edu/hosteddocs/hungary/1949%20Hungarian%20constitution.pdf with Hungarian Constitution 1989–90, Law XX of 1949 as amended, https://lapa.princeton.edu/hosteddocs/hungary/1989-90%20constitution_english.pdf.

22. In the Soviet period, the parliament was limited to two ceremonial meetings per year, during which it rubber-stamped proposed legislation without debate. A parliament that met nine months per year would finally have the chance to engage in actual legislative work.

23. To make these amendments, which required a two-thirds vote of the parliament, the governing parties needed parties in the political opposition to join them.

24. The agreement is simply called the "Paktum"(Pact) in discussion of this period.

25. There is some controversy here that ought to be explained. The MDF entered into this agreement without the Smallholders and Christian Democrats with whom they were in coalition. The SzDSz entered into this agreement without any of the other parties in opposition. While the MDF won about 25 percent of the popular vote and the SzDSz won about 21 percent, the pact between them excluded parties that had garnered between them the majority of voters: the Smallholders (12 percent), the Christian Democrats (6 percent), Fidesz (9 percent), and the Socialists (11 percent). The remaining 16 percent of the vote went to smaller parties that did not meet the 5 percent threshold for party representation. As a result, even though this MDF-SzDSz Pact brought together the leading government and opposition parties, for some of those left out, the Paktum had the air of a secret agreement that was not transparent. It remains the most controversial element of the transition, particularly for Fidesz, which was not included in the Paktum. For the election results of 1990, see http://www.ipu.org/parline/reports/arc/2141_90.htm.

26. This did not mean that all parties agreed on the particulars, which, of course, one would not expect in a normal democratic system. Instead, most of the parties agreed on the basic structure of governance, putting the most crucial institutional changes beyond the reach of a simple majority. Arato and Miklósi (2010) highlight the differences of opinion in the various political groups in the parliament at the time.

27. Andrew Arato has identified a constitution-producing process that operates in multiple stages, where one of the early stages involves outlining a set of principles that the constitution must adhere to as it becomes gradually more detailed. He calls this multistage model "post-sovereign constitution-making" (Arato 2006/2007). In his model, the parties first agree on governing principles, then they elect a body charged with writing a constitution according to those principles. The constitution that results is checked back against the initial principles for conformity therewith. In his view, the Hungarian constitution failed because it never actually produced this final constitu-

tional text. But, as I will argue below, the Constitutional Court attempted both to derive these principles and to check the results of the 1989–1990 constitution against them, thus completing the process. If one takes the court as more central to the process of constitution-making than Arato does, then it is easier to arrive at the conclusion that in fact all of his steps were followed.

28. Constitution of the Republic of Hungary, as Amended by Act No. XXXI of 1989, Article 3.

29. The principle of self-limitation was further manifested in a constitutional amendment made in 1995 that required the procedure for enacting a new constitution to be subject to a four-fifths majority in the parliament instead of the constitution-amending two-thirds. About this, more later.

30. Decision 23/1990 (X. 31) AB határozat, on capital punishment.

31. Sólyom's reference here to future constitutions was no doubt a reference to the fact that the 1989–1990 constitution had a preamble that indicated that it was temporary and that it should be replaced by a permanent constitution when the transitional period was over. The constitutional text envisioned a future constitution that would be based on the process started in the 1989–1990 constitutional-drafting period.

32. 1949 Constitution of the Republic of Hungary, as amended in 1989–1990, available in English translation at http://lapa.princeton.edu/hosteddocs/hungary/1989-90%20constitution_english.pdf. Note that the constitution retained the formal legal name of the Stalinst-era constitution despite the fact that it had been fundamentally changed by constitutional amendment in 1989–1990.

33. The second multiparty election brought the Socialists to power with a majority of seats in the parliament (33 percent of the party list votes and 209 total seats of the 396 available). Though the Socialists didn't need a coalition partner to govern, the SzDSz—which had received 20 percent of the party list votes and 29 of the total seats—agreed to form a coalition with the Socialists. For the election results in 1994, see http://www.ipu.org/parline-e/reports/arc/2141_94.htm.

34. This is what Prime Minister Viktor Orbán has called his mandate from the 2010 election. For the slogan, and some resistance, see Zilahy (2011).

35. The joint party list should not create the impression that there are really two distinct parties there. The Christian Democrats did not offer a separate parliamentary list in the national election nor did it put up candidates in most of the individual member districts. The KDNP's leadership is practically merged with the leadership of Fidesz and the two groups rarely disagree in public. Virtually all of Fidesz's radical legislation and constitution-making proposals since 2010 have been voted for unanimously by the Christian Democrats in parliament. As one Socialist politician said to me in a recent interview, the Christian Democrats are the "Christian wing" of Fidesz. From here on, I will refer to the government simply as a Fidesz government, which is also how the government refers to itself. It has not disputed its one-party formation.

36. Fidesz received 68 percent of the seats in the parliament despite the fact that Fidesz had about 40 percent popular approval on the eve of the election. Reduced

voter turnout produced a 53 percent majority for the Fidesz-KNDP party list. The disproportionate Hungarian electoral law then boosted that 53 percent majority to 68 percent of the parliamentary mandates. But Fidesz did not, as the party often implies in its public statements, receive 68 percent of the vote.

37. The continued legal validity of this provision was subject to some contestation in 2010. When the parliament amended the constitution in 1995 to set the bar at four-fifths before a constitutional drafting process could begin, the bill that passed the parliament containing the amendment specified that the four-fifths requirement was to sunset in 1998 when the government in power would be up for election again. (The law as it passed the parliament was 1995. évi XLIV. törvény.) But the actual amendment inserted into the constitution never mentioned that sunset provision. As a result, the four-fifths clause was still in the constitution at the time that Fidesz came to power, though some argued that it had formally lapsed in 1998. The fact that Fidesz voted to remove it from the constitution indicated that the leadership believed that the clause could be used to stop what they planned to do.

38. This statement, of course, presupposes that the four-fifths rule was still legally valid, something that was challenged at the time.

39. Amendment to Law XX of 1949 on the Constitution of the Republic of Hungary, July 5, 2010, *Magyar Közlöny*, no. 113 (2010).

40. For the decision of the Constitutional Court on retroactive taxes, see Hungarian Constitutional Court Decision 184/2010 (X. 28), *Magyar Közlöny*, no. 165 (2010). For the constitutional amendment restricting the jurisdiction of the court, see Law CXIX of 2010 on the amendment to Law XX of 1949 on the Constitution of the Republic of Hungary, *Magyar Közlöny*, no. 177 (2010).

41. The process is slightly more complicated than this. Decisions by the electoral commission at that time could be appealed to the Constitutional Court for review, so the Constitutional Court was really the final body to approve a referendum. But, as we have seen, by the time any public referendum might have emerged to challenge Fidesz, the court was already packed with government supporters.

42. Law CIV of 2010 on the Freedom of the Press and the Fundamental Rules of Media Content and Law CLXXXV of 2010 on Media Services and Mass Media. The laws are translated at the website of the Venice Commission: https://www.venice.coe.int/webforms/documents/?pdf=CDL-REF(2015)011-e.

43. This paragraph discusses Constitutional Court Decision 61/2011 (VII. 13.). A thorough analysis of this decision that I have relied on heavily here can be found in Halmai (2012).

44. What is "post-sovereign constitution-making"? As Arato (2006/2007, 539) writes: "What gradually emerged . . . was the new reliance on two drafting stages that foresaw from the outset the production of two constitutions, an interim and a final one, where the rules of the first constrain the making of the second. The existence of a fully developed, explicitly interim constitution is the most important component and documentary evidence of the new paradigm of constitution-making." A more

detailed analysis can be found in his later book *Constitution Under Occupation* (Arato 2009).

45. The term "democratic opposition" is what the parties to the left of Fidesz call themselves to distinguish themselves from the entire parliamentary opposition, a designation that would include the neo-fascist party Jobbik. As a result, Jobbik is specifically excluded from the "democratic opposition" designation.

46. Recall, however, that under the Hungarian electoral law valid at the time of the 2010 election, majorities became supermajorities and strong contenders were reduced in influence in the parliament that resulted. Fidesz got 53 percent of the party list votes and 262 of the seats while the Socialists got 21 percent of the vote and 59 of the seats. See http://www.electionresources.org/hu/assembly.php?election=2010. While much of the disparity comes from the fact that Fidesz swept the single-member districts, the lopsided effect comes from a combination of the disproportionate election law in place at the time and the way that district boundaries were drawn.

47. By this time, only one independent radio station, KlubRádió, and one independent TV station, ATV, were operating in Hungary. While the print media were more diverse, they, as well as the broadcast and internet-based media, were governed by the new media law that allowed the Fidesz-only Media Council to impose bankrupting fines on any news broadcast that was not "balanced." Later, after the constitution was adopted, the Constitutional Court struck down the content restrictions on the print media, but at the time when it would have been most crucial to have a robust debate—during the month when the constitution was open for discussion—even the print media were under the Media Council's sword of Damocles.

48. The government had asked the Venice Commission (the Commission for Democracy Through Law) of the Council of Europe for its advice on three small issues in the new constitution before the new draft was made public. The Venice Commission saw no serious objections to the three proposals, though it also noted with some testiness that much depended on how these three proposals fit into the new constitution, which they did not have a chance to review. For the Venice Commission's initial report on the three questions, see http://www.venice.coe.int/webforms/documents/?pdf=CDL-AD%282011%29001-e. There was no time for the Venice Commission to review the draft constitution in its entirety, which was only done some months later upon a request from the Parliamentary Assembly of the Council of Europe. For the final report on the entire new constitution, see http://www.venice.coe.int/webforms/documents/?pdf=CDL-AD%282011%29016-e.

49. The government was required to submit the draft constitution to the European Commission for its review as well. But the English translation of the constitution that was submitted to the European Commission omitted the controversial preamble, through which only ethnic Hungarians were established as the constituent power. In addition, the preamble laid symbolic claim to Hungary's historic lands and peoples (now in the territory of neighboring states), repudiated the constitution

and all laws that were in effect between 1949 and 1990, and established Christianity, family, and nation as the key principles of the new state. The draft also contained a number of misleading translations that disguised some of the more objectionable features of the new constitution. For a list of the misleading translation mistakes in the version of the constitution originally provided to the European Union, see http://www.ekint.org/ekint_files/File/tanulmanyok/alkotmanyozas/list_of_all_the_omissions_and_mistranslation s.pdf. For the current official translation, see http://www.kormany.hu/download/2/ab/30000/Alap_angol.pdf. For an alternative translation, see http://tasz.hu/files/tasz/imce/alternative_translation_of_the_draft_constituion.pdf.

50. The questions were:

1. Should the new constitution declare only rights or should it also declare obligations of citizens (work, study, national defense, environment)?
2. Should the new constitution restrict the extent of sovereign debt and thus accept responsibility for future generations?
3. Should the new constitution bring under its protection common values such as family, labor, home, order, and health?
4. Should the new constitution grant voting rights to the parent of a minor on behalf of his/her child?
5. Should the new constitution permit taxing the cost of raising children?
6. Should the new constitution undertake responsibility for future generations?
7. Should the constitution declare that only companies with a transparent ownership should have access to state funds?
8. Should the new constitution express the value of national togetherness with Hungarians living beyond our borders?
9. Should the new constitution provide protection for the biodiversity of the Carpathian Basin?
10. Should the new constitution provide special protection of national assets, especially arable land and water supplies?
11. Should the courts have powers to give life prison sentences that cannot be changed?
12. Should the new constitution define sanctions for no-shows before a parliamentary committee for a hearing?

Virtually none of the topics addressed by these questions made it into the constitution at all.

51. The government had promised anonymity to those who responded. But later, the ombudsman for data protection, shortly before his office was abolished, discovered that the questionnaires contained a QR barcode that could be read by any QR scanning device. This QR barcode contained the name and address of the person who received the questionnaire, so the responses were *not* anonymous. But now the

government knows precisely who is in the government's camp and who was not in favor of its various constitutional proposals.

52. The term "ordinary judiciary" is customarily used in systems that have constitutional courts to distinguish the courts that do not have constitutional jurisdiction—the "ordinary courts"—from the one court that does—the Constitutional Court.

53. There is a backstory here. After the constitution was enacted, and just before it went into effect, the parliament adopted an act called "Transitional Provisions of the Constitution." The Transitional Provisions were supposed to be added to the constitution to provide information about how the new constitutional system would be phased in; instead the Transitional Provisions also included a number of permanent amendments to the constitution. In its decision of 45/2012, the Constitutional Court declared that the permanent amendments included in the Transitional Provisions failed for formal reasons to properly amend the constitution and so were unconstitutional. So the government announced that it would seek to introduce a new constitutional amendment, done in the proper manner, *again* giving constitutional power to the head of the National Judicial Office to assign any case to any judge. In the meantime, between the nullification of the Transitional Provisions and the new constitutional amendment, the head of the National Judicial Office would have to rely on her statutory power in the cardinal act on the judiciary to accomplish the same goal. In the end, under international pressure, the power to assign any case to any court was removed from the powers of the head of the National Judicial Office.

54. The lowering of the judicial retirement age was declared unconstitutional by the Constitutional Court, citing the "historic constitution" that the constitutional judges are supposed to honor. According to the court, the retirement age of judges had been set at seventy in the mid-nineteenth century and it was a violation of the principle of legal security to change it without any time for the judges to adjust. The decision of the Constitutional Court—to which Prime Minister Orbán responded with defiance by announcing "the system remains"—was further supported by a decision of the European Court of Justice that found the sudden lowering of the retirement age to be a violation of EU law as well. Faced with this overwhelming judicial pressure, the government finally backed down and agreed to reinstate the judges—but not to their former leadership positions, which had already been filled. For an analysis of the Constitutional Court Decision 33/2012 (VII. 17.) AB határozat, see Scheppele (2012b). In fact, in the end, almost none of the judges returned to their prior positions.

55. During an election campaign, each party is allowed to send one delegate to the electoral commission, but the number of members of the electoral commission has been set so that Fidesz is guaranteed to still win every vote.

56. For an explanation of the two Constitutional Court decisions, see Uitz (2013).

57. Among the rules that I have not mentioned in the main text are the elimination of the second round voting in single-member districts making them into first-past-the-post elections (which will throw those seats to Fidesz unless the fractious opposition can unite behind a single candidate) and the restrictions on media coverage of the campaign (which

channel all funding for election ads to the private media dominated by Fidesz and all free media spots to the Fidesz-dominated public media).

58. For more on the Canadian actions and the reactions of those familiar with the Roma issues in Hungary, see Drache (2013).

59. For example, according to German sources, 68,892 Hungarians lived in Germany in 2010 but by 2017 that number had grown to 207,035 (Daily News Hungary, 2019). In addition to these figures, the number of Roma seeking refugee status in Canada sharply increased early in the Fidesz government's tenure: "In 2011, 4,427 of 24,416 new Canadian refugee cases were from Hungary, up from 2,300 a year earlier, according to the Immigration and Refugee Board" (Westhead 2012). Given that the population of Hungary is only about ten million people, these are large numbers, relatively speaking. And the surges are new.

References

Arato, Andrew. 2006/2007. "Post-Sovereign Constitution-Making and Its Pathology in Iraq." *New York Law School Law Review* 51: 535–555.

———. 2009. *Constitution Making Under Occupation: The Politics of Imposed Revolution in Iraq.* New York: Columbia University Press.

Arato, Andrew, and Zoltán Miklósi. 2010. "Constitution Making and Transitional Politics in Hungary." In *Framing the State in Times of Transition*, edited by Laurel Miller, 350–390. Washington, DC: Endowment of the U.S. Institute for Peace.

Baer, David. 2012. "The Fate of Hungary's Deregistered Churches." *Hungarian Spectrum*, August 13, 2012. https://hungarianspectrum.org/2012/08/13/david-baer-the-fate-of-hungarys-deregistered-churches/.

Bánkuti, Miklós, Gábor Halmai, and Kim Lane Scheppele. 2012. "Disabling the Constitution." *Journal of Democracy* 23 (3): 138–146.

Bozoki, András, ed. 1999–2000. *A Rendszerváltás Forgatókönyve: Kerekaszta Tárgyalások 1989.* Volumes 1–8. Budapest: Uj Mandatum.

Daily News Hungary. 2018. "Hungarian Parliament Passes Seventh Constitutional Amendment: Banning Homelessness." June 20, 2018. https://dailynewshungary.com/hungarian-parliament-passes-seventh-constitutional-amendment-banning-homelessness/.

Daily News Hungary. 2019. "Is Germany the Second Home of Hungarians?" January 10, 2019. https://dailynewshungary.com/is-germany-the-second-home-of-hungarians/.

Drache, Judy Young. 2013. "The Roma of Hungary: A Canadian View." *Hungarian Spectrum*, February 9, 2013. https://hungarianspectrum.wordpress.com/2013/02/09/the-roma-of-hungary-a-canadian-view-by-judy-young-drach/.

Halmai, Gábor. 2012. "Unconstitutional Constitutional Amendments: Constitutional Courts as Guardians of the Constitution?" *Constellations* (19) 2: 182–203.

Hungarian Constitution 1949, Law XX of 1949, available at https://lapa.princeton.edu/hosteddocs/hungary/1949%20Hungarian%20constitution.pdf.

Hungarian Constitution 1989–90, Law XX of 1949 as amended, available at https://lapa.princeton.edu/hosteddocs/hungary/1989-90%20constitution_english.pdf.

Kilényi, Géza, and Vanda Lamm. 1990. *Democratic Changes in Hungary: Basic Legislation on a Peaceful Transition from Bolshevism to Democracy*. Budapest: Hungarian Academy of Sciences.

Kis, János. 1998. "Between Reform and Revolution." *East European Politics and Societies* 12 (2): 300–383.

Kulcsár, Kálmán. 1994. *Két világ között: Rendszerváltás Magyarországon, 1988–1990*. Budapest: Akadémiai Kiadó.

Levinson, Sanford. 2006. *Our Undemocratic Constitution: Where the Constitution Goes Wrong (and How We the People Can Correct It)*. New York: Oxford University Press.

———. 2012. *Framed: America's 51 Constitutions and the Crisis of Governance*. New York: Oxford University Press.

Liphshiz, Cnaan. 2013. "Anti-Semitism Pushing out Hungarian Jews, Vienna Community Says." *Jewish Telegraph Agency*, February 3, 2013. https://www.jta.org/2013/02/03/global/anti-semitism-pushing-out-hungarian-jews-vienna-community-says.

Llewellyn, Karl N. 1960. *The Bramble Bush: On Our Law and Its Study*. Dobbs Ferry, NY: Oceana.

Rawls, John. 1971. *A Theory of Justice*. Cambridge, MA: Harvard University Press.

Rousseau, Jean-Jacques. 2003. *The Social Contract and Discourses*. Everyman's Library. London: J. M. Dent.

Scheppele, Kim Lane. 2006. "Guardians of the Constitution: Constitutional Court Presidents and the Struggle for the Rule of Law in Post-Soviet Europe." *University of Pennsylvania Law Review* 154 (6): 1757–1851.

———. 2012a. "First, Let's Pick All the Judges." Blog post at krugman.blogs.nytimes.com/2012/03/10/first-lets-pick-all-the-judges/.

———. 2012b. "How to Evade the Constitution." Blog post at verfassungsblog.de/evade-constitution-case-hungarian-constitutional-courts-decision-judicial-retirement-age/.

———. 2012c. "The New Hungarian Secret Police." Blog post at krugman.blogs.nytimes.com/2012/04/19/the-new-hungarian-secret-police/.

———. 2012d. "On the Unconstitutionality of Constitutional Change: An Essay in Honor of László Sólyom." In *Liber Amicorum in Honor of László Sólyom*, edited by Pál Sonnevend, Balázs Schanda, and Zoltán Csehi. Budapest.

———. 2014. "Legal but not Fair," Blog post at https://krugman.blogs.nytimes.com/2014/04/13/legal-but-not-fair-hungary/.

Schmitt, Carl. 2008. *Constitutional Theory*. Translated and edited by Jeffrey Seitzer. Durham, NC: Duke University Press.

Sieyès, Emmanuel-Joseph. 2003. "What Is the Third Estate?" In *Sieyès: Political Writings*, edited and translated by Michael Sonenscher, 92–162. Indianapolis, IN: Hackett.

Sólyom, László. 2000. "Introduction to the Decisions of the Constitutional Court of the Republic of Hungary." In *Constitutional Judiciary in a New Democracy: The Hungarian Constitutional Court*, edited by László Sólyom and Georg Brunner, 1–64. Ann Arbor: University of Michigan Press.

———. "On Capital Punishment." Hungarian Constitutional Court Decision 23/1990, October 31, 1990. Translated in *Constitutional Judiciary in a New Democracy: The Hungarian Constitutional Court*, edited by László Sólyom and Georg Brunner, 118–138. Ann Arbor: University of Michigan Press.

Szigetvári, Viktor, Csaba Tordai, and Balazs Vetô. 2011. "Beyond Democracy." Available at freehungary.hu/index.php/archives-new/613-beyond-democracy-the-new-electoral-law.

Uitz, Renata. 2013. "The Return of the Hungarian Constitutional Court." Blog post at verfassungsblog.de/the-return-of-the-hungarian-constitutional-court/.

Westhead, Rick. 2012. "Why the Roma Are Fleeing Hungary and Why Canada Is Shunning Them." *Toronto Star*, October 13, 2012.

Zilahy, Péter. 2011. "Young Hungarians Are Intent on Writing Their Own Future." Opinion. *Guardian*, December 17, 2011. https://www.theguardian.com/commentisfree/2011/dec/17/young-hungarians-viktor-orban.

CHAPTER 7

Communist Federations

Valerie Bunce

> Ethnic identities are cultural forms of expression that can be mobilized, politicized, and verified in state institutions—or not.
>
> —Lise Morjé Howard (2012)

Communism as a Radical Project

It is very easy to forget, in view of its sorry record of economic and political stagnation during its last few decades on the European stage, that Communism in the Soviet Union and Eastern Europe began as a bold experiment. Here, I refer to such remarkable innovations as the Leninist Party, the ideological mission of building a socialist order and socialist citizens, and the reliance not on the bourgeoisie but rather on a single party, state ownership of the means of production, and central planning as the drivers of socioeconomic transformation. Communism in Europe was, in short, a new type of dictatorship, and one that was, moreover, very successful in its early years in promoting rapid social and economic change. These achievements, plus its creation of a powerful political elite and, in the Soviet case, a superpower that could stand up to Hitler and then the West, made the Communist model extremely influential abroad. Beginning in the 1970s, however, two trends began to take shape that eventually undercut the sustainability and the external appeal of the Communist model. The first was an economic slowdown in the Soviet Union and Eastern Europe, and the second was the global diffusion of democracy and neoliberal economic policies (Simmons, Dobbin, and Garrett

2008). As a result, both the Communist model itself and its ability to win adherents abroad came to an end (see Bunce 1999).

There was, however, another, equally audacious innovation that the European Communists introduced—in this case, involving the introduction of new institutions that were to address the relationship between socioeconomic inequality and cultural diversity. Here, I refer to the remarkable decision by the Bolshevik leadership, once it emerged triumphant in the civil war in the early 1920s, to build an ethnofederal state in the ashes of the Russian Empire (see, e.g., Carr 1954; Brubaker 1996; Bunce 1999; Suny 1994, 1999a, 1999b; Slezkine 1994; Martin 2001; Hirsch 2005; Hale 2008). This was a state that shared certain features with all federal systems. For example, there was a central government with its own institutions of representation and decision-making, and the territory of the state was divided into a series of subunits that also had their own institutions of representation and decision-making. Moreover, and also typical of all federations, there was a division of, as well as some overlap between, powers reserved for the center and for the subunits. However, the Soviet version of federalism added a distinctive feature: the alignment of those subunits with the spatial distribution of cultural communities. Thus, the Bolsheviks added to their already very ambitious agenda of socioeconomic transformation the construction of a new type of nation-state that used federalism to represent and empower—and, in many instances, build—nations within the state. They took on this innovative national and state project, moreover, despite the fact that such tasks were not in a strict sense part of their Marxist job description (but see Carr 1954).

Like its socioeconomic counterpart, the ethnofederal experiment proved to be very influential, not just in shaping the evolution of the Soviet Union but also in convincing leaders in other states with diverse populations to adopt a similar approach. This was the case, moreover, whether these regimes were Communist or democratic. Thus, just as Communist-era Yugoslavia and Czechoslovakia emulated the Soviet model of ethnofederalism, so did, for example (but in many cases not consciously), Nigeria, Spain, Burundi, Lebanon, Cyprus, Northern Ireland, Belgium, and the Russian Federation (see, e.g., Conversi 1993; Díez Medrano 1995; Guibernau 1995; Moreno 2001; Bose 2002; McGarry and O'Leary 2002; Zahar 2005; Rothchild and Roeder 2005a, 2005b; Hale 2008; Howard 2012).[1] Indeed, this approach to addressing the challenges posed by cultural diversity within states had even more extensive impact. For example, it was championed by some theorists of divided societies, albeit ones that focused their attention on diversity in democratic orders

(Lijphart, 1969, 1977, 1996). At the same time, as we have seen in such cases as Bosnia and Iraq, many members of the international community also embraced ethnofederal arrangements when, following the end of the Cold War, they took on increased responsibilities for rebuilding states and regimes after internal wars (Lijphart 1969, 1977, 1996; Hartzell 1999; Csergo 2007; Rothchild and Roeder 2005a, 2005b; Jung 2010).

Thus, while the international influence of the Leninist Party and Communism's distinctive approach to dictatorship and development began to decline by the 1980s and certainly following the end of the Cold War, the same cannot be said for the impact of the ethnofederal model. The durability of this approach to the management of cultural diversity is surprising. First, a central goal of political leaders of culturally diverse countries and powerful actors in the international system is to maintain existing state borders. This is because, once state boundaries come into question, the likelihood of domestic and international conflict increases sharply. Second, as we saw from 1989 to 1992, all of the European Communist states that were ethnofederal—and only those Communist states—experienced both a change in the regime and a change in state borders. Indeed, this pattern of regime transition and the eruption of conflicts, often violent, over existing state borders even materialized within those subunits of these states that were themselves ethnofederal in design—for example, Georgia and Moldova in the case of the Soviet Union and Serbia in the case of Yugoslavia. Moreover, while the Russian ethnofederal republic managed to maintain its existing boundaries in its transition to independent statehood, it also experienced along the way significant secessionist pressures emanating from movements within some of its ethnically defined subunits (see Bunce 2004a, 2004b, 2007; Treisman 1997).

The purpose of this chapter is to analyze the design, origins, and consequences of ethnofederalism in the European Communist experience. I begin by summarizing the key features of the ethnofederal state, focusing primarily on the Soviet Union, but also bringing in the Yugoslav case as well because of the modifications in the model that the Yugoslav leadership introduced. I then turn to the question of why the Bolsheviks took this constitutional approach to the management of cultural diversity. Of interest here is both what motivated their decision to build this kind of system and the goals they thought would be served by taking this approach to state-building. I then assess the extent to which this state, in the short term and in the longer term, met those goals. I close the chapter by addressing the question of whether the relationship between ethnofederalism and the dissolution of the state in the Communist world is a function of the ethnofederal design of the state itself or the fact that the Communist experiment combined this type of state with dictatorial politics. Could it be argued, for example, that ethnofederalism sustains rather than undermines multinational states when it is combined with a democratic political system? This question seems highly salient at a time when movements to achieve ethnic homogeneity within nations seem to have renewed force in many lands.

Defining Ethnofederalism

In the Communist context, "ethnofederalism" referred to a type of federal state in which each of the constitutive subunits was defined by—and, indeed, named for—a specific cultural community. Two principles served as the building blocks of ethnofederalism. One was that there was a purposive coincidence between the geographical boundaries of political subunits, on the one hand, and, on the other, the spatial distribution of nations and what was often in practice in the less-developed areas of these states, proto-nations. The other was that the institutions of ethnofederalism were designed to serve a range of political and socioeconomic purposes—for example, sometimes creating but also in every case representing and empowering cultural communities; developing an indigenous stratum of political, economic, social, and cultural leaders; and promoting rapid and equitable economic and social change.

There are several important aspects of ethnofederalism in the Communist world that need to be highlighted. One is that this approach to federalism, as noted briefly in the Introduction, contrasts sharply with several other variants on federalism that we find in the world today. One is ethnofederalism that is based strictly upon linguistic cleavages, rather than, say, ethnicity, religion, or other cultural markers. An example here is India (see Bajpai 1997; Lijphart 1996). Another is asymmetric ethnofederalism, as we see in, say, Canada and Spain. Here, only some of the subunits that compose the state are defined in cultural terms, and these subunits are different from their counterparts in having significant cultural and political autonomy (see, e.g. Moreno 2001; Díez Medrano 1995). Finally, there are "a-national" federal systems, as in the United States and Germany, wherein political subunits are defined in purely spatial terms. National institutions neither assign nor recognize any distinctive "cultural" content for any of the states in the United

States or to any of the Lander in Germany (even if many residents believe their state is distinctively best). As a result, representation at the subnational level flows strictly from place of residence, rather than from this factor in conjunction with membership in a particular titular nation.

These variations recognized, however, the examples we provided lead us to an important point that will be relevant later in this chapter. It is very rare for dictatorships to go the federal, let alone the ethnofederal, route. This is largely because, just as federalism creates subnational institutions that have some potential for establishing autonomy from the center and thereby providing a base of operations for resisting central directives, so nationally defined federalism introduces further constraints on the powers of authoritarian leaders. For example, by highlighting the importance of culture and anchoring it in both space and institutions, ethnofederalism works against the ability of authoritarian leaders in culturally diverse countries (depending upon their approach to governance) to mobilize support and remain in power by using such familiar methods as suppressing cultural differences, building a statewide and nonethnic identity, and/or ruling on behalf of one cultural community in particular. In this sense, while authoritarian regimes vary from one to another and while the strategies their leaders use to manage diversity also vary, ethnofederalism would, on the face of it, be an equally threatening prospect for the rulers of, say, Bahrain, Syria, China, and Saddam Hussein's Iraq.

A second important fact on the ground in these ethnofederal experiments in the Communist world is that cultural communities within each of these states varied significantly in their size, geographical dispersion, level of socioeconomic development and potential for supporting or compromising the goals of building socialism and a viable state. For example, while the Russians were large, concentrated in the western half of the country, but also well-represented in the east as well, relatively developed in socioeconomic terms, and served as the core national group within the Bolshevik Party, the Georgians were much smaller and concentrated in the southwest, poorer, and more supportive of the Mensheviks. The implication here is that it was far from easy, whether we focus on the demographic, geographical, or ideological characteristics of nations within the Soviet Union (and Yugoslavia), to draw an ethnofederal map. Once the boundaries were drawn, moreover, they were subject to change in the future.

Third, it was the leaders of the Communist Party, influenced by ethnographic data and political and economic considerations, that decided which of the many cultural communities that made up the state would be officially recognized and which (in a subset of cases) would receive a political unit in their name (see, e.g., Slezkine 1994; Hirsch 2005). Moreover, in both Yugoslavia and the Soviet Union, in part because of the variations in the size, distribution, development, and political sympathies of cultural groupings, a decision was made to expand ethnofederalism beyond a simple two-tiered model composed of the center and the republics. For example, the Serbian republic in Yugoslavia had several nationally defined subunits that were attached to it in administrative terms (that is, Kosovo and Vojvodina, with the former recognizing a sizable Albanian community and the latter a significant Hungarian minority) and that had more restricted powers than Serbia (though this changed after a new constitution was put in place following the death of Tito in 1980). The same was the case for the Soviet Union with respect to the Russian and Georgian republics. As a result, we see in these cases ethnofederal republics nested within the ethnofederal state.

Fourth, it is important to recognize the institutional complexity of ethnofederalism as a result of its location within a Communist political and economic order. Thus, in addition to representational and decision-making units at the republican (and subrepublican) levels, the subunits of the ethnofederation had their own Communist parties and their own academies of sciences. The purpose of ethnofederalism, therefore, was to link these units with the center and its objectives; to represent them and their economic interests; to develop nations and local economies and societies; and to build an intellectual, social, and political elite stratum. In this way, ethnofederalism is best understood as a project in national, state, and economic and political regime-building.

Fifth, there were variations in ethnofederal designs—over time and across country. Thus, just as the boundaries of the subunits changed over time in the Soviet Union (especially in the Caucasus), so the degree of constitutionally defined autonomy of the provinces that were located below these subunits changed over time in Yugoslavia. At the same time, as already noted, in contrast to Czechoslovakia, the Yugoslav and Soviet federations featured several tiers of nationally defined subunits (and in the Soviet case, there were also "a-national" tiers within the Russian republic). Just as important, especially for understanding subsequent patterns of state dissolution, are two more distinctions that we can draw between federalism in Yugoslavia, on the one hand, and federalism in the Soviet Union and Czechoslovakia, on the other (see Bunce 1999). The Yugoslav federation is better understood, especially after

1965 and even more so after the death of Tito in 1980, as a confederation—in some ways not unlike the contemporary European Union. In particular, the economic, political, social, and cultural autonomy of the subunits was substantial, and the center was, as a consequence, relatively weak. By contrast, in the other ethnofederations, the center was stronger. It is telling, for example, that in the other two federations, the economy was structured in largely functional terms, whereas in Yugoslavia it was much more segmented by republic. At the same time, the Yugoslav approach was distinctive in its treatment of the "core" republic (see Bunce 1999). While all the Yugoslav republics were equal in their institutional endowments, whether we focus on political, social, economic, or cultural institutions, the same was not true for the Soviet Union or Czechoslovakia. In those two countries, the largest and most politically influential nation (in part because of where the capital of the country was located) and its designated republic—that is, the Russian and the Czech republics, respectively, as opposed to Serbia in the Yugoslav federation—did not have their own cultural and political institutions. Instead, the first two republics served merely as the seat of the "all-union" institutions, including, for example, the Communist Party, the economic ministries, the parliament, the secret police, and the military.

This contrast, which like the economic one helps explain why Yugoslavia dissolved through war whereas the other federations broke up in more peaceful ways, can be explained by differences in political pressures on the ground at the time that these federations formed. One issue was that, for Tito and his allies, Serbia needed to be sufficiently empowered to serve as a counterweight to Croatian nationalism. At the same time, Serbia had to be rewarded for making two sacrifices: giving up independent statehood in order to join the socialist Yugoslav state and accepting republican boundaries that did not encase the entire Serbian population of the country. Thus, an institutional "deal" was struck that, in contrast to the situation of Russia within the Soviet ethnofederation, gave Serbia the full complement of institutions that all the other Yugoslav republics received (and see Vujacic 1996, 2015; Vujacic and Zaslavsky 1991). By contrast, in the Soviet case, limiting the Russian republic to serving as the host for all-union institutions served two functions: using Russia to safeguard the Soviet project (which was no small concern in such a huge state), while reassuring non-Russians at the same time that Russia would lack the specifically Russian institutions that would allow it to continue its historical role of political, economic, and cultural domination over the entire country (Dunlop 1998). As for Czechoslovakia, there was not just the issue of the historical domination of the Czechs during the interwar period, but also the threats to Communist hegemony posed by 1968; that is, the necessity of using an empowered Slovak republic to rein in the Czech party and population. In this sense, the logic of introducing ethnofederalism in Czechoslovakia after 1968 was two-pronged: constrain the Czechs, but also court the Slovaks (who received from the deal not just new institutions and legitimation of their national heritage, but also a disproportionate supply of economic resources from the center and from the Soviet Union) (see Bunce 1984/1985).

We can now turn our attention to a final aspect of ethnofederalism in the Communist world that needs to be addressed. Few people would challenge the argument that, in a democracy, federalism has the effect of empowering subunits and thereby imposing significant constraints on the powers of the central government. The question is whether the same argument can be made in the case of a dictatorship. This is in fact a difficult question to answer. On the one hand, in the Communist cases, the center in theory and certainly more so in practice was the dominant political and economic player. This is because the architects of the Communist ethnofederations in Europe were motivated by a desire not simply to represent and empower nations but also to use these nations and their institutions to extend the center's control over the periphery. There were three key factors, moreover, that reinforced the ability of the center—that is, the Communist Party—to use ethnofederalism as a mechanism of spatial, ideological, and national control. One was the overarching ideological mission of building a common, socialist identity; another was the administrative principle of democratic centralism, wherein diverse opinions were tolerated until a decision was made and all units of the system were then expected to play the role of transmission belts for the implementation of central policy; and a final one was the center's control over the all-union economic and political institutions. With respect to the final point, it is important to recognize that Communist regimes, whether federal or unitary, had an unusually dense institutional landscape. There were no examples of what could be termed either political vacuums or "floating institutions." Instead, every institution was embedded in a hierarchy that ran from the bottom to the top of the system, whether that institution was defined in functional terms (as with the economy) or in territorial ones (as in the cases of the party, social and cultural institutions, and representative political bodies).

What also augmented the power of the center was the fact that in these federations, similar to what happens in other federations, but in a more extreme way because of the dictatorship and its institutional design, political and economic bargaining took place largely through vertical rather than horizontal interactions. In this sense, the Communist version of ethnofederalism closely resembled an empire. Thus, bargaining within these federations over power and money was largely a dyadic dynamic involving each republic and the center, rather than a process that took place either among republics or between the center, on the one hand, and a group of republics, on the other. What also blocked horizontal politics (as well as economics) was the fact that each republic represented a specific nation that had its own institutions and, because of that and the structure of the local economy, well-defined interests. While the nature of these subunits contributed to their ability to serve as counterweights to the center's power, it also served the opposite function, especially in the early years of Communism. It made coalition formation among the republics very hard as a result of the obstacles posed by the center's political and economic monopoly; the generation of divergent interests among the republics, as a result of the varying cultural and socioeconomic profiles; the construction of "hard" boundaries demarcating the republics; and perceptions among leaders of the republics that in the struggle for the center's favors they were involved in a zero-sum game. As a result, the structure of ethnofederalism served as a powerful tool for maximizing centralized control.

Finally, the center in the Soviet Union and Yugoslavia benefited from the existence of multiple tiers in the ethnofederal system. While there was a national pecking order in these two countries because the second tier enjoyed more rights and more autonomy than the tier below it and attached to it in a geographical and institutional sense, it was also the case that this third tier played an important role in defending the power of the center. In particular, this tier existed in order to counter the power of republics—by, for example, privileging a specific minority group, even when it was outnumbered by another group, including the group after which the republic had been named. In this way, some of the ethnically based provinces served as Moscow's eyes and ears in republican politics. This is precisely what we saw, for example, in the case of Abkhazia, an autonomous province within the Georgian republic, whose rulers were Abkhaz, but whose population was primarily Georgian. Because Abkhaz were a minority within their own province, but allied with Moscow against the Georgian majority in the province and in the republic, moreover, they were in a position to view any weakening of Moscow's control over the state with considerable alarm. While they had a lot to gain from a strong Moscow and a subservient Georgia, they had a lot to lose from a Moscow in retreat and a Georgia on the road to statehood (Dale 1996; Bunce 2007). What we saw, in short, was a security dilemma (Posen 1993).

There are good reasons, therefore, to argue that the subunits within these ethnofederations were in fact relatively weak. However, in some ways ethnofederalism did generate some constraints on the center. One way this happened was through the creation in each republic of titular leaders (though this was less the case in certain subunits, such as Chechnya within the Russian federal republic, where Russians held virtually all of the important political and economic posts) (see Evangelista 2002; Lieven 1998). Moreover, as already noted, in the case of Yugoslavia, the republics had a great deal more institutional autonomy than was the case for their counterparts in Czechoslovakia and the Soviet Union. Finally, the mere existence of the republics and their significant institutional and national endowments, coupled with the significant slowdown in the circulation of elites during the last several decades of Communism (especially in the Soviet Union and Czechoslovakia), laid the groundwork for a gradual and cumulatively significant redistribution of power and economic resources from the center to the next tier of the ethnofederation. This "republicanization" of politics and economics—that is, the creation over time at the republican level of well-defined nations, complete with their own political and cultural leaders and virtually all of the defining institutions of statehood, including demarcated boundaries of authority—is a dynamic that we will address in great detail later in this chapter.

A final factor also worked to slowly but surely augment the power of the republics that were nested within these ethnofederations. Titular nations that were given political units at the second tier of the Communist ethnofederations—that is, the constituent republics—had certain constitutional rights, such as self-determination. This was a peculiarity of the Communist ethnofederations that reflected the impact of three factors that played a role in the early decisions to constitute an ethnofederal state. One was the support of this principle by the Bolsheviks prior to their seizure of power. Another was their need to maintain this commitment, once they seized power and faced a civil war in which the key issues were whether they could stay in power at all and whether they would be able to project that power beyond a few major cities in the western portion of Russia to the point of reconstituting a rapidly disintegrating Russian Empire. Yet another factor were developments across Europe; that is, the disintegration of the other European empires during World War I, nationalist uprisings along the borders of the

Russian Empire, and the long shadow cast by Woodrow Wilson over Europe and his support of national self-determination. While an expedient decision, given the political context within which the Bolsheviks operated, their continued commitment to national self-determination when they built an ethnofederal state was in some respects costly. Like the institutional design of the republics, so this constitutional principle served as an important investment in the construction of new states and nations within the Soviet and later the Yugoslav and Czechoslovak states. Here, it is telling that, when nationalist mobilizations erupted in conjunction with the unraveling of the Soviet and Yugoslav states in particular, it was that principle that nationalist leaders cited to justify their cause and that constrained the ability of the center to declare these mobilizations as illegitimate.

Why Ethnofederalism?

Why did the new leaders of the Soviet Union decide to introduce an ethnofederal state (see especially Carr 1954; Brubaker 1996; Martin 2001; Suny 1994)? This was a decision that, not surprisingly, divided the Bolsheviks. On the one hand, there were compelling arguments against moving in this direction. The most obvious one was that this approach to state-building was untried. Why should they risk such an experiment, given their difficult position by the end of the civil war? Here, I refer to the facts that the Bolshevik hold on power was tenuous; the economy was in shambles; the society had suffered enormously as a result of World War I, the civil war, and extensive disease; and these decisions needed to be addressed in a time of not just significant nationalist mobilization within and all along the borders of the Russian Empire but also the rise of new states in the wreckage of neighboring empires. Moreover, the Bolsheviks faced two other threats: the hostility of the West and the many costs associated with having won power in what was in effect "the wrong kind of country" in which to build Communism; that is, an agrarian empire, not an industrialized state.

There were also good reasons to assume, as many Bolsheviks argued at the time, that the costs of ethnofederalism would outweigh its possible benefits. By legitimating and institutionalizing national diversity, ethnofederalism worked against the development of a common socialist identity—an identity that could play a pivotal role in defending the revolution, its goals of equality and development, and, of course, Communist

Party rule. Ethnofederalism, moreover, promised to invest heavily in the development of national, rather than class identities and nationally based, rather than class-based coalitions. In the process, it could encourage simultaneous territorially and nationally based resistance to the extraordinarily ambitious policies of the center and its ruling Communist Party. For example, just as investing in nations in ways that leveled the developmental and political playing field made some sense as a strategy to promote development and link citizens to the new order and its radical agenda, so this approach could in fact give some nations reasons to revolt—for instance, those that had been privileged in the old order, those that were not given political units of their own, and those nations that became minorities within the designated political subunits—and other nations precisely the resources they needed to carve out autonomy and to launch a revolt—for example, those national communities that received significant institutional and socioeconomic investments. Finally, every imaginable approach to building an ethnofederal state in the Soviet Union, as elsewhere, involved decisions that were inherently exclusionary, as well as inclusionary, and, therefore, divisive. There were too many nations and proto-nations to be given political units, and most of them were too dispersed for these units to achieve anything close to cultural homogeneity.

From these vantage points, therefore, ethnofederalism appeared to be the worst kind of decision that the Bolsheviks could make about designing their new state. It appeared to be at once a luxury and a gamble. However, there were strong arguments in support of this approach, and these were the arguments that won the day. To understand why they did, we need to recognize two points at the outset. First, in the context of the civil war and given the need to provide incentives for rebellious publics to side with them and not the alternatives, the Bolsheviks had in fact assembled in the territories they controlled and hoped to control a rudimentary form of an ethnofederal state. In this sense, the foundations for their innovative state project had already been laid. Second, as a result of the historical development of this part of the world, when the Soviet and then the Yugoslav leaders came to power (this was less an issue for the Czechoslovak leadership), they confronted societies that were remarkably diverse in two ways. One was socioeconomic diversity, and the other was cultural diversity. What made these two types of diversity so politically and economically important for revolutionaries committed to building a new regime, state, and socioeconomic order was that: (1) these differences correlated highly with one another, such that some nations were much more developed than others; and (2) these cultural and socioeconomic differences were expressed as well in geographical terms. What this meant is that, if the national question in the Soviet Union and Yugoslavia in particular was very hard to address, it was also an issue that *had* to be addressed. This was because the national issue was inextricably linked to the other central concerns of the newly empowered Communist leaders, including their ability to stay in power, build a new regime, define and defend state boundaries, and promote social and economic change. At the same time, as noted earlier, there was a matter of revolutionary legitimacy. Both the Bolsheviks and the Yugoslav Communists had won power not just because of their commitment to socioeconomic and political equality, but also because of their commitment to the empowerment of subjugated nations and the establishment of equality among national communities.

If these considerations made it hard for the Bolsheviks to embrace an "a-national" approach to state-building and economic development, so did the likely economic costs of proceeding in such a direction. By ignoring national diversity and by deciding against investing in the development of nations, the regime could undercut its mission of social and economic transformation by reinforcing existing spatial, socioeconomic, and cultural inequalities. In the process, the regime would contribute to further segmentation of already quite segmented economies, produce lower rates of growth, and encourage the rise of popular resentments that were likely to be politically important because they were anchored in the spatial distribution of nations and the spatial structure of the economy.

By delegitimating national identities, furthermore, this approach to state-building carried one more cost—in this case, ideological. Here is where we need to recognize that the Bolsheviks took Marxist ideology seriously. Because they had won power only to face the daunting prospect of needing to establish the very socioeconomic and political conditions that were supposed to have been in place for them to have emerged as Russia's rulers, they felt compelled to follow their "premature" victory with policies that created those missing stages of development and that promised to help—or force—Russia to move quickly through them. In this way, the superstructure—that is, politics—had to create the base—that is, the required socioeconomic conditions—rather than the reverse. If the Marxist understanding of stages of development led the Bolsheviks in power to build a penetrative and loyal party and use that party, plus ideology, terror, state ownership of the economy, and central planning, in order to generate the needed class structure and the industrialized economy that the building of socialism required, so it also led them to identify two more tasks that they needed to fulfill in order to play catch-up with history; that is, building well-defined nations and building strong states. Thus, the Bolsheviks were gradualists in the sense of believing in the importance of stages of development, but they were radicals in the sense that they felt they needed to use all the power at their disposal to move quickly through those stages and thereby arrive at the promised land. As a result, ethnofederalism, with its considerable investment in national development, went hand in hand with the party-state's commitment to rapid socioeconomic transformation (see especially Carr 1954; Martin 2001).

One reason the Bolsheviks were in a hurry is that they were vulnerable—to challenges within the party and from below in Russia and to the threats posed by a West that had quickly provided concrete evidence of its opposition to Bolshevik rule. It is here where we discover a final factor that tilted the Bolshevik leadership in favor of the ethnofederal model; that is, the lessons that the Bolsheviks learned from their own revolution, which had sparked nationalist-based secessionist movements in the western portions of the Russian Empire, and from similar processes associated with decline and then the disintegration of the Habsburg and the Ottoman Empires. Here, the key issue was how, given their fragile hold on power, they could demobilize not just those national communities whose leaders had secessionist agendas, but also attach these nations, along with the many others that made up the far-flung Russian Empire, to the new Soviet state and its ideological project. They could, of course, have decided to trim back the empire to its core groups, thereby forfeiting not just the Baltic areas and sections of Poland (which did happen), but also, possibly, Belarus, Ukraine, the Caucasus, and Central Asia. However, their logic was likely that Ukraine and the Caucasus were too important to forfeit, and that downsizing significantly in a territorial sense could tempt further interventions by the West while encouraging a national and territorial form of a bank run. As so often happens with empires and states and political units that, as with the emerging Soviet state, straddle the two, heightened concerns about security often lead to decisions to engage in territorial expansion.

Once we combine these considerations, we can conclude that the ethnofederal approach to nation- and state-building allowed the Bolsheviks to be both good Marxists and clever politicians. The latter was particularly the case, moreover, since, as noted above, just as ethnofederalism invested heavily in the development of nations, so it embedded those nations and their institutions in a more elaborate hierarchy that limited the ability of these nations to carve out autonomy, mobilize against the center, form coalitions with one another, and thereby use their institutional resources to threaten the sustainability of the regime and the state. Moreover, many of these nations had strong incentives to support the Communist regime. Like the peasants who went to the cities once the Communists began to implement their agenda of rapid industrialization, so the nations that acquired a written language, literacy, leaders, and economic opportunities as a result of the policies of the Communists developed identities and interests that supported the Communist experiment. In this sense, especially for the less-developed nations within the federation, ethnofederalism fused the national with the socialist project (Darden and Grzymala-Busse 2006; Bunce 2005). As a result, the nations that benefited from Communism were in a position to serve as powerful counterweights to those nations that had been more developed when the Communist period began, perceived tensions between the socialist project and their nationalist aspirations, and, that, as a result, were more prone to resisting the center and engaging in popular unrest. In this way, as Terry Martin (2001) has argued, ethnofederalism in the Soviet Union was both a bold and an unprecedented experiment in state-sponsored affirmative action.

Finally, as an added lure, the right of national self-determination reassured the leaders of national communities that they indeed had power—or at least expanded economic and political opportunities—within the Communist project. This was especially the case, since this constitutional principle was associated in practice with elaborate political, economic, social, and cultural institutions of the sort that one sees in nation-states. Returning to the period of the 1920s, moreover, one can also suggest that ethnofederalism was a way to build a bridge between the Communist socioeconomic project, on the one hand, and the widespread appeals of Wilsonian principles, on the other.

The Functions and Impact of Ethnofederalism

Our discussion of the rationale behind the decision to build an ethnofederal state suggests that this approach to state-building was intended to serve a remarkable array of functions—in particular, to promote economic growth, defend the state and the socialist regime, and build nations that had strong identities but that also came to share with one another a common, ideologically based identity. The question then becomes: did the architects of the

Soviet, Yugoslav, and Czechoslovak states get the results they wanted from their ethnofederal experiments? Here, I would make a two-stage argument. First, especially in the early decades of Communist Party rule, Communist leaders did reap considerable benefits from ethnofederalism. Thus, despite Western hostility to the Communist project, nationalist uprisings preceding and sometimes following the empowerment of the Communists, political repression and the enormous dislocations produced by war, Stalinist terror and draconian developmental policies, these three states managed to survive. Moreover, the economies of these states grew rapidly (though this was far less the case for the more developed Czechoslovakia), and the nations that composed these states developed rapidly as well (particularly the ones that, like the Central Asians in the Soviet Union, the Macedonians and Albanians within Yugoslavia, and the Slovaks within Czechoslovakia, had started the socialist project with fewer economic and social advantages). With respect to the issue of a common socialist identity, however, the results were more checkered, particularly if we focus on the richer areas of these states, such as Slovenia and Croatia in Yugoslavia; the Baltic countries in the Soviet Union; and the Czech lands in Czechoslovakia. In these cases, the "gain" scores from participation in a socialist economy were less impressive, and this undermined in turn the party's claim that political repression was a small price to be paid for significant improvements in education, expanded opportunities for social mobility, guaranteed employment, a generous welfare state, and legitimation of national differences. In this sense, it was in the poorer areas of these states and in areas where the Communists built nations, rather than ruling ones that were already well-defined, that we find not just the growth of national identity, but also its close ties to a widespread acceptance of a common socialist identity.

On the whole, therefore, the achievements of these regimes were remarkable—and very much in line with the most optimistic hopes of the architects that built these states. Moreover, many of these achievements can be explained in terms of the mutually supportive impact of the two models that the Communists invented in order to achieve their ideological, economic, and political objectives: that is, their developmental model and the ethnofederal design of the state. Thus, if we were to freeze our assessment of ethnofederalism in the 1960s for the Soviet Union and the 1970s for Yugoslavia, we would conclude that the Communist leaders in these two countries were remarkably accurate in their positive predictions about the benefits of ethnofederalism. Moreover, I would underscore another aspect of this record that can be easily lost as a result of knowing the "end" of the European Communist story. For most regimes and states in the world, especially those featuring, like the Communist ethnofederations, enormous cultural and socioeconomic diversity, this lengthy run of success—that is, forty and thirty years, respectively, for the Soviet Union and Yugoslavia—would be a source of considerable envy. To embellish this point further, it is also important to note that the Soviet Union—and not China—still holds the record for the longest-lived regime governed by a Communist party.

Once we take a much longer-term perspective, however, we discover that the ledger of ethnofederalism appears to be more mixed. Here, I refer to several developments. One is the collapse of Communist Party hegemony in the Soviet Union, Yugoslavia, and Czechoslovakia from 1989 to 1990. However, this was a development that also took place in neighboring Communist regimes that had unitary states. Second, what was distinctive about our three ethnofederations is that it was only in these three cases that the end of Communism was accompanied by the dissolution of the state. As a result, it appears that in the long run, ethnofederalism failed to accomplish two of its central goals; that is, to safeguard the regime and the territorial integrity of the state. Moreover, what followed this dynamic was a prolonged war in Yugoslavia, as well as a series of conflicts within the Soviet Union; the rise in all three ethnofederations of new political and economic regimes that in every case (but sometimes only years after the end of the state) rejected the ideas of a common socialist identity and the Communist economic model; and a transition to new states and new political and economic regimes that led for at least a decade after Communism to what is best termed de-development, rather than rapid socioeconomic transformation.

The question then becomes: was ethnofederalism responsible for these failings? Here, I would offer three answers (and see Bunce 1999). First, ethnofederalism contributed in important ways to the end of Communism in Europe. That recognized, however, its role in these processes was not decisive. Second and by contrast, ethnofederalism was in fact a necessary condition for the disintegration of the Soviet, Yugoslav, and Czechoslovak states into their republican parts. Finally, it is not self-evident that these states would have dissolved had the hegemony of the Communist Party—for whatever reason—been maintained. Let me now provide some elaboration of these three conclusions.

A key issue in the evolution of these three ethnofederal states was the growing economic and political weakness of the center. As these regimes evolved, they were less able to generate economic growth and therefore provide the economic resources and the social opportunities for the upward mobility that had in the early years played the key role in generating, at the least, popular compliance and, at the most, outright appreciation for what the regime and its policies had accomplished. Economic performance was undermined in part by the developmental model and its inability to generate sustained growth as a result of its tendency to foster corruption and its inability, given state ownership and central planning, to shift from the task of increasing the factors to production (which was the key issue in the early years) to the efficient utilization of those factors of production (which was the key issue, once a more developed economy was in place). However, ethnofederalism also played a role in the processes of economic decline. Among other things, these states encouraged a remarkable duplication of economic institutions, which contributed to economic inefficiency. This is precisely what one would expect in a system that in effect constructed proto-states in all of its subunits. If duplication was a drain on the economy, however, so were the obstacles that ethnofederalism had erected to a rational division of economic labors among the republics. Finally, because many of the republics were run in effect by ethnopolitical machines, they had incentives and the institutional capacity to hide capital, falsify economic data, and use economic resources from the center to pay off their friends and families. As a result of these and other problems, these economies began to decline. Vested interests in the status quo on the part of not just party leaders, but also planners, factory managers, and the working class, not to mention leaders of the republics, however, created powerful centers of resistance to the introduction, let alone the implementation of needed market-oriented reforms. As a result, the center lost one of the presumed benefits of ethnofederalism—that is, better information—and one of its key levers for extracting the compliance of its publics and its subunits—that is, the redistribution of economic resources. In this sense, it is not surprising that the story of the collapse of Communism began not just in Poland but also in the Soviet Union and Yugoslavia.

At the same time, pressures built on Communist rulers to maintain their coalitions at the top in difficult economic circumstances by embracing a policy of "stability in cadres" that involved giving allies in the party two things that they coveted but had never had: job security and predictable access to rents. However, by slowing down the circulation of political leaders, republic-level elites lost any hope for upward political mobility, had fewer incentives, as a result, to prove themselves to their superiors, and faced the prospect at the same time of diminishing resources supplied by the center. The predictable outcome was to hoard resources and to build ethnopolitical machines that were notable for their corruption and their ability to carve out economic and political autonomy from the center. At the same time, they were also well endowed with virtually all the institutions that are associated with statehood, including geographically bounded political authority, a well-defined nation, educational institutions, an often self-sufficient local economy, and a well-established political, social, economic, and cultural elite stratum. It is not surprising, therefore, that, as the center weakened, the political and economic autonomy of the republics grew, along with public unrest, and the ability of the center to contain these challenges to its hegemony declined.

Also important was the fact that the republics, because of their growing autonomy and their very different political, economic, and social circumstances, began to follow very different political and economic trajectories the last decade of Communism. This variation, we must remember, was expressed in spatial and national terms and, therefore, unusually hard to reconcile, especially by a center that was losing its control. As a result, the republics became too "different," as well as too independent, to be easily incorporated into a common state or regime project. For example, just as the Baltic republics had very little in common with Kazakhstan in the Soviet Union by the 1980s, so in Yugoslavia by the 1980s the political economy and the regime and state preferences of citizens in Slovenia were very different from what existed in Serbia. As for Czechoslovakia, similar distinctions were drawn, especially given the fact that the Slovaks had gained so much more from the ethnofederal experiment than had the Czech lands.

For all these reasons, therefore, it is not accidental (to recycle a familiar Communist phrase) that, once the center either divided because of these difficulties together with changes in the constitution (as in Yugoslavia in the 1980s) or responded to these mounting problems by launching bold and divisive reforms (as with Gorbachev, beginning in 1986), popular unrest erupted in all three of the ethnofederations. Moreover, because of that institutional context, unrest took on specific forms that threatened both the state and the regime. Thus, particularly in the Soviet Union and Yugoslavia, popular mobilizations quickly became nationalist mobilizations that were rooted in specific republics and that sought, at the least, greater autonomy within the federation or, at most, independent statehood. What we did not tend to see in these ethnofederations, once again particularly in the Yugoslav and Soviet contexts, were, for example, class-based mobilizations, mobilizations by national communities that did not have institutional representation within the federation, or uprisings that crossed national or republican lines. Thus, it was clear that it was the structure of the ethnofederal state that defined the playing field, including the players themselves and the kinds of national, spatial, and ideological demands that they put forward. In this way, the structure of ethnofederalism insured that the debates about the future direction of the regime would be diverse and divisive, and that the exit of Communism would necessarily go hand in hand with the dissolution of the state. Finally and also a function of ethnofederal structures, the states that arose from the wreckage of these regime and state experiments featured precisely the boundaries that had designated the republics and, in some cases, the ethnically defined provinces during the Communist era. Indeed, the best predictor of where secessionist movements arose and where new states formed was not the national map of these countries but, rather, their administrative maps.

A final indicator of the reorganizing power of ethnofederalism in disorganized times is another pattern that we find in the Soviet Union and Yugoslavia in particular. In the years when many of these republics were seceding from the union and in the years following the transition to statehood, the leaders of these republics, then countries, often confronted the problem of restive minorities. In virtually every case, these challenges to the borders of the new state were carried out by national communities that had institutional recognition and resources during the Communist era (with the conflict between Azerbaijan and Armenia with respect to Nagorno-Karabagh being an exception). Here, I refer not just to the eventual secession of Montenegro from rump Yugoslavia, with Montenegro serving as the final republic to depart from the Yugoslav confederation, but also to the secessionist demands put forward by ethnically defined provinces that had been nested within republics during the Communist era—for example, Transniestr (Moldova); South Ossetia and Abkhazia (Georgia); Chechnya and Tatarstan (Russia); and Kosovo (Serbia) (see, e.g., Cerovic 2001; Cornell 2001; Gorenburg 2003; Giuliano 2000; Treisman 1997; Toft 2003; Jenne 2006; Bunce 2007; Hale 2008; Pula 2001; but see Barany 2002). What we saw, in short, was a continuation to the next administrative tier (where it existed) of the very dynamics that had led to the dissolution of the state into its republican components. This second round of secession, however, was less successful in producing new states. As Charles King (2001) has argued, one reason for this, aside from the international community's unwillingness to accord recognition to these "statelets," is that both sides in the conflict enjoy significant rents from a situation of semi-sovereignty (also see Lake and Rothchild 1998).

There are several themes that need to be highlighted in this discussion. First, the collapse of Communism was a process that was several decades in the making, rather than sudden, and it was largely a function of the rising costs associated with the Communist developmental model. Second, those costs for the regime were in many ways exaggerated by ethnofederalism, because of the role of the republics in contributing to economic decline, imposing more constraints on the center's ability to improve economic efficiency and introduce reforms, creating national and territorial bases for contesting a common socialist identity and political-economic project, and sponsoring diverse visions and coalitions associated with them about how the regime and state should develop in the future. Finally, ethnofederalism laid the foundations for the dissolution of the state—a process that was sped up by the end of Communist Party hegemony. In particular, when Communist regimes endowed nations with institutions, they provided all the resources that these nations would need to construct states of their own—that is, state successors to their republics—in the wreckage of the Communist experiment (see especially Bunce and Watts 2005 for a comparison of nations with and without institutions). In this sense, the Bolsheviks were correct to see ethnofederalism as an exercise in building their regime and their state. Where they miscalculated was in not foreseeing the longer-term costs of their successes in these endeavors; that is, the fact that what they had really accomplished was the fulfillment of nation-, state-, and regime-building *projects.*

Thus, we would conclude that, if ethnofederalism helped undermine the regime, it bears full responsibility for dissolving the state. This argument leads, in turn, to a rejection of two clichés that figure prominently in discussions of the end of the Communist experiment in Europe. One is that nationalist uprisings took place in the Communist world because nationalist aspirations had been thwarted for so long, and the other is that such developments are the norm in multinational dictatorships and/or empires that, for whatever reason, experience a weakening of the central government or dominant power (see, e.g., Roshwald 2001). In the first instance, it is clear that ethnofederalism in the Communist world built nations and states within the state, provided these units with leadership and institutions, froze identities and interests along national-territorial lines, and built highly compartmentalized and distinctive politics and economics by republic. In the second instance, it is clear that minorities without such institutional endowments in the

Communist dictatorships—for example, Hungarians in Romania—lacked the incentives and capacity to mount the kinds of challenges to the state that we saw in Yugoslavia, Czechoslovakia, and the Soviet Union.

Conclusions: Dictatorship, Democracy, and Ethnofederalism

The purpose of this chapter has been to analyze the origins, design, and impact of three Communist ethnofederations: the Soviet Union, Yugoslavia, and Czechoslovakia. Rather than summarize what has already been argued, allow me to conclude this discussion by addressing at least in skeletal fashion the scope conditions of my arguments. Put simply: would an ethnofederal approach be as likely to undermine the regime and the state if the regime was democratic rather than authoritarian? Is ethnofederalism a problem, therefore, in countries such as Bosnia, Belgium, Nigeria, and Lebanon?

There are many reasons why the Communist experience with ethnofederalism should not travel well to democratic contexts. One is that Communism was a highly repressive dictatorship, especially in its early years, and it was distinctive with respect to its ambitious ideological mission and the fused, centralized, and extraordinarily penetrative political and economic system that Communist leaders built to achieve that mission and, not incidentally, to stay in power. As the discussion above recognized, these defining elements of Communism led them in some respects to invent ethnofederalism. At the same time, it was the partnership between ethnofederalism and the political and socioeconomic project of Communism in Europe that was responsible for building but also eventually disassembling the regime and the state. The other consideration is that the costs attached to ethnofederalism, while growing over time as a result in part of the design of the state as well as the regime, increased in response to a particular Communist problem—that is, the economic and social slowdown following on the heels of rapid change.

These arguments about the interactive consequences of ethnofederalism and the Communist political economy recognized, however, I would nonetheless claim that at least some of the costs associated with this approach to the management of cultural diversity can also appear in democratic systems that feature ethnofederal elements. Most obviously, ethnofederalism, whether in a democratic or an authoritarian political setting, can never be configured in ways that either succeed in representing every cultural community within the state or in producing culturally homogeneous units. As a result, ethnofederalism always leaves some individuals and groups out in the cold—because they are not officially recognized, their identities are not primarily expressed in national terms, and/or they have the bad luck of living in the "wrong" subunit. In this sense, ethnofederalism—or any political approach to managing diversity that rests on the provision of group rights and culturally defined institutions—always rests on some form of favoritism. As Amartya Sen (2006, 203) has summarized: "Gifts of inclusion often go with the adversity of exclusion." Indeed, it is precisely the same trade-off that we find, more generally, in all nationalist movements (Marx 2003).

Another problem is that ethnofederal institutions, whatever their regime context, encourage a freezing of identities, values, and interests, and, therefore, a narrowing of the opportunities that individuals and groups have to discover and express the diversity of their identities and their preferences. In this sense, ethnofederalism and, more generally, power-sharing arrangements can lead to a "miniaturization" of human beings (Sen 2006, 185; also see Zahar 2005; Rothchild and Roeder 2005a, 2005b; Howard 2012). Because they are stuck in an "ethnocracy trap" (Howard 2012), it is very hard for them to build collaborative relationships that extend beyond their national community—not just in the political realm, but also in the societal and economic spheres (Varshney 2002). As a result, ethnofederalism can work against the development of trust among different cultural communities and among citizens who purportedly share the same state; the formation of governments that are broadly representative, as well as stable, flexible, and effective; and even the generation of strong economic performance (also see Gerring, Thacker, and Moreno 2005; Anderson 2001; Roeder 2005).

What further contributes to these costs is the fact that the effectiveness of power-sharing arrangements, such as ethnofederalism, depends significantly not just on the ability of these institutions to legitimate and represent cultural differences, but also on the desire and the willingness of political leaders who speak for these communities to work with one another. It was precisely their inability to do so that, for example, ultimately led to the dissolution of the Soviet, Yugoslav, and Czechoslovak states. Why they could not do so was largely a function, moreover, of the ways in which ethnofederal institutions, whether in a democratic or an authoritarian political context, limit opportunities for cross-community interaction, generate identities and interests that diverge along national lines, and provide leaders of national groups with incentives to engage in ethnic outbidding (Chandra 2004; Roeder

1998). Collaboration among leaders of different national communities, therefore, is discouraged.

Ethnofederalism can also weaken rather than safeguard states. Here, there are two issues. One is that ethnofederalism, even in a democratic context, makes secession easier, because it encourages, as noted above, differentiation among political units, isolates these units and their associated cultural communities from one another, and encourages leaders to play up differences among these communities rather than locate values and interests that they share. It can be countered, of course, that secession is not necessarily a bad thing, especially if it produces a closer alignment between national and state boundaries. However, secession is usually an ugly business. This is because local leaders often want it more than their followers; political leaders at the center fear a bank run if they accede to any nationalist demands and are tempted, as a result, to use force; and some people, because of identities and interests that diverge from those of their neighbors, fear losing the protection of the center and residing in a new and smaller state.

The other issue is that ethnofederalism bears a close family resemblance to empires in both structural and behavioral terms. In a structural sense, I refer, as argued earlier, to the power of horizontal relationships and the weakness of vertical ones. What we find, in short, is a center presiding over a "siloization" of culture, politics, and often economics. However, one can also think of empire as an issue of legitimacy. Thus, when the Soviet Union began to dissolve, the perception of many citizens was that the state had ceased to be effective and that it had lost, as a result, both its right and its capacity to rule (see especially Beissinger 2002). As a result, it was argued that the Soviet Union had transitioned from being a state—that is, an entity that was widely perceived as legitimate with respect to its claim to exercise spatially bounded political authority—to being an empire—that is, a political unit experiencing growing contestation over and thus deregulation of its monopoly over space and political authority. Ethnofederal arrangements, I would argue, make such reinterpretations of the state project much more likely. This is not just because of the investments in leaders and institutions at the subnational level; it is also because it is so easy—or at least easier than in a unitary state—to support the goal of "going it alone." Moreover, because they have limited opportunities for winning and exercising power at the center, leaders in the subunits in an ethnofederation can easily settle on the next best thing: becoming leaders of their own states (see Horowitz 1985).

In addition, ethnofederalism can encourage the development of corrupt and exclusionary ethnopolitical machines. This is largely because ethnofederal institutions provide leaders with ample rents to reproduce their coalitions over time. It is striking here, for example, that in the Russian Federation, there is evidence that the ethnically defined republics have been less likely to experience turnover in parties and governments, more likely to have one-party systems and to have powerful executives that are subjected to fewer institutional constraints, and, finally, more prone to corruption (see, e.g., Petrov 2013; Bunce 2013). In this state at least, ethnofederalism has weakened party systems and civil societies, undermined political competition, and supported a turn toward more dictatorial politics.

Finally, there is a tension between the principles underlying liberal democracy and those that define ethnofederalism (Howard 2012). Here, there are several problems. One is that competition is not fully open. This is because political posts are often reserved for members of specific national groups. Indeed, in many ethnofederations, this is also true for state institutions, which in theory should be staffed on the basis of considerations of merit. At the same time, group rights can work against the principle of individual rights. This issue returns us to an earlier problem. Individuals who are not members of the group are in some sense stripped of their rights. At the same time, all individuals in an ethnofederation are discouraged from fully exploring, let alone expressing their diverse identities, values, and interests. Instead, the design of the state has narrowed their world.

Thus, while ethnofederalism proved to be especially costly in the Communist world, insofar as the durability of these dictatorial regimes and these states were concerned, some of these costs, it can be suggested, could materialize in democratic orders as well. As a result, though accommodation of many forms of diversity within democratic societies may well be generally desirable, there are reasons to question whether this approach to the political management of cultural diversity is advisable, even in democratic political settings.

Notes

My thanks to Peter Holquist and Rogers Smith for their helpful comments on an earlier version of this essay.

1. In this evaluation, we will leave out the case of Czechoslovakia. This is because ethnofederalism was introduced there following the crisis in 1968. As a result, it is

better understood as a model for containing a political and economic crisis that arose during socialism than as a model designed to build a new socialist order.

References

Anderson, Liam. 2001. "The Implications of Institutional Design for Macroeconomic Performance: Reassessing the Claims of Consensus Democracy." *Comparative Political Studies* 34 (4): 429–452.

Bajpai, Kanti. 1997. "Diversity, Democracy and Devolution in India." In *Government Policies and Ethnic Relations in Asia and the Pacific*, edited by Michael E. Brown and Sumit Ganguly, 33–81. Cambridge, MA: MIT Press.

Barany, Zolton. 2002. "Ethnic Mobilization Without Prerequisites: The East European Gypsies." *World Politics* 54 (April): 277–307.

Beissinger, Mark. 2002. *Nationalist Mobilization and the Collapse of the Soviet State*. New York: Cambridge University Press.

Bose, Sumantra. 2002. *Bosnia After Dayton: Nationalist Partition and International Intervention*. London: Hurst.

Brubaker, Rogers. 1996. *Nationalism Reframed: Nationhood and the National Question in the New Europe*. New York: Cambridge University Press.

———. 2004. *Ethnicity Without Groups*. Cambridge, MA: Harvard University Press.

Bunce, Valerie. 1984/1985. "The Empire Strikes Back: The Transformation of the Soviet Bloc from a Soviet Asset to a Liability." *International Organization* 39 (Winter): 1–46.

———. 1999. *Subversive Institutions: The Design and the Destruction of Socialism and the State*. Cambridge: Cambridge University Press.

———. 2004a. "Federalism, Nationalism and Secession: The Communist and Postcommunist Experience." In *Federalism, Unitarism and Territorial Cleavages*, edited by Ugo Amoretti and Nancy Bermeo, 417–440. Baltimore: Johns Hopkins University Press.

———. 2004b. "Is Ethnofederalism the Solution or the Problem?" In *Nationalism After Communism: Lessons Learned*, edited by Alina Mungiu-Pippidi and Ivan Krastev, 179–198. Budapest: Central European University Press.

———. 2005. "The National Idea: Imperial Legacies and Postcommunist Pathways in Eastern Europe." *East European Politics and Societies* 19 (3): 406–442.

———. 2007. "Minority Politics in Ethnofederal States: Cooperation, Autonomy or Secession?" Einaudi Center for International Studies, Cornell University, Working Paper Series 08-07, July 2007. www.einaudi.cornell.edu/files/workingpapers/08-2007.pdf.

———. 2013. "Regime Transition, Political Institutions and Minority Politics in Russia." In *Managing Ethnic Diversity in Russia*, edited by Oleh Protsyk and Benedikt Harzl, 263–275. London: Routledge.

Bunce, Valerie, and Stephen Watts. 2005. "Managing Diversity and Sustaining Democracy in the Postcommunist World." In *Sustainable Peace: Power and Democracy After Civil Wars*, edited by Philip G. Roeder and Donald Rothchild, 133–158. Ithaca, NY: Cornell University Press.

Carr, Edward Hallett. 1954. *The Bolshevik Revolution, 1917–1923*. London: Macmillan.

Cerovic, Stojan. 2001. "Serbia, Montenegro: Reintegration, Divorce or Something Else?" *U.S. Institute of Peace: Special Report*, April 2, 2001.

Chandra, Kanchan. 2004. *Why Ethnic Parties Succeed*. Cambridge: Cambridge University Press.

Conversi, Daniele. 1993. "Domino Effect or Internal Developments? The Influences of International Events and Political Ideologies on Catalan and Basque Nationalism." *Western European Politics* 16 (3): 245–270.

Cornell, Svante. 2001. *Small Nations and Great Powers: A Study of Ethnopolitical Conflict in the Caucasus*. Surrey, England: Curzon.

Csergo, Zsuzsa. 2007. *Talk of the Nation: Language and Conflict in Romania and Slovakia*. Ithaca, NY: Cornell University Press.

Dale, Catherine. 1996. "Abkhazia and Southern Ossetia: Dynamics of the Conflicts." In *Conflicts in the Caucasus*, edited by Pavel Baev and Ole Berthelsen, 13–26. Oslo: International Peace Research Institute.

Darden, Keith, and Anna Grzymale-Busse. 2006. "The Great Divide: Literacy, Nationalism and the Communist Collapse." *World Politics* 59 (1): 83–115.

Díez Medrano, Juan. 1995. *Divided Nations: Class, Politics, and Nationalism in the Basque Country and Catalonia*. Ithaca, NY: Cornell University Press.

Dunlop, John. 1998. *Russia Confronts Chechnya: Roots of a Separatist Conflict*. Cambridge: Cambridge University Press.

Evangelista, Matthew. 2002. *The Chechen Wars: Will Russia Go the Way of the Soviet Union?* Washington, DC: Brookings Institution.

Gerring, John, Strom C. Thacker, and Carola Moreno. 2005. "Centripetal Democratic Governance: A Theory and Global Inquiry." *American Political Science Review* 99 (4): 567–582.

Giuliano, Elise. 2000. "Who Determines the Self in the Politics of Self-Determination? Identity and Preference Formation in Tatarstan's Nationalist Mobilization." *Comparative Politics* 32 (3): 295–316.

———. 2003. *Minority Ethnic Mobilization in the Russian Federation*. New York: Cambridge University Press.

Guibernau, Montserrat. 1995. "Spain: A Federation in the Making?" In *Federalism: The Multiethnic Challenge*, edited by Graham Smith, 239–254. London: Longman.

Hale, Henry E. 2008. "The Double-Edged Sword of Ethnofederalism: Ukraine and the USSR in Comparative Perspective." *Comparative Politics* 40 (3): 293–312.

Hartzell, Caroline A. 1999. "Explaining the Stability of Negotiated Settlements in Intrastate Wars." *Journal of Conflict Resolution* 43 (1): 3–22.

Hirsch, Francine. 2005. *Empire of Nations: Ethnographic Knowledge and the Making of the Soviet Union*. Ithaca, NY: Cornell University Press.

Horowitz, Donald. 1985. *Ethnic Groups in Conflict*. Berkeley: University of California Press.

Howard, Lise Morjé. 2012. "The Ethnocracy Trap." *Journal of Democracy* 23 (4): 155–169.

Jenne, Erin K. 2006. *Ethnic Bargaining: The Paradox of Minority Empowerment*. Ithaca, NY: Cornell University Press.

Jung, Jai Kwan. 2010. "The Perils of Power-Sharing in the Transition from Civil War to Peace and Democracy." Paper delivered at the SGIR 7th Pan European Conference on International Relations, Stockholm, Sweden, September 9–11, 2010.

King, Charles. 2001. "The Benefits of Ethnic War: Understanding Eurasia's Unrecognized States." *World Politics* 53 (4): 524–552.

Lake, David A., and Donald Rothchild. 1998. "Spreading Fear: The Genesis of Transnational Ethnic Conflict." In *The International Spread of Ethnic Conflict: Fear, Diffusion, and Escalation*, edited by David A. Lake and Donald Rothchild, 3–32. Princeton, NJ: Princeton University Press.

Lieven, Anatol. 1998. *Chechnya: Tombstone of Russian Power*. New Haven, CT: Yale University Press.

Lijphart, Arend. 1969. "Consociational Democracy." *World Politics* 21 (2): 207–225.

———. 1977. *Democracy in Plural Societies: A Comparative Exploration*. New Haven, CT: Yale University Press.

———. 1996. "The Puzzle of Indian Democracy: A Consociational Interpretation." *American Political Science Review* 90 (2): 258–268.

Martin, Terry. 2001. *The Affirmative Action Empire: Nations and Nationalism in the Soviet Union, 1023–1939*. Ithaca, NY: Cornell University Press.

Marx, Anthony. 2003. *Faith in the Nation: Exclusionary Origins of Nationalism*. Oxford: Oxford University Press.

McGarry, John, and Brendan O'Leary. 2002. "Federation as a Method of Ethnic Conflict Resolution." Paper presented at the Annual Meeting of the American Political Science Association, September 4, 2002.

Moreno, Luis. 2001. "Ethnoterritorial Concurrence in Multinational Societies: The Spanish *Comunidades Autónomas*." In *Multinational Democracies*, edited by Alain G. Gagnon and James Tully, 201–221. Cambridge: Cambridge University Press.

Petrov, Nikolai. 2013. "Governance and the Types of Political Regimes in the Ethnic Regions in Russia." In *Managing Ethnic Diversity in Russia*, edited by Oleh Protsyk and Benedikt Harzl, 111–129. London: Routledge.

Posen, Barry R. 1993. "The Security Dilemma and Ethnic Conflict." *Survival* 35 (1): 27–47.

Pula, Besnik. 2001. "Contested Sovereignty and State Disintegration: The Rise of the Albanian Secessionist Movement in Kosova." Master's thesis, Georgetown University.

Roeder, Philip G. 1998. "Liberalization and Ethnic Entrepreneurs in the Soviet Successor States." In *The Myth of "Ethnic Conflict": Politics, Economics and "Cultural" Violence*, edited by Beverly Crawford and Ronnie D. Lipschutz, 75–107. Berkeley: International and Area Studies, University of California at Berkeley.

———. 2005. "Power Dividing as an Alternative to Ethnic Power-Sharing." In *Sustainable Peace: Power and Democracy After Civil Wars*, edited by Philip G. Roeder and Donald Rothchild, 51–82. Ithaca, NY: Cornell University Press.

Roeder, Philip G., and Donald Rothchild, eds. 2005. *Sustainable Peace: Power and Democracy After Civil Wars.* Ithaca, NY: Cornell University Press.

Roshwald, Aviel. 2001. *Ethnic Nationalism and the Fall of Empires: Central Europe, Russia and the Middle East, 1914–1923.* London: Routledge.

Rothchild, Donald, and Philip G. Roeder. 2005a. "Dilemmas of State-Building in Divided Societies." In *Sustainable Peace: Power and Democracy After Civil Wars*, edited by Philip G. Roeder and Donald Rothchild, 1–26. Ithaca, NY: Cornell University Press.

———. 2005b. "Power-Sharing as an Impediment to Peace and Democracy." In *Sustainable Peace: Power and Democracy After Civil Wars*, edited by Philip G. Roeder and Donald Rothchild, 29–50. Ithaca, NY: Cornell University Press.

Sen, Amartya. 2006. *Identity and Violence: The Illusion of Destiny.* London: Penguin Books.

Simmons, Beth A., Frank Dobbin, and Geoffrey Garrett, eds. *The Global Diffusion of Markets and Democracy.* Cambridge: Cambridge University Press.

Slezkine, Yuri. 1994. *Arctic Mirrors: Russia and the Small Peoples of the North.* Ithaca, NY: Cornell University Press.

Suny, Ronald Grigor. 1994. *The Making of the Georgian Nation.* 2nd ed. Bloomington: Indiana University Press.

———. 1999a. "The Emergence of Political Society in Georgia." In *Transcaucasia, Nationalism and Social Change: Essays in the History of Armenia, Azerbaijan and Georgia*, edited by Ronald Grigor Suny, 109–140. Ann Arbor: University of Michigan Press.

———. 1999b. "On the Road to Independence: Cultural Cohesion and Ethnic Revival in a Multinational Society." In *Transcaucasia, Nationalism and Social Change: Essays in the History of Armenia, Azerbaijan and Georgia*, edited by Ronald Grigor Suny, 377–400. Ann Arbor: University of Michigan Press.

Toft, Monica. 2003. *The Geography of Ethnic Violence.* Princeton, NJ: Princeton University Press.

Treisman, Daniel. 1997. "Russia's "Ethnic Revival': The Separatist Activism of Regional Leaders in a Postcommunist Order." *World Politics* 49 (2): 212–249.

Varshney, Ashutosh. 2002. *Ethnic Conflict and Civic Life: Hindus and Muslims in India.* New Haven, CT: Yale University Press.

Vujacic, Veljko. 1996. "Historical Legacies, Nationalist Mobilization, and Political Outcomes in Russia and Serbia: A Weberian View." *Theory and Society* 25 (6): 763–801.

———. 2015. *Nationalism, Myth and the State in Russia and Serbia: Antecedents of the Dissolution of the Soviet Union and Yugoslavia.* Cambridge: Cambridge University Press.

Vujacic, Veljko, and Victor Zaslavsky. 1991. "The Causes of Disintegration in the USSR and Yugoslavia." *Telos* 88 (Summer): 120–140.

Zahar, Marie-Joëlle. 2005. "Power-Sharing in Lebanon: Foreign Protectors, Domestic Peace, and Democratic Failures." In *Sustainable Peace: Power and Democracy After Civil Wars*, edited by Philip G. Roeder and Donald Rothchild, 219–240. Ithaca, NY: Cornell University Press.

CHAPTER 8

Constitutional Moments and the Paradox of Constitutionalism in Multinational Democracies (Spain, 2006–2019)

Jaime Lluch

The Paradox of Constitutionalism

Most formulations of the paradox of constitutionalism are based on the observation that at times there can be a collision between constituent power and constitutional form, or a clash between politics and law, or between democracy and constitutionalism. Such a collision can lead to a clash of legitimacies between an established constitutional form and the constituent power represented by the democratic will of a people in a well-defined territory, as Kim Scheppele argues elsewhere in this volume. Moreover, modern constitutions often aim not only to establish a form of governmental authority but also to "reconstitute the people in a particular way. The notion of a *constitutional* identity of a people, and particularly its relation to the *constituent* power possessed by the people, is perplexing" (Loughlin and Walker 2007, 1; emphasis in original). There is the suggestion, in the first place, that to the degree that there are "natural" units of "peoples," constitutional texts can reshape and mold these "natural" boundaries between "peoples." Political identities can thus be "constitutionalized," given that there is some space for malleability and fluidity, but, conversely, constitutional form itself is not unchallengeable (Loughlin and Walker 2007, 2; Lluch 2018).

Therefore, "if the *influence* of constitutional form lies in its ability to refine the meaning and import of collective political identity, its *authority* must nevertheless in some measure depend upon its continuing capacity faithfully to reflect that collective political identity. The formal constitution that establishes unconditional authority, therefore, must always remain provisional. The legal norm remains subject to the political exception, which is an expression of the constituent power of a people to make, and therefore also to break, the constituted authority of the state" (Loughlin and Walker 2007, 2).

Modern constitutions come into existence as a result of a singular founding act, usually a constitutional convention or constituent assembly. The act serves to define the institutional parameters of a new polity and the rules for coexistence. But who is the "people" that authorized this founding moment, acting under what authority? "Does that founding authority extend through time to bind subsequent generations? Does the authorizing agent manifest itself only for the purpose of a foundational act and, its business concluded, extinguish itself? Or does that agent maintain a continuing presence within the polity, such that it may reassert itself to modify, or radically alter, the terms of the original foundation?" (Loughlin and Walker 2007, 3).

At first glance, one possible interpretation is that the constituent power of the people would seem to be circumscribed by the constituted power of the governmental form. But established constitutional forms may also be challenged and questioned. "It is in coming to terms with these realities of power in modern societies that constituent power insinuates itself into the discourse of constitutionalism, whether in the form of oppositional politics in their various guises and the (counter)constitutional visions they implicitly or explicitly espouse or, more generally, by ensuring that the intrinsic tension between the abstract rationalities of constitutional design and the quotidian rationalities of governing remains exposed" (Loughlin and Walker 2007, 4; Lluch 2018).

As the Introduction to this volume argues, the history of constitution-making has shown that constitution-makers seek to provide answers to at least six overarching questions. Constitutionalism in contemporary multinational democracies such as Canada, Spain, Belgium, and the United Kingdom generally seeks to answer at least three of these questions in relation to the accommodation of national diversity in such states: Who has the authority to write a constitution? Who has the authority to enact a constitution in a way that makes it authoritative and legitimate? And what sorts of governing institutions should a constitution establish in order to facilitate the accommodation of national diversity?[1]

The Paradox of Constitutionalism and Multinational Democracies

In contemporary multinational democracies such as Spain, Canada, Belgium, Italy, and the United Kingdom, the political aspirations of substate national societies for accommodation by the state, for a special status autonomy, for asymmetric federalism, or for a more satisfactory representational scheme in the administrative organs of the central state have been formulated as demands for constitutional reform in the last thirty or forty years (Tierney 2006, 17). Such demands, in the context of the social and political peculiarities of multinational democracies, add an additional level of intricacy to the contemporary debates concerning the relationship between constituent power and constitutional form. Contemporary multinational democracies, thus, are the universe of cases covered by the scope conditions of this chapter.

The dominant constitutional and political view in substate national societies such as Scotland, Quebec, the Basque Country, Catalonia, Northern Ireland, and South Tyrol challenges contemporary assumptions about the nation-state—namely, the "monistic demos" thesis. The traditional assumptions of contemporary republican theory are disputed in these substate national societies: the notion of a "monistic conception of the nation as the embodiment of a unified demos" is rejected. In contemporary multinational democracies, there is a distinctive historiographical account of the state's origins—a "conceptualization of this founding moment as a union of pre-existing peoples subsequent to which sub-state national societies within the state continued to develop as discrete *demoi*" (Tierney 2007, 232).

Thus, substate nationalists present "particular challenges to constitutional form which do not generally arise in uninational states" (Tierney 2007, 236). The minority nation–majority nation dynamics one observes in multinational democracies add an additional level of complexity to the contemporary debates concerning the relationship between constituent power and constitutional form.

These debates about the relationship between constituent power and constitutional form matter especially in multinational polities because the challenge posed by substate national societies to the central state has been formulated in three varieties of substate nationalism: independentist, autonomist, and pro-federation nationalism (Lluch 2010, 2012, 2014). Substate national movements tend to bifurcate or, at times, trifurcate, into two or three basic political orientations: independence,[2] autonomy,[3] and, oftentimes, pro-federation.[4] While independentist nationalism still remains a vital force in societies such as Quebec and the Basque Country, and more recently in Scotland and in Catalonia, at the same time substate national movements have also sought an autonomous special status (as in South Tyrol) or greater power as a constituent unit of a fully formed federation (as in Québec at present). Nonsecessionist orientations are present within such substate national movements. In fact, even when it appears a strategy of secessionism is being advanced, "the constitutional outcome it in fact seeks is often a heavily compromised version of statehood which bears little resemblance to the traditional Westphalian model" (Tierney 2006, 93).

The trend toward accommodation within the state has led to the rethinking and reformulation of increasingly complex constitutional models of accommodation within existing states. The search for these sophisticated institutional designs of mutual accommodation may as a matter of fact pose a more radical challenge to the state and its constitutional self-understanding than secession itself. "Such demands, if taken seriously by the state, can call into question many of the constitution's most profound self-understandings including even the conception of unitary citizenship which has been an article of faith for state-building processes" (Tierney 2006, 96). Autonomist and pro-federation substate nationalisms may question central tenets of the constitutional ideology of the central state and may lead to the development of a "metaconstitutional" discourse—that challenges the state's traditional constitutional discourse. All of this leads to a rethinking of the possibilities for evolution and development of new models of constitutional accommodation in multinational polities. To encourage such accommodation, it would be best to minimize the tension between constituent power and constitutional form, especially in constitutional disputes between the central state and the governments of substate national societies.

In this chapter, I seek to go beyond the interesting observation by constitutional theorists that this paradox of constitutionalism is one of the great paradoxes of contemporary constitution-making and to show how politics and law actually interact in a number of concrete situations in multinational polities. I will show that the clash between constituent power and constitutional form can have an important effect on politics, and thus that constitutionalism can have an effect on the development and evolution of substate nationalism, and, conversely, substate nationalism can mobilize itself with the aim of impacting constitutionalism. There is a mutual interaction between law and politics, and the best method we can use to account for this interaction is to integrate comparative politics and comparative constitutional law (Lluch 2018).

Spain in recent years has become a laboratory for observing this interaction between politics and law, and a virtual natural experiment to understand how the clash of legitimacies between constituent power and constitutional form can have a substantial impact on nationalist politics, both at the state level and the substate level. Spain is also interesting because in the constitutional standoff between Catalonia and the Spanish state in the period 2006–2019, the tension between constituent power and constitutional form was expressed in two varieties: first, in the clash between an organic statute of autonomy and a constitution (the Catalan Statute of Autonomy of 2006 versus the interpretation of the Spanish Constitution expressed in the Spanish Constitutional Court (Decision 31/2010 of June 28, 2010). This political drama has been playing itself out especially since 2006. Second, in the case of constitutive referenda, as the constitutional standoff between the Catalan government (which has been insisting all along on its right to hold a referendum and acted accordingly on October 1, 2017) and the Spanish government (which has been very consistent in asserting that a referendum is not constitutionally permissible). The first variety arises out of the conflict between constituent power and constitutional form that is crystallized around a "constitutional moment." The second arises out of the tension between constituent power and constitutional form that arises in a "constituent moment." Each of these two varieties of the paradox of constitutionalism has an important effect on substate and state nationalisms.

After the October 1, 2017, referendum produced an over 90% vote for independence, though with only 43% turnout, the Catalans declared independence on October 27, and the Spanish government sought to impose direct rule, invoking Article 155 of the Constitution for the first time. But a December 21, 2017, election produced another Catalan nationalist victory and though former Catalan president Carles Puigdemont had to flee the country, nationalists regained control from Spain in June 2018. At this writing the dispute continues, with Catalan's new president, Quim Torra, a Puigdemont ally, seeking another referendum. At the same time, there is a center-left government in Madrid, led by Pedro Sánchez of the PSOE. It has adopted a more conciliatory tone, seeking avenues of constitutional accommodation within the Spanish Constitution, but faces rising far right opposition.

Bridging Comparative Constitutional Law and Comparative Politics

Constitutionalism has traditionally been the primary mechanism for facilitating the mutual accommodation of substate and state national societies in plurinational states (Tierney 2006, 17). However, as recently noted, in multinational democracies (which are a subset of the genus of "divided societies"), if we are to address the complexities of constitutional mutual accommodation, "*comparative constitutional law* must expand its intellectual agenda to encompass issues that have hitherto been the exclusive domain of *comparative politics* in order to be of relevance" (Choudhry 2008a, 13; emphasis added). In addressing the politics of accommodation and constitutionalism in multinational democracies, therefore, "there is a need to bridge comparative politics and comparative constitutional law through a genuinely interdisciplinary conversation" (Choudhry 2008a, 13). Indeed, "the work of constitutional law and comparative constitutional law cannot carry forward in intellectual isolation from the work of other disciplines of political science, sociology" (Jackson and Tushnet 2002, xviii). Studying constitutionalism and politics in such settings calls for disciplinary syncretism. Comparativists who try to bridge two disciplines are required to "speak in the 'familiar and recognizable vocabularies' of more than one disciplinary community," and this may well seem like a daunting task, but it is bound to yield substantial cumulative knowledge (Adams and Bomhoff 2012, 12).

As Sujit Choudhry (2008b, 172) has noted, a "legal approach to the accommodation of minority nationalism has both its strengths and weaknesses." He further states that we "face genuine difficulty in constituting and regulating moments of constitutive constitutional politics, because at those moments, the very concept of political community those rules reflect is placed in contention by the minority nation." Therefore, Choudhry concludes, it is at this point that "we come up against the limitations inherent in constitutionalism itself, at least with regard to its ability to accommodate minority nationalism."

Another of these challenges is directed toward a narrow form of legal formalism that pervades much of contemporary constitutional scholarship: mainstream theorists are asked to reimagine the very concept of the plurinational constitutional state. "In methodological terms, this challenge critiques the artificial distinction between the legal and the political: constitutional formalism, it is argued, is itself conditioned by, and dependent upon, politically-informed assumptions about reality which may themselves by false . . . '[C]onstitutionalism, no less than nationalism, is a functional myth'" (Tierney 2007, 237). Thus, there is a need for a more historically or sociologically contextualized account of constitution-making. It follows that "if the plurinational constitution is to be legitimate in the eyes of all of the state's constituent *demoi*, elite state actors must be prepared to embrace the idea of the constitution as a living, reflexive instrument. This requires lawyers to broaden their methods and engage with historical and sociological arguments as useful tools in the task of constitutional interpretation" (Tierney 2007, 237).

This chapter adopts a syncretistic approach to the multiple dimensions of the politics of accommodation, which opens up new intellectual vistas and makes us appreciate the contribution that political science perspectives can make to law and how law and jurisprudence can enrich the study of politics.

Constitutional Moments and Substate and State Nationalisms

There are two senses in which *constitutionalism* is a critical dimension of the politics of mutual accommodation in multinational polities. First, constitutions tend to constitute the very demos that governs itself under and through the constitutional regime. Constitutions can constitute a demos by projecting a given vision of political community with the aim of altering the very self-understanding of citizens, often encapsulated in "constitutional moments." Second, constitutions "enable decision making by creating the institutions of government [such as the kind of federal system it creates], by allocating powers to them, by setting out rules of procedure to enable these institutions to make decisions, and by defining how these institutions interact" (Choudhry 2008a, 5). Sovereign states are themselves engaged in a process of majority nation-building aimed at producing a common national identity across the entire territory of the state. "Constitutional moments" are critical periods given that "constitutions have played a central role in this process [of majority nation-building], both in the regulative sense of creating institutions with state-wide authority to permit the creation and enforcement of these policies, and in the constitutive sense of projecting an image of political community meant to be internalized by citizens" (Choudhry 2008a, 30).

A "constitutional moment" is a higher-order constitutional event, which impacts the relationship between the central state—largely controlled by the majority nation—and the minority nation embedded within the same state (Ackerman 1991). It is of a higher order than ordinary legislative activity. Such "constitutional moments" are relatively rare, and they represent a critical event that crystallizes the nature of the relationship between the central state and the embedded minority nations. These critical constitutional transformative events include the adoption of a new constitution, the adoption or proposal of significant constitutional amendments, the adoption or proposal of a new organic statute for the government of the embedded minority nation, the proposal and organization of a referendum on sovereignty for a substate territorial unit, and so on (Lluch 2010). The very process of debating and negotiating a constitutional moment is critical because such moments "help to create the political community on whose existence the constitutional order which results from that process depends" (Choudhry 2008a, 6).

Note that these critical constitutional transformative events may be either positive or negative in their final outcome. That is, the event could have led to the actual enactment of a constitutional amendment, organic statute, and so on, or the event could have been the proposal of such an amendment or the like, even if it was later rejected. What matters is that the event set in motion the public policy discussion and critical reevaluation of the relationship between majority and minority nations, both coexisting in a dialogical relationship within the same state.

Some constitutional moments are often interpreted by the minority nationalists as an instance of majority nation nationalism, and, thus, these constitutional events impact the intersubjective relations of reciprocity between minority nationalists and majority nation nationalism. Importantly, such constitutional moments often dramatize and encapsulate the tension between constituent power and constitutional form, or the tension between democracy and law, in multidemoi polities. They may also lead to a clash of legitimacies between an established constitutional form and the constituent power represented by the democratic will of the people in a well-defined territorial substate unit.

As scholars have shown previously, in the period from 1976 to 2010, both the Catalan and Quebecois national movements experienced the foundation and growth of new political orientations within the institutional component of their national movements, espoused by nationalist political parties (Lluch 2010). The transformation of Esquerra Republicana de Catalunya (ERC) into a secessionist party during the late 1980s represented the establishment for the first time in the Catalan parliamentary sphere of a genuinely secessionist formation, where none had existed before. The founding of Action démocratique du Québec (ADQ) in 1994, out of discontented elements that came out of the federalist party in Quebec, resulted in the creation of an autonomist formation that was more decentralizing in its program and nationalist animus than the federalist party out of which it emerged. These developments in two different national movements that successfully established new political orientations that represented the radicalization of nationalists' preferences show that constitutional moments can have important political effects.

Intersubjective relations of reciprocity between substate nationalists and majority nation nationalism are essential for understanding the "trigger" event that serves as the immediate catalyst that inaugurated the process that led to the founding and growth of independentism in the parliamentary sphere in Catalonia in the 1980s. The central state constitutional moment of 1975–1982 was interpreted by the minority nationalists in Catalonia as an instance of nonaccommodation and nonreciprocity (Lluch 2010). Similarly, during 1982–1992, three remarkable central state constitutional transformative events occurred in Canada: the final "patriation" of the Canadian Constitution and the adoption of the Canadian Charter of Rights and Freedoms in 1982; the negotiation and ultimate failure of the Meech Lake Accord from 1987 to 1990; and the proposal and ultimate failure of the Charlottetown Accord in 1992. These had an important effect on politics in Quebec, leading to the creation of an autonomist party (Lluch 2010).

Substate nationalists inhabit an imagined community that is a "moral polity" where reciprocities are expected and notions of collective dignity, the commonweal, and mutual accommodation are essential (Lluch 2014a, 2012a). The perception by these substate nationalists that their expectations of reciprocity have been violated is a factor that contributes to the increasing radicalization of substate nationalists' political preferences.

The research discussed above concerns constitutional moments and political developments that took place in the 1980s and 1990s. Recent developments in Spain, especially during 2006–2019, have given us another opportunity to further understand how the clash of legitimacies between constituent power and constitutional form can have a substantial impact on nationalist politics, both at the state level and the substate level. I will first examine how the tension between constituent power and constitutional form is expressed in the clash between an organic statute of autonomy and a constitution (the Catalan Statute of Autonomy of 2006 versus the interpretation of the Spanish Constitution expressed in the Spanish Constitutional Court decision of June 2010). Second, I will refer to the longstanding and unresolved constitutional standoff between the Catalan government and the Spanish government on the issue of holding a referendum.

The Catalan Statute of Autonomy of 2006 and the Spanish Constitution of 1978

The Spanish territorial model established in the 1978 constitution, the State of Autonomies, has been unsatisfactory for a number of years in the eyes of the main political parties in Catalonia. In Catalonia, the major parties until 2010 were: Esquerra Republicana de Catalunya (ERC); the federation Convergència i Unió (CiU), consisting of Convergència Democràtica de Catalunya (CDC) and Unió Democràtica de Catalunya (UDC); Partit dels Socialistes de Catalunya (PSC); and Iniciativa per Catalunya-Verds (IC-V).[5] "The autonomy achieved at the foundational moment of the Spanish constitutional state was closer to the administrative decentralization than to a model of national minorities' accommodation; . . . national pluralism was not implemented by the State central authorities" (Lopez Bofill 2014). Moreover, autonomy did not ensure the protection of the Catalan language and culture, given the overwhelming presence of Spanish in the public sphere. In the financial and fiscal sphere, the system established has been perceived as inadequate. There has been a "persistent transfer of resources to the Spanish central government as a 'solidarity' contribution with the outcome of a fiscal imbalance with the center of almost 17 billion euro, or 9.8% of the Catalan GDP. As an average, during more than 30 years of autonomy, for every euro that Catalans paid in taxes only 57 cents were spent in the region" (Lopez Bofill 2014).

During a number of years, the major Catalan parties had been putting forward proposals for reform of their statute of autonomy. By September 2005, the parties were able to come to an agreement, and in September 2005 a major proposal for the reform of the Catalan Statute of Autonomy was passed by the Catalan parliament. A total of 120 out of 135 members of parliament voted for the September 2005 Catalan Statute of Autonomy (CSA), including the representatives of practically all the Catalan parties, except the People's Party (Partido Popular, PP). The new CSA was a complex document of 110 pages in length and containing a preamble, a preliminary title, and the following seven titles in its final version (2006):

Title I. Rights, Obligations and Governing Principles (Articles 15–54)
Title II. Institutions (Articles 55–94)
Title III. Judicial Power in Catalonia (Articles 95–109)
Title IV. Powers (Articles 110–173)
Title V. Institutional Relations of the *Generalitat* (Articles 174–200)
Title VI. Funding of the *Generalitat* (Articles 201–221)
Title VII. Reform of the *Estatut* (Articles 222–223)

The new CSA proposal sought (1) the recognition of Catalonia as a "nation" and to increase the symbolic, linguistic, and identity elements of Catalonia within the Spanish state; (2) the protection of the Catalan self-government powers vis-à-vis the central government's constitutional powers; and (3) the improvement of the finance system in order to limit the "solidarity" contribution.

In the quasi-federal system that is the State of Autonomies, the amendment of an autonomous community's statute of autonomy must be enacted by the Spanish parliament (Cortes Generales) under the shape of a Spanish state law (*Ley Orgánica*). The new CSA of 2005 was amended extensively by both houses of parliament (the Congress of Deputies, whose members must approve the autonomy statute's amendment by overall majority, and the Senate). According to one study, 64.7 percent of the articles in the proposal that came out of the Catalan parliament in September 2005 were amended by the Spanish Congress of Deputies.

The approval by the Spanish parliament was possible since the Spanish prime minister, the socialist José Luis Rodríguez Zapatero, arrived at an agreement with the Catalan leader Artur Mas about the definition of the nation, the Catalan language regulation, the allocation of powers, and financing. This agreement, however, represented a step back from the principles that had inspired the new CSA of September 2005 (the national recognition, the protection against the central state's infringement against

Catalan self-government's exclusive competences, the measures adopted in order to strengthen the Catalan language's social use, and the effort to limit "solidarity" revenue transfers from Catalonia to the central state). The so-called Mas-Zapatero agreement on the amendment of the Catalan Statute of Autonomy engaged the socialist parliamentarian groups in the Congress and Senate, which at that time were the majority of both houses. Other minority political groups represented in the Spanish parliament gave support to the Catalan statute's amendment as well (the left-wing political groups and those that represented national minorities such as the Basque and the Galician, besides the support of the Catalan nationalist group of CiU in the Congress and the Senate). But the main opposition party in the Spanish parliament, the conservative People's Party (Partido Popular, PP) strongly contested the new CSA's amendment process. The People's Party fostered a fierce campaign against the statute's approval in the course of the winter and spring of 2006, which sometimes included vitriolic language and a campaign to boycott Catalan products, such as the Cava (Lopez Bofill 2014, 79).

The final form of the new CSA of 2006 was enacted by the Spanish parliament and ratified by the Catalan people in a referendum that was held on July 18, 2006, in Catalonia, at which 73.9 percent of the votes were in favor, 20.8 percent against, and 5.3 percent blank votes, with 48.85 percent participation (Argelaguet 2014, 115).

The new CSA of 2006 was therefore the quintessential example of the invocation of *constituent power* to express the democratic will of a people in a territory with a substate national society. The text was approved by 120 out of 135 members of the Catalan parliament in 2005, was then subsequently approved by the Spanish parliament in 2006, and by the Catalan people in a referendum (2006).

The People's Party voted against the statute's amendment project in the Spanish parliament and, after its enactment by the Spanish parliament and the ratification by the Catalan people, the PP parliamentarian groups in the Congress and Senate challenged the constitutionality of the new Catalan statute before the Spanish Constitutional Court (SCC) in Madrid.

After four years of deliberation, the court finally issued the decision on the statute of Catalonia in June 2010. The decision—Spanish Constitutional Court Decision 31/2010 of June 28, 2010—has 881 pages, of which 250 contain its legal rationale. The court nullified fourteen key provisions of this statute and interpreted another twenty-seven key provisions in accordance with the 1978 Spanish Constitution. The decision undermined the aims and the basic structure of the CSA of 2006. The SCC decision of June 2010 and its interpretation of the constitutional form embodied in the Spanish Constitution of 1978 dramatized the clash between constituent power and constitutional form in contemporary Spanish constitutionalism.

According to the interpretation given by Professor Hector Lopez Bofill (2014, 71–72), a constitutionalist at Universitat Pompeu Fabra,

> The recognition of Catalonia as a "nation" was curtailed since the judgment held that the term "nation" used in the Statute's preamble had no legal standing. The Court insisted that according to the Spanish constitutional framework there is only one nation, Spain, which is the unique holder of sovereign power through the will of the Spanish people represented in the Spanish Parliament. The term "nation" mentioned in the Catalan Statute's preamble was therefore rejected by the Spanish Constitutional Court if it contained any attribute of sovereign power. Nevertheless, it was considered compatible with constitutional provisions insofar as it referred to what the Spanish Constitution defines as a "nationality": a community that can exercise a right to autonomy under the framework set by the Spanish Constitution. The interpretation given by the Court to the term "nation" as a "nationality" was extended to any aspect of the Statute in which the national character of Catalonia was mentioned such as the reference to the "national situation" or the regulation of the "national symbols." The struggle for a political recognition of Catalonia within a plurinational conception of Spain was therefore rejected by the Spanish Constitutional Court ruling.

Regarding "historical rights" referred to in Article 5 of the Catalan statute, "the Court's decision deliberately excluded this provision from the recognition that the Spanish Constitution makes of historical rights in Navarra and the three Basque provinces, on which the independent financing system of these territories is based. Avoiding any possible correspondence between the Catalan 'historical rights' and the constitutionally enshrined historical rights of the above-mentioned territories," the court rebuffed the Catalan statute's aims not just in the field concerning the recognition of identity elements within the Spanish state but also in the improvement of the Catalan financing system (Lopez Bofill 2014, 71).

> Concerning linguistic rights, the ruling abolished the preferential status for Catalan in the Catalan public administration and media. Even though the decision maintained the pre-eminence of the Catalan language in the area of education and its vehicular character, the Court subjected the Statute's provisions to the recognition of the Spanish language as vehicular in education at the same level as Catalan. The [Constitutional Court's] decision [on the statute] regarding language policy was the beginning of a sequence of judgments issued by Spanish ordinary courts that have threatened the policy established from 1983 by the Catalan government of making Catalan the main language of communication and learning in Catalonia's public schools. This policy was considered a key tool in order to preserve the Catalan language after 40 years of [prohibition] during General Franco's dictatorship. However, according to the Constitutional Court ruling, Spanish should increase its presence as a language of learning [menacing the social use of Catalan among students and thus in the future]. (Lopez Bofill 2014, 72)

As for the allocation of powers, the Constitutional Court's ruling on the Catalan statute "closed the door" to the statute's intention "of modulating the competences framework between the state and the Autonomous Community" of Catalonia. The ruling deactivated practically all the new aspects that the statute had sought to introduce, by explicitly specifying an inferior position of the Statutes of Autonomy within the block of constitutionality and promoting the role of the Constitutional Court in the interpretation of the system of the allocation of powers. Therefore, it rejected all of the statute's attempts to broaden the material content of the autonomous community's exclusive powers and "to ensure that, as far as possible, the central government would not use its own powers to intervene in these areas." The ruling stated that the Constitutional Court enhanced its interpretative monopoly on the general categories regarding the functional definition of competences, watering down the range of exclusivity applied to the competences recognized under the new CSA of 2006. "Regarding institutions, the ruling questioned the articles related to the Judicial Power altogether and declared them unconstitutional" (Lopez Bofill 2014, 72; SCC Decision 31/2010; *Revista Catalana de Dret Públic* 2010).

Finally, the financing system was also heavily modified by the Spanish Constitutional Court's decision since it reduced the legal effect of the statute's provisions in this area. The statute's norms are not enforceable against the Spanish parliament, which is sovereign to regulate the contribution of every autonomous community to the "solidarity" fund, and the financial transfers. In practice, the Constitutional Court's decision on the financing system was contrary to one of the central purposes of the new CSA of 2006: to do a structural reform of Catalonia's financing system and to avoid the burden of fiscal transfers and the enormous fiscal imbalance with the center that has a deleterious effect on the substate territory's economy (Lopez Bofill 2014; SCC Decision 31/2010).

The Political Effect of the Paradox of Constitutionalism in Spain, 2006–2013

The Spanish Constitutional Court ruling on Catalonia's statute was contested by a huge demonstration that filled Barcelona's center on July 10, 2010, with an estimated attendance of more than one million people. Even though the call for independence began to be present in the demonstration, the march's slogan "We are a nation, we decide" still sought to defend the will of the Catalan people expressed in the new CSA of 2006. Even Catalonia's prime minister at that time, a member of the PSC opposed to Catalan independence, José Montilla, expressed his "disappointment and indignation" with the Spanish Constitutional Court's ruling and supported the march summoning the Catalan people to demonstrate in order to defend the full implementation of the statute (Lopez Bofill 2014, 72).

The constitutional moment of 2006–2010 was interpreted by many in Catalonia as an instance of majority nation nationalism, and, thus, it impacted the intersubjective relations of reciprocity between minority nationalists and majority nation nationalism. Importantly, it embodied the tension between constituent power and constitutional form. Many scholars and political analysts would concur that the constitutional moment of 2006–2010 served as the "trigger" event that was the immediate catalyst for the dramatic growth of independentism in the parliamentary sphere in Catalonia after. A 2014 article in *El País*, for example, concluded that the point of inflection was reached in 2010, and the trigger event was the 2010 Constitutional Court decision (Verdú 2014).

In late November 2010, elections were held in the Parliament of Catalonia, and a new political plurality emerged. CiU, the moderate Catalan nationalist coalition, won 62 seats out of 135. However, it had to govern in minority, hoping to receive some support from other parties. The political commitment of the new president, Artur Mas, was to get a new fiscal pact and try to cope successfully with the economic crisis that was having two important effects: it was eroding the living conditions of many families and it was jeopardizing the finances of the government that allowed implementing welfare policies (Argelaguet 2014, 117).

On September 11, 2012, during the Catalonia's National Day celebrations, hundreds of thousands of people took to the streets of Barcelona calling for Catalonia's independence from Spain. After this massive demonstration, President Mas dissolved the regional parliament and called for elections. His coalition, Convergència i Unió (CiU), included for the very first time in 2012 the demand for statehood in its electoral manifesto (Lopez Bofill 2014, 71–72).

On November 25, 2012, in the elections to the parliament of Catalonia, CiU received 30.7 percent of the votes and 50 seats (out of 135); ERC, 13.7 percent and 21 seats; PSC, 14.4 percent and 20 seats; PP, 13.0 percent and 19 seats; ICV-EUiA (Iniciativa per Catalunya Verds–Esquerra Unida i Alternativa, or Initiative for Catalonia Greens–Alternative and United Left), 9.9 percent and 13 seats; C's (Ciudadanos–Partido de la Ciudadanía, or Citizens–Citizenship's Party), 7.6 percent and 9 seats; and, finally, CUP (Candidatura d'Unitat Popular, or Popular Unity Candidature), 3.5 percent and 3 seats (Argelaguet 2014, 109, citing government of Catalonia sources).[6] Jordi Argelaguet (2014, 109) explains: "These results show that in Catalonia a clear majority of the parties [were] defending the so-called 'right to decide' (CiU, ERC, ICV and CUP), that is, they believe that the people of Catalonia have the right to choose its political future and, moreover, they [were] committed to holding a referendum on independence."

One of the first decisions of the new parliament was to approve, on January 22, 2013, Resolution 5/X, entitled "The Declaration of Sovereignty and Right to Decide of the People of Catalonia."[7] Its centerpiece states that "the people of Catalonia has, for reasons of democratic legitimacy, the nature of a sovereign political and legal subject." "This resolution—adopted by 85 votes in favor (CiU, ERC, ICV-EUiA and a member of CUP), 41 against (PSC, PPC, and C's) and 2 abstentions (CUP)[8]—came into collision with the Spanish Constitution, which establishes that the Spanish people are sovereign" (Argelaguet 2014, 109).

The new parliament of Catalonia of 2012 reflected the growth of the secessionist option that had occurred in Catalan society in recent years,

Table 8.1. Constitutional Preferences of the Relationship Between Catalonia and Spain According to Centre d'Estudis d'Opinió Surveys (2006–2013)

	Region	*Autonomous community*	*State within federal Spain*	*Independent state*	*DK/NA*	*N*	*Source*
2006*	8.1	38.2	33.4	13.9	6.3	2.000	REO, 346
2006	6.8	40.0	32.8	15.9	4.5	2.000	REO, 367
2007	5.1	37.8	33.8	17.3	6.0	2.000	REO, 404
2008	7.1	38.3	31.8	17.4	5.4	2.000	REO, 466
2009	5.9	37.0	29.9	21.6	5.6	2.000	REO, 544
2010	5.9	34.7	30.9	25.2	3.4	2.500	REO, 612
2011	5.7	30.3	30.4	28.2	5.4	2.500	REO, 651
2012	4.0	19.1	25.5	44.3	7.1	2.500	REO, 705
2013	4.4	20.7	22.4	46.4	6.1	2.000	REO, 712

Source: Argelaguet (2014).
* This is the first survey of the CEO's Barometer Series, in March 2006. The other surveys are the last wave of the Barometer in each year. In 2013, it is the first wave of the Barometer.

especially since the Constitutional Court ruling of June 2010. Data from Centre d'Estudis d'Opinió (CEO) of the Catalan government show the dramatic growth of Catalanist sentiment and independentism. The CEO is a well-respected instrumentality in charge of measuring public opinion. While nonpartisan, it is a branch of the Catalan government. It is the counterpart of the Centro de Investigaciones Sociológicas (CIS) in Madrid (Lluch 2018).

Table 8.1 shows the dramatic upswing in the citizenry's political orientation. Pro-independence alternative has grown from 13.9 percent to 46.4 percent in 2013. Correspondingly, the pro-autonomism orientation (which represents the status quo—the State of Autonomies) has suffered a drop from 38.2 percent in 2006 to 20.7 percent in 2013. The pro-federalism orientation has also suffered a dramatic descent from 33.4 percent to 22.4 percent.

I conclude that these data indicate that the pro-independence orientation has been growing since 2010, and its upward turning point can be located in or around 2010–2011, which is right after the constitutional moment of 2006–2010. This provides support for my thesis that the latter was the "trigger" event and the immediate catalyst for the dramatic growth of independentism in Catalonia after 2010.

Table 8.2. Subjective National Identity in Catalonia (1979–2013)

	Only Catalan	*Cat > Spa*	*Cat= Spa*	*Spa> Cat*	*Only Spanish*	*DK/ NA*	*N*	*Source & study number*
1979	14.9	11.7	35.4	6.7	31.3		1.079	DATA
1982	9.3	11.7	41.2	8.7	23.1		1.176	DATA
1984	7.1	22.4	46.2	8.8	12.5	3.0	4.872	CIS, 1413
1988	11.1	28.2	40.4	8.4	9.1	2.7	2.896	CIS, 1750
1992	15.6	23.4	35.7	8.3	14.9	2.0	2.489	CIS, 1998
1995	13.4	23.1	41.0	7.0	13.8	1.7	1.593	CIS, 2199
1999	14.0	21.8	43.1	6.1	11.5	3.3	1.368	CIS, 2374
2001	15.4	25.8	35.9	6.2	14.7	2.0	2.778	CIS, 2410
2003	13.9	24.7	43.2	6.7	9.8	1.8	3.571	CIS, 2543
2006	13.8	24.7	41.6	7.6	8.8	4.5	1.965	CIS, 2660
2006	14.2	27.7	42.5	5.2	6.6	3.9	2.000	REO, 346
2006	14.5	27.2	44.3	4.7	6.1	3.2	2.000	REO, 367
2007	17.1	29.4	41.2	5.1	3.9	3.4	2.000	REO, 404
2008	16.4	25.7	45.3	5.4	4.7	2.5	2.000	REO, 466
2009	19.1	25.6	42.7	4.5	5.7	2.4	2.000	REO, 544
2010	20.3	25.5	42.5	3.9	5.5	2.3	2.500	REO, 612
2011	20.5	29.5	39.3	3.3	5.0	2.4	2.500	REO, 651
2012	29.6	28.7	35.0	2.5	2.0	2.3	2.500	REO, 705
2013	29.1	27.9	35.1	2.7	2.9	3.2	2.000	REO, 712

Note: DATA and CIS surveys are based on personal interviews; CEO, on CATI (computer assisted telephone interviews).
Source: Argelaguet (2014).

Table 8.2 shows subjective national identity in Catalonia, based on the "Linz-Moreno" question, which allows us to examine an indicator on the identification of individuals with two political communities that claim to be nations, as in this case, Spain and Catalonia. There have been some changes: between 2006 and 2013, the Catalan identity has grown while the Spanish one has declined significantly.

Table 8.3 shows the growth in the pro-independence orientation in Catalan politics. As I have noted previously, in 1989 for the first time in contemporary Catalan history, a fully pro-independence political party (Esquerra Republicana de Catalunya) made its appearance in the parliamentary sphere. This political orientation has been gaining support in the electorate: in the 1990s it was about one-third, and in 2013, it was measured at 54.7 percent.

Table 8.3. Evolution of the Options About the Independence of Catalonia

	2001	2011 (June)	2011 (Oct.)	2012 (Jan.)	2012 (June)	2012 (Nov.)	2013 (Feb.)
Yes, in favor	35.9	42.9	45.4	44.6	51.1	57.0	54.7
No, against	48.1	28.2	24.7	24.7	21.1	20.5	20.7
Nonvoting	—	23.3	23.8	24.2	21.1	14.3	17.0
Other answers	—	0.5	0.6	1.0	1.0	0.6	1.4
DK	13.3	4.4	4.6	4.6	4.7	6.2	5.2
NA	2.8	0.8	1.0	0.9	1.1	1.5	1.0
(N)	2.777	2.500	2.500	2.500	2.500	2.500	2.000
Source	CIS	CEO	CEO	CEO	CEO	CEO	CEO
Study number	2410	652	661	677	694	705	712

Note: The Centro de Investigaciones Sociológicas (CIS) survey is an interview face to face; the Centre d'Estudis d'Opinió (CEO) survey is a CATI one.
Source: Argelaguet (2014).

Conclusion

The shift since 2010 in Catalan public opinion about constitutional preferences is remarkable, and I argue that the constitutional moment of 2006–2010 was the "trigger" event and the immediate catalyst for this dramatic growth. The paradox of constitutionalism in Spain during 2006–2010 has had a concrete political effect: it shows how politics and law actually interact, and how it can serve as a catalyst for the growth of the pro-secessionism orientation in substate nationalism in multinational polities.

These events also confirm one of the theoretical points made in previous work: substate nationalists inhabit an imagined community that is a "moral polity" where reciprocities are expected and notions of collective dignity, the commonweal, and mutual accommodation are essential. The perception by these substate nationalists that their expectations of reciprocity have been violated is a factor that contributes to the increasing radicalization of substate nationalists' political preferences.

However, it needs to be recognized after the "trigger" event of the constitutional moment of 2006–2010, other factors came into play, which had an additional effect on the growth of substate secessionism in Spain. Some of these factors

> affect strictly political issues such as election results and formation of new governments, or they are related to public policy (bills, public investment in the area) . . . or economic factors (the economic crisis and its impact on the finances of the government of Catalonia, with all its consequences); or, even, they affect some symbolic elements (expressions of opposition to the action of the head of the state, for example). Also, this process is completed with the structuring of a wide social movement in favor of independence, which showed a high capacity for action in the public sphere and for exerting pressure on political parties. (Argelaguet 2014, 114)

From 2012 to the present, there is constitutional standoff between the Catalan government (which insists on the Catalan people's "right to decide" and hence to hold a referendum, and attempted one on October 1, 2017) and the Spanish government (which insists that this is not constitutionally permissible).[9] Chapter 3, Section 148 (17) of the Spanish Constitution states that "authorization of popular consultations through the holding of referendums" is one of the prerogatives of the central state. A new constitutional moment configured itself since 2013, and this new instance of the paradox of constitutionalism has had a palpable effect on substate nationalist politics.

Unlike the Scottish case, where an agreement between the Scottish prime minister Alex Salmond and the British prime minister David Cameron was signed on October 15, 2012, in order to provide the legal framework for the holding of Scotland's independence referendum, the Spanish government, whether of the left or the right, has taken a stand against the Catalan proposal to hold a referendum on independence. The Spanish government's strong opposition is supported by the interpretation of the Spanish Constitutional Court defending the most restrictive point of view on the issue of the right to self-determination of other nations currently existing within the Spanish state (Lopez Bofill 2014). What is the normative status of constitutional referenda within multinational polities, which may call into question fundamental constitutional presuppositions of existing states? Is there a right to holding constitutional referenda in multinational polities? How do we determine what is the demos entitled to participate in such a referendum (Tierney 2012)? These are some of the questions that will be on the constitutional and political agenda in Spain during 2019–2020 and beyond.

Notes

1. For a thorough comparative perspective on some of the basic arguments and evidence presented here, and an expansive exposition of the causal relation between the sorts of constitutional moments mentioned in this chapter and substate party system realignments, based on an explicitly comparative research design, please see Lluch (2018). Puerto Rico's status as a territory acquired by the United States is in important respects distinct from that of Catalonia, but there too constitutional moments have triggered substate party shifts.

2. "Independence" is the realization of full political sovereignty for a nation. For stateless nations, it is the attainment of separate statehood, independent from the majority nation with which they have coexisted within the same state for some time. Also, proposals for sovereignty association and associated statehood are variants of the independence option.

3. Autonomy proposals are political arrangements that generally renounce independence—at least for the medium to short term—but which seek to promote the self-government of a territorial unit populated by a polity with national characteristics. Contemporary instances of actually existing autonomy relationships include Åland Islands/Finland and Puerto Rico/United States, among others. Most cases of actually existing autonomy arrangements can be clearly distinguished from classic *federations*. Generally speaking, moreover, "autonomy is always a fragmented order, whereas a constituent . . . [unit of a federation] is always part of a whole. . . . The ties in a . . . [federation] are always stronger than those in an autonomy" (Suksi 1998, 25). Autonomist parties seek a special status and special powers within a defined geographical territory, but a status that does not constitute a constituent unit of a classic federation.

4. Pro-federation nationalists seek to have their nation remain (or become) a constituent unit of classic *federations*, which constitute a particular species within the genus of "federal political systems," wherein neither the federal nor the constituent units' governments (cantons, provinces, *Länder*, and so on) are constitutionally subordinate to the other—that is, each has sovereign powers derived directly from the constitution rather than any other level of government, each is given the power to relate directly with its citizens in the exercise of its legislative, executive, and taxing competences, and each is elected directly by its citizens.

5. These are the Republican Left of Catalonia (ERC), Democratic Convergence of Catalonia (CDC), Democratic Union of Catalonia (UDC), Socialists' Party of Catalonia (PSC), and Initiative for Catalonia-Greens (IC-V).

6. CiU is a moderate center to right Catalan nationalist coalition; ERC, a pro-independence and leftist party; PSC, a Catalan socialist party with narrow links to PSOE, the regional branch of the PP; ICV-EUiA, a coalition between a post-Communist and green party with a coalition of leftist groups led by the Party of the Communists of Catalonia (PCC); C's, a Spanish nationalist and populist party; and

CUP, an extreme left and pro-independence party. SI (Solidaritat per la Independència, or Solidarity for Independence) is a pro-independence party.

7. This complete declaration is available at http://www.parlament.cat/web/documentacio/altres-versions/resolucions-versions.

8. Five members of the parliament belonging to PSC did not participate in the vote because they did not want to vote against the "right to decide" as was suggested by their party. Two deputies belonging to CUP abstained because they rejected the references to EU and some other aspects of the declaration.

9. On the possible constitutional avenues for holding a referendum, see, for example, a series of reports by the Institut d'Estudis Autonòmics (Institute of Autonomic Studies) of the Catalan government, such as Institut d'Estudis Autonòmics (2013); also, reports by the Consultative Council for the National Transition of the Catalan government, especially Consell Assessor per a la Transició Nacional (2013).

References

Ackerman, Bruce. 1991. *We the People*. Cambridge, MA: Harvard University Press.

Adams, Maurice, and Jacco Bomfoff, eds. 2012. *Practice and Theory in Comparative Law*. Cambridge: Cambridge University Press.

Argelaguet, Jordi. 2014. "From Autonomism to Independentism: The Growth of Secessionism in Catalonia (2010–2013)." In *Constitutionalism and the Politics of Accommodation in Multinational Democracies*, edited by Jaime Lluch, 108–135. St. Antony's Series. Houndmills, UK: Palgrave Macmillan.

Choudhry, Sujit. 2008a. "Bridging Comparative Politics and Comparative Constitutional Law: Constitutional Design in Divided Societies." In *Constitutional Design for Divided Societies: Integration or Accommodation?*, edited by Sujit Choudhry, 3–40. Oxford: Oxford University Press.

———. 2008b. "Does the World Need More Canada? The Politics of the Canadian Model in Constitutional Politics and Political Theory." In *Constitutional Design for Divided Societies: Integration or Accommodation?*, edited by Sujit Choudhry, 141–172. Oxford: Oxford University Press.

Consell Assessor per a la Transició Nacional, Generalitat de Catalunya. 2013. "La Consulta sobre el Futur Politic de Catalunya." Barcelona, July 25, 2013.

———. 2014. "Las Vías de Integración de Catalunya en la Unión Europea." Barcelona, April 14, 2014.

Cordell, Karl, and Stefan Wolff, eds. 2011. *Routledge Handbook of Ethnic Conflict*. London: Routledge.

Dorsen, Norman, Michel Rosenfeld, András Sajó, and Susanne Baer. 2010. *Comparative Constitutionalism: Cases and Materials*, 2nd ed. St. Paul, MN: West.

Elias, Anwen. 2006. *Europeanising the Nation: Minority Nationalist Party Responses to European Integration in Wales, Galicia, and Corsica*. Ph.D. diss., EUI, Florence.

Gagnon, Alain-G. 2003. "Undermining Federalism and Feeding Minority Nationalism: The Impact of Majority Nationalism in Canada." In *The Conditions of Diversity in Multinational Democracies*, edited by Alain-G. Gagnon, Montserrat Guibernau, and François Rocher, 295–314. Montreal: Institute for Research on Public Policy.

Ghai, Yash, ed. 2000. *Autonomy and Ethnicity: Negotiating Competing Claims in Multiethnic States*. Cambridge: Cambridge University Press.

Hepburn, Eve. 2007. *The New Politics of Autonomy: Territorial Strategies and the Uses of European Integration by Political Parties in Scotland, Bavaria, and Sardinia, 1979–2005*. Ph.D. diss., EUI, Florence.

Holmes, Stephen. 2012. "Constitutions and Constitutionalism." In *The Oxford Handbook of Comparative Constitutional Law*, edited by Michel Rosenfeld and András Sajó, 189–216. Oxford: Oxford University Press.

Institut d'Estudis Autonòmics, Generalitat de Catalunya. 2013. "Informe sobre els procediments legals a través dels quals els ciutadans i les ciutadanes de Catalunya poden ser consultats sobre llur futur polític col·lectiu." Barcelona, March 11, 2013.

Jackson, Vicki C., and Mark Tushnet, eds. 2002. *Defining the Field of Comparative Constitutional Law*. Westport, CT: Praeger.

Keating, Michael. 2001. *Plurinational Democracy*. Oxford: Oxford University Press.

Lijphart, Arend. 1968. *The Politics of Accommodation: Pluralism and Democracy in the Netherlands*. Berkeley: University of California Press.

Linz, Juan, Alfred Stepan, and Yogendra Yadav. 2011. *Crafting State Nations: India and Other Multinational Democracies*. Baltimore: Johns Hopkins University Press.

Lopez Bofill, Hector. 2014. "The Limits of Constitutionalism: Politics, Economics, and Secessionism in Catalonia (2006–2013)." In *Constitutionalism and the Politics of Accommodation in Multinational Democracies*, edited by Jaime Lluch, 70–83. St. Antony's Series. Houndmills, UK: Palgrave Macmillan.

Loughlin, Martin. 2010. "What Is Constitutionalism?" In *The Twilight of Constitutionalism?*, edited by Petra Dobner and Martin Loughlin, 47–69. Oxford: Oxford University Press.

Loughlin, Martin, and Neil Walker, eds. 2007. *The Paradox of Constitutionalism*. Oxford: Oxford University Press.

Lluch, Jaime. 2010. "How Nationalism Evolves: Explaining the Establishment of New Varieties of Nationalism Within the National Movements of Quebec and Catalonia." *Nationalities Papers: The Journal of Nationalism and Ethnicity* 38 (3): 337–359.

———. 2012a. "Autonomism and Federalism." *Publius: The Journal of Federalism* 42 (1): 134–161.

———. 2012b. "The Internal Variation in Substate National Movements and the Moral Polity of the Nationalist." *European Political Science Review* 4 (3).

———, ed. 2014a. *Constitutionalism and the Politics of Accommodation in Multinational Democracies*. St. Antony's College Series. Houndmills, UK: Palgrave Macmillan.

——. 2014b. *Visions of Sovereignty: Varieties of Minority Nationalism in Multinational Democracies*. Philadelphia: University of Pennsylvania Press.

——. 2018. "State-Nations, the Legitimacy-Legality Constitutional Conundrum, and Sub-State Party System Realignments: Catalonia and Puerto Rico (2005–2018)." *Revista Jurídica UPR* 87 (1): 266–302.

McGarry, John, Brendan O'Leary, and Richard Simeon. 2008. "Integration or Accommodation? The enduring debate in conflict regulation." In *Constitutional Design for Divided Societies: Integration or Accommodation?*, edited by Sujit Choudhry, 41–90. Oxford: Oxford University Press.

Nimni, Ephraim. 2011. "Stateless Nations in a World of Nation-States." In *Routledge Handbook of Ethnic Conflict*, edited by Karl Cordell and Stefan Wolff. London: Routledge.

Poiares Maduro, Miguel. 2005. "The Importance of Being Called a Constitution: Constitutional Authority and the Authority of Constitutionalism." *International Journal of Constitutional Law* 3 (2–3): 332–356.

Revista Catalana de Dret Públic. 2010. Especial Sentencia 31/2010 del Tribunal Constitucional, sobre el Estatuto de Autonomía de Cataluña de 2006. Barcelona: Escola d'Administració Pública de Catalunya.

Revista d'Estudis Autonòmics i Federals. Especial sobre la Sentencia de l'Estatut d'Autonomia de Catalunya, No. 12 (March 2011).

Suksi, Markku, ed. 1998. *Autonomy: Applications and Implications*. The Hague: Kluwer Law International.

Taylor, Charles. 1994. "The Politics of Recognition." In *Multiculturalism: Examining the Politics of Recognition*, edited by Amy Gutman. Princeton, NJ: Princeton University Press.

Tierney, Stephen. 2006. *Constitutional Law and National Pluralism*. Oxford: Oxford University Press.

——. 2007. "'We the Peoples': Constituent Power and Constitutionalism in Plurinational States." In *The Paradox of Constitutionalism*, edited by Martin Loughlin and Neil Walker, 229–246. Oxford: Oxford University Press.

——. 2012. *Constitutional Referendums*. Oxford: Oxford University Press.

Verdú, Daniel. 2014."El viaje hacia el soberanismo." *El País*, July 22, 2014.

Walker, Neil. 2008. "Taking Constitutionalism Beyond the State." *Political Studies* 56: 519–543.

Walker, Graham. 1993. "The Constitutional Good: Constitutionalism's Equivocal Moral Imperative." *Polity* 26 (1): 91–111.

CHAPTER 9

Constituting the State in Postcolonial Africa: Fifty Years of Constitution-Making Toward an African Constitutionalism

Heinz Klug

Constitution-making has become a growing practice and increasing focus of academic study since the end of the Cold War. While this academic interest spans both empirical and normative approaches the general focus has been on constitutional design, the notion that constitutions are, or at least should be, the product of a rational process of institutional choice. While there was once an assumption that all constitutions were simply reflections of national character and identity, the reemergence of constitutional review post–World War II, as well as the explosion of constitution-making and constitutional revision at the end of the Cold War, accelerating again in the mid-2000s, brought a greater comparative focus and global perspective to studies of constitutionalism. From a comparative perspective there has been a focus on the empowerment of the judiciary (see Hirschl 2004) and the related question of constitutional interpretation (see Goldsworthy 2006). A more global perspective is reflected also in recent works that adopt a transnational approach, often considering broad themes—such as judicial independence (see Sajo 2004) or the legitimacy of courts (see Huls, Adams, and Bomhoff 2009)—or questions of convergence and divergence in constitutional decision-making (see Jackson 2010). What is common across these literatures is a focus on the courts. While this rich literature focuses on the emergence and spread of constitutional review as one of the key elements of post–World War II and post–Cold War constitutionalism, there is much less written on the broader question of constitutional orders and the sources of variation in different constitution-building processes.

Another focus in the post–Cold War era is on democratization reflected in the discussion of democratic waves, in which constitution-making is seen as the product or maybe the handmaiden of dramatic shifts in global political culture. Part of this focus has been a reversion to a notion of nation-building that I argue needs to be distinguished from state reconstruction and from what I want to describe as a post–Cold War conception of constitutional democracy. Constitution-building from this latter perspective envisions a broad process that in most societies may be understood to include the whole range of political and legal struggles and debates that characterize a democratic transition and undergird the emergence of a new constitutional order. A constitutional order, Mark Tushnet (2003, 1) argues, is "more like the small-c British constitution than it is like the document called the United States Constitution" and may be broadly understood as encompassing "relatively stable political arrangements and guiding principles." While the immediate goal of many of these processes is the staging of a free and fair election to determine the will of the people, there needs to be more of a focus on the nature of democratic representation and the differences between electing a constitution-making body, a legislature, or a single executive to rule over a continuing process of democratization. Despite a general assumption that written constitutions somehow mark the climax of these recent processes of democratization, there is little acknowledgment of the role that constitution-making in a broader sense plays in both enabling the transition to democracy and underpinning its sustainability.

At least until recently, the project of nation-building, with its roots in the early formation of the nation-state and so often etched in the blood of those minorities who have resisted its historical trajectory, seems out of place in a post–Cold War era in which constitutionalism had become the preferred means of maintaining the shared imperatives of multicultural societies. While there has always continued to be a broad commitment to maintaining the internationally recognized boundaries of nation-states, despite their often colonial origins, the idea of forging a single national identity as the primary social bond among the inhabitants of most modern states was for a time not accepted as a goal whose achievement might justify the suppression of individual rights or even minority interests. Instead, the emphasis in international human rights documents and in the constitutional options that have flowed from them is to guarantee individual rights and to provide different means—

from devolution of power to the protection of cultural, language, and other minority rights—to accommodate the interests of communities who will not be able to achieve significant or dominant protection of their interests through the regular electoral processes of representative democracy.

As discussed elsewhere in this volume, the recent surge of nationalist movements labeled "populist," which often seek to restrict immigration and to alter constitutions to favor dominant ethnocultural groups, is challenging these trends, though how far the dominant trends of the late twentieth century will be shifted remains unclear. In this context, the renewed emphasis on nation-building implies either a mistaken reliance on the history of post–World War II reconstruction in Europe and Japan or a simple means of emphasizing the desire to achieve stable governance over a defined nation-state without recognizing the implications for the nature of the democratic goals suggested as the outcome of the process. Such nation-building goals may be particularly understandable in the context of economic stresses, demographic transformations, and especially failed states and the concern that these areas are becoming sources of transnational violence. But it is important to resist this impulse if it threatens to shift the aim of these transitional processes toward simply strengthening the nation-state and away from the broader goal of achieving an inclusive democracy that will be responsive to the needs, wishes, and concerns of all the country's citizens.

Unlike debates over nation-building, when the focus shifts to constitution-making the tendency is to think in terms of constitutional design, whether from a normative, empirical, or comparative perspective (see Ginsburg 2012). This focus on constitutional design seems to imagine the process of constitution-making as an act of pure rationality,[1] an example of human society's capacity of self-definition. While this is an inherently attractive and uplifting vision of constitution-making, it ignores Karl Marx's ([1852] 1973) most enduring insight, that "men" make their own history but one burdened and shaped by what has gone before.[2] It is this vision of agency bounded by constraints, both historical and contextual that leads me to call for an approach to constitution-making that is both grounded in the particular history of each particular society and seeks to identify broader themes through a comparative approach that is rooted in a thick descriptive or granular understanding of particular local and regional contexts. This is particularly important in the case of Africa, a vast continent that is often viewed in the media through a single lens, described by some as "Afro-pessimism" (see Mamdani 1996). At the same time, a narrow focus on constitutional design and the new constitutional documents that are the product of different constitution-making processes may produce, particularly in the hands of lawyers and many human rights activists, a countervailing celebration of text without the necessary recognition of institutional limitations and historical contexts that may challenge any newly adopted constitutional vision.

Martin Chanock (2010, 127) has characterized the dominant analysis and practice of constitution-making in Africa as top-down, resulting in "the writing of increasingly complex constitutions, with increasingly sophisticated institutions and rights guarantees, which have, as has been shown time and time again, floated meaninglessly above the societies for which they have been designated, until the bubble bursts in outbreaks of violence." This critical, yet clear-eyed, view of Africa's postcolonial constitutional experience poses a direct challenge to us. Whether in our analysis of constitution-making or in the project of constitution-making, how do we bring our commitments to a better future into a more effective engagement with the patterns of historical experience and society in Africa? Chanock (2010, 127) himself suggests that "constitutionalism must be based on a rule of law that builds from the bottom up rather than a bill of rights handed down . . . [and that] African constitutionalism must be based on a common law with which people identify." In taking up this challenge I will argue in this chapter that an analysis of constitution-making in Africa must be rooted in an understanding of the state in Africa as well as through an embrace of a contextualized and comparative approach to the history of postcolonial constitutionalism in Africa.

Before proceeding, however, it is necessary to clarify two preliminary issues. First, Africa is a vast and diverse continent and any notion of a singular culture, historical trajectory, or constitutional form would, on its face, be a gross and unjustifiable simplification. Even if it is possible to identify a number of broad historical patterns and alternatives etched into the political landscape of Africa by the colonial experience and nationalist struggles that saw the emergence of independent African states from 1957 until the formal end of apartheid in South Africa in 1994, these commonalities overlay vast cultural, economic, ethnic, language, and political differences. Furthermore, the emergence of postcolonial independent states spans a period of nearly half a century and while the Cold War was a common element through most of this period, it was the end of the Cold War in 1989 that allowed the decolonization of Namibia and the democratic transition from apartheid, while simultaneously fragmenting the established postcolonial order throughout Africa, leading to a second, more autochthonous, wave of constitution-making in sub-Saharan Africa. While heralded as a wave of democratization in which single-party and military-dominated states witnessed multiparty elections and the installation of new democratic governments that could address what the World Bank had identified in 1989 as Africa's governance problem (World Bank 1989), the subsequent civil and military conflicts, as well as state failure, genocide, and international interventions, make it clear that the malaise lies deeper than the simple design of democratic constitutions. The recent emergence and subsequent disappointments of the Arab Spring in North Africa add yet another dimension to this constitutional foment.

Second, not only did Africans share a variety of colonial experiences—depending on the identity of the colonial power and the extent of colonial settlement—they also shared an important factor in the process of decolonization, a process of constitution-making in which the key element was the transfer of power to those struggling to be free from colonization. Thus, the first postcolonial constitutions were largely negotiated instruments in which the nationalist parties were centrally concerned with their ability to exercise power as representatives of a new nation and accepted many specific constitutional formulations largely designed by the retreating colonial authorities. Even if these constitutions sought, in a variety of creative ways, to address what their designers thought were the underlying problems facing the newly independent states—such as ethnic diversity and legal pluralism—their foreshortened lives reflect the fact that they were not embraced by either those who were to govern through the institutions and structures they created or the governed, who often rejoiced at their demise, rather than defending them as reflecting their own social and political aspirations.

Constitution-Making in Africa

Chanock's challenge is, of course, only the latest in a series of analyses that have questioned the place of constitutions and constitution-making in Africa. While H. W. O. Okoth-Ogendo (1991) eloquently critiqued the first wave of postcolonial constitutions as producing "constitutions without constitutionalism," other participants in a conference on "State and Constitutionalism in Africa," held in Harare, Zimbabwe, in May 1989, on the verge of the second wave of constitution-making in postcolonial Africa, heralded the possibility of a new, popular democratic constitutionalism, described by Issa Shivji (1991b,

39–40) as a "new concept of constitutionalism [that] should rest on [an] accountable/responsive state and collective rights/freedoms." Other African voices, including Muna Ndulo (2001), who sees constitution-making in Africa as essential to the establishment of good governance necessary for economic development, and Yash Ghai, who as both an analyst and practioner of constitution-making in Africa, has sought to promote popular participation in the constitution-making process, have seen constitution-making as a means to build effective government and a culture of human rights in Africa. In my own work on South Africa I have reflected on the process of constitution-making and how it took place within a global context that framed the opportunities for local innovation as well as a national history and culture that shaped alternatives and imposed a certain path dependency on the options that were embraced (Klug 2000, 2010). Despite these and many other contributions to our understanding of constitution-making in Africa, today achieving a deeper analysis of the processes and impacts of constitution-making in Africa requires us to both reorient our understanding of constitutions and place this perspective within a broader, comparative view of the postcolonial state in Africa.

Constitutions have been classically understood and normatively embraced as reflections of the society they constitute. Muna Ndulo (2001, 108) quotes the late chief justice of South Africa Ismail Mohammed describing a constitution as "not simply a statute which mechanically defines the structure of government and the relations between the government and the governed . . . [but as a] 'mirror reflecting the soul,' the identification of the ideals and aspirations of a nation." While this popular and symbolic notion of a constitution is central to the legitimating function of constitutionalism and is regularly embraced by constitution-makers, judicial interpreters of constitutional meaning and advocates of constitutional patriotism or those who perceive constitutionalism in the United States as civic religion, I want to embrace a more sociological conception of constitutions as social phenomena that serve the essential role of organizing, establishing, and conserving public and social power in society. Chris Thornhill's (2011, 372) *A Sociology of Constitutions* concludes "that constitutions are functional preconditions for the positive abstraction of political power and, as such, they are also, over longer periods of time, highly probable preconditions of institutions using power: that is states." Similarly, my argument will place processes of constitution-making within a broader context than that framed by a focus on constitutional design and instead suggest that constitution-makers attempt to understand the process within which they are embedded from a more holistic perspective. In the case of Africa this broader view requires a renewed appreciation of the character of the postcolonial state and specifically its genealogy in colonialism and decolonization.

The puzzle for me is to explain the similarities in Africa's postcolonial constitutional experience—weak administrations, patrimonial forms of leadership and governance, coups and authoritarianism—despite repeated adoptions of formal democratic constitutions. While Martin Chanock's (2010, 127) point that "working constitutionalist democracies are rare" and that "failure to establish democratic constitutionalist states is not a peculiarly African failure" is well taken, any attempt to understand constitution-making in Africa must begin by seeking to understand both the sources of commonality and possible sources of variation that constitution-makers and observers should know. The remainder of this chapter will first seek to explain possible sources of commonality in the particular history and form of the state in Africa. It will then turn to a discussion of constitution-making and use the South African example to explore possible sources of variation in constitution-making processes that might provide a basis for imagining an alternative path to democratic constitutionalism in Africa.

Conceiving the State in Africa

One explanation for the phenomena of thin constitutionalism in Africa, reflected in both the Harare discussions in 1989 and Martin Chanock's (2010, 127) characterization of the products of constitution-making "floating meaninglessly above the societies for which they have been designated" is that there is a fundamental incongruence between the new institutional architecture they offer and the institutional legacies that remain dominant within those societies. If constitution-makers fail to address the particular institutional and historical form of governance that dominates a society, it should not be a surprise that past legacies may frustrate the aspirations of new constitutions. In the literature on the state in Africa there are two key perspectives that I believe are of direct significance for the task of identifying and conceptualizing issues important to constitution-making. First, there is the view that the colonial state in Africa has a particular form and that the common features of this form define patterns of governance despite the vast diversity of African societies. Second, that the history of constitutionalism in postcolonial Africa reflects the continued influence of both this colonial legacy as well as the common history of decolonization, or what Crawford Young (2012) describes in his book *The Postcolonial State in Africa: Fifty Years of Independence, 1960–2010* as "the code of decolonization."

In his earlier book *The African Colonial State in Comparative Perspective*, Young (1994, 281) argued that although the colonial state in Africa is not unique among colonial states, "when we assemble its traits, examine its trajectory, and weave together the determinants of its structure and behavior, a singular historical personality looms before us." In this work, Young (1994, 278–281) identifies seven key characteristics of what he terms "Bula Matari" (he who crushes rocks), colonialist Henry Stanley's nickname and a telling metaphor for capturing "the crushing, relentless force of the emerging colonial state in Africa" (Young 1994, 1). These characteristics include: the late nineteenth-century division of Africa under the emergent international doctrine of "effective occupation" which compelled an "immediate requirement of confirming propriety title by forcible demonstration of dominance; ruthless extractive action; an active role in forcing rural Africans into labor service; advanced technologies of dominance reflected in sheer military supremacy; spheres of policy thought permeated by a virulent racism that constructed Africans as savage; unsparing efforts to "monopolize the production of meaning and thus the construction of culture" (281); and finally, a "syndrome of citizen attitudes and expectations" produced by the particular "sequencing of decolonization" (279) and the reliance by the late colonial state on developmentalism and a paternalistic bestowal of state welfare in its attempt to gain legitimacy, while remaining an "alien and predatory other" (280). Similarly, for Mahmood Mamdani (1996, 16–18), the colonial state has a particular essence that lies in its institutional segregation, creating what he terms a "bifurcated state" reflecting the dynamics of direct and indirect rule. The apartheid state in South Africa is in Mamdani's analysis not exceptional but rather reflects the fundamental logic of the colonial state in Africa.

The second perspective highlights the process of decolonization as a source of explanation of the form taken by the postcolonial state in Africa. For Crawford Young (2012, 89–96), the "code of decolonization" was set by the United Nations General Assembly resolution on the granting of independence to colonial territories and peoples in 1960, which produced a focus on territoriality, representative institutions, universal suffrage, the centrality of political parties, sovereignty, and "finally, speed became of the essence" (96). As Issa Shivji (1991a, 253) argued in his conclusion to the edited collection of papers that came out of the 1989 Harare conference, *State and Constitutionalism: An African Debate on Democracy*, "from civilian to military regimes and from one-party 'socialist' to one-party 'capitalist' states, the role of constitutions [in Africa] has lain in constituting the sovereignty of the states . . . or in simply effecting the transfer . . . or re-ordering . . . of political power." Describing the limited notion of constitutionalism that dominated the process of decolonization, Sam Nolutshungu (1991, 92–93) argues that the idea of "constitutional function"—what the constitution was supposed to do—was fragmentary and undeveloped, while the idea of "constitutional moment"—focused on the transfer of power—meant that constitutional debate was "dominated by the need for a settlement between parties to a political dispute." Summarizing this perspective, Issa Shivji (1991a, 254) concludes that "while we have had great use, if not reverence, for the documents called constitutions there has been little regard for constitutional principles or constitutionalism. Constitutional documents have neither been an outcome of a clash of principles nor are they seen as embodying a political commitment to a global societal vision."

The postcolonial state, from these perspectives, is embedded in the legacies of colonialism, and whether it is through the specific process of decolonization or broader processes of path dependency and legal continuity, the impact has produced a fundamental disconnect between the formal constitutional product or process of constitution-making and the nature of the state and institutions of governance that have emerged in the postcolonial period. Evaluating the literature on the postcolonial state in Africa, Crawford Young (2012, 70–71) argues that the "postcolonial state was thus a hybrid creature" that took three forms. The first combines "residues of the colonial state . . . [and] practices of ruling group management of power that drew on customary repertoires." Second, a "neopatrimonial practice permeated the political realm," producing a "predatory extraction of public resources and severely compromising state capacity to function according to normative state precepts" (70–71). Third, a form of hybridity "privileges the blend of democratic norms ostensibly embraced by the state and the reality of a range of authoritarian practices that limit their scope" (71). In his book *Citizen and Subject: Contemporary Africa and the Legacy of Late Colonialism*, Mahmood Mamdani (1996, 301) extends his analysis of the bifurcated nature of the colonial state to argue that the postcolonial state in Africa rests on a specific mode of rule reflected in the continued division between state and traditional authority and the interaction of a rural-urban division that is both geographic and institutional—producing a decentralized despotism in the colonial era and requiring for the project of democratization a transcendence of the "dualism of power around which the bifurcated state is organized."

Legal Pluralism, the Rule of Law, and the Promise of Constitution-Making

While the literature on the postcolonial state produces a clear picture of the historical linkages between the colonial period and the history of independent Africa, it also enables us to understand how the joint legacies of colonialism and the process of decolonization effectively displaced the design of constitution-makers in the process of decolonization. There is, however, another literature that views a number of alternative legacies, of the traditional rule of law in the one instance and in more recent judicial biography to argue that judicial independence and the daily operation of the law may provide a basis for the building of the rule of law and respect for constitutionalism in Africa. On the one hand, there is Jennifer Widner's (2001, 24) book *Building the Rule of Law*, which explores the biography of Justice Francis Nyalali of Tanzania to detail the construction of a new institutional order through struggles to "establish the separation of powers, the independence of the judiciary, and the rule of law in common law Africa." Widner's work provides a valuable perspective on the ways in which the judiciary in at least one postcolonial state was able to build legal institutions and respect for the formal rule of law despite the structural limitations and politics of the one-party state and legal pluralism.

If Widner's approach emphasizes the slow task of institution building and incremental constitutional change, there are a number of academics who have argued that even if law served the colonial project, its institutional practices provide the basis for constitutionalism in the postcolonial era. Both Stephen Ellmann and Jens Meierhenrich have argued that the tradition of the judiciary as well as the depth of legal tradition in the country since the arrival of settlers at the Cape in 1652 respectively provides a path-dependent legacy of legitimacy and law upon which South Africa's post-apartheid rule of law and constitutionalism may be rooted (see generally Meierhenrich 2008). While Ellmann (2010) has acknowledged, based on Chanock's work, that "race was at the heart of the entire enterprise of South African judging" prior to 1994, Meierhenrich's conception of the legacy of law in colonial South Africa and under apartheid providing a basis for a post-apartheid rule of law, stands in contrast to Martin Chanock's (2001, 538) more pessimistic view, when he warns that if law "is seen as the means through which solutions to conflicts, which the political processes may have failed to compromise, are to be found . . . the idealizing language of law conceals not only the ambitions of the state, but also its incapacities, which are the major threat to a rule of law."

The link between the promise of the rule of law and constitutionalism is highlighted in postcolonial Africa by the question of legal pluralism and the accommodation of traditional authority. Muna Ndulo (2001, 109) notes that "in a typical African state a large percentage of the people remain outside the formal structures of the state . . . within a traditional social and cultural context" and calls for the incorporation of traditional authority into the new constitutional orders as a means of enhancing the legitimacy of local government. While Mahmood Mamdani warns that this recognition is a basic element of the inherited, bifurcated state, Martin Chanock (2010, 141) recognizes that "culture is a dialogue between aspirations and sedimented traditions" and argues that it "is from this dialogue, including a dialogue with the imported individualizing discourse and centralizing ambitions of bills of rights, that we might find the basis for a rule of law, and, ultimately, a constitutional democracy." In South Africa this dialogue between a constitutionally recognized "customary law" and the post-apartheid legal order is ongoing, while the evolution of "customary law" through processes of development, legislative alteration and incorporation, invalidation, and harmonization is being increasingly documented and recognized (see Sloth-Nielsen and Mwambene 2010).

Given the impact of colonialism and decolonization on the creation and emergence of a postcolonial state, as well as the impact of these legacies on the constitution-making processes that swept Africa after 1989, how might we develop a broad yet contextualized understanding of constitution-making in Africa today? Instead of engaging in detailed description of the different processes, including documenting the varying approaches to constitution-making, from constitutional conventions to constitutional commissions and constitutional assemblies, I want to explore sources of variation in constitution-making processes that might provide alternative pathways through which the postcolonial state may be reconfigured. Through repeated processes of conflict and constitutional reconstruction as well as new commitments at the regional and continental level through regional bodies and the African Union, there is the possibility that an African constitutionalism may be emerging.

Five Sources of Variation in Constitution-Making

Building a constitutional democracy encompasses a far broader range of issues than drafting and adopting a new constitution (see Ghai and Galli 2006). Yet, it is the process of constitution-making that has become a key element in the political transitions that have followed the end of the Cold War (Benomar 2004, 81). At the same time there has been a resuscitation, despite long recognized critiques, of the tendency to propagate and adopt model forms of institutions and rights that experts are convinced address this or that problem of governance or social conflict. While different examples may very well inform participants or serve to shape their own imaginations of the possible, the tendency to promote model solutions rather than to learn and adapt comparative experiences to the richness of each new national, cultural, political, and temporal context often undermines the very goal of attempting to reconstruct a particular polity through constitutional change. To understand the place of constitution-making in building a democratic future I believe we need to focus less on this or that successful model and instead consider the different mechanisms and paths that have been employed in achieving at least some degree of sustainability in different democratic and constitutional transitions. From this perspective constitution-drafting may be a central feature of a broader process of constitution-building that includes a variety of different elements. It is the exploration of the specifics of these different elements that will enable us to develop a better understanding of the variations in different processes of constitution-building, enabling us to use different historical examples to inform the decisions facing constitution-builders in Africa and around the globe.

Drawing on the South African experience, we may identify five sources of variation in the process of constitution-building that might help us understand the relevance of different aspects of this particular historical experience. First, there is a temporal dimension, which may be characterized as having two distinct forms—a macro and a micro form. In macro terms, the democratic transition takes place within a specific historical era that holds significant consequences for both its very possibility as well as the particular scope of alternatives that might be available in the international political culture of that era. In micro terms, there are the specific time frames of the process of constitution-making, which will themselves have clear consequences for the political choices and opportunities available to the parties. Second, there is a question of process, in which the procedures of constitution-making, chosen from a range of historic options, are deployed by the various parties to achieve specific advantages over their opponents but may also be deployed as a means to ensure that the political transition is kept alive. Third, participation in the constitution-building process was an aspect that was important both for those who were active in the actual constitution-making process, from political activists to the legal representatives of the political parties and their political principals, and for the broader society that was called upon to accept and legitimate the constitutional product as the basis of a future social compact. Fourth, there was the recognition and use of constitutional principles as an essential element of the constitution-making process. While many of the constitutional principles may have been inherent in the contrasting positions of the different political groupings, the decision to explicitly debate and adopt constitutional principles within the context of the constitution-building process had a profound impact on the substance and legitimacy of the outcome. Finally, the substantive dimension, involving constitutional and institutional choices that are required to be made in the constitution-making process involves contestation over alternative institutional designs and the substantive elements of the constitution, all of which had a significant and continuing impact on the overall process of constitution-building.

The Temporal Dimension

The timing of a constitution-building process is a significant determinant of the outcome and is best understood as having two distinct dimensions. On the one hand, an international dimension frames the broad environment in which the local political process of state reconstruction is taking place. From the end of the Second World War through to the Cold War, the era of decolonization and the post–Cold War period, the political opportunities and constraints that affected local political options varied greatly. In the post–Cold War era the process of state reconstruction has been framed first by a wave of market-oriented democratization and more recently by the shattering effects of 9/11 and the global war on terror. As Saïd Arjomand (1992) has argued, this macro temporal dimension may be understood in terms of the formation and transmission of an international political culture. While he acknowledges the influence of a society's pre-constitutional institutional structure and the increasing syncretism of later constitutions, Arjomand (1992, 75) argues that given the impact of the prevalent international political culture on constitution-making the timing of any constitution-making process is more "consequential than the institutional structures of different countries."

The significance of this argument is evident in the consolidation of international political culture since the collapse of state socialism. The ideologically inspired diversity of constitutional alternatives—one-party states, military dictatorships, liberal democracies, people's democracies, and so on—characteristic of the Cold War period and reflected in the increasing syncretism of postcolonial constitutions gave way to an increasing hegemonization. By the early 1990s liberal constitutional principles were hegemonic, with constitutional review by an independent judiciary increasingly becoming a prerequisite for international constitutional respectability (see Beatty 1994, 1–56; Held 1991). In this sense we may understand constitutions as being "sediments of diverse historical processes, crystalized into a small number of indigenous and borrowed principles" (Arjomand 1992, 49). In South Africa the emergence of a hegemonic culture of constitutionalism in the international political culture of the late 1980s had a dramatic impact in shaping the boundaries of constitutional possibility and in reshaping the specific constitutional initiatives and objectives of different social groups and institutions.

However, these principles, and the practices associated with them, only "become effective social forces to the extent that they are borne by social groups and institutions" (Arjomand 1992, 49), highlighting the significance of a more local and immediate temporality—the timing of specific aspects of the constitution-making process itself. Even as we acknowledge the significance of the emergence of a hegemonic international political culture it is important to understand that its integration into the political life of any society will be shaped by the specifics of each particular political transition, including the degree and nature of public participation in the process.[3] South Africans debating constitutional reform had always drawn freely on the international lexicon of constitutional options. In the 1970s and 1980s, the Buthelezi Commission in Natal discussed consociationalism, federalism, and bills of rights (Mare and Hamilton 1988, 163–170), the National Party (NP) referred to the Swiss canton system and consociationalism,[4] and the African National Congress (ANC) asserted the right of South Africa's black majority to self-determination.[5] While these were all respectable elements of the international political culture at that time, the ANC's argument, with its emphasis on decolonization, had direct implications for the constitution-making process, implying that it would be for the "people" of South Africa to decide on the specifics of a future political system including the possibility of a one-party state, state socialism, or any other form of state recognized in the international system.

The end of the era of decolonization, the unraveling of military dictatorships in Latin America, and the collapse of state socialism coincided with an increasing assertion of democratic principles in the international political arena. This was closely associated with the growth of an international human rights movement and the increasing legitimation of bills of rights at both the regional and national level.[6] Tied to this development was the emergence of constitutional review as the essential element in the institutionalization of individual human rights and the constitutionalization of bills of rights (see Rosenfeld 1993; Beatty 1994). These developments within international political culture were reflected in a number of different processes. The adoption of a set of "constitutional principles" by the Western Contact Group on Namibia[7]—establishing a minimum framework as a precondition for an internationally acceptable resolution of the Namibian conflict—saw the international community's first application of substantive principles, beyond a simple exercise of self-determination through a national plebiscite, in the context of decolonization. These 1982 constitutional principles became part and parcel of the UN peace plan for Namibia through Security Council Resolution 632 of February 16, 1989,[8] and were subsequently adopted by the Namibian Constituent Assembly. A second process was the development of the Conference on Security and Cooperation in Europe (CSCE) human rights system, particularly through the follow-up process of intergovernmental conferences provided for in the Helsinki Final Act (Buergenthal 1991).

Most significant of these was the Vienna Follow-up Meeting, which lasted from 1986 to 1989. Taking place in the context of transformation within the Soviet Union under Gorbachev, the Vienna meeting saw a dramatic breakthrough on issues of human rights with agreement on the holding of conferences to address the "human dimension of the CSCE" and the establishment of the Human Dimension Mechanism to deal directly with allegations of failure by a party to uphold its human dimension commitments (Buergenthal 1991, 370). Moving beyond a traditional human rights framework, the Copenhagen Meeting of the Conference on the Human Dimension agreed that "pluralistic democracy and the rule of law are essential for ensuring respect for all human rights and fundamental freedoms" (CSCE 1990, 1307; see Halberstam 1993). A third and significant development in the African context was the World Bank's 1989 conclusion, following a three-year study of Africa's economic malaise, that no economic strategy would reverse Africa's economic decline unless political conditions on the continent improved. This conclusion, placing the blame for economic decline on the lack of public accountability and disrespect for individual rights, pointed directly to a new focus on the rule of law as an essential component of good governance (see Wani 1993).

Each constitution-building process is thus subject to a variety of temporal influences including the broad international configuration of political power and ideology as well as the particular life cycle of internal leadership and social conditions. It is through this perspective that we can understand the significance of the decision by the ANC to develop its own set of constitutional principles and to seek the adoption of an internationally recognized framework for negotiations in South Africa. As a result, the apartheid regime saw the opportunity of gaining international recognition of even a modified version of its 1983 "tricameral" constitution collapse with the adoption of the Harare Declaration[9] and the subsequent incorporation of these principles into the UN Declaration on Apartheid in December 1989.[10] These developments held important implications for the second, more immediate, temporal dimension in that they set the stage upon which the parties negotiated for a specific constitution-making process. While international political culture provided no determinative process for constitution-making, the shift to democratic participation that had occurred through the 1980s made it very difficult for those who wished to confine the process to a limited negotiated solution between the principle parties. It was in this context that the demand for a constituent assembly carried enormous political weight both internally and internationally. But, given the reluctance of the governing minority to accept a process that would limit their influence on the outcome, the compromise of a two-stage process became the only way to avoid stalemate and to ensure the peaceful continuation of the political transition.

A Question of Process

Constitution-making must be understood, to a large extent, as a process. This process includes far broader aspects of any particular political transition than merely the negotiation and drafting of a new constitution. While it is possible to identify a range of different paths and mechanisms—including negotiating the cessation of hostilities, establishing transitional arrangements, arranging and holding a democratic election, negotiating and drafting a new constitution, and implementing and sustaining the new democratic order, each of which will have had an important impact on the failure or success of a country's political reconstruction—there are a range of specific historically determined constitution-making processes that are regularly proposed or argued for. These alternatives range from acts of simple imposition or legal transplant to different forms of negotiating forums or democratically elected bodies as well as forms of public involvement in, or endorsement of, the ultimate product. Each of these alternatives holds profound consequences for both the possibility of reaching agreement to embark on a constitution-building process and for the likely outcomes, including the degree of legitimacy and durability of the new governing parties and institutions.

Deciding how to achieve a new constitutional framework, including both a future text and related institutions, is determined first by the relative power and legitimacy of the different participants in any particular conflict, democratic transition, or constitution-building exercise. While holding an election is the recognized means to establish legitimate claims on power, this will also narrow the scope of available compromises as each side recognizes the extent or limits of its own claims. Relying on an expression of democratic will is limited too by the necessity in many circumstances to address the needs of ethnic or indigenous minorities whose legitimate claims are in tension with the popular demands of the majority. Furthermore, the very means of measuring electoral support, such as proportional or first-past-the-post elections and the appropriate spatial distribution of constituencies or electoral contests, are all matters of intense conflict. These difficulties require recognition of different mechanisms that might be employed in achieving an initial electoral contest that will be inclusive and allow the participation of all the major contestants in the conflict, as well as an understanding that their participation might depend on at least some guarantees that their power as a significant party to the conflict will not be completely erased by the expression of the popular will. This concern is extremely important in contexts in which an ethnic or other minority might hold economic or military power but is likely to be defeated in a simple majority vote election, but is also significant in those situations in which a minority has legitimate claims to some form of autonomy, based on concerns of historic exclusion or cultural vulnerability.

South African history provides a rich example of the different forms of constitution-making processes that have been relied upon at different times. In rough outline we may trace four alternative processes of constitution-making and adoption that have characterized the history of written constitutions in South Africa. First, there has been a significant history of imposed constitutions, from the Republic of South Africa Constitution Act of 1961 through the imposition of "Bantustan" constitutions in the Transkei, Ciskei, Bophuthatswana, and Venda, to the contested imposition of the 1983 "tricameral" constitution. Second, there is a history of negotiated constitutions beginning with the first constitution of the Union of South Africa in 1910 to the negotiated 1993 "interim" constitution that provided the basis for the country's democratic transition. Third, there is the single example of a constitution produced by a democratically elected Constitutional Assembly in 1996. Finally, the South African experience has involved a number of different processes through which these constitutions have been adopted, from the enactment of the Union Constitution by the British Parliament in 1909 to the assertion of sovereignty by the white minority parliament in declaring a republican constitution in 1961 and continuing through the adoption of the "final" constitution by the Constitutional Assembly in 1996.

Aside from these formal processes of constitutional adoption, a number of significant political and legal processes have been used to facilitate or confirm the legitimacy of these constitutions. While the apartheid government frequently used referenda based on the "whites only" electoral list to endorse its constitutional goals—from the decision to form a parliamentary republic in the 1960 referendum to the 1992 "whites only" referendum to decide whether to pursue constitutional negotiations—the threat of turning to a public endorsement by 60 percent in a national referendum on a "final" constitution if the 1994–1996 constitution-making process failed served to ensure a spirit of collaboration in the Constitutional Assembly. Finally, the South African experience has produced a couple of unique legal processes designed to facilitate the constitution-making process or to ensure that the process retains the support of the contesting parties. In the first instance, adoption of the 1993 "interim" constitution involved a dual process in which the Multi-Party Negotiating Forum at Kempton Park first reached agreement on the constitution and then in accordance with the demand by the government that there be "legal continuity" the constitution was formally adopted by the "tricameral" parliament in Cape Town and signed into law by President F. W. De Klerk. In the second instance, the constitution adopted by the Constitutional Assembly could not become law until it was certified by the Constitutional Court as being substantially in accordance with the thirty-four constitutional principles contained in Schedule 4 of the "interim" constitution.

In addition to the historic processes that have been part of South Africa's experiences in constitution-building, the various parties in South Africa had long advocated a range of alternative constitution-making processes. On the one extreme are those who contested the very sovereignty of the apartheid state (Mutiti 1985), leading to the argument that the only legitimate means of adopting a new constitution was to elect a constituent assembly free of any negotiated constraints and to acknowledge that only such a body would have the "power constituent" to adopt a new constitution. At the other extreme there was an argument that any elected body would be effectively "undemocratic since the majority would then bind minorities who would not be in control of their own destinies. The Inkatha Freedom Party (IFP) was particularly concerned about this, viewing the very notion of a democratically elected constituent assembly as inherently undemocratic (IFP 1992b). Since, from the perspective of the IFP, the very purpose of a justiciable constitution and a bill of rights is to protect minorities from the tyranny of the majority, the minorities to be protected must give their prior assent to any constitutional framework. In other words, the IFP and every other minor party at the negotiating table—regardless of the extent of their political support—would have to give their consent before a final constitution could be adopted. Recognizing the practical and political difficulties of obtaining universal consensus, the IFP called for a depoliticized process of constitution-making with a group of constitutional experts retained to produce a constitution that would then be adopted by all parties and endorsed in a national plebiscite (IFP 1992a).

The apartheid government, however, insisted that any future dispensation be negotiated and that no democratic election could be held before the adoption of a negotiated constitution provided the legal basis for such an election. This insistence on a negotiating body, what in other contexts may be described as a constitutional convention, to determine the content of a future constitution would enable the white minority to avoid their effective exclusion, which any first-past-the-post election would have entailed. At the same time, the idea of a simple elite pact held the danger of undermining the legitimacy of a future constitution, particularly in a context in which democratic participation had become a central claim for the liberation movement and its allies as well as an integral part of the global political culture of the late 1980s and early 1990s. It was this tension that led to the compromise of a two-stage process in which an "interim" constitution was negotiated in a process that was effectively a constitutional convention and followed two years later by a "final" constitution produced by the Constitutional Assembly, composed of the elected members of both houses of parliament—effectively an elected constituent assembly. The key "legal" link between these two processes was the inclusion of a set of constitutional principles in the interim constitution and the requirement that the newly created Constitutional Court would be required to certify that the product of the Constitutional Assembly adhered to those principles.

Participation as an Element of Constitution-Building

While it is true, as many point out, that South Africa was privileged to have a leadership that had the moral authority and ability to craft compromises as well as a legacy of negotiating skills that had been honed in the labor movement and in exile, this does not explain the popular embrace of constitutional democracy and rights that has been so key to South Africa's success in sustaining its constitution. To understand this, it is necessary to reflect on the dialectical relationship between interparty negotiations and simultaneous processes of popular participation that both highlighted the salience of particular issues and led to shifts in popular perceptions and demands that ultimately brought the parties closer to mutual understanding. Popular participation in the early part of the transition ranged from mass demonstrations, promoted by the ANC as organized mass action in support of the ANC's demands, as well as a multitude of smaller engagements. A key aspect of this less visible process was a series of conferences on constitutional issues organized by the ANC Constitutional Committee, including members of ANC branches, trade union and other community activists, as well as local and international academics brought together to discuss key constitutional issues. These were supplemented by many local meetings to discuss the options being considered both internally among policy-makers in the ANC and in engagements with the government and other parties.

These informal forms of participation were institutionalized in the second phase of constitution-making through a process of public consultations, education, and requests for comments that accompanied the work of the elected Constitutional Assembly under the slogan: "You've made your mark, now have your say." The Constitutional Assembly's public participation program encompassed a full range of media and other outreach efforts, including: weekly radio broadcasts that reached ten million listeners each week; 160,000 copies of the Assembly's newspaper, *Constitutional Talk*, which was published twice a month; thirty-seven television programs; thousands of hits on the Assembly's web page; and, hundreds of public meetings and visits to far-flung corners of the country. A nationwide survey conducted in April 1996 concluded that approximately eighteen and a half million South Africans, approximately 73 percent of adults, had been reached by this campaign and that 84 percent of the survey respondents had, to varying degrees, become invested in the process (Murray 2001, 107; see also Hassan 1998, 239–250).

The ambiguous nature of this participation was, however, epitomized by a full-page newspaper advertisement showing Nelson Mandela standing in front of his home talking on his cell phone with the caption stating that he was phoning in his comments and contribution to the Constitutional Assembly. While the advertisement was clearly an attempt to encourage members of the public to participate in the Constitutional Assemblies public participation program—which included a dedicated phone-in line for comments and suggestions on the draft constitution—it was manifestly bizarre to suggest that President Nelson Mandela would be making his input to the constitution-making process by leaving a message on an answering machine. For some this only highlighted the fact that while the Constitutional Assembly received over two million submissions from the public, including eleven thousand that Christina Murray (2001, 107) describes as substantive, it is clear that these were not a significant source of ideas for the constitution-making process, even if they were all read. To this extent, Murray notes that the posters declaring that "the Constitution is being written by the most important person in the country: You" might be fairly described as misleading. Despite these criticisms, Murray points out that the program may be understood as "having broader, less instrumental goals," including that South Africans should feel that the constitution belongs to them (112).

Although an ethos of participation pervaded South Africa's extended constitution-making process, it may be fairly concluded that the various forms of participation served less as a receptor of popular demand than as a process of integration through which the imagination of all parties steadily evolved toward the embrace of potentially sustainable alternatives. While this interactive process may be demonstrated in various arenas from the conflict over regional powers to the protection of minority rights, it is in the debate over property rights that it may be most clearly demonstrated. In the face of massive dispossession, the liberation movements had long promised the return of the land to the people. The apartheid government was equally adamant that a future constitution must protect existing property rights. Refusing to accept the constitutionalization of apartheid's spoils, the ANC finally accepted the protection of property but only with the guarantee of restitution for people whose land rights were denied or dispossessed under discriminatory laws from 1913 to 1994. Even then it took public demonstrations by land claimants and threats to refuse to include any property clause at all before the "white" parties accepted the imperative to include a promise of restitution and even the promise of land redistribution in the final constitution. That promise has never been fulfilled, but in the summer of 2018, the ANC was again seeking to achieve it, this time via constitutional amendments—affirming that that the processes of political developments were continuing along this established constitutional path. In each area of major contestation the constitutional outcome has long been the product of an iterative process in which demands and compromises were combined with threats and public engagements in which principles were appealed to and their content expounded from different and often conflicting perspectives.

Constitutional Principles as an Element of Constitution-Building

The South African experience demonstrates, I believe, that a focus on constitutional principles and the need to frame a democratic transition within the realm of a set of broadly agreed upon principles provides a potential means of entrapping unnegotiable conflicts into ongoing but manageable constitutional struggles. The key element in this process, drawing participants in and enabling them to sustain their own visions of a viable alternative to the existing situation, is the practice of constitutional imagination in which the different concepts and options are invested with meanings most in accord with the hopes and aspirations of the different parties. Despite often divergent understandings and deliberately open-ended agreements over meaning, the framing of constitutional principles in the South African case, I will argue, both facilitated the progress of the transition to democracy and provided the means of incorporating often inconsistent and conflicting ideas about the parameters of the future, whether in the forms of explicit guarantees or institutional arrangements. It was this principled ambiguity that allowed the conflict to be "civilized," despite continuing violence and vociferous, if not fundamental, disagreement.

The constitutional principles that have framed the post–Cold War transitions to democracy stem from a range of sources, including local constitutional histories and the evolving international standards reflected in the post–World War II human rights agreements, the Helsinki process, and the experience of decolonization. For southern Africa the first explicit articulation of constitutional principles as a basis for negotiating a democratic transition emerged in the form of the 1982 principles produced by the Western Contact Group for Namibia. Given the legal status of Namibia, as a former German colony, League of Nations mandate, and, finally, illegally occupied territory—after the United Nations' withdrawal of the mandate was recognized as binding by the International Court of Justice—it was often assumed that the idea of constitutional principles would be unique to that conflict. While the implementation of UN Security Council Resolution 435 led to these principles being adopted as the guiding principles of the Namibian Constitutional Assembly, which drew up Namibia's constitution after the 1990 elections, the idea of constitutional principles as a means of framing a democratic transition would become key to South Africa's surprisingly successful transition to democracy.

Although it is possible to claim that the idea of constitutional principles was foreshadowed in South Africa by the presentation of the African Claims document—demands framed around the promises of the Atlantic Charter—by the African National Congress in 1944, or even by the ANC's adoption of the Freedom Charter in 1955, in fact, neither of these documents offered binding promises or institutional assurances to opponents of the ANC. It was only with the publication of the ANC's "Constitutional Guidelines" in 1988 that there is an attempt to offer a broad framework for a future system of governance and rights. It was the internationalization of these principles through the Harare Declaration of the OAU's liberation subcommittee and in the UN General Assembly's Declaration Against Apartheid in 1989 that created a clear set of parameters within which the process of building a democratic South Africa could begin to be negotiated.

The publication of the ANC's "Constitutional Guidelines" in 1988 can thus be seen as an opening gambit in the process of negotiations as well as an intervention designed to preclude internal options that the apartheid government was then considering. The 1988 "Constitutional Guidelines" served both as a signal to ANC activists and supporters of the possibility of a negotiated transition and as a promise to those in South Africa who feared the possibility of a future ANC government, of its democratic intentions. Among the principles adopted by the ANC were commitments to democracy, cultural diversity, basic rights and freedoms in a bill of rights, as well as a mixed economy—including a private sector. While the "Constitutional Guidelines" made clear that the ANC's vision of these principles included mechanisms to address the legacies of apartheid, including affirmative action and land reform as features of a "constitutional duty to eradicate race discrimination" and "the economic and social inequalities produced by racial discrimination," the document nevertheless reassured both domestic and international observers whose understanding of the ANC had been shaped by the Cold War that the ANC would embrace a constitutional democracy.[11] In this way it may be argued that the 1988 "Constitutional Guidelines" initiated the process through which the idea of constitutional principles became central to enabling the transition to democracy.

The Harare Declaration, which began the process of internationalizing the ANC's 1988 principles, took the process a step further, outlining what would be an internationally acceptable process of democratization in South Africa (see ANC 1990, 34–40). In addition to the constitutional principles, the Harare Declaration included a set of conditions designed to enable a climate of negotiations: the release of political prisoners and detainees; the lifting of prohibitions and restrictions on organizations and individuals; the removal of troops from the black townships; the end of the state of emergency and repeal of legislation that circumscribed political activity; and finally, the ceasing of political executions. It also provided guidelines to the process of negotiations toward a democratic order and new constitution, including the establishment of an interim government to oversee the transition. This latter demand failed to recognize that the apartheid government would not agree to relinquish political power until there were some guarantees as to the shape a future South Africa would take. This problem pushed the question of the constitution-making process to the top of the political agenda but provided no means to resolve the different visions of who should participate in what form of process to create a new constitution. It did, however, make it clear that any resolution of the conflict would need to meet minimum international standards if South Africa was to be accepted back into the world community.

Even then the debate over constitutional principles had only begun. While the parties failed to all agree on the Declaration of Intent, a minimal set of principles adopted at their first formal meeting—the Convention for a Democratic South Africa (CODESA) in December 1991—the debate over principles begun at that time would become central to the negotiations in the Multi-Party Negotiating Forum that convened in early 1993 and led to the adoption of the 1993 "interim" constitution under which South Africa's first democratic elections were held and Nelson Mandela was elected president. Still the role of constitutional principles was not exhausted, as an even larger number of constitutional principles had been included in an appendix to the 1993 constitution for the purpose of providing a framework for the work of the newly elected bicameral legislature, serving in joint sitting as a constitutional assembly with the mandate to produce a "final" constitution within two years.

While agreeing on a list of thirty-four constitutional principles and including them in Schedule 4 of the interim constitution was less difficult than first predicted, the key issue remained how they would work to resolve the dual problems of process and substance. Although it could be argued that the principles provided clear substantive criteria to constitution-makers, it was less clear how they would serve to bind the process. It was the decision to require a new constitutional court to certify that the final constitution, produced and adopted by a democratically elected constituent assembly, adhered to the requirements of the constitutional principles in Schedule 4, which created the degree of confidence necessary for the democratic transition to go forward. Thus, in the end the Constitutional Court, in applying the constitutional principles to determine whether the final constitution could be certified and adopted, served as a last check before President Mandela signed the constitution into law as the last formal act of the democratic transition. While this was by no means the sole source of mutual confidence between the once-warring parties, its importance for creating the atmosphere of trust so crucial to the political transition cannot be overestimated.

Although the constitutional principles negotiated by the South African parties represent a vast and often contradictory range of possibilities, the very process of negotiating and providing justification for their inclusion had a significant impact on the parameters of constitutional imagination in South Africa. Some would claim, however, that the inclusion of some principles provided the basis for continued sectarian claims by ethnic minorities or traditionalists by embracing perspectives that were seemingly in conflict with the broader democratic thrust of the process. Yet, the international frame within which these principles were located, I would argue, gave weight to those who insisted on a democratic interpretation of the overall framework. It was this interaction between local demands and global norms that enabled the constitutional principles to play very different roles at different moments in the political transition. At one moment they enabled parties to feel that their most urgent demands had been included, while at other moments the emergence of an internationally defined interpretation of a particular principle would force an understanding of the principle at odds with the initial claim. In this sense the dimension of constitutional principles clearly embraces an important temporal element in addition to the broader substantive implications of the principles.

The effect of combining the debate over constitutional principles with the requirement that any future constitutional dispensation meet minimum international standards, as defined by international human rights principles, was to frame the parameters of acceptable options. This framing had a powerful impact on the shape of the debate over different constitutional options and the available alternatives. The debate over the claim of self-determination, made in the context of the negotiations by ethnically defined parties, provides an interesting example of this process.

Recognition of a claim of self-determination, particularly in the context of decolonization, provided significant support for the claimants in the international arena. However, the minority groups who claimed the right of self-determination in South Africa in the early 1990s found themselves precluded from asserting this right. Despite the fact that only a few years later the international community would recognize ethnically based claims to self-determination in the context of the wars in the former Yugoslavia, before this shift in interpretation, the right of self-determination had been framed by the process of decolonization. Under this rubric international law required that the right of self-determination be exercised by all inhabitants within the internationally recognized borders of a former colony.

In this context the ANC was able to assert that the only internationally recognized right of self-determination in South Africa was the right of all South Africans, regardless of race or ethnic origin, to participate in a democratic process to determine the country's future. The effect of this broader norm on the claims of self-determination by Afrikaners and other minorities was to force them to accept reassurances that their "right of self-determination" would be respected so long as it fell within the democratic norms of the constitution and could be negotiated with a new democratic government. Confining the constitutional imagination of participants in the South African process was not limited to the claims of minority groups. The ANC had long asserted its demand that the land and key industries be nationalized so that the wealth of the country might be redistributed, yet given the domination of market-oriented perspectives after the fall of the Berlin Wall, it was impossible for the ANC to simultaneously embrace the now dominant understanding of international human rights and exclude claims to property rights and free economic activity. Thus, if, on the one hand, the inclusion of internationally recognized constitutional principles precluded demands for ethnic self-determination or consociationalism, on the other hand, it was the very same principles that frustrated popular demands to nationalize the land and key national industries. At the same time, gender activists, who formed a cross-party coalition of women demanding that gender equality not be overridden by claims of tradition, were empowered by the inclusion of these broader international norms that favored gender equality over "traditional authority."

Adopting a list of constitutional principles does not guarantee the future, but it does provide a process and a framework within which areas of commonality may be defined and questions of difference may be located. Providing an institutional mechanism through which these principles may be brought to bear on either the debate over constitutional provisions or as a means to evaluate the final product adopted by a democratically elected constitution-making body provided a zone of comfort for those who did not feel that their central concerns were likely to be adequately reflected in the democratic process—whether they be past elites or excluded minorities. Another important role that the debate over constitutional principles plays is in postponing or mediating the necessity of making a hard or immediate decision on what might be effectively nonnegotiable issues. The adoption of a broad principle allows the conflicting parties to put aside an issue for further debate while working on issues over which there might be greater agreement. This postponement, coupled with continuing engagement between the parties, is an important component in building the basic elements of trust between opposing groups that is central to the ultimate success of a democracy-building project.

Constitutional principles are rarely definitive and contain in most cases a degree of constructive ambiguity that enables all parties to feel that they might be able to live with the outcome of the process. At times the different parties in South Africa held diametrically opposite understandings of the meaning of particular principles, but it was precisely this often acknowledged ambiguity that allowed the process to go forward. One of the effects of the process of negotiating constitutional principles is to slowly entrap the political conflict in a process of argumentation and alternative legal propositions. This has the effect of both precluding some outcomes and mediating the differences between what might be considered acceptable alternatives, often influenced as much by international understandings as the particular historical and material parameters of the local conflict. Finally, the commitment to constitutional principles promotes constitutional engagement over exit and the ever-present threat of violence this implies. Such commitment and engagement appear to be continuing to provide boundaries to disputes and so to aid South African constitutional negotiations today.

Institutional Design and Substantive Choices

Last, but not least is the element of institutional design and substantive choices involved in the actual construction of a constitutional system. While the ideals of participation and democratic process may provide some guidelines for those embarking on a constitution-building exercise, the scope of institutional and substantive choices is framed to a large extent by a combination of elements including the legacy of existing institutions, the imagination of those pursuing new institutional designs and substantive options, as well as the availability of different alternatives. A good example of this was the debate, in the South African context, over the relationship between the center and periphery, referred to as federalism, regionalism, and, finally, as cooperative government. While the apartheid state had attempted to Balkanize the country into racially and ethnically distinct portions, the different participants in the political transition fought for very different visions of a future country. The ANC sought a unified central authority that could challenge and dismantle the legacies of segregation and geographic apartheid, while the NP and the IFP sought different forms of "federalism" or local autonomy as a means to protect ethnic or local centers of power. The international arena, of course, provided a vast array of options from the supremacy of central government in the United Kingdom to the relative autonomy of states in the United States or forms of consociationalism and autonomy in Belgium or Switzerland.

The outcome in South Africa is unlike its Indian and Canadian forebears, which retained central authority while allocating regional powers. The South African Constitution follows more closely in the footsteps of the German Constitution, placing less emphasis on geographic autonomy and more on the integration of geographic jurisdictions into separate, functionally determined roles, in a continuum of governance over specifically defined issues. While provision is made for some exclusive regional powers these are by and large of minor significance, all important and contested issues being included in the category of concurrent competence. How the constitution-makers came to this compromise provides an interesting insight into the processes that shape the selection of different options. Before describing how this compromise was reached it is important to understand just how far apart the main parties were. First, the apartheid government initially seemed set on guaranteeing some form of minority protection. The government and its negotiators pursued this goal by promoting a version of local autonomy drawing on the Belgium and Swiss experiences. Second, the IFP sought a more geographically based form of autonomy, since their claims were framed in terms of the original geography of the Zulu Kingdom. However, despite their assertions that they wanted a "federal" solution, the degree of autonomy they suggested in their constitutional proposals would have required the creation of a confederation of essentially independent entities. Finally, the ANC equated all these claims for ethnic authority as forms of neo- apartheid and saw the claim for federalism as an attempt to prevent the emergence of a united South Africa—one of the basic premises of the nationalist movement.

The breakthrough in the debate over regionalism flowed directly from a study tour of the parties by invitation of the German government that led the ANC to reconsider its hostility to all forms of regionalism. While the ANC had already accepted the existence of distinct regions in the country, it now began to envision how authority could be shared between the center and the regions. The German model provided a more integrative approach as compared to either the U.S. or Canadian forms of federalism and allowed the ANC to reimagine the problem in terms of the allocation of authority between different levels of government according to the needs and capacities of governance at each level. The eventual adoption of the National Council of Provinces, modeled on the Bundesrat, and the conception of cooperative government as a uniquely South African form of regionalism provided a means to achieve agreement on what at first seemed a nonnegotiable conflict. While the analogy to the German system provided an essential source of legitimacy for this new conception, in fact the final institutional design and substantive distribution of powers remains quite different. Thus the existence of an acceptable alternative approach, as well as the ability of the parties to reshape this model to serve as a unique form of "cooperative government" that includes all levels of government from the national government through the provinces to metropolitan areas, local municipalities, and villages, demonstrates how contingent and yet bounded this element of constitution-building is.

Conclusion: Africa in Comparative Context

Africa's experience may also be placed in comparative context with processes in other parts of the globe and in relation to other countries that have been through a process of constitution-building in the post–World War II era. While most countries have experienced some form of constitutional change during this historical period, there are a few cases that highlight some of the elements of constitution-building that I believe may provide a useful framework for a comparative discussion of constitution-making. Despite the clear and specific impact of national histories and domestic politics on the particular outcomes of constitution-making exercises in different countries, a number of broad trajectories may be identified as a means of exploring the effect these different sources of variation may have on constitution-building. For the purposes of this discussion I will limit this exploration of the significance of these elements or sources of variation to the very brief consideration of just three issues: the relationship between the degree and nature of participation in the constitution-making process and the impact on the constitution's legitimacy or effectiveness; the effect of history and timing on the inclusion or form of particular rights; and, finally, the acceptance or rejection of the notion of constitutional supremacy and the role of the courts in defining the meaning of the constitution. Likewise, I will choose from a limited number of jurisdictions to highlight these points.

There are a vast range of constitution-making processes yet the immediate source of a constitution and the process from which it emerges seem to be of great significance to its eventual implementation and legitimacy. While both the German and Japanese postwar constitutions, located within the context of civil law legal systems are considered to be generally successful, the status of these constitutions is quite different. On the one hand, it is acknowledged that the German Basic Law enjoys enormous legitimacy and plays a central role in the life of the country. On the other hand, the Japanese Constitution is, in comparison, rarely invoked, especially in regard to its bill of rights, and the Japanese courts play a far less important role in the implementation of the constitution as compared to the German Constitutional Court. In this comparison I would argue that although the Allied occupation forces in both Europe and the Pacific played significant roles in the two constitution-making processes, the fact that the German process was essentially handed over to German participants, with only a general insistence by the Allied powers that the Basic Law include a federal structure of government and a bill of rights, contrasts markedly with the role that General MacArthur and his staff played in imposing the constitution on Japan. These examples also stand in marked contrast to the Indian and South African experiences where elected constitution-making bodies ensured that their respective constitution-making exercises were to some degree grounded in overtly democratic processes. In fact, the stability of the Indian Constitution has been remarkable, despite serious political tensions internally and an international context in which most of the postcolonial constitutions of the same era have suffered ignoble fates through military coups or other disruptions.

The effect of the temporal dimension and its interaction with constitutional principles and alternative formulations of rights may be illustrated by considering how different constitution- making processes reflected claims for self-determination and property rights. While the principle of self-determination had its origins in the recognition of the rights of national minorities in post–World War I Europe and the League of Nations, the evolution of this principle in the postcolonial setting meant that white minorities in Zimbabwe and South Africa could not claim a right to self-government.

Instead, the post-independent Zimbabwe Constitution gave the white minority twenty seats in parliament for a transitional period of ten years. In contrast, the claim of self-determination by Afrikaners in South Africa was only given partial recognition, and it is an open question whether in a post–Dayton Accord world—in which the global powers returned to a notion of ethnic self-determination—the claims of self-determination by ethnic minorities in southern Africa might not have had more power. Similarly, when it came to debating whether property rights should be included in the South African bill of rights there seems to have been little alternative than to accept the dominant market-oriented notions of property that marked the immediate post–Cold War era.

Despite the availability of reasonable alternatives from the Canadian Charter's omission of property rights to the German Basic Law's adoption of a specific notion of the social function of property, making the right to property subject to public need, the insistence that property rights be protected—over the objections of the majority whose property rights had long been denied—reveals the significant influence of both the temporal dimension and the power of international norms. Even when South Africa's constitution-makers adopted a set of clear qualifications based on the historic dispossession of property, including an affirmative duty to pursue land reform and the recognition of those rights previously denied, Nelson Mandela's government committed itself to a policy of "willing buyer, willing seller" as a means of distinguishing itself from the controversial land reform policies being adopted at the same time by Robert Mugabe's government in Zimbabwe.

Finally, the idea of constitutional supremacy has become a central tenet of post–Cold War constitutionalism. This principle has had implications for both the role of the courts in these new constitutional orders and the constitution-making process itself. First, the adoption of constitutional supremacy often confronts a long tradition of parliamentary sovereignty with its claim that the democratic representatives of the people should have the final say. Second, this requires recognition not only of the legal but also the political consequences of a supreme constitution, from the constraining of legislative authority to the empowerment of the courts. Third, these consequences have direct implications for a constitution-building process in which the negotiators have to strike a delicate balance between popular demands and the authority and power of politicians. While the ANC had come to recognize the value of an entrenched bill of rights, this was still compatible with the idea that the elected representatives of the people would be sovereign; yet the idea of constitutional supremacy emerged as a founding provision of the final constitution. In contrast, the Lancaster House Constitution that was passed by the British Parliament granting independence to Zimbabwe in 1980 retained the notion of parliamentary sovereignty.

In Kenya the constitutional commission that drew up the "Bomas Draft" constitution with a massive public participation program failed to get the draft adopted in the face of opposition from the sitting parliamentarians who felt they had lost control of the process. It was only once the politicians were reincorporated into the process and the draft constitution tailored to address some of their concerns, as well as in the face of disastrous postelection violence in 2007, that Kenya was able to produce a constitution that incorporated a significant majority, gained broad credibility from its acceptance in a nationwide referendum in August 2010, and enshrined the notion of constitutional supremacy. From these experiences I would conclude that the acceptance of constitutional supremacy, as well as broad legitimacy for the product of constitution-building in South Africa and India, can be linked to the nature of their constitution-making processes. Democratically elected constituent assemblies, including political participants from across these societies, produced a level of inclusion and a degree of assurance based on the common acceptance and entrenchment of the rules governing the new order, that sustains the idea of constitutional supremacy and practice of constitutionalism.

Notes

1. "Rational design" here invokes the logic of enlightenment rationality, which asks of the present not how it fits into a wider scheme, or what it says about tomorrow, or even whether it is the beginning of a new world but rather "what difference does today introduce with respect to yesterday?" (Foucault 1984, 33–34). Michel Foucault (1984, 39) describes this perspective as part of an attitude of modernity that has continued to be embroiled in "struggles with attitudes of 'countermodernity.'" See generally Hamilton (1992).

2. Marx's ([1852] 1973, 146) formulation reads: "Men make their own history, but not of their own free will; not under circumstances they themselves have chosen but under the given and inherited circumstances with which they are directly confronted. The tradition of the dead generations weighs like a nightmare on the minds of the living."

3. Cf. Franklin and Baun (1995), whose study acknowledges the existence of international models but concludes that "constitutionalism is largely a cultural phenomenon and not simply the product of properly designed institutions and structures of government" (231). The potential success of democratic constitutionalism is ascribed by the authors to "favorable economic conditions and a certain amount of external security," which they consider "important factors supporting the establishment of democratic regimes in postwar West Germany and Japan" (232).

4. See the statement of Chris Rencken, MP and spokesman for the National Party, to the *Weekly Mail*, November 22, 1985, that a constitutional "model tailored specifically for the country's poly-ethnic nature may very well include elements of federalism, confederation, consociationalism, proportionalism, and even elements of the Swiss canton system" (quoted in Cooper et al. 1986).

5. The principle of self-determination was incorporated into the ANC's 1949 Programme of Action but found its first application to South Africa in a resolution

demanding the right of self-determination submitted by ANC president J. T. Gumede, J. A. La Guma, and D. Colraine to the inaugural congress of the League Against Imperialism in Brussels in February 1927 (Meli 1988, 74–75; see generally Klug 1990).

6. Although the international human rights movement has grown steadily since the Second World War, the recent hegemony of fundamental rights as a basis for constitutional reconstruction is quite dramatic when compared to the situation in the mid-1970s when it was possible to argue that constitutional bills of rights were increasingly being abandoned (see Nwabueze 1977, 309).

7. See "Principles Concerning the Constituent Assembly and the Constitution for an Independent Namibia," transmitted to the Secretary-General of the United Nations on July 12, 1982, UN Doc. S/15287; but cf. Wiechers (1991).

8. See UN Security Council, Resolution S/20412 of January 23, 1989, para 35.

9. "Harare Declaration: Declaration of the OAU Ad-hoc Committee on Southern Africa on the Question of South Africa, Harare, Zimbabwe, August 21, 1989," reprinted in ANC (1990, 34).

10. Declaration on Apartheid and Its Destructive Consequences in Southern Africa, GA Resolution S-16/1, December 14, 1989, reprinted in Secretary-General, Second Report, UN Doc. A/45/1052 (1991), Annex III.

11. See African National Congress, "Constitutional Guidelines for a Democratic South Africa" (1988), reprinted in ANC (1990).

References

ANC (African National Congress). 1990. *The Road to Peace: Resource Material on Negotiations*. Johannesburg: ANC Department of Political Education.

Arjomand, Saïd Amir. 1992. "Constitutions and the Struggle for Political Order: A Study in the Modernization of Political Traditions." *European Journal of Sociology* 33 (1): 39–82.

Beatty, David M, ed. 1994. *Human Rights and Judicial Review: A Comparative Perspective*. International Studies in Human Rights, vol. 34. Dordrecht, Netherlands: Martinus Nijhoff.

Benomar, Jamal. 2004. "Constitution-Making After Conflict: Lessons for Iraq." *Journal of Democracy* 15 (2): 81–95.

Buergenthal, Thomas. 1991. "The CSCE Rights System." *George Washington University Journal of International Law and Economics* 25 (2): 333–386.

Chanock, Martin. 2001. *The Making of South African Legal Culture, 1902–1936: Fear, Favour and Prejudice*. Cambridge: Cambridge University Press.

———. 2010. "Constitutionalism, Democracy and Africa: Constitutionalism Upside Down." *Law in Context* 28 (2): 126–144.

Cooper, Carole, et al. 1986. *Race Relations Survey: 1985*. Johannesburg: South African Institute of Race Relations.

CSCE (Conference on Security and Cooperation in Europe). 1990. "Document of the Copenhagen Meeting of the Conference on the Human Dimension of the CSCE, June 29, 1990." Reprinted in *International Legal Materials* 29 (5): 1305–1322.

Ellmann, Stephen. 2010. "A Bittersweet Heritage: Learning from the Making of South African Legal Culture." *Law in Context* 28 (2): 76–94.

Foucault, Michel. 1984. *The Foucault Reader*. Edited by Paul Rabinow. New York: Pantheon Books.

Franklin, Daniel P., and Michael J. Baun. 1995. *Political Culture and Constitutionalism: A Comparative Approach*. Abingdon-on-Thames, UK: Routledge.

Ghai, Yash, and Guido Galli. 2006. *Constitution Building Processes and Democratization*. IDEA Policy Paper. Available at idea.int/sites/default/files/publications/constitution-building-processes-and-democratization.pdf.

Ginsburg, Tom, ed. 2012. *Comparative Constitutional Design*. Cambridge: Cambridge University Press.

Goldsworthy, Jeffrey, ed. 2006. *Interpreting Constitutions: A Comparative Study*. Oxford: Oxford University Press.

Halberstam, Malvina. 1993. "The Copenhagen Document: Intervention in Support of Democracy." *Harvard International Law Journal* 34 (1): 163–176.

Hamilton, Peter. 1992. "The Enlightenment and the Birth of Social Science." In *Formations of Modernity*, edited by Stuart Hall and Bram Gieben, 17–70. Oxford: Polity Press in association with the Open University.

Hassan, Ebrahim. 1998. *The Soul of a Nation: Constitution-Making in South Africa*. Oxford: Oxford University Press.

Held, David. 1991. "Democracy, the Nation-State and the Global System." In *Political Theory Today*, edited by David Held, 197–235. Stanford, CA: Stanford University Press.

Hirschl, Ran. 2004. *Towards Juristocracy: The Origins and Consequences of the New Constitutionalism*. Cambridge, MA: Harvard University Press.

Huls, Nick, Maurice Adams, and Jacco Bomhoff, eds. 2009. *The Legitimacy of Highest Courts' Rulings: Judicial Deliberations and Beyond*. The Hague: T. M. C. Asser Press.

IFP (Inkatha Freedom Party). 1992a. "Position Paper of the Inkatha Freedom Party for Submission at the CODESA Meeting of February 6, 1992." Reprinted in South African Supplement, Release 92-2 (A. P. Blaustein, March 1992), to *Constitutions of the the Countries of the World*, edited by A. P. Blaustein and G. H. Flanz. Dobbs Ferry, NY: Oceana, 1971–.

———. 1992b. "Why the Inkatha Freedom Party Objects to the Idea of the New Constitution Being Written by a Popularly Elected Assembly (Whether Called 'Constituent Assembly' or Called by Any Other Name)." Undated submission to CODESA (Convention for a Democratic South Africa) Working Group 2.

Jackson, Vicki C. 2010. *Constitutional Engagement in a Transnational Era*. Oxford: Oxford University Press.

Klug, Heinz. 1990. "Self-Determination and the Struggle Against Apartheid." *Wisconsin International Law Journal* 8 (2): 251–300.

———. 2000. *Constituting Democracy: Law, Globalism and South Africa's Political Reconstruction*. Cambridge: Cambridge University Press.

———. 2010. *The Constitution of South Africa: A Contextual Analysis*. London: Bloomsbury.

Mamdani, Mahmood. 1996. *Citizen and Subject: Contemporary Africa and the Legacy of Late Colonialism*. Princeton, NJ: Princeton University Press.

Mare, Gerhard, and Georgina Hamilton. 1988. *An Appetite for Power: Buthelezi's Inkatha and South Africa*. Bloomington: Indiana University Press.

Marx, Karl. (1852) 1973. "The Eighteenth Brumaire of Louis Bonaparte." Reprinted in *Surveys from Exile*, vol. 2, *Political Writings*, edited by David Fernbach, 143–249. Brooklyn, NY: Verso.

Meierhenrich, Jens. 2008. *The Legacies of Law: Long-Run Consequences of Legal Development in South Africa, 1652–2000*. Cambridge: Cambridge University Press.

Meli, Francis. 1988. *South Africa Belongs to Us: A History of the ANC*. Harare: Zimbabwe Publishing House.

Murray, Christina. 2001. "Negotiating Beyond Deadlock: From the Constitutional Assembly to the Court." In *The Post-Apartheid Constitutions: Perspectives on South Africa's Basic Law*, edited by Penelope Andrews and Stephen Ellmann, 103–127. Johannesburg: Witwatersrand University Press.

Mutiti, Mudimuranwa A. B. 1985. *South Africa: Is It a Sovereign Independent State?* Harare: Aroclar.

Ndulo, Muna. 2001. "Constitution-Making in Africa: Assessing Both the Process and the Content." *Public Administration and Development* 21 (2): 101–117.

Nolutshungu, Sam C. 1991. "The Constitutional Question in South Africa." In *State and Constitutionalism: An African Debate on Democracy*, edited by Issa G. Shivji, 91–100. Harare: SAPES.

Nwabueze, B. O. 1977. *Judicialism in Commonwealth Africa: The Role of the Courts in Government*. New York: St. Martin's Press.

Okoth-Ogendo, H. W. O. 1991. "Constitutions Without Constitutionalism: Reflections on an African Political Paradox." In *State and Constitutionalism: An African Debate on Democracy*, edited by Issa G. Shivji, 3–25. Harare: SAPES.

Rosenfeld, Michel. 1993. "Modern Constitutionalism as Interplay Between Identity and Diversity: An Introduction." *Cardozo Law Review* 14 (3): 497–532.

Sajo, Andras, ed. 2004. *Judicial Integrity*. Leiden: Martinus Nijhoff.

Shivji, Issa G. 1991a. "Contradictory Class Perspectives in the Debate on Democracy." In *State and Constitutionalism: An African Debate on Democracy*, edited by Issa G. Shivji, 253–260. Harare: SAPES.

———. 1991b. "State and Constitutionalism: A New Democratic Perspective." In *State and Constitutionalism: An African Debate on Democracy*, edited by Issa G. Shivji, 27–54. Harare: SAPES.

Sloth-Nielsen, Julia, and Lea Mwambene. 2010. "Talking the Talk and Walking the Walk: How Can the Development of African Customary Law Be Understood?" *Law in Context* 28 (2): 27–46.

Thornhill, Chris. 2011. *A Sociology of Constitutions: Constitutions and State Legitimacy in Historical-Sociological Perspective*. Cambridge: Cambridge University Press.

Tushnet, Mark. 2003. *The New Constitutional Order*. Princeton, NJ: Princeton University Press.

Wani, Ibrahim J. 1993. "The Rule of Law and Economic Development in Africa." *East African Journal of Peace and Human Rights* 1 (1): 52–79.

Widner, Jennifer A. 2001. *Building the Rule of Law: Francis Nyalali and the Road to Judicial Independence in Africa*. New York: W. W. Norton.

Wiechers, Marinus. 1991. "Namibia: The 1982 Constitutional Principles and Their Legal Significance." In *Namibia: Constitutional and International Law Issues*, edited by Dawid van Wyk, Marinus Wiechers, and Romaine Hill, 1–21. Pretoria, SA: VerLoren van Themaat Centre for Public Law Studies.

World Bank. 1989. *From crisis to sustainable growth - sub Saharan Africa: a long-term perspective study*. Washington, DC: The World Bank.

Young, Crawford. 1994. *The African Colonial State in Comparative Perspective*. New Haven, CT: Yale University Press.

———. 2012. *The Postcolonial State in Africa: Fifty Years of Independence, 1960–2010*. Madison: University of Wisconsin Press.

Conclusion

Rogers M. Smith

By 2019, some months after the final revisions in the preceding chapters, recent developments further heightened the significance of the themes they develop. The chapters confirm that, even though modern constitutionalism inescapably involves responses to all of the six tasks of constitutional formation that we identified in the Introduction, those responses have varied greatly in different countries and in the same countries over time, as David Law and Mila Versteeg maintain. Different sorts of political bodies and actors contribute to constitution writing and to constitutional authorization. These range from the special conventions used to write and adopt the original U.S. Constitution, to the adoption of a new Hungarian constitution in 2011 by the Fidesz-dominated parliament, to the elaboratedly negotiated, multistage constitutional process in South Africa, among many options (including, as in many of the American States, the combination of a special convention and a popular referendum to create a new Ecuadorian constitution in 2008). Constitutions also vary widely in how easily alterable they are, with America's original hard-to-amend model abandoned in most parliamentary systems; and they differ even on whether they can be regarded as largely "written." Though written constitutions have become the norm, exceptions like Great Britain and Israel persist. Moreover, often much is "unwritten" in the operation of written constitutions, even in the case of the U.S. Constitution, as Akhil Amar (2012) has argued.

Patterns in global constitution-making and global constitutional developments are nonetheless discernible. In terms of representative institutions, parliamentary models originally inspired chiefly by Britain and France remain globally more influential than the American structure of separation of powers. But some regimes are purely parliamentary (though South Africa labels as its "president" the legislatively chosen leader who is the equivalent of "prime minister" in other regimes, and Spain's prime minister, who must be sworn in by the monarch, can be officially referred to as "president" as well). Other constitutional systems, like Hungary and Russia, are officially presidential/prime minister hybrids, but where the power lies can vary greatly with who the occupants of those offices are, whatever the formal allocations of authority may be. (It matters if the formal title is followed by the name "Putin.") The modern constitutions discussed here also provide examples of the widely varying judicial structures, electoral systems, and divisions of power between levels of government, national, subnational, and, especially in the case of the European Union nations, supranational. Moreover, as the contrast between authoritarian and democratic constitutional systems and debates over the meaning of human dignity values make clear, modern constitution-makers have been motivated by a significant range of political purposes.

In the latter regard, even the limited sample of modern constitutions explored here confirms the broad arc of development in modern constitutionalism discussed in the Introduction, including the sobering reality that this developmental path today may be at a critical juncture. Up through the first decade of the twenty-first century, scholars could describe that arc as, overall, a movement toward more democratic constitutional systems with more independent judiciaries, and toward ones with a greater proliferation of positive rights that displayed socially transformative potential. Sanford Levinson and Emily Zackin have affirmed here that, when one looks at the American states, with their adoption of initiative and referendum and the various kinds of positive rights, this arc of constitutional development is visible even in the United States. The texts of many constitutions in formerly Communist nations also fit these patterns, at least on their faces. So does the influential Constitution of South Africa. These features are truer yet for those new constitutions in Latin America adopted during the years when many countries on the continent were veering "left," even as North Atlantic nations were moving in neoliberal directions.

Today, however, the rise of the right-wing populist movements and leaders on virtually every inhabited continent, including Jair Bolosonaro in Brazil, Viktor Orbán in Hungary, and Donald Trump in the United States, among many others, has disrupted those trends. Orbán (2014) argued explicitly that "the new state we are building is an illiberal state" that "applies a specific, national, particular approach" to constitutional governance, though one that he insisted complied with core values of democracy and human rights. As

Kim Scheppele has shown, his approach involves visibly subordinating the courts to his leadership. Tom Ginsburg's contention that authoritarian regimes can find some components of constitutionalism useful, even as they reject what liberals see as its most vital features, is confirmed in this and many other instances.

Even so, some contributors here, particularly Law and Versteeg, and to a lesser degree Heinz Klug, are not convinced that these disturbing developments are so broad and deep as to amount to a clear global trend away from liberal constitutional democracies, or even from the more recent left-leaning transformative constitutions. They simply stress, again, that modern constitutions take many forms. Others like Scheppele are more militant about the dangers of recent populist trends, because they are less sanguine that they can be contained without strenuous resistance to them. The most intensely nationalist forms of modern populism are often linked, moreover, to the phenomena that Valerie Bunce and Jaime Lluch explore in different contexts, the challenges to contemporary constitutional systems raised by demands for recognition of a variety of ethnocultural groups, including ones that seek regional autonomy or even independence, such as in Catalonia.

A willingness to give constitutional recognition to diverse communities, often with accommodations for long-disadvantaged ones, is one of the hallmarks of modern transformative constitutionalism as it has emerged particularly under the influence of the Indian and South African constitutions. Yet for that reason, it can fuel reactionary responses by more exclusionary nationalist constitutionalist visions and movements, as many fear to be true of Nahendra Modi's Bharatiya Janata Party in India, with its animus against Muslims, and even Xi Jinping's version of Chinese Communism, with its hostility to rule-of-law reformers, to Uighurs, and to autonomy for Hong Kong and Tibet, among other examples. Perhaps the modern emphasis on values of human dignity that Christopher McCrudden finds in many recent national constitutions can mitigate these dangers. Yet, as he stresses, governments and political leaders can and do interpret dignity in many ways and in behalf of many causes.

Still, as Orbán's elaboration of Hungarian "illiberal democracy" shows, these recent constitutional developments, dismaying to liberals, do not alter the fact that the basic features of modern constitutionalism—the creation of fundamental charters to authorize both institutions of popular self-governance and the protection of basic rights via the rule of law—are now endorsed, at least rhetorically, all around the world. Here skeptics and proponents of the global influence of the U.S. Constitution can find common ground: most if not all agree that this was decidedly not the case when modern constitutionalism began in the eighteenth century. In soaring words if not reassuring deeds, the core principles of modern constitutionalism that the American and French revolutionaries jointly initiated still reign triumphant in the twenty-first century.

What recent developments remind us, however, is that from their inception, modern constitutions have often failed in the eyes of many to fulfill these principles and aspirations, even as others have continued to reject those principles as the right standards to guide political life. Nations governed by modern constitutions have often fallen short of providing democratic self-governance, protection of rights for all, and the rule of law, in ways that have long created pressures for constitutional change. Perhaps it is not surprising that today many constitutions are being rewritten by forms of politics that many see as threatening to those core constitutional values and institutions, even as political leaders continue to proclaim support for modern constitutional principles and claim to be strengthening their practical efficacy. If so, we must conclude that the endeavors of modern constitutionalism, in all the cases considered here and in many others as well, are not only both enduring and evolving. They are also incomplete and embattled in ways that make them central to the political present and future of the modern world.

References

Amar, Akhil. 2012. *America's Unwritten Constitution: The Precedents and Principles We Live By*. New York: Basic Books.

Orbán, Viktor. 2014. "Speech at the XXV Bálványos Free Summer University and Youth Camp." July 26, 2014. https://budapestbeacon.com/full-text-of-viktor-orbans-speech-at-baile-tusnad-tusnadfurdo-of-26-july-2014/.

CONTRIBUTORS

Richard R. Beeman was the John Walsh Centennial Professor of History at the University of Pennsylvania. Author of eight books and many articles, he also served as dean of the College of Arts and Sciences at Penn and director of its Center for Early American Studies. He was a member of the Board of Trustees of the National Constitution Center and of the Executive Committee of the Penn Program on Democracy, Citizenship, and Constitutionalism, now the Andrea Mitchell Center for the Study of Democracy, from their inception.

Valerie Bunce is the Aaron Binenkorb Chair of International Studies Emerita at Cornell University. Her research analyzes transitions to democracy, democracy promotion, democratic breakdowns, authoritarian politics and the cross-national diffusion of political change in Eastern Europe, Russia, Ukraine and the Caucasus. Her current work focuses on Russian aggression in Ukraine and in the 2016 U.S. election as measures designed, respectively, to protect Putin's power at home and to pay the United States back for using elections to topple dictators in Russia's zone of influence.

Tom Ginsburg is the Leo Spitz Professor of International Law at the University of Chicago, where he also holds an appointment in the Political Science Department. He holds B.A., J.D., and Ph.D. degrees from the University of California at Berkeley. He is the author of many articles and four multiple-award-winning books, most recently *How to Save a Constitutional Democracy* with Aziz Z. Huq (University of Chicago Press, 2018). He currently codirects the Comparative Constitutions Project, an NSF-funded data set cataloging the world's constitutions since 1789.

Heinz Klug is Evjue-Bascom Professor of Law at the University of Wisconsin–Madison and is an honorary visiting professor in the School of Law at the University of the Witwatersrand, Johannesburg, South Africa. Growing up in Durban, South Africa, he participated in the anti-apartheid struggle, spent eleven years in exile, and returned to South Africa in 1990 as a member of the ANC Land Commission and researcher for the chairperson of the ANC Constitutional Committee. He has published widely, including: *Comparative Constitutional Law in Context* (with Stephen Ross and Helen Irving, Lexis-Nexis, 2014); *The South African Constitution: A Contextual Analysis* (Hart, 2010); and *Constituting Democracy: Law, Globalism, and South Africa's Political Reconstruction* (Cambridge University Press, 2000).

David S. Law is the Sir Y. K. Pao Chair in Public Law at the University of Hong Kong and Chancellor's Professor at the University of California, Irvine. He holds a Ph.D. in political science from Stanford, a B.C.L. in European and Comparative Law from the University of Oxford, and a J.D. from Harvard Law School. Until 2019, he served as the Charles Nagel Chair in Constitutional Law and Political Science at Washington University in St. Louis. His works have been translated into Chinese, Spanish, Japanese, and Romanian and include *Nihon no saikosai wo kaibou suru* (The Japanese Supreme Court and Judicial Review) (Gendaijinbunsha, 2013) and *Constituciones aparentes* (with Mila Versteeg) (Universidad Externado, 2018). He is the editor of the forthcoming *Constitutionalism in Context* (Cambridge University Press, 2020) and co-editor of the forthcoming *Oxford Handbook of Constitutional Law in Asia* (Oxford University Press, 2020).

Sanford Levinson is the W. St. John Garwood and W. St. John Garwood Jr. Centennial Chair in Law, University of Texas Law School, and a professor of government at the University of Texas at Austin. His most recent books are *Fault Lines in the Constitution* with Cynthia Levinson (Peachtree Publishing, 2017) and *Democracy and Dysfunction* with Jack Balkin (University of Chicago Press, 2019). He was awarded the Lifetime Achievement Award from the Law and Courts Section of the American Political Science Association in 2010.

Jaime Lluch (Ph.D., J.D., Yale University) is an associate professor in the Department of Political Science at the University of Puerto Rico. He is a comparativist who works on the constitutional and political accommodation of national diversity in multinational democracies, comparative federalism, migration and citizenship in comparative perspective, European and EU politics, and comparative public law. He is the author of the award-winning

Visions of Sovereignty: Nationalism and Accommodation in Multinational Democracies (University of Pennsylvania Press, 2014) and the editor of *Constitutionalism and the Politics of Accommodation in Multinational Democracies* (Palgrave Macmillan, 2014).

Christopher McCrudden is a professor of human rights and equality law at Queen's University Belfast and William W. Cook Global Professor at the University of Michigan Law School. His most recent book is *Litigating Religions* (Oxford University Press, 2018). He is a member of the Royal Irish Academy and a fellow of the British Academy, and was awarded a CBE by the queen in 2019 for services to human rights.

Kim Lane Scheppele is the Laurance S. Rockefeller Professor of Sociology and International Affairs in the Woodrow Wilson School and the University Center for Human Values at Princeton University. Scheppele's work focuses on the intersection of constitutional and international law, particularly in constitutional systems under stress. She has published widely in law reviews, as well as disciplinary and interdisciplinary journals in the social sciences and won the Kalven Prize for influential socio-legal scholarship from the Law and Society Association in 2014. An elected member of the American Academy of Arts and Sciences and the International Academy of Comparative Law, Scheppele has taught in the law schools at Harvard, Yale, the University of Pennsylvania, the University of Michigan, Erasmus-Rotterdam and Humboldt-Berlin.

Rogers M. Smith is the Christopher H. Browne Distinguished Professor of Political Science at the University of Pennsylvania. He founded the Penn Program on Democracy, Citizenship, and Constitutionalism, now the Andrea Mitchell Center for the Study of Democracy, in 2006 and chaired it for a decade. He is the author or coauthor of over ninety articles and eight books, most recently *That Is Not Who We Are! Populism and Peoplehood* (Yale University Press, 2020).

Mila Versteeg is the Class of 1941 Research Professor of Law at the University of Virginia School of Law and a Carnegie Fellow at the Andrew Carnegie Foundation of New York (for 2017–2019). Most of her research deals with the origins, evolution, and effectiveness of provisions in the world's constitutions. Her publications have appeared in, among others, the *California Law Review*, the *New York University Law Review*, the *University of Chicago Law Review*, the *American Political Science Review*, the *American Journal of Political Science*, the *Journal of Legal Studies*, the *Journal of Law and Economics*, the *American Journal of International Law*, and the *Journal of Law, Economics and Organizations.*

Emily Zackin is an assistant professor at the Krieger School of Arts & Sciences at Johns Hopkins University. She earned her Ph.D. in politics from Princeton University, and her B.A, from Swarthmore College. Professor Zackin is the author of *Looking for Rights in All the Wrong Places: Why State Constitutions Contain America's Positive Rights* (Princeton University Press, 2013), which focuses on three political movements that added positive rights to state constitutions.

INDEX

An "f," "n," or "t" following a page number indicates a figure, endnote, or table, respectively.

ACKNOWLEDGMENTS

This volume would not have been conceived, much less completed, without the intellectual and administrative leadership of the late Richard Beeman, who chaired the Planning Committee of the Penn Program on Democracy, Citizenship, and Constitutionalism, now the Andrea Mitchell Center for the Study of Democracy, for which the chapters were originally prepared. Rick was passionately dedicated to the American Constitution and the cause of democratic constitutionalism more generally, commitments that today seem more crucial than ever. All the authors represented here join in dedicating *Modern Constitutions* to him.

This work also benefited enormously from the editorial assistance of Matthew Roth, associate director of the Andrea Mitchell Center, and the guidance and support of Peter Agree at the University of Pennsylvania Press. Anthony Grasso provided valuable research assistance that aided the drafting of the Introduction, completed by Rogers Smith after Rick's passing. All responsibility for any shortcomings falls to the surviving coeditor.

www.ingramcontent.com/pod-product-compliance
Lightning Source LLC
LaVergne TN
LVHW091525200926
848483LV00002B/304